ID0605469

Preventing Classroom Discipline Problems

A Classroom Management Handbook

Third Edition

Howard Seeman

The Scarecrow Press, Inc.
Technomic Books
Lanham, Maryland, and London
2000

SCARECROW PRESS, INC.
Technomic Books

Published in the United States of America
by Scarecrow Press, Inc.
4720 Boston Way, Lanham, Maryland 20706
http://www.scarecrowpress.com

4 Pleydell Gardens, Folkestone
Kent CT20 2DN, England

British Library Cataloguing in Publication Information Available

Library of Congress Cataloging-in-Publication Data

Main entry under title:
       Preventing Classroom Disciple Problems: A Classroom Management
       Handbook, Third Edition

Library of Congress Catalog Card No. 99-64546
ISBN No. 1-56676-834-9

♾™ The paper used in this publication meets the minimum requirements of
American National Standard for Information Sciences—Permanence of
Paper for Printed Library Materials, ANSI/NISO Z39.48–1992.
Manufactured in the United States of America.

*To Dr. Albert Cullum, who, all too well,
understood the vulnerability of childhood
and healed so many*

TABLE OF CONTENTS

PART III
Preventing and Handling the Sources of Disruptive Behavior

PART IV
Special Features:
Training Tools That Can Be Used with This Book

PREFACE TO THE THIRD EDITION

Unfortunately, since the writing of the second edition, school violence has become almost a weekly headline and our children are in more trouble; thus, the burden on our teachers is even heavier. Schools report that "discipline problems" are still their major concern, but the problems have become more severe. Every day in America about 8,500 children are reported abused or neglected. These are the students who enter our classrooms. Lack of adequate training of teachers in classroom management then contributes to our students acting out, many withdrawing, and now a dropout rate of about 2,850 students per day![1] These "hanging out" students quickly get into trouble: Violent crime among 14–17 year olds is up 46.3%.[2] One survey finds 12% of students saying they now carry weapons in school for protection.[3] Research indicates that in the United States one teacher in five has been assaulted or threatened with violence.[4]

These issues have become so prominent in the nation's concerns that they were highlighted on national television by the President of the United States:

> "Character education must be taught in our schools. . . . And we must continue to promote order and discipline . . . remove disruptive students from the class-room, and have zero tolerance for guns and drugs." (President Clinton's *State of the Union Address,* Feb. 4, 1997)

The following are all new additions to this third edition:

1. Chapter 1:
   - C. For Substitute Teachers
   - K. For Parents:
     1. When *Your* Child Is a "Discipline Problem"
     2. When It's the *Other* Students

---

[1] *The New York Teacher,* June 1996.

[2] James Alan Fox, "Trends in Juvenile Violence," *A Report to the U.S. Attorney General,* June 1996.

[3] Harris Poll, Erin Donovan, June 1996.

[4] Wild, Jerry, *Anger Management in Schools* (Technomic Publishing Co., 1996).

- Appendix D. "Am I Going to Have a Lot of Discipline Problems?" A Pretest for Diagnosis and Prevention
- Appendix E. An Indexed Inventory of the Sources of Disruptive Behavior and Their Remedies
- Appendix F. A Checklist for Student Teachers, "Your First Day!"
- Appendix G. A Glossary of Technical Terms Used in Schools
- Bibliography

The following have all been expanded and updated in this third edition:

1. All the exercises and checklists of all the chapters.
2. All of the sections: Especially for Grades K–6 in all of the chapters.
3. All of the following chapters and sections:
   - Chapter 1, Using This Book as a Handbook
   - Chapter 2B, A Summary and Critique of the Literature
   - Chapter 3; Chapter 5; Chapter 6A; Chapter 7E
   - Chapter 9H.; Chapter 10D and E; Chapter 12A
   - Chapter 12B. The Debates about: "What's Most Effective"?
   - Chapter 13B.5; Chapter 14H.; Chapter 17; Appendix G
   - Bibliography

Foremost, I want to thank Mary-Ann L. Feller, a wonderful conscientious teacher, who skillfully suggested additional ideas for grades K–6 for this third edition. I also thank Carmen Mason, a great teacher and "god mother" to many students, for her suggestions for many rewards for the upper grades; Dr. Susan Roth; Karla Beatty for editorial services; Professor Sandrea DeMinco for her helpful library assistance in my research; and the children that I have the privilege to take care of and play with, who are always my dear teachers. In addition, I thank my wife, Dr. Karen Beatty, for reading what I write, for helping me with suggestions, and for tolerating, my sometimes oversensitive need for organization. And finally, my daughter, Jaimelyn, for heightening my motivation for living, in general.

PREFACE TO THE SECOND EDITION

Since the publication of the first edition of this book in 1988, "discipline problems" continue to be a major issue in our schools across the nation. In 1993, discipline problems were still rated as the second biggest problem in our schools, second only to drug abuse. It was rated even higher than teachers' and parents' concerns about proper financial support for schools or even curriculum standards.[5] For example, in New York State in 1993, teachers reported a 91% increase in the use of profanity, an 87% increase of student defiance, and a 63% increase in violence directed at other students over the past five years.[6] Crime in these schools increased at every grade level (except K–6), up 20.9% in the middle schools, and up 39.5% in the high schools.[7]

We are all familiar with the pattern of how often a child is a discipline problem today, becomes truant the next day, hangs out with other truants, gets in trouble, goes to family court, or becomes a hardened criminal or victim of crime or drug abuse. In New York State in 1993, the violent crime arrest rate per 100,000 for juveniles increased from 664 to 980. The percentage of teens neither in school nor the workforce increased from 5.4% to 6.1%.[8]

The second edition of this book has not only been updated but contains many new additions to the original text:

1. In Chapter 1, new "road maps" about how to use this book as a handbook have been written to include other educators not in the first edition: education majors, student teachers, teachers K–6, aides (paraprofessionals), consultants, school psychologists, and guidance counselors; also, the section "for parents" has been expanded.

2. A review of the current literature in Chapter 2, section B now includes new recent writings on discipline problems. Also, Appendix C, A Resource Bibliography, has been updated.

[5] G. H. Gallup. "Gallup Poll of Public's Attitudes Toward Public Schools" (1993).
[6] *The New York Teacher*, p. 13 (May 17, 1993).
[7] *The New York Teacher*, c. 5A (November 16, 1992).
[8] *The New York Teacher*, p. 15 (May 17, 1993).

3. A new section appears in Chapter 4: C. What to Do Instead of Making Miscalls, with section C1: How to Refer Students to Professional Help.
4. Almost every chapter now includes a special section: Especially for Grades K–6. And new exercises, especially for elementary school teachers, have been added to each chapter.
5. In Chapter 12, new sections have been added on preventing and handling students who have "crushes" on teachers, wear hats, bring personal stereos or beepers to class, who "dis" (criticize) each other, and are "high" or are dealing drugs. Also, now "inappropriate punishments" appear here.
6. In Chapters 1, 3, and Appendix E new sections appear that are especially for student teachers.
7. A new questionnaire that administrators can use to assess their staff's needs regarding discipline problems is now included in Appendix B.
8. A Glossary has been added as Appendix D, Technical Terms Used in Schools.

My appreciation for the help provided to me in writing this second edition mainly goes to all of the students and educators who used the first edition and openly gave me valuable suggestions for the text, as they successfully used it from coast to coast. The second edition will be even more useful to their colleagues, thanks to them. Also, a special Thank you goes to Denise Sands Baez, Ron Manyin, Carmen Mason, Noreen Cavaliere, and my wife, Karen Beatty, and daughter, Jaimelyn, who understood "my absence" when I needed to work on this project.

PREFACE TO THE FIRST EDITION

In national surveys of the public's attitude toward education since 1974, discipline has been cited as a major problem. Concern about discipline consistently has been rated higher than concerns about drug abuse, poor curriculum, academic standards, and even lack of appropriate financial support.[9] In one survey, teachers throughout the state of New York cited "managing disruptive children" as the most stressful problem in their professional lives; indeed, the problem was rated as the highest stress factor among these teachers, regardless of their age, type of school district, sex, marital status, or grade level.[10] Similar findings have also appeared in studies of Chicago teachers[11] and teachers in Great Britain.[12] (The reader should also note the latest statistics on this subject in the Preface to the Second Edition.)

Unfortunately, remedies usually require far-reaching changes. For instance, attempts to mediate discipline problems by establishing crisis intervention teams, student grievance committees, parent councils on discipline, or in-school or out-of-school suspension programs usually require many administrative and procedural changes, long-range planning, and considerable time and coordinated effort on the part of all staff. Because there seem to be few suggestions that offer immediate help, the problem is very frustrating to teachers and to teacher-educators who need help now.

Often, the problem of disruptive classroom behavior has been skirted. Though it has been the major problem nationally for over a decade, there are very few in-service or student teacher training courses that focus on this real

[9] G. H. Gallup. "Gallup Poll of Public Opinion, 1974–1983," published in *New York State United Teacher* (official publication of the New York United Federation of Teachers), vol. 43, no. 2, p. 7 (November 1983).

[10] G. H. Gallup. "Gallup Poll," in *New York State United Teacher,* vol. 39, no 2, p. 5 (November 1979).

[11] D. J. Cichon and R. H. Kloff. "The Teaching Events Stress Inventory" (Paper presented at the meeting of the American Educational Research Association Conference, Toronto, Ontario (March 1978), ERIC Document Reproduction Service, no 160, p. 662.

[12] C. Kyriacou and J. Sutcliffe. "Teacher Stress: Prevalence, Sources and Symptoms," *British Journal of Educational Psychology,* 48:159–167 (1978).

obstacle to viable learning. Sometimes, the problem is covered over with the attitude that: "If you're just a good teacher, you just won't have such problems; and if you have such problems, you're just a bad teacher!" Or, even worse, to compound this avoidance of the problem, there is the attitude: "Good teachers just know what to do; you can't train a teacher how to be; some teachers 'just have it' and some 'just don't' " Or the problem is too simply called "classroom management," and teachers are only taught how to make neat bulletin boards, how to have orderly routines, and to keep neat desks and rows—as if that will answer, e.g., the problem of what to do when Johnny says, "Go to hell!"

This book attempts to meet the issue of discipline problems head-on. It presents suggestions for preventing and handling these problems that can be immediately applied by the present teacher, or by teacher-educators working with teachers and prospective teachers who are facing these problems *now*. The book can either be used as a "self-help guide" for the classroom teacher, Kindergarten to 12th grade, or as a "training manual" for teacher-educators and administrators who wish to help the classroom teacher with these problems. Each chapter offers: an explanation of the problem; a description of the skills needed to remedy the problem; actual reports from teachers who had these problems and struggled to learn these skills; and training exercises and checklists that help the mastery of the skills.

This book is based on the realization that helping teachers prevent discipline problems requires more than offering theoretical explanations and "do this-solutions" to the problem. Instead, it specifically trains teachers' perceptions and behavior so that they can be more effective and competent, and yet can react spontaneously according to their own style in the classroom. In this sense, the book offers not just understanding, but skills, and ways to practice these skills, so that a teacher can develop competent trained responses that *naturally prevent* and handle disruptive behavior. The reader who heeds the design of this book can avoid the usual two alternatives open to most teachers: learn to prevent and handle discipline problems through years of trial and error, or fail at handling and preventing such problems, suffer "burn-out," and simply leave the profession, as so many do.

A skim-reading or misreading of this book may give the reader the misconception that this book is about controlling kids. It is not. The recommendations that follow present a framework that is an amalgam of support for humanistic education without neglect for practical solutions to disruptive behavior. To avoid the latter would not protect the education process itself. A good teacher needs to be in control, even if s/he is only attempting to be a facilitator and co-learner of the feelings and thoughts of others. To be systematic, constructively assertive and organized are not by implication the ingredients of a totalitarian teacher. Instead, to be able to perform these skills are *the prerequisites* for being more humanistic, flexible, and creatively spontaneous.[13]

The recommendations and training design that follow have been formulated over a period of twenty years. These include the author's six years of experience as both an English and Social Studies teacher in three high schools, service as a substitute teacher in about ten junior and senior high schools in lower Manhattan, New York City, and, since 1970, as an instructor and field supervisor of student teachers and teachers who were upset by discipline problems. The sections of the book in each chapter entitled Teachers Share Their Growing Pains contain teachers' actual problems and how they have used the author's recommendations to prevent and handle them. Also, the training design and its recommendations have been successfully employed in the author's consultant work throughout the United States. Thus, the suggestions offered here are not from an "ivory tower" perspective. The book is written from an understanding of what the job of the teacher is firsthand. Some teachers deserve "purple hearts" for surviving up in front of that room. I know what it's like: from filling out bus passes, to losing the bathroom pass, to taking attendance; from kids calling out, and throwing things, to being conned, or provoked by the infamous unanimous low hum done by all the kids under their breath. These experiences have been the training ground for this book.

I wish to thank my wife, Dr. Karen Beatty, for her support and intelligent advice, and Dr. Albert Cullum for modelling the kind of teacher that has helped me upgrade and keep high standards in education. I also wish to thank friends and colleagues who have supported and encouraged my work, especially: Professor Anthony Patti, Professor George Schoengood, Dr. Brenda Byrne, Dr. Daniel J. Wiener, Drs. Susan and Jay Roth, Dr. Robert Weintraub, Ms. Karla Beatty, Ms. Susan Kirby, Ron and Ruth Manyin, Mr. Terence Brunson, my parents, and my students.

---

[13] For more on this point, see p. 140.

PART I

*Understanding the Problem and
the Proper Approach*

CHAPTER 1: USING THIS BOOK AS A HANDBOOK

A. For Education Majors and Student Teachers

The reader should first notice that Part II (Chapters 6, 7, 8, and 9) describes the sources of discipline problems and that Part III (Chapters 10, 11, 12, 13, and 14) is ways to handle and prevent the problems previously presented in Part II.

You are probably experiencing a lot of anticipatory anxiety about how you will handle all kinds of discipline problems, and you're picturing some very "rough" kids. These future fears are very normal. I had the same fears. The first thing you may want to read is Chapter 3, You're Not Alone, #1. Then read Chapter 4 and practice the exercises imagining your first time teaching. Then you can read Chapters 2, 3, and 5. Again, do the exercises you feel you need most help with, but do them imagining you are now actually a teacher. In Appendix F, you will find a checklist for you (as you actually get ready to teach your first day): "Especially for Student Teachers." If you have particular immediate concerns, locate that concern in the index or Appendix E and simply read the text according to your needs. To diagnose the problems you may encounter due to your style, read Appendix A, and take the pretest in Appendix D. Finally, ask your department or instructor to get a copy of the **video,** by the author, that is cued to this book (see Appendix B at the end of this book) and see that **video,** if you can.

B. For New Teachers or Veteran Teachers Experiencing Difficulties on the Job

The reader should first notice that Part II (Chapters 6, 7, 8, and 9) describes the sources of discipline problems and that Part III (Chapters 10, 11, 12, 13, and 14) is ways to handle and prevent the problems previously presented in Part II.

If you're a teacher about to have a nervous breakdown and need immediate help, skip the first few chapters and read Chapter 4 first. This will help you

3

eliminate many causes of discipline problems quickly and easily without much revision in your routines, or rules, or general style. Then, skip all of Part II and read Chapter 10, sections A, B, C, and D. These sections will help you handle some frequent disturbances without involving you in major revisions, or school policy, or deeper understanding that you can always gain later after you feel some control and more patience. Then, read Chapter 12, sections A, B, and C. These sections will also give you a quick remedy for usually the most pressing and disturbing disruptions to your teaching. Also, skim Chapter 13B for specific problems that you may be having. All these short sections, when "under your belt," should save you from "going under" fairly quickly. Once you feel that your crisis state is over, you should then go back and read and practice the other sections of the book that handle much more of the general problem but take more time and practice. When you are ready for the other sections, read them in order from where you skipped: Chapters 2, 3, 5, 6, 7, etc. To help you focus on which of these several chapters are specifically helpful for you, you may first answer the two questionnaires in Appendix A, and Appendix D.

On the other hand, if you are a teacher who is experiencing problems but are not in crisis and can take your time to solve these problems, read the book and do the exercises in the order the book is written. You should probably underline parts that you wish to remember or put in practice that particularly relate to you. If you're lucky, you have found this book in August, or just before the new semester, or new marking period. If so, changing your rules or routines will be easier. If you wish to put some of the books ideas into practice "midstream," it may be a little more difficult. But this can be done by simply preparing a short talk to the class about why you've decided to change a rule or routine if they feel: "you already said one thing, and now are saying another." Tell them your new thoughts about the changes, even some of your new feelings, and follow through from this new self-made start. Once you feel you have read and practiced the training exercises and have implemented your new rules and routines, you might wish to consult Appendix E every so often. There, you can check yourself by using the: Indexed, Systematic Inventory of the Sources of Disruptive Behavior and Their Remedies. Finally, try to get a copy of the **video,** by the author, that is cued to this book (see Appendix B at the end of this book) and see that **video,** if you can; or recommend it to your school administration.

C. For Substitute Teachers

The reader should first notice that Part II (Chapters 6, 7, 8, and 9) describes the sources of discipline problems and that Part III (Chapters 10, 11, 12, 13, and 14) is ways to handle and prevent the problems previously presented in Part II.

If <u>you are going to be</u>, <u>or are</u>, <u>a substitute teacher</u>, <u>or a cluster teacher</u>, or if you have to do a short-term coverage for another teacher, skip the whole book for now and read Chapter 15 first, especially the sections most relevant to your job or concerns. This chapter is meant mostly for the per diem sub who is covering for a teacher for just one day or subs for a different teacher every day.

However, if you wind up covering for the same teacher more than just one day, or covering the same classes for an extended period of time, then you are becoming more like the students' regular teacher. And, as you become more regular, the job description widens, and your abilities increase to create a relationship with the students and to prevent and handle disruptive behavior. Therefore, as this happens, then, begin to read and make use of the sections of this book that I suggest to New Teachers (Chapter 1B, just above this section).

D. For Teachers K–6

The reader should first notice that Part II (Chapters 6, 7, 8, and 9) describes the <u>sources</u> of discipline problems and that Part III (Chapters 10, 11, 12, 13, and 14) is ways to handle and prevent the problems previously presented in Part II.

Teachers of grades K–6, although you experience some of the same disruptive behaviors as teachers of grades 7–12, you encounter different kinds of disruptive behaviors, and these behaviors often occur for different reasons. Therefore, for almost every chapter, a section appears: Especially for Grades K–6. (These sections have been specially revised and expanded for this edition.[14]) If you teach K–6, you can read each chapter as suggested in section B above, but then you can revise this information for each chapter by reading this special section for grades K–6 that appears at the end of each chapter. The same principles and concepts apply, but the situations are often a little different and often come from different sources. Finally, ask your instructor or department chair to get a copy of the **video,** by the author, that is cued to this book (see Appendix B at the end of this book) and see that **video,** if you can.

E. For Paraprofessionals, Aides

The reader should first notice that Part II (Chapters 6, 7, 8, and 9) describes the <u>sources</u> of discipline problems and that Part III (Chapters 10, 11, 12, 13,

[14] With the consultancy of Mary-Ann L. Feller (see her bio at the back of the book).

and 14) is ways to handle and prevent the problems previously presented in Part II.

You are often in a frustrating situation. You see what you call (or do not call) discipline problems, but since you are not the teacher, you have less power to stop, prevent, or handle these situations. Your ability to identify, prevent, or handle disruptive behaviors will depend on how much authority and control your teacher gives you regarding such situations. Of course, as in any human relations negotiation, show your teacher-partner that you respect him or her. It may often be appropriate for you to swallow your irritation and follow your teacher. After all, s/he has the license, and all of the blame and responsibility falls on the teacher, not you. In any event, the first step in negotiating with your teacher is always to listen first, even (especially) when you're angry. If you can ask a respectful question about the situation you are disturbed by and just listen to your teacher's feelings and reasons, you may then be more likely to get some listening in return. You might hear information you are lacking (and vice versa) that helps each of you better own the decisions about the children in the class. When the class feels you are not united on your opinions, rules, ways of giving approval, etc., they will go between you and after the "weakest link". This inconsistency confuses the kids and un-educates them socially and emotionally. As with parents, try to follow and present a united team and save the discussions over disagreements for a private time—when at all possible. Of course, generally, each of you should back each other (or stay out of it) when the other was not there at the time a situation occurs. Show the children you believe in each other's judgments. You can wait, or fill the other in later, after you have backed each other.

The first chapter you should probably read is Chapter 4. This will help you clarify when you should call a situation a discipline problem. Then, at the proper time, see if you and your teacher can agree. You may both try Exercise Three at the end of the chapter and work to get your answers similar. Then you should read each chapter in order, especially the sections for grades K–6. You might wish to underline parts you agree with or that are particularly helpful for your class. With respect for your teacher's ability and knowledge, you might show him or her the parts you underlined. Allow your teacher to defend him/herself, and you should assume that, if the suggestion is useful, s/he will incorporate it. If your teacher refuses to budge, try again to present your opinion as only your opinion; perhaps explain why you are "uncomfort-able" with the present situation. Then try to back your teacher for the sake of the children's need for consistency. Even if you are correct and the teacher is not, to angrily keep the conflict going will often hurt the children more than your inability to get them your "correct" way. That's why your job is so difficult. I respect your situation. I understand. And if you can do some of the above, you're an excellent paraprofessional. Finally, try to ask your principal to get a copy of the **video,** by the author, that is cued to this book (see Appendix B at the end of this book) and see that **video,** if you can.

F. For Instructors and Consultants of Inservice or Graduate Workshops or Courses

The reader should first notice that Part II (Chapters 6, 7, 8, and 9) describes the sources of discipline problems and that Part III (Chapters 10, 11, 12, 13, and 14) is ways to handle and prevent the problems previously presented in Part II.

My first suggestion is to teach the workshop or class sitting in a circle, not rows. This seating arrangement will allow the teachers in the course to see one another and help them realize they are not alone with the problem. The key to teaching a course on this problem is to find ways for the teachers to feel comfortable enough to share their vulnerabilities and problems with each other. The first meeting of the course should be spent learning each others' first names, hearing why each has come to the course, and allowing each to vent their angers and frustrations around discipline problems they have had. This book is organized as follows: Part II (Chapters 6, 7, 8, and 9) describes the sources of discipline problems, and Part III (Chapters 10, 11, 12, 13, and 14) is ways to handle and prevent the problems previously presented in Part II.

Everyone should first try to locate the chapters in Part III that are the answers to the chapters in Part II. Then, the first chapter they should read is Chapter 3: You're Not Alone. When they return to the course after reading that chapter, let them share their own "horror" stories. As each one tells his or her story, do not allow the class to lapse into giving each other advice or judgments of any kind. These latter responses will only close down the trust level of the class and prevent any future ability to use the class to help one another. Just keep asking the class: "Who else has had similar problems or feelings?" This strategy needs to be followed until the class has vented much of their anger and frustration. Until then, they will be deaf to hearing you or learning from this book.

Once you feel the class feels unalone, has more trust with one another, and can't wait for solutions, have them read Chapter 2: Why Many Attempts Have Been Inadequate. This chapter is designed to prevent you and the class from helping each other in unproductive ways. You, as the instructor, should read this chapter carefully and underline it. If your course doesn't seem to be going well, usually you are down a path that this chapter has warned against. Orally go over the chapter in class with your teachers and clarify how you will proceed and what will and won't be helpful to try.

Next, have your class answer the two questionnaires provided in Appendix

A and Appendix D. Tally their answers on the chalkboard for each questionnaire, so they can, again, see that they are not alone. Then, you can refer students to look at the section that is specifically their concern, or seek immediate help in the Index.

Next, work with the class on Chapter 4: <u>When Should You Call It: "A Discipline Problem?"</u>. Again, after each reading, have them share what it is they got from the reading, and how any of it reminds them of themselves. You can use the exercises at the end of the chapter as a homework assignment at the end of the lesson.

Then, have them read Chapter 5: <u>From the Horse's Mouth</u>. They will now be more ready to hear the "kid's point of view" on this subject. Then, have the class read the book in its order (each meeting of the course) from Chapters 6–14. Again, let them share, follow the warnings 1–10 (on pp. 19–23) in Chapter 2, and use the training exercises at the end of each chapter as homework assignments, or assess specific skills by using Appendix E. If you follow these suggestions, the course should go well, especially if you also use your own style as you make use of this book. My best wishes to you; you will not only be saving teachers from burnout, youngsters' learning, and parents from upset, but society's foundation. Please feel free to write to me[15] if I may be able to help more. Finally, try to get a copy of the **video,** by the author, that is cued to this book (see Appendix B at the end of this book) and have your students see that **video,** if they can.

G. For School Psychologists and Guidance Counselors

The reader should first notice that Part II (Chapters 6, 7, 8, and 9) describes the <u>sources</u> of discipline problems and that Part III (Chapters 10, 11, 12, 13, and 14) is ways to handle and prevent the problems previously presented in Part II.

You are both in the same boat. "Disruptive" children, or teachers or parents who have "disruptive" children, will either be referred to you individually, or you will be seen as the one with "expertise" and be asked to conduct a course or workshop on "discipline problems." This is a difficult job. Two immediate suggestions are: 1) read section E above if you are asked to conduct such a workshop and 2) write for a reprint of the article "A Teacher Inservice Model for Problem Solving in Classroom Discipline: Suggestions for the School Psychologists (Craig L. Frisky, *Education Foundations,* 1403 Norman Hall, University of Florida, Gainesville, FL 32611-2053).

If you are working individually with either a child, teacher, or parent,

---

[15] Professor Howard Seeman, Lehman College, Department of Middle and High School Education, Bedford Park Blvd., Bronx, NY 10465. e-mail: HOKAJA@aol.com

obviously, first simply listen a lot. There is usually anger in these situations, and you will have a "deaf" client and have little or no influence over them until they vent. Of course, empathize with the feelings even if you cannot support the facts of the behavior. If you have been asked to see a disruptive student, of course, counsel him or her according to your training; work on the causes of the behavior or the feelings involved. Perhaps you can influence the student's teacher about rewards, punishments, needs for attention, etc. Or you may want to influence the teacher regarding what s/he calls a discipline problem. In these cases, you will need to support the teacher while you influence the teacher by referring to specific chapters: 10, 12, and 13 and then chapters 4, 7, 8, 9, 11, and 14. Lend this book to the teacher; be supportive. Tell him or her many teachers (who have seen you privately) need help in these areas: "You're not alone." If the teacher is recalcitrant, then the only thing you can do is help the student learn how to deal with such difficult teachers; s/he will meet many in his/her life, and it is a skill for the student to be able to cope with such situations.

Actually, you can do no more than this: try to organize and conduct a workshop on this area for your school or district. The first thing to do here is make copies of the Questionnaire in Appendix A of this book. Have it filled out by the staff and post the results anonymously. This will spark the need for such a workshop. At the first session of the workshop, simply follow the guidelines in section F above for Instructors of Inservice Workshops. Finally, try to get a copy of the **video,** by the author, that is cued to this book (see Appendix B at the end of this book) and see that **video,** if you can. You can show it to teachers who are asking you for help with handling disruptive behavior.

H. For Administrators

The reader should first notice that Part II (Chapters 6, 7, 8, and 9) describes the sources of discipline problems and that Part III (Chapters 10, 11, 12, 13, and 14) is ways to handle and prevent the problems previously presented in Part II.

You will find it helpful to read section G above since you are often in the same role as the school psychologist or guidance counselor. The first thing to do to help your school is to administer the Questionnaire in Appendix A to your staff and post the results anonymously. This will help them all feel unalone with these problems. Hopefully, this will be enough to spark a workshop in your school on the subject. You should look at the suggestions: about warnings and punishments in Chapter 12A and B, about rewards in Chapter 12C; the suggestions about conflict resolution education in Chapter 12D; and the specifics in Chapter 13 so that you can back up such input if your staff feels that these policies are useful.

Or, you yourself can read the book in the order it is written. You might make notes in the margin of names of teachers to whom you should refer certain sections or pages. Then, use Appendix E to direct teachers to specific sources or skills that may be appropriate. You might notice that Mr. Smith needs to work on skill 4B-7, and, thus, should read the chapter that works on that skill. You might also suggest he try the exercises at the end of the chapter to practice that skill. If you are going to observe a teacher, take Appendix E with you and use it as an evaluative checklist. You can also use Appendix E to refer to what you see going on in your school at a faculty meeting. You may also consult Appendix E as a guide to what to look for as you interview a new teacher for your staff. Or use the questionnaire in Appendix D to help you "diagnose" this teacher's style. If it would be helpful to you, please write me at Lehman College, Department of Middle and High School Education, Bedford Park Blvd., Bronx, NY 10468. e-mail: HOKAJA@aol.com

You should also especially consult: Chapter 10A., School Violence; Chapter 12B, Suspensions; and Appendix C, Legal Parameters.

If you have only a little money in your budget, a fast, inexpensive way to improve the classrooom management in your school quickly, without re-vamping the whole school's philosophy, is to get the **video,** cued to this book, to help your teachers get immediate, easy, practical help to prevent classrom discipline problems, to cut down on all the referrals to you or your dean (see Appendix B at the end of this book).

However, if a workshop does not form, and you can't work with each teacher individually, show the **video** at a staff meeting, which will motivate your teachers to improve their classroom management methods. Then, have available in the library or teacher's lounge some copies of this book for them to use on their own without any stigma.

I. For Supervisors of Student Teachers

The reader should first notice that Part II (Chapters 6, 7, 8, and 9) describes the sources of discipline problems and that Part III (Chapters 10, 11, 12, 13, and 14) is ways to handle and prevent the problems previously presented in Part II.

You may wish to start with a few special features of this book before you and your students read the whole text. Special sections specifically useful for student teachers are located in Chapter 1A; Chapter 3, and Appendices E, F, and G.

Have your student teachers all answer the questionnaires in Appendix A and Appendix D, and refer them to their appropriate weakness, worry, or pitfall. Then read the book in the order it was written. You might wish to make notes in the margin of names of student teachers (from your observations of them) you might refer certain sections or pages to. Use Appendix E as an evaluative checklist during your observations, and then assign the appropriate chapters and exercises accordingly. If you have a student teachers' seminar, you may wish to lecture on "the Sources of Disruptive Behavior." If so, after having read Part II, you can use Appendix E as your lecture notes. I would also advise that you follow the suggestions I gave in this chapter, section F: For Instructors and Consultants of Inservice or Graduate Workshops or Courses as guidelines for running your student teaching seminar. If you can, try to show your student teachers the **video,** by the author, cued to this book (see Appendix B, at the end of this book).

J. For Instructors of Education Courses

The reader should first notice that Part II (Chapters 6, 7, 8, and 9) describes the sources of discipline problems and that Part III (Chapters 10, 11, 12, 13, and 14) is ways to handle and prevent the problems previously presented in Part II.

First, you can read the introductions to each chapter of the text. Then you should follow the guidelines I gave in this chapter, section F, as guidelines for running your class. However, since these students will not have yet had experience as teachers, you should have them share either their fantasies of problems they might have or problems they have observed. This sharing can come from the answers that they give to the two questionnaires in the back of this book in Appendix A and Appendix D. Have them do these as exercises before they share with each other. Otherwise, follow the guidelines I gave in this chapter, section F above. As a first assignment, you might ask them to list behaviors that are slightly discipline problems, usually discipline problems, surely discipline problems. When they bring these lists to class, ask them to read examples from their list without identifying the category that they put each under. See if their classmates put each example cited under the same category. They won't! This will point out that we need to decide: when should you call it a "discipline problem"? Then, have them read Chapter 4, sections A and B as their first reading assignment. After they have read it, you can discuss the best definition of a "discipline problem" and then assign Chapter 4, sections C, D, E, and F.

Then you should probably assign Chapter 2 and teach it in class. Then have them read Chapters 3 and 5 and discuss these. With these latter chapters you might ask them about which descriptions make them most worried, or which they relate to most.

Then you can assign Chapters 6, 7, 8, etc. in the order the book is written, and assign the exercises for each chapter as homework. If you wish to give them either a written examination or a performance examination (have them role play: if the children do this, what do you do?), you will find that Appendix

E is excellent for designing such examinations. If you can obtain the **Video,** by the author, cued to this book, show it to your class, as they read the chapters (see Appendix B, at the back of this book).

K. For Parents

The reader should first notice that Part II (Chapters 6, 7, 8, and 9) describes the sources of discipline problems and that Part III (Chapters 10, 11, 12, 13, and 14) is ways to handle and prevent the problems previously presented in Part II.

1. When your child is a "discipline problem"

You have a special and unique role in this problem. Probably you have gotten bad reports from teachers about your son or daughter. Your child is probably frustrated and angry with school and certain teachers. Now, his or her frustrations and anger, and your frustrations and anger are driving both of you (and maybe even your spouse) farther apart. What should you do, and how can you best make use of this book?

Consult these chapters in this order:

1. Read Chapter 5 first. This will sensitize you to how your child might see the situation and why he or she tends to "act out" in certain situations, with certain teachers.
2. If your child generally feels "picked on" by some teachers, read Chapter 4.
3. Read both of these chapters before you try to talk to your child about his or her behavior. By reading Chapter 4 especially, you may find some justice in your child's complaints.
4, Probably your next step is to talk with your child. I suggest that you approach this talk mostly as a listener, nonjudgmentally, and not ready to "lay down the law." It's best to assume that your child is "right" with some of his or her complaints, though not all right. Listen with the understanding gained in Chapters 4 and 5.
5. End the first talk with your child with the attitude: I've listened to your side, let me think about what you said and are feeling.
6. Then, read Chapter 6. This chapter will help you see your child in the context of his or her growing-up problems in general and in terms of natural environmental stresses. Here, you'll see that your child is not alone, and your empathy will be heightened for your child, his or her teachers, and educators in general.
7. Now you'll need to analyze both (a) the specific school sources of your child's tendencies to "act out" and (b) the areas that may be appropriately the irresponsibility or misbehavior of your child.

If it's mostly (a):

1. Skim Chapters 10, 11, 12, 13, and 14, which will give you good advice about what to discuss with your child's teacher, and how you might positively suggest to the teacher revisions to his/her methods or style that may have become the catalyst for your child's disruptiveness.
2. You can use Appendix E to check off these revisions when you confer with your child's teacher.
3. Then read Chapter 12D to help you at home if your child has frequent fights with siblings or with playmates.
4. Read Chapter 12E if you feel your child often succumbs to destructive peer pressure.
5. Read Chapter 12F if you feel your child tends to be victimized by bullies.
6. Read Chapter 12G if <u>you</u> sometimes have trouble asserting yourself with your child (or others).
7. Read Chapter 12H if your child is in elementary school.
8. Finally, for background reading, after the crisis has settled down, you may find these sections generally informative: Chapter 2B; Appendices C and G and the Bibliography.
9. For specific help with a particular problem, consult the Index.

If it's (b) above:

1. You will need to understand why your child gets angry and frustrated, and give him or her the proper rewards, punishments, and supports at home with you that make acting out no longer as worthwhile as doing well and behaving.
2. You and the teacher now need to be a team (and you and your spouse/partner need to be a team) that consistently gives reinforcement for good behavior[16] and non-reinforcement (e.g., deprivation of privileges and punishments) for bad behavior.
3. In this team effort with the teacher, you may wish to advocate change in the teacher's style (with respect for his/her point of view) from your reading of this book. Do this gently and with the attitude of "a possible suggestion."
4. Then aim to back up the teacher's goals, demands, homework, etc., with warnings and reprimands followed up at home.
5. Here, it will be helpful for you also to follow the guidelines in Chapter 12, sections A and C, but revise these concrete rewards and warnings according to what you can follow through with at home (which is often more than the teacher can do at school). Always assume that your son or daughter is acting out because of needs, or that they are getting more by

---

[16] For useful tips on positive reinforcement, see Chapter 12C on "Rewards." Then, Chapter 12B can be read for general background information on this issue.

acting out than behaving. You need to discover these needs and care about these feelings and make behaving more rewarding than misbehaving.

6. Listen to your child warmly and nonjudgmentally and provide more rewards for behaving well than acting out.

7. Finally, try to have your school or PTA get a copy of the **video,** by the author, that is cued to this book (see Appendix B at the end of this book) and get parents (and teachers) to see that **video,** if you can.

This book is designed to remedy (a) those classroom-teacher situations that inadvertently cause and/or reinforce disruptive behavior. It can help to prevent and handle these problems. It is not specifically designed to handle nor prevent problems that may (b) have their sources elsewhere. Obviously, use this book for (a). For more on (b), you can work on items 1–6 above. And if you have the courage, you need to examine what you and your spouse (or child caregiver) have inadvertently taught your child about dealing with anger and conflict resolution in general. Unfortunately, children learn to handle anger and conflict destructively when they watch adults display the following kinds of behavior:

• expressing anger physically (e.g., by hitting)
• or by expressing anger by name-calling or "put downs"
• not listening to each other's feelings
• judging, criticizing, or making fun of each other's feelings
• not allowing the constructive verbal expression of frustration or anger
• interrupting each other when the other is trying to express important feelings
• trying to be strong by not showing feelings in general
• trying to win arguments, rather than trying to see the other's point of view
• never admitting mistakes, short comings, or apologizing
• not negotiating when there is a conflict in their wants and preferences
• trying to look good, or "cool" to cover feelings of inadequacy
• dogmatically insisting that their particular point of view, taste, or value system is better than any other

If many of the above are true in your home, you should carefully read Chapter 12D, especially, 5, A and B in that chapter.

For more help with (b) above, I also recommend: Thomas Gordon's Parent Effectiveness Training (New York: Penguin,1975). And, if you need help with a teenager in more serious trouble, e.g., drug abuse, consult: Paulene Ness's Tough Love (Abingdon Press, 1984). If you are particularly worried about a teenage girl and sex, and peer pressure, etc., Mary Pipher's Reviving Ophelia (Ballantine, 1995) is very insightful. Finally, to help you to keep having a constructive influence with your children, How to Talk So Kids Will Listen & Listen So Kids Will Talk by Faber (Avon Books, 1982) is very useful.

Usually the sources of school misbehavior are always at least some of (a), as well as (b).

2. When it's the other students

If it's not your child that's the "discipline problem," it may be another student or students. In this case, your child is, instead, a victim of classroom disruptive behavior. His or her learning is being impaired by other students' disruptions. The teacher is having to take time away from teaching to handle these disruptive students. Or, maybe worse, your child is the victim of other students who, e.g., hit your child or generally bother your child while s/he is trying to learn. In this case, I suggest the following guidelines in using this book:

1. It's always best never to act alone. Talk to other parents whose children are in the same class. See if you hear a consensus about this problem. Try to decide if the teacher is working on the problem adequately already. Share your frustrations with the other parents/guardians so that you gain some emotional strength, so that you do not feel alone about what you may need to do.

2. If you feel that not enough is being done, or not fast enough, first try to get these parents to all bring up this issue at their individual, periodic teacher's conference when each parent gets some time to talk to each teacher privately. (This meeting [if you can] is always better than writing the teacher a letter.) If this meeting is too far away in time, or has little effect, try to arrange for a special meeting with the teacher and the concerned parents of the class. (It's best if you first talk to the teacher before you go to the principal or assistant principal. That way, at the meeting, you'll have a less defensive teacher listening to you.) You may discuss the problem with the school psychologist, but hopefully he or she keeps your confidentiality and recommends similar guidelines that are explained here.

3. When you gather parents for this meeting, contact all the parents, not just the parents of the "victims" or just the parents of the "troublemakers." The meeting should not be about specific kids, but about behaviors: What are the proper behaviors for this class? What kinds of behaviors are not to be tolerated? What warnings, rewards, and punishments does that teacher carry out to prevent disruptive behavior? (See Chapter 12A and C.) Are these congruent, fair, appropriate, consistent, and followed through? (see Chapters 8 and 11).

4. Do not get into arguing about what behaviors already happened, or which kids did these, or who started it, etc. Start with: what all the people

involved would like to see enforced from now on. <u>Don't</u>: get into the history of what happened, or what should have been done, or who is to blame.

5. Assume that the teacher and some of the parents at this meeting (if they show up!) will be defensive. The teacher may argue and defend him/herself. The parents that you think are responsible may argue with you and complain, "it's not my fault," "it's not my kid." That's okay and to be expected in front of other people. But usually much of what is said at such meetings <u>does</u> sink in and have a useful effect. Much of what is heard will be implemented when the teacher has time to digest the meeting and when the parents get home and can talk to their child and/or spouse privately.

6. Often, what comes out of such meetings are some agreements on norms of behavior, rewards, and punishments, and generally agreements about the questions above (in 3). Now, both parents and teachers need to note what will be on the contract (the warnings, rewards, and punishments) with these students. The teacher must carry these contracts out, and you, as parents, must follow through with your child regarding these contracts <u>at home</u>. It may be that the warnings are, e.g., that at the third infraction, the parent will not allow the child to watch TV for a day; or the reward will be for "turning over a new leaf" that the parent, e.g., takes the child to a special movie. The main point is that the teacher and parents agree to work in concert to reinforce the appropriate behavior and to extinguish the inappropriate behavior. (Of course, hopefully, the parent/guardians at home are also in concert <u>with each other</u>.)

7. Then, the <u>teacher</u> should be urged supportively to consult this book as follows:

   • Follow the suggestions in the chapters that are suggested in Chapter 1B.
   • Regarding setting up these contracts, the teacher will find Chapter 12 very helpful (and especially Chapter 12H, if the problem is in grades K–6).

8. Then, give the problem some time to be resolved. During this time, try to compliment the teacher or the child regarding any small improvements. Give complaining a rest.

9. However, if the problem persists, or the understandings above are not enforced, or the problem gets worse, it may be time now to talk to the assistant principal or the principal. If you decide that this step is now necessary, make sure that you have really tried all of the above. Then use the same guidelines above when you meet with any of these administrative staff. Keep in mind that if you decide to take this step, most likely the administration will somewhat defend the teacher involved and, also,

that you may have to tolerate the teacher feeling threatened. Then, the teacher may work on the problem in compliance only out of feeling coercion (which is always less productive than when the teacher acts out of feeling alliance). Though the administration may defend the teacher at the meeting, rest assured that if there is any truth to your complaints, some pressure will be put on that teacher.[17] (Hopefully, the administration is not dealing with a completely recalcitrant teacher, e.g., who has tenure, is very stubborn, or who is just waiting out his or her time to retire.)

10. Finally, try to get your school or PTA to get a copy of the **video,** by the author, that is cued to this book (see Appendix B at the end of this book) and get parents (and teachers) to see that **video,** if you can.

---

[17] You can refer the administration to their specific section of this book, so that they can better work with this teacher: Chapter 1H: For Administrators.

CHAPTER 2: WHY MANY ATTEMPTS HAVE BEEN INADEQUATE

A. What We Need to Do and Be Careful About

In 1977, a report by the American Association of School Administrators identified more than fifty different strategies that schools were trying to deal with discipline problems. To date, that number has more than doubled. These strategies include: token reward systems, assertive discipline systems, conflict resolution training, administrators working with discipline committees, crisis intervention teams, student grievance and appeals committees, parent councils on discipline, in-school and out-of-school suspensions, etc. And yet the problem persists as the number one deterrent to our educational process. Why is this? Some sociologists or psychologists may argue that it is not the case that educators are less capable, but that students (because of sociological or psychological factors) are just more disruptive than they used to be; it is not we who are worse, but the kids. Why then haven't we kept up with the necessary understanding of these factors or the art of preventing and handling these disruptions?

I think there are several answers to this question:

1. There has not been enough help for you, the teacher. That must be our main focus. Disruptive behavior first shows itself between student and teacher, even if its causes may sometimes be in the home environment. There is nothing wrong with parent effectiveness training, nor sociological analyses of the ills of our society. But the present stress of these problems falls mostly on you, the teacher. Even if such problems are passed along to our school administrators, they still reflect on us and our jobs as teachers. Although this book does not pretend to replace a supportive administration nor effective parenting before the children arrive in your room, it can give you some tools to use in the one arena you can control: your classroom.
2. Most teacher-education programs you have gone through do not have any courses devoted to handling discipline problems. If the subject is

approached, it is often swept under the rug with "group dynamics" or as "classroom management." The latter topic tends to gloss over the problem by treating it as if all would be solved with the proper lesson plan, a tidy classroom and bulletin board, and systematic classroom routines. These certainly help, but teachers receive little help regarding the key source of discipline problems: the complex interaction between student and teacher. We can have all of our "classroom management" techniques ready and in place, yet we still need to know how to handle and explain the fact that Tommy just told me, "Go to Hell!" Why doesn't he act that way toward Mr. Anderson? And Mr. Anderson doesn't even have a neat bulletin board!

3. A key part of the answer is that it is insufficient to train teachers in technique alone. One of the major sources of discipline problems is this complex human interaction between teacher and student. Thus, one of the major ways to prevent discipline problems is to train teachers how to form an educational, nonadversarial, even partnership, relationship with students. It is a fact that the same kids love some of their teachers, whereas they hate other teachers. And the fact is not explained by analysis of the differing techniques or routines of these teachers. Both Mr. X and Mr. Y may write the same classroom rules on the chalkboard, use behavior modification, even have the same clear and systematic classroom routines, yet kids may love Mr. X's class, but they dislike and act out in Mr. Y's class. The unavoidable conclusion is that who the teacher is, i.e., his or her delivery of the lesson plan (not just the lesson plan itself) with his or her jokes, affect and gestures, is the significant difference. We'd like to avoid this conclusion because we are saying that, in a way, it's the teacher's personality that is often a crucial factor here. Well, it is! But we need not avoid this issue out of our fear that this crucial factor is not teachable. We can understand and articulate this complex set of personal skills, affect and values, and train for these. As a matter of fact, that will be one of the basic things we will work on in this book.

4. What has also impeded the development of the art of preventing and handling discipline problems is that teachers differ as to when they think it is accurate to call a classroom situation a "discipline problem." Even the same teacher will identify the same situation sometimes as a discipline problem and sometimes not. One teacher's discipline problem will be described by another as "no big deal." This is not simply the "picture problem" we describe below in number 9 of this chapter. One teacher will consider Tommy doing his Spanish homework in his/her Math class a discipline problem, whereas others will not. Even the same teacher will consider this situation a discipline problem on Monday the third period but will not consider it to be one on Tuesday the sixth period. This is

because teachers are not clear with themselves, and certainly with each other, as to when it is appropriate to call a situation a discipline problem. The state of the art of preventing and handling discipline problems has been greatly impeded by this mire of equivocation. We will need to get clear as to when we should call it a discipline problem, as opposed to, for example, "an educational problem" or "a guidance problem."

5. Not enough help has been given in the area of prevention. Often, educators spend much energy on how to control disruptive behavior; some even suggest corporal punishment.[18] Instead, this book is based on always trying to discover the sources of discipline problems and preventing them rather than trying to extinguish them. The major recommendation will be to discover and train for that relationship between student and teacher that does not make them feel like enemies. Students have the right to feel satisfied in the classroom, and it is our job to deliver what is both satisfying and educational. In this sense, when students "turn off" to our lessons, it is we who should feel the demands of our job, not the students who should feel the power of our position.

6. There is another reason why we cannot avoid the crucial factor we discussed in 3 above: the teacher's personality. The effectiveness of any specific technique is only as cogent as that technique is congruent with the style and personality of the teacher who uses it. Students are not taught by techniques or lesson plans. They are taught by a person; that person is the teacher. A technique is as effective as it is congruent with the teacher who employs it. That is why one man's food can be another man's poison, or one teacher's well-delivered technique can be another's incongruent incitement to riot. That is why the kids in Mr. X's class heed him when he shouts, "If you call out again, you'll see me after class," whereas the same kids in Mr. Y's class, when he issues an identical injunction, just laugh. This is not just because Mr. X follows through on what he says.

It is also because the kids believe and feel Mr. X is "behind" what he says, whereas they do not feel that about Mr. Y. In short, the kids would say, "We listen to Mr. X because he doesn't bullshit, and you can just feel that." What they are feeling is that Mr. X's comment or technique is congruent with who he is. Carl Rogers defined congruence as that relationship in communication when the speaker's words and gestures seem to match or correspond to what the speaker is really feeling. A rule

---

[18] The frustration level regarding this issue is often so high that a survey showed the majority of teachers and parents favoring corporal punishment in the schools in 1972. See Robert J. Trotter, "This is Going to Hurt You More Than It Hurts Me," *Science News,* Vol. 102 (Nov. 18, 1972): 332–333. **For more on corporal punishment, see Chapter 12B.2, p. 295.**

or technique that is advocated by a teacher who does not feel personally in line with that rule will appear incongruent to students, lack cogency, and thus effectiveness. That is why this book cannot be a catalogue of recommended techniques, and why one teacher can't solve another's discipline problems with simply the advice: just do or say what I do. This is also why behavior modification techniques without attention to congruence go only so far and do not by themselves create an allied relationship between student and teacher. As a matter of fact, it is the lack of awareness of this key factor, congruence, or its awareness coupled with the belief it is not teachable, that has held back the state of the art of preventing and handling discipline over the years. Sure, technique is important, as is followthrough—so are systematic rewards and punishment, etc.—but if these are not delivered congruently, they will be ineffective. We must (and will here) train teachers to be congruent. It is this ingredient that fosters a relationship between student and teacher that keeps them from becoming enemies.

7. Along with the above point, we must also point to the problem of simple resistance. Teachers, who are also people, do not like to show their vulnerability. Mr. Y probably tried, unsuccessfully, what worked for Mr. X, but would rather say things are "fine now," than really share that he still has difficulties. Furthermore, it is difficult for us as teachers to change our style or techniques, or correct our incongruence; after all, the latter has to do with our personality. Most of us tend to teach the way we were taught. We came out of school saying, "I'm going to be like Mr. Smith whom I remember as my greatest teacher." The trouble is that we are not Mr. Smith. We are ourselves. We must find those techniques and lesson plans that are congruent with who we are. Our wonderful Mr. Smith was probably great because he was congruent. If we copy him, we won't be congruent. That is why we need more than understanding to be an effective teacher. We need training, so that we will naturally react with effectiveness and congruence. This kind of training must be more effective than our resistance to reveal our inabilities. We'll have to practice being effective and congruent. We'll have to overcome our stubbornness to do it as we've always done it. We'll also have to guard against our anxiety. When we get anxious, we usually go back to teaching the way we were taught, and once again we become incongruent.

8. Teachers need to learn how to practice their own behaviors that prevent and naturally handle disruptive behavior. That means teacher-educators need to spend less time in education courses on lesson plans and techniques and more time on giving teachers training and practice. That means doing, trying out, creating styles of teacher behaviors that work for each teacher. Teachers and prospective teachers need to take fewer notes from teacher-

educators. Instead, they need training designs in which they try out their own congruent behaviors for dealing effectively with student-teacher situations. For instance, teachers need help with their delivery of the lesson plan (like the comedian who works on his delivery) besides help with the written-out lesson plan itself.

9. Another factor that has impeded the development of the art of preventing and handling discipline problems is what I shall call "the picture problem." Simply speaking, when teachers describe their discipline problems or give advice to each other, they tend to think they understand one another and are talking about the same thing. Most of the time, the two teachers are usually picturing very different situations. For instance, Mr. X asks Mr. Y, "What do you do when you have a class clown?" Mr. Y pictures his Tommy, who is a good student and is funny, and whose timing even makes the lesson fun. So, Mr. Y responds: "Oh, I just ignore him," whereas Mr. X has a class clown who is failing, whose jokes are hostile, and whose timing purposely disrupts Mr. X's lesson. No wonder a teacher's advice is often inappropriate or often something the other teacher already tried. And, usually, this advice is more rewarding to the adviser, who loves to give advice. Consequently, teachers seldom seek advice from each other. It is this "picture problem," besides the issue of congruence, that has made it so difficult for teachers to get help from one another.

10. It is now clearer why so many attempts have failed to remedy this problem: many attempts are in the form of advice and judgments. These cannot accomplish much. Advice and judgments are usually off the mark if teachers and advisers picture different things or have different personalities that make many suggestions incongruent for them. Also, since many discipline problems have their source in very complex student-teacher interactions (not in a violated rule or routine), judgments and advice about what you should be doing usually are not helpful. If you are a troubled teacher, be careful about swallowing others' advice and judgment whole. If you are advising teachers or future teachers, your advice may only luckily hit the mark or have already been tried unsuccessfully. And your advice and judgments may alienate you from a teacher who now not only feels misunderstood but annoyed with your "shoulds." Also, advice and judgments usually leave the adviser feeling wiser and stronger and the advised dumber and weaker. A teacher left in this state has certainly not been left in a better state to handle discipline problems.[19]

---

[19] Teacher educators will find it useful to refer their teachers and student teachers back to these points in this chapter as "pitfalls" that we fall into as we often attempt inadequate or ineffective methods of handling discipline problems.

B. A Summary and Critique of the Literature

A description of the limits of various approaches to this problem would not be complete without a critique of some of the major books that have attempted to tackle this problem. (A more general Resource Bibliography can be found at the back of this book in Section SF.8.) Some of the most influential ones have been:

A. Canter, Lee and Marlene. *Assertive Discipline: A Take-Charge Approach for Today's Educator.* Seal Beach, California: Canter and Associates, 1976. (Updated for Parents, 1995)

B. Chernow, Fred and Carol. *Classroom Discipline and Control: 101 Practical Techniques.* West Nyack, New York: Parker Publishing Co., 1981. (Updated for Grades 4-8, 1986)

C. Collins, Myrtle. *Survival Kit for Teachers.* California: Goodyear Publishing Co., 1975.

D. Dobson, James. *Dare to Discipline.* Wheaton, Illinois: Tyndale House Publishers, 1970.

E. Dreikurs, Rudolf and Pearl Cassel. *Discipline without Tears: What to Do with Children Who Misbehave.* New York: Hawthorn Books, 1974.

F. Ernst, Ken. *Games Students Play and What to Do about Them.* Melbrae, California: Celestial Arts, 1973.

G. Glasser, William. *Schools without Failure.* New York: Harper and Row Publishers, 1969. (also Quality School Teacher, 1993)

H. Gordon, Thomas. *T.E.T: Teacher Effectiveness Training.* New York: McKay Publishing Co., 1975.

I. Johnson, Simon O. and Verna J. Johnson. *Better Discipline: A Practical Approach.* 2nd ed. Illinois: Charles C Thomas Publisher, 1990.

J. Keating, Barbara et al. *A Guide to Positive Development.* Boston: Allyn and Bacon, 1990.

K. Madsen, Charles and Clifford. *Teaching Discipline: Behavioral Principles Towards a Positive Approach.* 2nd ed. Boston: Allyn and Bacon, 1981.

L. Raths, Louis. *Values and Teaching.* Columbus: Charles E. Merrill Publishing Co., 1966. (also Thinking Strategies, 1986)

M. Weinstein, Carol Simon. *Secondary Classroom Management.* New York: McGrawHill, 1996.

N. Weinstein, Carol Simon and Andrew J. Mignano, Jr. *Elementary Classroom Management: Lessons from Research and Practice.* 2nd ed. New York: McGrawHill, 1997.

Although it is not possible in this short space to detail the approach of each book, let me at least give a brief description of the general tack each one takes toward trying to resolve classroom behavior problems.[20]

A. Canter's book recommends a logical system of conditioning and reinforcement with rules set up exclusively by the teacher with clear rewards and punishments. There is little regard for the inner emotions of the disruptive child, and the child is not in on the decision making. The teacher is in command and decides on the appropriate directive techniques, rewards, or punishments. "Teachers have the right to have this power and use it for their own needs in order to teach" (p. 2).

B. Chernow's book recommends specific behaviors a teacher should try for a multitude of situations and has a suggestion (in the form of "How to . . .") for resolving classroom routine problems, as well as mediating psychological problems. It's full of advice about homework, improving the physical environment, what to do about constant talkers, cheating, foul language, stealing, etc. Its approach seems eclectic; sometimes its advice is focused on prevention and sometimes on behavior modification. At other times, it takes almost a Rogerian-understanding approach by talking to the feelings that may be instigating the disruption. One might use this book by finding the situation listed in the table of contents that is your problem and read the author's advice.

C. Collins' book is similar to Chernow's in that it is also a book of advice and suggestions. However, Collins' book has many possible suggestions for almost every seemingly disruptive situation. It is like a shotgun catalogue of what you can try, given a particular classroom situation. It lists over forty classroom situations in alphabetical order: absence, anger, arguments, bathroom going, bus pass hand out, cheating, clowning, crushes on you, dress, etc. Then, you can turn to any one of these and listen to a number of possible things you might try for each one. There does not seem to be any unified philosophy or approach, other than the book's catalogue layout itself.

D. Dobson's book, like Canter's, also sees the teacher as controller of a conditioning system of rewards and punishments. Dobson even justifies the use of physical punishment in certain situations to teach standards of behavior and moral development. The book leans heavily on a rationale of Christian, religious principles (pp. 24–25, 107).

E. In Dreikurs and Cassel's book the teacher is a clarifier, boundary delineator, and ultimately an enforcer of behaviors that will enable the child and

---

[20] For a more detailed analysis of some of these books (though one that is less critical than mine), the reader is referred to Wolfgang and Glickman's *Solving Discipline Problems*. Boston: Allyn and Bacon, 1998.

society to get along and function well. The approach always is to try to get children to be responsible for their actions and then help each to find the best social contract for all concerned. The teacher diagnoses which "faulty goal" is motivating the unsocial behavior, and by questioning, directive statements, and modeling (not through reinforcement or punishment) "talks to" the rational capacities of the child. There is confidence here in the effect of showing the child the <u>logical consequences</u> of his or her actions.

F. Ernst's book recommends resolving discipline problems by seeing each child's behavior within the framework of transactional analysis (T.A.). What students do (so the book suggests) is to a great extent a reflex response to a "tape" of a similar past situation, a remembrance of, e.g., a parental reprimand. Each child is in the process of learning how to negotiate with the <u>Adult</u> part of himself as he deals with his Parent and <u>Child</u> parts. A student who is consistently disruptive does so because of an unproductive tension among these three inner parts of himself. The teacher needs to resolve this tension by affirming the capability of the <u>Child</u> and talking to the child's <u>Parent</u> and <u>Adult</u> through various forms of "stroking." With this approach, reinforcement and punishment take a back seat to understanding and listening.

G. Glasser's book suggests that the teacher's role is enforcer, one who encounters the disruptive child by pointing out the misbehavior and firmly directing the correct behavior. The child is shown the irresponsibility of the misbehavior in the context of a social contract that requires each individual to heed others' needs and rights. If the child does not heed these directive statements, the teacher is to follow with questions to the child that ultimately teach the child the irrationality of his or her behavior. Though Glasser mostly presupposes that just the child's rationality and enlightened awareness of social responsibility will do the trick, he also sometimes approves of reinforcement, but then only in terms of removing privileges from the child. He does not believe punishment is effective. But he will sometimes recommend that the child be isolated, not for punishment's sake, but, again, to leave the child to contemplate the irrational consequences of his or her actions in the context of social responsibility.

H. Gordon's book, in a way, suggests we apply Rogerian psychology to the classroom disruptive child. The teacher is a listener, facilitator, empathizer—not an enforcer, punisher, nor even controller. There is much faith put here in acceptance and being supportive. A disruptive child is not abused, judged, or criticized in this approach. Instead, he is given <u>understanding</u> regarding the emotions that are behind the misbehavior. Gordon delineates problems that are "student-owned" vs. teacher-owned to decide on one's approach. But he strongly disagrees with any use of rewards or punishments as ways to reinforce the good behavior. Instead, he believes that "I" messages from the teacher, empathy, and modeling the appropriate behavior will usually resolve the problem. He is against trying to control the child. The furthest he will go is to recommend the need for strong directive statements to the child or a reorganization of the child's environment. But, he warns, these moves must only be for "influencing" and for "support." If they suggest power, they are (according to Gordon) ineffective, even provocative of further misbehavior.

I. Johnson's book provides strategies for teachers and administrators to prevent discipline problems. It briefly discusses why students demonstrate negative behaviors and lists some reasons for the causes of discipline problems. It then describes various kinds of problems (tutorial, mentor) and enrichment activities. The fourth section of the book discusses discipline and minorities, and finally, a section is devoted to specific discipline problems, e.g., students who come unprepared, who talk while the teacher is giving directions, who lack note-taking skills, etc.

J. Keating's book recommends that the emphasis must be on self-discipline and on helping students make responsible decisions. It maintains that you can (as with any other area of the curriculum) teach students the concepts of self-discipline, show them how to make responsible decisions, and perform responsible behaviors—if they are given ample time to practice these and ample praise and recognition. Such students may need to be corrected and retaught at times, but the goal is self-discipline. Students are instructed about the proper behaviors regarding, e.g., achievement, social interactions, safety, care of the environment, etc. These behavioral expectations are developed, explained, taught, and practiced. Students are taught about the decisions and choices they make each day and how these impact their lives and their school. These learnings and behaviors are then reinforced by positive consequences, recognition, and privileges, and often logic is used to show the reason for doing the appropriate behavior. The author believes that, often, at the root of irresponsible behavior is simply "poor decision making." Students are encouraged to be involved in forming the "expectations" for their classroom and, thereby, their own behavior. They, therefore, become partners with the teacher to support, not the teacher's "rules," but the expectations agreed upon. The book then provides a step by step approach to implementing this philosophy, backed up with useful materials (lessons) that can be used in class with students.

K. Madsen's book suggests that the teacher control the environment. The teacher needs to condition the child with the proper commands, rewards, and punishments to teach the child not to misbehave. "If the teacher wants a student to behave a certain way, the teacher must structure the student's external world (i.e., control his environment) to ensure the desired outcome" (p. 7). Madsen is a behaviorist. He does not recommend searching the origins of the child's behavior, nor does he believe that supportive empathy will elicit the appropriate behavior. The approach is one of conditioning and reinforcement for behavior modification.

L. Raths' book suggests the teacher be a facilitator of various activities that clarify ways of behaving, attitudes, aspirations, and values. The rationale is that such activities will bring about an awareness of socially productive alternative ways of behaving. Raths believes that the causes of much misbehavior lie in the child's lack of the knowledge of right and wrong and a lack of ability to choose personal values within a moral context. As with Gordon, Raths (also influenced by Rogers) does not recommend that the teacher be a controller or judge. The role of the teacher is to facilitate behavioral and moral clarification via skilled exercises and dialogue in a supportive, nonjudgmental atmosphere. Raths has faith that this method will move the child through a process of choosing, then prizing, then acting appropriately (p. 30).

M. In Weinstein's book, about two thirds of the discussions are about the latest research (up to 1996) on effective classroom management. The other third integrates into these findings some "practical knowledge" culled from real secondary school teachers from varied subject areas. The research presented and the teachers' contributions are organized into these areas: the physical environment of the classroom; developing and teaching rules and routines; gaining students' cooperation; and making the most use of classroom time. There are also more specific discussions about managing seatwork, groupwork, and recitations. Then, there is one ending chapter that discusses what is best to do when the above planning is insufficient to protecting and restoring order. The final section of the book offers suggestions and guidelines for working with students' families and with students who have "serious" problems.

N. Weinstein and Mignano's book combines research with knowledge from four practicing teachers to introduce classroom management on the elementary school level. The great strength of this book is in the prevention of discipline problems. It is very useful to the teacher who is setting up a classroom, or who is not in crisis. Each chapter discusses a facet of elementary classroom management, from the impact of the physical environment, to managing different teaching models, to helping troubled students. Chapters include a realistic discussion and definition of an aspect of classroom management (using citations from research and the teachers); solid recommendations on pragmatic approaches to the management aspect; an outline-form summary of the chapter; an activity/practice section; and a reference list. The book offers both theoretical and practical suggestions on classroom management, all of which are reliable techniques. The book unfortunately does not offer immediate help to the teacher who is in the middle of a true discipline emergency. By its structure and content, the authors imply that prevention of discipline problems is all a teacher should need. Although there is a chapter entitled "When Prevention Is Not Enough: Protecting and Restoring Order" the problems presented, while real problems, are not generally of the scale that we are discussing in this text. The authors approach important issues, such as defiance and profanity, and the suggestions offered are good. The emphasis continues to be on prevention, but there is no offer of further resources if the situation is not resolved.

All of the above books are useful for some teachers and for some situations. However, some are limited as practical guides for preventing and handling discipline problems by several inadequacies:

(a) Of the above books, only N clearly defines when it is appropriate for a teacher to call a situation a "discipline problem." But, unfortunately, like so many other books, there is an overemphasis on an easy area: the physical environment of the classroom. And, some key source areas are neglected: the teacher's personality; congruence regarding rules, warnings, and the lesson plan delivery; and an adequate discussion of the baggage that students bring with them into the classroom from their families and peer relationships.

(b) None of the above books, with the exceptions of M and N, focus on prevention by trying to systematically articulate the specific causal events or sources of discipline problems. Many of the above (e.g., A, D, E, F, G, L) do offer a theoretical psychology for the causes of antisocial behavior or misbehavior. J, like G, assumes too much that misbehavior comes out of irrationality, that simply better decision making and awareness of unproductive consequences will be enough to make children behave according to the proper "expectations." Youngsters, unfortunately, are not just rational. They often act out merely by the push of immediate emotions and needs without any eye to the future consequences. The book adds forms of behavior modification to supplement this situation, but not enough is said about "congruence" or the inability, at times, to wait until consensus is built among student "expectations." J especially seems so reluctant to enforce rules. One wonders what is to be done if students don't join the "team" or what happens during the long time it takes to build a consensus of "expectations" while the teacher must continue to teach the academic curriculum. Such a consensus is difficult, especially in the upper grades, where students may be intentionally unfair to others and enjoy delay tactics to not get back to the subject matter lessons. (It is more advisable to allow students in the lower grades to create the rules for the class than it is advisable in the upper grades. For more on this valuable tact, see Chapter 12H. 1. But there is no systematic delineation of the concrete sources or initiating events of these behaviors. Whether they originate from outside school, inside school but right outside the classroom, or from inside the classroom (from its environment, or the teacher's interaction with the students, etc.)—knowing the concrete originating events of these behaviors would be very helpful. (Although I does discuss some useful sources of negative behavior, the strokes are too broad and not systematic.) M suggests that all its advice is "preventive" because it has a concluding chapter entitled: "When Prevention is Not Enough," implying that the previous chapters have covered the major, necessary sources of disruptive behavior. But, unfortunately, like so many other books, there is an overemphasis on an easy area: the physical environment of the classroom. And some key source areas are neglected: the teacher's personality; congruence regarding rules, warnings, and the lesson plan delivery; and an adequate discussion of the baggage that students bring with them into the classroom from their families and peer relationships. The book makes some useful points: that structuring the lesson activities effectively can do more to prevent disruptive behavior than concentrating on "discipline tactics" per se; that one behavior may not be a problem in one situation, but a problem in another; that different kinds of rewards can be used to motivate the proper behaviors; and that "leadership" is important. Unfortunately, these points are mentioned without any full systematic presentation of exactly how to apply these true guidelines. Sure, it seems impossible to track down all the possible sources that ignite these misbehaviors. Yet, for there to be an approach to this problem that is also preventive, a systematic list of these sources should be attempted (with instructions about congruence).

(c) None of the above books accounts for the fact that, for some reason, one technique or reprimand used by one teacher works, while the same technique or reprimand tried by another teacher not only fails but is laughed at by the students. Why is it that when Mr. Smith says, "That's enough!" the kids seem to stop, whereas when Mr. Brown says the same thing (even imitating the same tone of voice), the kids make fun of his anger? The theoretical framework in which the reprimand is practiced (whether it's Canter's, Dobson's, Dreikurs') seems irrelevant. Some teachers can make their statements work; some can't, no matter which of the books' strategies they try. And following through on reprimands doesn't seem to explain this fact sufficiently either. The fact is (as we shall discuss later) students believe a teacher's statement when they can see that the teacher is personally "congruent" with the statement. We will have to understand this important phenomenon that gives certain communications their impact. Without an understanding of this subtle power of credibility, and how to become good at it, the strategies of all of the above books often fall on deaf ears.

(d) Many of the books (E, F, G, H, L) are an attempt to transfer the efficacy possible in a one-on-one therapeutic situation to a classroom group situation.

Whether one tries to be a clarifier of the social contract, or use the framework of T.A., or Rogers', such approaches take a long time for such growth of rational awareness and self-control. Often, teachers do not have the time or the ability to work that closely with the individual disrupter.

(e) Many would argue that any behavior modification system of reward and punishment (books A, D, K) shows too little regard for the underlying emotions that are often the source of misbehavior. To look past these feelings and only at the behavior is to look past the child. Also, to condition the correct response, while possibly damaging the relationship with this disregard for feelings, can provoke anger that leads to further misbehavior. A regard for the feelings of the student would also require that, if a punishment were used, it should feel educationally appropriate and fair to the child.

Also, reward and punishment systems need to be careful about <u>punishments.</u> Those that only extinguish the wrong behavior, without showing the right behavior, only teach repression and held-in anger at the enforcer. Both of these reactions do not last long. They usually turn into active hostility when the enforcer's power slips. Any classroom discipline based only on power (rather than also on a good relationship between student and teacher) requires a kind of exhaustive energy on the part of the teacher that can't (nor should) last. Such teachers hate their jobs, and the kids know it and go after these teachers.

(f) On the other hand, solely the attempt to have a good, rational, empathetic relationship Books F, G, H, L), one that nurtures the student, is often not sufficient nor efficient for the teacher's responsibility to the rest of the students disrupted by the few. These authors shy too far away from any use of rewards and punishments. Children may often choose the short-term immediate gratification rather than the long-term socially best behavior—even if the former is illogical. Passive, nonverbal students are very difficult to process through such a verbal system as T.A. or T.E.T. And some hostile students may gain more acceptance in the social contract by being "bad."

To summarize, the above approaches are useful for some teachers, for some situations, but suffer from important inadequacies. In short, we might say that a complicated eclectic approach that uses the best of these approaches would be very useful. As we discussed above, we need to bring direct aid to <u>the teachers</u> who are on the front lines and let them know they are not alone (we shall in Chapter 3). We need to help teachers understand why kids seem to go after certain teachers (we shall in Chapter 5) and help them with deciding when to call it: "a discipline problem" (Chapter 4). Our eyes need to be always turned toward the sources of disruption, so we can spend our energies on prevention (Chapters 6–9). We will have to examine the complex interactions of student and teacher personalities and only try rules or routines that are congruent for each teacher (Chapters 10–13). As we work on these problems, we must respect the fact that teachers, like most people, are resistant to change and that this is a very anxious area for most. We must avoid advice and judgments, instead, provide guidelines for each to find his or her own congruent behaviors, routines, and rules. Then, we need to help teachers practice these, train for immediate, spontaneous classroom situations. We must listen carefully to these problems so that we don't mis-help because we are each, perhaps, picturing something different. Often, it might be better to ask a teacher to show us what happens in his or her classroom, rather than just tell us. Finally, we may have to sometimes use rewards and punishments, but only when we do not have time for a therapeutic teaching relationship. And, if we have to regretfully use the former, we will have to make sure we are congruent with our system, and the system is educationally appropriate.

CHAPTER 3: YOU'RE NOT ALONE
"Right in the middle of my lesson, this kid suddenly . . ."

We have already mentioned that since 1974 teachers across the country have named discipline problems as their major difficulty. So, you're certainly not alone. Yet few teachers will admit to each other that they have trouble controlling their classes. Teachers feel that such problems are a sign of a "bad teacher." Often, because they are afraid of looking bad, they are reluctant to discuss these problems with the people they often need to talk to the most: the school's dean or principal. Many teachers work very hard to design creative, motivated lessons, try (almost to the point of exhaustion) to enforce rules, and even plead with students—only to be frustrated, harassed, and even humiliated. Often, they feel it is not their fault. The kids seem disruptive before they enter the classroom, or the problems seem to come out of nowhere.

What follows is the start of this seeming "assault on the job" as it begins in student teaching, and then actual accounts of teachers in grades K–12 in all subjects who attempt to endure these difficulties. Teachers: for you, check the ones that you can relate to; you'll see, "it has happened to others too"; they may even seem relievingly funny. Teacher-educators: this is how it often feels to your student teachers and teachers you are trying to help. What would you suggest to these teachers? Parents: your child may be in these teacher-described situations. Here you need to be reminded that your son's or daughter's difficulties, although seemingly centered on him or her, are usually within a class or group problem, at least from the teacher's point of view. We all need to be more aware and empathetic of what it's like to be up in front of that classroom all day.

1. "I remember when I thought I was going to be this great teacher."
(the education student or student teacher)

Do you remember that? Or, are you now studying to become a future teacher? Well, perhaps you can relate to the following, sometimes the typical, story of "becoming a teacher":

I sat in my square tight desk in row three imagining: "If I were teaching behind that big desk up there, I'd do it my way and it would be so much better!"

Now that I'm almost there, I have pictured teaching my first class about twelve times already. I have pictured writing the aim of the lesson on the chalkboard. It would be important and motivational, written clearly, with a certain flair. I would have all my rules listed in yellow chalk on the side board in order of importance, ending with perhaps a little joke. In light blue chalk I would have written out my marking system. No, it would all be on two ditto sheets handed out as each came in the door. No, maybe I'd better give them to each kid on the first seat and ask them to:

"Please pass the extras back." No, "Pass the extras back." I don't need "please," I'm their teacher.

As my first big day actually approached, I prepared three lecture topics and four clever methods about getting across the significance of the Boston Tea Party. I also prepared two class participation debates from brilliant questions I had created and two small cartoons they would interpret. My hope was to fill the first forty-minute period with this. (I was terrified that there would be ten minutes left until the bell rang and I would run out!)

Luckily, my five months of student teaching had been easy. So far, I only had to teach twice and luckily just review lessons. But these kids wouldn't be like those kids. These kids tomorrow morning would be youngsters, with open minds, thirsting for knowledge. I'd just have to feed them nourishing ideas. Teaching them would simply be just showing them how to learn. I'd make a great contribution. They'd say: "There's a great teacher, really nice; one you can talk to."

My alarm clock rang. I was exhausted. I changed my mind again as to what to wear and put on the blue dotted tie with the off-white shirt, instead of the tie with the little animal on it and the shirt with snaps. I ran to the train with my new attache case filled with extra pens, stenciled puzzles, and extra paper. As I got on the train I repeated: "Control them, but don't be a dictator." "Come across confident but human." "Help the kids who need it, but don't make them feel self conscious."

When I got to the school the side doors wouldn't open; so I ran around to the front. When I got in, the time clock wouldn't hit my card right (it looked like I had worked on Sunday). Then, the wrong roll book was in my mailbox and my homeroom was moved to the annex (which had locked faculty bathrooms that used a different key). Then, I was supposed to "note" these twelve new school rules and procedural changes on these six very light blue printed ditto sheets.

The bell rang. I was a little late to my first class. They were all there before me. "Go to Hell teacher" was written on the chalkboard. There was no chalk anywhere. In the middle of trying to present myself, I was interrupted by latecomers three times (one winked, one waved, and one just danced in).

I got scared and tight. To protect myself, I tried to let them know I was their teacher, not just any person on their block. I tried to show them I knew a lot of information. After all, all these college courses, notes, and facts I learned should gain me respect. However, I became afraid when I didn't know an answer.

Two kids fell asleep in the back of the room, and some tilted their chairs back, and drove me crazy. If I said, "You're disturbing the class!" they'd say "I wasn't bothering anybody!" I had no "comeback." I'd spend hours preparing lessons that I really got involved in. But the class would just digress from my lesson and irritate me like crazy.

Kids would come in angry at their mothers, so they got angry at me. Or they had just had a fight with another student, or a previous teacher—and I got the tail end of it. No one really asked kids for passes in the hallway or stopped kids from hanging out. Even if my own class was fine, the loose school rules would mess my class up.

I had trouble getting from my 3rd period room, 132, to my fourth period room, 323, on time. By the tame I got to room 323, they were all there. The desks were out of order, and the chalkboard had Economics notes all over it that I had to erase.

My rules started falling apart. Whatever I said didn't seem to matter to them. I forgot some of the warnings I gave or couldn't decide what to do if a kid said, "Oh yeah!" I had trouble taking stands. I tried to be myself, but I didn't know how much of myself I could be. Sometimes, the second I would start the lesson, they'd "turn off."

I would prepare very logical lessons, but somehow I'd get disorganized. Then, they'd start playing games and act like wise guys. Either they were all "asleep," or they'd all start calling out.

I became more and more a policeman and less a teacher and couldn't get close to them. I got a sore throat from yelling and was exhausted at the end of each day. I found myself only looking forward to weekends or vacations and dreading Mondays.

I was overwhelmed by trying to handle absences, kids arguing back at me, going to the bathroom, cheating, clowning, coming in high, chewing gum, passing notes, smoking, and swearing. I had little time to really prepare lessons while trying to fill out bus passes, cut cards, roll books, late passes, the bathroom sign-out book, and ethnic survey reports.

Whenever I needed the dean or the principal, they were never to be found. If the dean did see a kid that I sent him, he would joke with the kid, make light of the problem, and send the kid back to me making me look like a fool. All I got from the dean or the principal was: "Make sure the kids don't wear hats in school!"

I kept hoping that my education supervisor would rescue me. I never thought being an education student or student teacher would be like this!

The above fantasy represents the following kinds of normal uncertainties and fears of student teachers:

Some Uncertainties of Most Student Teachers

1. Will students recognize my lack of confidence?
2. Will I be able to control the group?
3. How strict should I be?
4. How lenient should I be?
5. Should I attempt to impress the cooperating teacher?
6. Will my voice be too loud?
7. Am I speaking clearly?
8. What may happen when I turn my back to write on the chalkboard?
9. What attention-seeking students should I ignore?
10. How should I introduce myself?
11. What should I tell them about myself?
12. When should I ignore my plan book?
13. How should I handle a defiant student?
14. Will they like me?
15. Will they respect me?
16. Should I play with them at recess?
17. How can I de-emphasize the teacher image and be more real with them without losing control of the class?
18. What will happen if the regular classroom teacher leaves the room?
19. What if I don't agree with the cooperating teacher?
20. How am I going to get the students involved?
21. What if I lose my temper with the class?
22. What should I do if a kid says I'm being racist?
23. What if I can't operate the projector or the computer?
24. Should I let the children call me by my first name?
25. Should I give weekend homework assignments?
26. Will I have to play the piano?
27. Should I dress simply or with flair, or be myself a lot, or dress like "the teacher"?
28. What should I do when the principal enters the room?
29. How should I conduct myself with parents?
30. How should I handle the following kinds of problems:

A. Fighting in class	B. Arguments
C. Cheating	D. Gum chewing
E. Students "high" in class	F. Personal stereos
G. Eating in class	H. Students who don't do the homework
I. Students who call out	J. Name calling

K. Cursing   L. Students talking during
                                        my lesson
M. Students throwing things   N. "Class clowns"
O. Withdrawn students   P. Asserting myself

You may want to survey your fellow student teachers and see if they would check off the same "uncertainties" above that you would. You're not alone.

Hopefully, things don't go as bad as depicted in the fantasy above. However, the following are actual reports from real teachers who have various kinds of discipline problems.[21] As you know, it's rough out there in front of a class. We will not analyze them. Let's just listen to how it feels and perhaps share with them what we're worried about or what has happened to us.

2. "A circle of wrestlers" (Kindergarten)

I was reading a story—using a lot of "Would you do this?" "Have you ever seen . . .?"

I was feeling fine—maybe tired and perhaps anticipating the end of the day.

The children were sitting around the rim of a round rug. They were listening in an interested manner, but they were all so very eager to answer the questions that everyone started to interrupt everyone else and to call out.

As the children started to call out and interrupt each other, they also began moving into the center of the circle and at this precise time the "problem" occurred. Lewis hit Michael because he was accidentally kicked. Michael, who loves to retaliate, began hitting Lewis, and the "rumpus" began, "free-for-all"—with all the children crunched together in the circle. It was very difficult to get to the fighters. The circle of children appeared to be a circle of wrestlers.

It seemed necessary to grab either Lewis or Michael and then hopefully everything would go back to its original state. After Lewis was caught, Michael simmered down, but the others were tumbling all over each other.

At first, I felt scared. I was afraid someone would get seriously hurt. Then my fear turned to anger. How could these children do this!

3. "The room was very peaceful." (1st grade, Writing)

I was walking around the room helping the children with some written work. I was feeling very good. Everyone was really into doing a good job. I

---

[21]These are descriptions of classroom incidents from teachers who have been teaching less than five years and were enrolled in graduate education courses at Lehman College, New York City. They taught in Manhattan, the Bronx (many in the South Bronx), and lower Westchester from 1976 to 1985.

was feeling satisfied. The kids were all working. They seemed to be enjoying themselves. I sensed they were feeling successful. The room was very peaceful.

I heard some noise at one of the tables. One of the boys had begun to push the child next to him. I asked him to stop and get back to work. He then tore up his paper and threw it on the floor. When I gave him a new sheet of paper and reprimanded him for tearing the old one, he pushed his desk over and began crying and yelling.

I felt really that he had invaded my nice little group of kids. I was angry and disgusted. At first, I didn't really want to know his problem; I just wanted him to "fit in."

I was outraged that he had thrown his desk over. I yelled at him that he could have hurt someone (but I really felt how dare he do this to me). This caused him to continue his yelling and kicking at his desk. When I tried to restrain him physically, he fought against me. I then tried to calm him down by calming myself down. I told him that I would sit down and help him with his work.

Honestly, at one point, I felt afraid that I wouldn't be able to calm him down. He was really getting wild. I felt kind of inadequate. But, as I began to stop being mad, I realized that maybe he was afraid also, that he couldn't do the work or that I wasn't paying enough attention to him.

4. "The class laughed." (1st grade, Math)

I was gathering material for my lesson. I was going to teach math and introduce the concept of addition. I was going to use different objects. It was Monday and I was a bit tired, but I had planned my lesson well. All the kids were sitting down in a circle and listening to what I had to say about addition. The tone of the room was quiet. There were two boys playing around not disturbing the class, but disturbing me.

Since the boys were disturbing my lesson, I had to give them some attention, and as I gave them attention the other children began to lose interest in the lesson. So, instead of having a problem with two children, I had a problem with four or five children.

I asked the children to sit down in their chairs quietly. They just wouldn't. I yelled at them, but the class laughed and cheered the two boys. I felt like two cents and wanted to punish the whole class. Finally, I grabbed one of the boys and scared him, and that got the whole class scared.

5. "Larry picked up his desk . . .!" (2nd Grade, Social Studies)

I was being videotaped teaching social studies. I had planned a great lesson integrating music and the geography of our city. I felt nervous about the taping, but confident about the lesson. I had taught the class the song "NYC," using it to talk about things that we observe in the city. I started the videotape and we began to review the song. In the middle of the first verse, Larry lay back on his desk and started to howl like a wolf. In my school, the policy is that a student cannot be sent out of the room to sit in the hall. In addition, my principal, Mr. Smith, had already given up on Larry and told me that he refused to see him in the office. I was on my own and on tape!

I continued with the song until we got to the part about "the Hudson at sundown." When I started discussion, I left the piano and moved around the room, stopping at Larry's desk to rest my hand gently on his shoulder. This often calmed him down and thankfully seemed to work that day. The class had a lot of ideas and quickly got the concept that the Hudson was a river and that Manhattan was an island. I was excited because the children were really getting into the topic and on their own were using the maps of New York City that they had brought in. Just as we started to talk about what had to be on the other side of Manhattan for it to be an island, Larry picked up his desk by about an inch and dropped it onto the floor. (Even though he was the right age for second grade, he was my size, which made it difficult when he got physical.) I tried resting my hand on his shoulder again, but it didn't work and he kept slamming the desk. Ignoring the noise, the class and I decided that Manhattan was an island because it was surrounded by water.

After the discussion, I went back to the piano to conclude the lesson by singing the song once more. I was relieved that Larry calmed down again when the piano started. Once the class was singing, however, he started both howling and slamming his desk. By now I was so frustrated I was ready to cry. He hadn't quite managed to completely sabotage my lesson, but he had ruined my videotape!

After the lesson, I sent the other children to get their snacks and asked to talk to Larry in the hall. When he finally got there, I asked him why he hadn't taken a walk when he got out of control the way we had agreed in our behavior contract. He said he didn't know. I asked him to stay in the hall until he did know and I went back into the room. He began loudly kicking the door and the door frame. When I ignored him, he ripped work off the hallway bulletin boards. Just then Mr. Smith happened to walk down the hall, but his only comment was to tell Larry to stop. When Larry ignored Mr. Smith, he just looked at me, shrugged, and said, "Take him back inside the room."

I felt abandoned by my administration, angry at the child, and like a failure as a teacher. I struggled through the rest of the day feeling totally incompetent. When I got home, I called my mother and told her I was never going back. I did go back, but I never managed to feel successful with that student or good about that year of teaching.

6. "A lot of yelling." (3rd grade, Math)

I was teaching a math lesson. I was in a good mood and confident that no problems would arise. The students were listening and participating in the lesson by answering questions verbally and writing on the chalkboard. There was an occasional bit of chatter in the room, but on the whole the class was quiet.

I gave the class an assignment in their math workbooks. When they were finished, they were told to come up to my desk, one at a time, and we'd go over the assignment individually. Students started talking to one another and rushing in line to have me look at their work. The noise continued even at my many requests for quiet in the room. I yelled at them.

I stood in front of the class and asked them to quiet down. I told them that when everyone was finished they would be allowed to whisper. They still talked. It didn't work.

I was annoyed and then became extremely angry when the class would not follow my directions. It took a lot of yelling to get them to quiet down.

7. "Talking out of turn." (4th grade, Math)

I was teaching a math lesson. I called up several children to the chalkboard to explain how they solved the math problems.

This particular student kept talking out of turn. He kept saying that math was stupid and didn't make any sense. He had always been deficient in math. He did little things to get the other students' attention; he made noises and put on strange faces.

I told him to stop. Even though he may not have been interested in learning, he had no right to prevent the other students from learning. He stopped for a little while, but then he resumed. Finally, I sent him out of the room. He sat in another classroom.

I felt very annoyed. This was not the first time with this student. I had tried to be as hopeful as I could that his behavior would improve.

8. "Rocking back and forth." (4th grade, Language skills in an open classroom)

I was teaching a Language Skills Group. It was a lesson on punctuation. I was bored and they were bored. The children were listening to my explanation of a "period." In other parts of the room, other higher level groups were engaged in similar activities. The room was fairly quiet, except for some pencil tapping and a hummer.

One child was rocking back and forth in his chair. I noticed this out of the corner of my eye, but being involved in what I was doing, I ignored it. Soon the child next to him began to do the same thing. I stopped the lesson and said, "Don't do that! First it's dangerous and secondly, it's distracting." At which point, a third child leaned all the way back and his chair fell over, which caused everyone else to fall off their chairs laughing.

When I noticed and said something I was starting to feel frustrated and upset. I feared what the next step would be: someone falling off their chair and everyone getting crazy. I felt like I was losing control of myself and the kids. I wanted to scream at them or tell them to just leave, but I couldn't because of the other teachers in the large room.

I felt I was in a situation completely out of my control and that I was not handling it at all. It was just happening, and I thought: in twenty minutes it would be lunch time and it would be all over, I hope! I stopped everything and looked at them and said something stupid like, "Well, that's just what I was talking about. Kenny, are you O.K.? Well now, let's get back to work." I don't think I handled it at all. Teachers from the other groups around the room turned and looked at me. I think we got back to work, but I don't even remember.

9. "Now, I really have problems!" (5th grade, Math)

I was teaching a math class. A girl got up out of her seat, danced around me or something, and then wrote on the board behind me. Until then, I was feeling fine and enthusiastic. She just got up out of nowhere. The kids were listening to me. The tone was fine. She just got up and did this, and that's it!

My first reaction was to stare at her as if she was insane. I then tapped her on the backside with the corner of an eraser, to sit down. She sat down and all appeared O.K. It definitely did not work because the next day I received a letter from her father who was really "pissed." He said that if I had tendencies to "throw" an eraser, then I had capabilities of throwing chairs, and desks, and maybe even kids. So, now that the father is on her side, it's a bad situation. She feels she has the right to do as she pleases, and now, I really have problems.

10. "I was lucky!" (6th grade, Math)

I was going over some worksheets on fractions. I was in a good mood because it was a Friday afternoon, last period. Four students were in the room talking quietly among themselves, going over some classroom assignment from another teacher. There were no troubles because the period was just beginning.

Then, a fifth student, a boy, came in about five minutes late. He had gotten into trouble with his classroom math-lab teacher for copying someone else's homework and getting caught. The other kids knew about it and started making fun of him. I tried to calm them down, but they were all "hyped up" for the weekend, and tempers started flying (and fists too) between two of the boys.

First, I tried to break the boys apart and couldn't. I was lucky that a male teacher was in the lab (next door) at the time and he separated the boys.

I was really angry and scared and said something to myself like, "Why do these bitches have to start my weekend off in a bad mood?"

I felt lucky that another teacher was there to help me out. I was wondering what would have happened if one of the kids took a swing at me!

11. "I was drained." (7th grade, Homeroom)

The discipline problem began immediately on my first day with the class. They had had four other teachers in the last week. I was beginning my first day as an English teacher in an I.S. open classroom. There are sixteen 7th and 8th grade classes in one large area with no real walls. I was formerly licensed as an Early Childhood teacher and had taught 1st, 2nd, 3rd, and 5th grade. I was feeling very frightened and anxious the whole weekend before beginning my new assignment. I had no idea of what I was supposed to teach and no materials.

The children had just walked into the homeroom, and they didn't know who I was. I introduced myself and explained that I was going to be here permanently, but they didn't believe me, after having four teachers in one week. There was a lot of noise from all sixteen classes in the area. In my own section, there seemed to be more movement and noise than anywhere else.

One child was escorted into the room by the dean because I had to be warned that he was a severe problem. He started right away to refuse to sit down or do any work. He got into a few small arguments (hitting and cursing) immediately. I had to grab his arm to stop him from stabbing a girl with a pencil. While I held onto him, the rest of the class became wild. They were out of their seats and shouting to each other.

I was terrified that the boy would get away from me and hurt someone. I was feeling very inadequate and felt I would never be able to gain control of these children.

I couldn't let go of the boy so I told another child to get the dean. There was no way to reason with the child, so I held on and shouted over the noise for the other children to be seated. They didn't listen. The dean came in and took the boy out of the room.

During the incident, I was angry at the other children for not understanding that they had to remain calm when I tried to contain the child. I was drained of all energy and strength. I just wanted to sit down and cry, but I knew I had to suppress my emotions and keep on working.

12. "I felt like a wild man." (7th grade)

I was in the hall as the class was entering the room. I was quite tired because it was Friday, the 8th period. I had just had a rough experience with the previous group. (It was my first year as a teacher.)

The students came in very noisy, running from the hall into the room. They were supposed to copy their homework from the board, but few were doing it. A couple of kids started "play-fighting."

Since the class came in so wild, I needed to calm them down so we could start the lesson. So I came in yelling and screaming and started to chase a boy who was running around the room. This further excited the students, and they seemed to be yelling and screaming over me and chasing me!

First I yelled and screamed louder, but this only intensified the noise level as they shouted over me. Finally, I sent for an assistant principal who settled them down. But as soon as he left, it all started again, even worse! Nothing I did worked. I felt extremely angry.

As it continued, I felt ridiculous, ashamed, angry, and frustrated. It had to be one of the most frustrating experiences of my life. I almost hit a kid—I think I did punch a kid very hard in his arm. I felt like a wild man and very incompetent.

13. "I picked John up." (7th grade, Math)

I was teaching the concept of set notation. I was using everyday examples and having students give their definition for certain words. I felt great. I had two free periods before this class. The kids were listening, participating in the class discussion, and writing formal definitions in their notebooks.

A particular student, John, refused to take his notebook out and copy notes. John was sitting in the last row in the room. During the lesson, he moved his desk and chair from the back of the room to the front. He began calling out things that didn't have anything to do with the lesson. He started shaking the other students' desks as they were writing. He lined up three chairs, lay down, and began singing!

First, I ignored John, but he was persistent. He was then informed that he would receive a zero for the day and he would be asked to bring his mother. This didn't work either. He informed me that he lives with his <u>grandmother</u> and she was too old to do anything. I sat down and wrote a note to the assistant principal explaining why I was sending John to his office. John immediately informed me that he was not leaving the room! By this time, I had reached the boiling point. I told everyone to remain seated until I got back. In a rage, I picked John up (he was about 80 lb) and took him to the assistant principal's office myself. What a day!

14. "I just lost my head." (8th grade, English)

I was teaching grammar, or some basically uninteresting subject, feeling tired and distracted. I was trying very hard to keep it a structured class and still get the kids involved. Deep down, I was just hoping that some of the kids would be enthusiastic about what I was teaching, even if I wasn't.

The majority of the students were not listening, and there was a lot of quiet rumblings in the room (talking, horsing around). I could tell the kids didn't want to be there and there was an uneasy tone in the classroom. I felt it hard to be assertive because I wanted the kids to be with me, not against me.

Well, the students were immediately bored without even giving the subject a chance. No one was understanding anything! They started to misbehave in petty ways and I got quite irritated. The tension in the room was building, and I saw what was going on, but I couldn't decide how to deal with it. One kid in particular began calling out and passing notes and being disruptive. I got more upset.

At first, I just lost my head and started yelling. I found this had a 50/50 chance of breaking through. My immediate reaction was fear and anxiety. I felt like I couldn't handle it. As it persisted, I got more frustrated and angrier. I was nervous about the whole situation and about how I appeared to the students. "Success" to me, is measured by how I get along with the kids.

15. "I turned on the whole class." (9th grade, Biology)

Before the discipline problem occurred, I had just walked into the classroom. I was in pretty good spirits, on my way to Bio. 9-3. The kids were all talking excitedly about something. Although it was hard to understand what they were saying, I am sure it wasn't bio! In fact, after I walked in, they were still jabbering away. It took everything short of shooting off a pistol to quiet them down.

I started the class in my usual way of telling everyone what today's lesson was to be all about. We were doing the "Reproductive System" and would be discussing human sexual reproduction. Then, one of the students said: "Why don't you just call it f—ing so that we all can understand?" Immediately I turned on the kid and called him a very low intelligent version of a monkey and I said a few more words in rapid fire staccato. Then, I turned on the whole class and was received by boos and jeers. When I turned my back, I was struck by a sharp pointed object, a pencil, and then spit balls, etc.

At first, I felt angry, and then fear, because the whole class was against me. This had never occurred to me before and I didn't know how to act. I turned and gave everyone a cold stare and dared the people who threw it to stand up. (Secretly hoping no one would be so brave.) Luckily, no one did.

I told the class that I would make believe that it didn't happen, but if such a thing ever did again, I would punish the whole class until I found out.

I don't think I showed it, but I was scared. I realized that I had to keep my composure and boy was I relieved when the bell rang.

16. "I had trouble not laughing myself." (9th grade, Business course)

We were discussing the different economic systems. I was leading the discussion with the students doing a good job participating. The kids were listening and answering my leading questions. The room was filled with "active" noises (straining to be called upon, some buzzing).

During the discussion, I noticed that one group of boys was snickering whenever something was said. All the levity seemed to be centering around one boy. While the discussion progressed, I watched the group carefully because it was becoming annoying. Finally, I noticed that Brian was making outrageous faces and that's what was causing the annoyance.

When the snickering first began, I was angry because Brian was disturbing a good class. He was involving some of the students around him. As I watched Brian, I also found some of the faces were really funny, and I had trouble not laughing myself.

I decided to make an example out of Brian. I stopped the discussion and said to Brian, "Do you know what detention is like?" He said that he didn't! I replied, "Good, then tomorrow at 7:45 A.M. you can find out!" With this, he blushed, but someone jeered at me. Then, others started to make wise cracks. It all got worse.

17. "I was more embarrassed." (9th grade, Math)

I was feeling pretty good. I was relaxed and going over some work with fractions. They were given some problems to do and we were going over them together. It was a fairly small group of about fifteen students. The students were paying attention, and each person was getting an opportunity to answer questions. We were in a fairly relaxed atmosphere in which there was a little talk going on at times, but the class certainly was under control. There didn't seem to be any problems at all.

Then, one of the students, a very big and bright boy, George, made a joke about one of the other students (a much smaller boy), who I think gave a wrong answer. One of the girls defended the smaller boy and called George a "bully who only picked on little people!" She was pretty angry when she said this and was cursing also. When George heard this, he became enraged. He began cursing at the top of his voice, threatening to kill her and do violent things. He was shaking with rage. He got out of his seat and walked in back of the room and out of sight of the rest of the students. One student went over to him to calm him down. He continued to curse but out of ear shot of the class. His rage did not subside and he just stared out the window.

At first, I tried to make light of the whole situation. It started out very harmless and didn't seem to be any big deal. But the boy's masculinity was attacked, and he didn't know how to handle it. I tried to be calm as the situation worsened and try to get them to settle down and be cool. But neither of them was in any mood to settle down. When George walked back to the back, I was glad and I think I tried to coax him to go back to his seat.

When it first began, I didn't feel bad at all. As the situation got worse, I got angry that this would happen in my class! I think I was more embarrassed than anything. I didn't really feel anything bad would happen, but another teacher happened to walk by my room at the time, and that got me. I was worried I'd look bad.

18. "Thank God!" (10th grade, Typing)

I was teaching a lesson. I was very happy and felt very attractive that day. I was teaching how to type a business letter. It was 2:00 P.M. on a Friday. They were listening and they were very happy, responsive, humorous, and energetic. No trouble at all.

I asked the students questions. Then I asked Rafael (18 years old) to answer one. Instead of answering the question, he asked me out to the movies in front of the entire class! Everyone clapped and waited for my response. It might have looked like a joke, but Rafael was serious. Others had told me that he had a crush on me. I was afraid to answer or move at first. I didn't want to reject the student nor change the mood of the classroom. I must have blushed too. I was shocked and didn't react—after all, I couldn't believe it! I must have had a blank look on my face. Then, he asked the question again! Everyone waited for my answer. I started to look around me as if he had directed the question to someone else. Then I said, "What will I tell my 400-lb boyfriend? Thanks but I'm afraid I can't." It worked! The student accepted the answer and the class laughed. Thank God! I was so relieved that I was able to hide behind my humor.

19. "Hangman." (10th grade, Math)

I was teaching math, going over questions and helping students with problems in comprehension. As is usually the case with math classes, some kids listen and others play "hangman."

More and more people drifted into the "hangman" player category until everyone was totally oblivious to what was going on in class.

I tried the old "you're only cheating yourself" routine. I told them: "When the final comes, it will be evident to me who has studied and who has not. If you're lost now, you had better listen and get back on the ball if you intend to pass this course."

At first, I felt frustrated then I felt angry. I then asked all those who were more interested in playing games than passing the course to please leave and I would enter the "F" right now. Luckily, no one left!

20. "I tried to make a lesson of it." (10th grade, English)

I was not teaching. They had just changed classes, and I was standing in my doorway. I was feeling fine and relaxed. I had just taught an English class and was waiting for the next class to come in. The class had left the room peacefully, and the class coming in was arriving peacefully enough; very few problems had occurred that day.

A student entered the room in a disgruntled manner. He was mumbling to himself and obviously in a perplexed mood. Not knowing what his problem was, I asked. It was a carryover from the previous class and was not my problem. The rest of the class was seated, and when I asked the problem, I got it full blast. In a loud argumentative voice, I was told how the previous teacher didn't have to throw him in his seat just because he had lost his paper. The student exploded and was letting his anger out on me.

I felt that I didn't start this problem, why should I put up with this crap. I felt like sending him back to the other teacher.

At first, I said: "Don't worry about it," but that didn't seem to please him. He just tried more to convince me that he was right. Since trying to calm him while I taught didn't work, I tried to appeal to his feelings and make a lesson of it to the whole class. But now I couldn't seem to settle them down.

21. "Praying that the bell would ring." (10th grade, Consumer Economics)

Before this particular incident, the class was just finishing an examination. Everything was quiet; some of the students had already left because they were finished. I was feeling very bored. I usually feel this way when I give full-period tests. I was walking around the room trying to keep the students' minds on their own tests. The kids were very quiet as they usually are during tests. It was a particularly hard test, and they were spending more time on it than usual.

Everything was fine until I noticed some of the students starting to snicker and glance in the direction of one particular student I will call John. Rather than confronting the students about what was so funny, I decided to casually walk over to where John was sitting. Without letting him know, I watched him until he glanced down toward the floor. I walked over to him and saw that he had his notebook opened to the chapter that he was being tested on. The period was almost over so I said to him, "John, let me have your test." He must have realized that he was caught because he snapped back at me, "I'm not finished yet!" I felt that he was questioning my authority in front of the other students, so I took his paper away and gave him a zero for "breaking the testing rules."

John is the type who does not need much provocation to explode, and explode he did. He started pounding on his desk and screaming profanities. He got up and started to pound the walls. He became completely irrational and started to threaten me, under his breath.

I was in a state of shock. I just stood there watching, not believing what I was seeing and hearing. My first reaction, after the shock wore off, was that of fear for myself and the other students.

I decided that in his state of mind, yelling or any type of physical restraint was ridiculous. He was irrational and could not be talked with. So I decided that I would just try to sit at my desk and wait for the muting to subside or the bell to ring. Meanwhile the remaining students just sat there.

The bell finally rang, and I collected the other papers and dismissed the rest of the class along with John. He was still fuming, and out in the halls I could hear him beating lockers with his fists.

I felt a deep sense of frustration during the whole incident because I was supposed to be an educated adult, able to cope with the classroom situation, and I could do nothing. I was also petrified and praying that the bell would ring and he would go to a neutral corner.

22. "The kids began to turn around." (11th grade, American History)

I was teaching about the primary election. I was explaining about the candidates. I was feeling fine. The kids were listening very quietly and they seemed to be interested. There was no trouble at all in the class.

The only problem was a girl talking in the back of the room. She was joking with a boy and she started to laugh. The kids began to turn around and lose interest.

I asked the girl to keep quiet or go out of the room until she could calm down. She cursed me out under her breath. I felt in trouble, in a battle, and a little scared. She sat there, I went on. But she kept talking to this boy when I would turn to write on the chalkboard. I was afraid to start with her again, so I decided to wait it out (it felt terrible) until the bell rang, luckily, in five minutes. The class loved the whole thing. I really was angry and humiliated.

23. "Guilty it was my fault." (11th grade, Algebra)

I was teaching math at the board—lecturing. I felt I was losing the class, because I know they were confused about what I was going over. They were taking notes and listening to me teach. The tone of the room was restless because of the confusion of material.

A couple of students were apparently getting bored and started talking. After awhile, their voices got louder and the class could not go on.

I felt angry because I felt they should be listening to what I was saying at the board. But I guess I also felt frustrated, feeling possibly guilty it was my fault for these outbursts.

I stopped teaching and just stood in front of the room and stared at these two students. I then gave one of my one-minute lectures on: "What I expect from my students and the level of maturity that one should have to be in this class!" I then tried to continue the class. Some laughed at my lecture. I felt I couldn't keep lecturing or teaching. Luckily, the bell rang. I don't know what to do tomorrow when that class comes back.

24. "The students no longer feared me." (12th grade, Economics)

I was teaching my class without any of the usual disturbances. I was rather content with teaching students that wanted to learn. But many just didn't. Prior to the discipline problem, the kids were docile, obedient, and attentive. The room was quiet and there were no problems.

CHAPTER 4: WHEN SHOULD YOU CALL IT: "A DISCIPLINE PROBLEM"?

A. Not All Disruptions Are "Discipline Problems"

Of course, the preceding twenty-four situations in Chapter 3 are examples of classroom disruptions. But are they all discipline problems? "Of course they are," you reply. Well, maybe they are by the time the initial event becomes full blown and hasn't been handled. But is the initial disruption a discipline problem? "What do you mean?" you ask. "If it's a classroom disruption, it's a discipline problem," you probably reply. Well, is that always true? Is everything that disrupts this person up in front of the room a discipline problem? Is it possible that there are some initial disruptions that are not per se discipline problems, but by calling them that, and then acting on them as if they were, we then incite a real discipline problem? We need to consider this possibility. We need to clarify when an initial disruption is a discipline problem, so we will know how and when to act accordingly. Let's take a closer look.

It is clear that there are many kinds of problems that occur in classrooms. There are individual emotional problems that require the aid of a guidance counselor. There are problems of evaluation that often require tough decisions regarding proper grading of students. There are motivational problems that require creative methods to encourage learning. And then, there are discipline problems that often require immediate assertive action on the part of the teacher, even if this action is as minimal as saying, "See me after class!"

When, however, is it clear that a particular classroom situation is a discipline problem, rather than a guidance problem, or an evaluation problem, or a motivational problem? Of course, sometimes these problems are entangled with one another. For example, some situations that might initially require disciplinary action also affect the evaluation of a student who might be having a problem with motivation and may later require the help of a guidance counselor. Classroom situations often are many things all at once. Yet, sometimes, they are clearly one kind of problem rather than another. But, whether these problems are simple or complex, it would be very helpful to have some guidelines regarding their proper identification. After all, each kind of problem requires a very different professional response.

51

Most of us probably feel pretty clear as to when a situation is a "guidance problem" or when it is an "education problem" (evaluation or motivation), but we are not clear as to when it should be called a "discipline problem," in other words, we are often not sure when we should respond to students with disciplinary action, rather than refer them to the guidance counselor or try to motivate them better, or lower their grades. Not only do teachers differ among each other as to whether a specific situation is a discipline problem, but individual teachers seem to change their minds depending on their mood or on the class or student. The same teacher will decide that situation A is a discipline problem one minute and not the next.

For instance, which of the situations below would you call a discipline problem?

Right in the middle of your explaining something to the class:

1. A student in the fifth row, last seat, puts his head on his desk and proceeds to quietly fall asleep.
2. A student in the front seat, third row, seems bored and quietly puts her pen down and proceeds to rest her head on her desk.
3. A student in the back of the room is doing her math homework in your Spanish class.
4. A student in the first seat, first row, is making believe he is taking notes while he is really looking at a *Playboy* magazine in his lap.
5. A student comes to class with neither pen nor pencil and proceeds to ask other students if he can borrow one.
6. A student calls out the answer to a question even before you have finished formulating the question to the class.
7. A student comes in late to class with a late pass and walks in front of you as you're teaching.
8. A student grimaces, as an aside, to show her boredom with your lesson.

Which of these do you think require immediate, assertive, disciplinary action? Which do you think you should let slide? Which is a guidance or education problem? Is it really best in terms of fairness and consistency to say it always depends on the student? If it "always depends . . . ," is it not this way of deciding that gets our kids so angry with us? Is every situation that disrupts us a discipline problem? Isn't it possible for us to get disrupted and it not be a discipline problem? Isn't it true that our calling attention to some behavior and going after it is often more disruptive to our teaching than if we had left the behavior alone?

These are difficult questions, but they show us that we are in serious need of guidelines to help us decide when it is best to call a problem a discipline problem. Our confusions here have often caused us to act like the man in the following situation.

Mr. Blurt is in the middle of frying some eggs on the stove, when suddenly the entire shelf above the stove begins to dislodge from the wall and fall. Mr. Blurt immediately gets very annoyed and anxious about how disruptive this is to his meal and impulsively grabs for a hammer in a nearby drawer. Without thinking, he strikes angrily with the hammer at the fastener that has become loose in the wall. He now notices things are now worse. The plaster wall has begun to break up and the shelf is even weaker. He notices that the supposed nail that he struck with the hammer was actually a screw. In his haste, he has struck a screw with a hammer, instead of using a screwdriver. But, after all, a screwdriver would have taken too long. Mr. Blurt, in his haste, could not be bothered with fitting the end of a screwdriver carefully to the notch of a screw and turning it slowly. But, now the situation is much worse. The blow of the hammer has closed up the notch in file screw and cracked the wall it was screwed into. As the shelf begins to fall into Mr. Blurt's food, his meal is even more disrupted!

Miscalling a situation a "discipline problem" when it might be better handled as a guidance or education problem is like hitting a screw with a hammer. When classroom situations annoy us, we get anxious and disrupted. We want to stop the behavior as fast as possible. So, like Mr. Blurt, we blurt out whatever impulsively comes to our minds: "Johnny, you back there with your head on your desk, pay attention! What do you think this is . . . ?" At this point, the entire class has stopped taking notes and is now looking and laughing at Johnny. Johnny probably engages in a five-minute argument with you that begins with: "Hey, I wasn't bothering anybody. What are you getting on me for? Get off my case!" And on, and on . . . Things have gotten worse. Now, your lesson is really disrupted, and probably the most disruptive behavior in the classroom was yours!

It is true; a major source of discipline problems is often the teacher who miscalls a situation a discipline problem when it might have best been handled as a guidance or education problem. We need a good working definition of discipline problems to separate these from what we shall label "miscalls." Often, the reformulation of how we categorize and identify data is the first step needed to better deal with that data. How we identify things decides our approach and expectations, even our habitual responses. Perhaps, if we can come up with a better working definition of discipline problem, one more pragmatic for our tasks, our work will be more effective.

I would like to suggest that we will be better at dealing with discipline problems and not ourselves be the source of them, if we call a discipline problem:

> a behavior (not merely the expression of a feeling) that disrupts (or is potentially disruptive to) the learning of the rest of the class (not just the learning of the

disrupter), or disrupts the role responsibilities of the teacher (not just the personal feelings of the teacher).

Any situation that falls under this category is best handled by some kind of immediate assertive response on the part of the teacher, even if only, "See me after class!" Situations that do not fail under this category are best considered guidance or education problems. In a sense, the latter are screws that require much time and patience to be turned around. The former are more like nails; they are best handled by immediate assertive moves. Some examples of discipline problems then are: (a) students who call out and disrupt other students' learning or your teaching; (b) kids who throw things that disrupt the class; (c) students who come in late and disrupt your teaching; and (d) students who make wisecracks that disrupt your teaching; etc.

On the other hand, a "miscall" would be:

a guidance problem that requires psychological help, a teaming disability, a grading or credit decision, or a strategy for better student motivation that is mishandled as a discipline problem.

Or we may define a "miscall" as the converse of a discipline problem:

a behavior (or merely the expression of a feeling) that does not disrupt (or potentially disrupt) the learning of the rest of the class (though the learning of that individual student may be in trouble), and that does not disrupt the role responsibilities of the teacher (though it may be personally disruptive to him or her as a "person").

A "miscall" is identifying and treating a classroom situation as a discipline problem when, for all practical purposes, it is not. Let us look back at our examples on page 52, number 8: a student who grimaces, as an aside, to show her boredom with your lesson, is not a discipline problem. To identify it as such is to make a miscall. If we follow the definition of a miscall above, notice this is a behavior (actually it is the mere expression of a feeling) that does not disrupt the learning of the rest of the class. Unless her grimace is imitated by the rest of the class, it is not even potentially disruptive.

Furthermore, it does not disrupt the role responsibilities of the teacher. The teacher needs to explain, to clarify, to write on the chalkboard, to answer questions, to grade, etc. None of these role responsibilities need be disrupted. The problem is that here the teacher, as a person, is probably personally disrupted. He's insulted that someone is bored with his wonderful lesson. But this is not a discipline problem; it's at best a personal problem for the teacher. Or this student is bored because her life is upset in general. But, then, it's a guidance problem. Or she's bored because she's not motivated. But, then, it's an education problem. Perhaps, if the student applies herself more, she'd be less bored? Maybe the teacher should give a test on this lesson and let the student's grade be the catalyst? But then, it's an education problem, not a discipline problem that requires immediate assertive action in front of the entire class.

In other words, there are:

A. Guidance problems that require individual psychological intervention
B. Education problems that can be handled by grades or credit evaluation or better motivational techniques
C. Personal disruptions that are disruptive to you as a <u>person</u>, not as <u>teacher</u> (in other words, not really disruptive to your role responsibilities as teacher)
D. And then there are discipline problems.

To handle (A, B, or C) as (D), right in front of your class, is to commit a miscall, and become, yourself, the major source of actual discipline problems. Then, you really do have a behavior that disrupts the learning of the class or disrupts the role responsibilities of the teacher. But then, the behavior that is the problem is the teacher's!

Many of us have not made these distinctions before. It might, therefore, be helpful to take some time here to further clarify what it is we are saying: we are contending that different kinds of problems require different kinds of responses. To respond to a guidance problem by lowering the grade of a student would be to treat an individual psychological problem as if it were only an education problem about the evaluation of grades. We can feel that that is inappropriate. Similarly, it is inappropriate to reprimand a student in front of the class who: (a) is having an individual psychological problem; (b) deserves less credit or a lower grade, or needs more motivation; (c) bothers us personally, though not as teacher. This inappropriate response is what we are labeling a miscall. Certainly, behaviors do not come in neat little packages. A student who has psychological problems and does not do his homework and fails tests may require both individual counseling and also that we lower his grade. Similarly, a student who constantly calls out is both a discipline problem and may also need individual, psychological help. Yet our ability to see these distinctions can help us to make the appropriate response or, if necessary, responses.

We can further clarify these points if we again take a look at these previous examples of classroom situations along with our definition of discipline problem:

> a behavior (not merely the expression of a feeling) that disrupts (or is potentially disruptive to) the learning of the rest of the class (not just the learning of the disrupter), or disrupts the role responsibilities of the teacher (not just the personal feelings of the teacher).

1. A student in the fifth row, last seat, puts his head on his desk and proceeds to quietly fall asleep.

2. A student in the front seat, third row, seems bored and quietly puts her pen down and proceeds to rest her head on her desk.
3. A student in the back of the room is doing her math homework in your Spanish class.
4. A student in the first seat, first row, is making believe he is taking notes while he is really looking at a *Playboy* magazine in his lap.
5. A student comes to class with neither pen nor pencil and proceeds to ask other students if he can borrow one.
6. A student calls out the answer to a question even before you have finished formulating the question to the class.
7. A student comes in late to class with a late pass and walks in front of you as you're teaching.
8. A student grimaces, as an aside, to show her boredom with your lesson.

1. This is not a discipline problem if this student's sleeping does not disrupt the learning of the rest of the class. If he falls asleep and snores, he is a discipline problem. If this seems to be a pattern, it may require that he see a guidance counselor. Or, if in falling asleep, he fails to get the notes to pass your test, it may be necessary to give him a lower grade on his report card. But if he falls asleep and does not snore and no one in the class notices him so that he does not disturb the rest of the class, then he is not a discipline problem. To call attention to him would be a miscall, where your behavior will be more disruptive than this student's. But you may argue, "He bugs me!" Yes, of course he does. But if he is not interfering with your teaching, you can (if you choose and have the control) go right on teaching—though you feel personally insulted. If this student quietly falls asleep in the back of the room and does not disrupt the learning of the rest of the class nor your role responsibilities as teacher, then he should not be treated as a discipline problem. "But," you say, "isn't it my responsibility as teacher to safeguard this sleeping student's education?" Yes. But then, this student is a guidance problem or an education problem. You might wish to safeguard his education by referring him for psychological help, or by trying to motivate him more, or even by showing him the consequences of his sleeping in class in terms of lower grades. But, to call attention to him and reprimand him in front of the class will not safeguard his education, and it will be your miscall that becomes the major disruptive behavior. Calling attention to this unnoticed sleeping student fits our definition of a miscall well. His behavior is:

> a behavior (or merely the expression of a feeling) that does not disrupt (or potentially disrupt) the teaming of the rest of the class (though the teaming of that individual student may be in trouble), or that does not disrupt the role responsibilities of the teacher (though it may be personally disruptive to him or her as a "person").

On the other hand, if the rest of the class begins to notice our sleeper, or he snores, then we may consider him to be <u>potentially disruptive</u>, and thereby, <u>correctly,</u> handle him as a discipline problem. It would then be appropriate to call attention to this disruptive behavior in front of the class, even if we later decide to treat him also as a guidance or education problem.

2. We seem to have merely the expression of a feeling of boredom, not a disruptive behavior. Clearly, this is at least a problem of motivation. But, if her expression of this feeling (resting her head on the desk) distracts other students, since this time the student is not in the fifth row, last seat, then her behavior is at least potentially disruptive and may call for some mild disciplinary action.

3. We need to take a long, hard, honest look. Is this student's doing her math homework in your Spanish class disrupting the learning of the rest of the class? Since she is seated in the back of the room, probably none of the other students notice what she's doing. So, unless you call attention to her behavior, the answer is: no. Is she disruptive to the role responsibilities you have as teacher? Can you ignore her and go right on teaching? It seems that the answer is: yes. Is her doing her math homework in your Spanish class disruptive to you as a "person"? Do you find it personally insulting that she's not paying attention to you? Probably you do. But, if you reprimand her, you would be labeling what you feel as a personal disruption a discipline problem, which is a miscall. But, you might contend, "isn't it my role responsibility as teacher to see that she listens to my Spanish lesson, rather than do her math homework?" Well, maybe. Your role responsibility is to teach her and safeguard her education. It is possible that she's doing very well in your Spanish class, even understands well the lesson you're now teaching—but is failing math. She may have a math test next period that she's anxious about failing. Then, to make her listen to what she doesn't need right now would not be helpful to her education. Let's say she's doing poorly in your Spanish class and is doing well in her math class. Well then, it is kind of strange that she is choosing to do math rather than Spanish. Perhaps, if she continues in this pattern—if she really needs to listen to your Spanish lesson—she'll fail your Spanish test this Friday. Well then, fine; that will be incentive to pay attention in Spanish class. Perhaps, you may want to approach her after class and say, "Mary, I noticed you were doing your math homework during my Spanish lesson. Are you making the right decision about where to spend your energy? Are you going to do well on Friday's Spanish test?"

These tactics are all fine ways to handle Mary as a possible education problem. She may need to see the results of her priority decisions in terms of the grade on your Spanish test, or she may be helped by your questioning her priorities. But, if you wish to safeguard her education, your reprimand here would probably not be helpful. Other than the fact that her behavior is personally insulting, she is not disrupting the rest of the class or you as teacher. In fact, if you did reprimand her in front of the class, you would be disrupting the learning of the rest of the class and your teaching. Also, if the student is verbally adept, she might even say, "Hey, why are you getting on my case? Am I bothering anyone?" You might, unfortunately, respond, "But what about the Spanish test Friday?" She may then say, "Let me be the judge of how I'll be; let me worry about that." If you went after her further, you would have surely turned a possible education problem into a miscall.

4. Is the student perusing a *Playboy* magazine in his lap disrupting the learning of the rest of the class? This is difficult to answer. If the other students notice the magazine, then this behavior is disruptive to the rest of the class. Then, it is a discipline problem, and we will have to (later in the book) discuss how such situations might best be handled. But let's say you barely notice it. Let's say he's so careful about this deceit that no one else notices it, except you. Then, I think it would be the case that to treat it as a discipline problem would be committing a miscall. If you're capable of controlling your personal reactions, it does not have to interfere with your teaching. You are probably reacting strongly because it is a sex magazine. But, what if it were a sports magazine or his math homework that were in his lap in your Spanish class? Again, if his not taking notes and looking at the magazine is depriving him of learning your lesson, then (if your lesson is helpful in passing your test) he'll probably do poorly on your upcoming test. Obviously, to call attention to what he's doing, especially if you try to take the magazine away, would be more disruptive than anything he's doing. As long as his looking at the magazine is not disrupting the rest of the class, or you <u>as teacher</u>, we may have an education or even a guidance problem here, but not a discipline problem.

5. This is the classic example of the unprepared student. Perhaps the first time he is unprepared, you give him a pencil. If the pattern persists, however, you do not wish to keep doing that. Is this a discipline problem or an education problem? If it's true that being "unprepared" means unprepared to do the work and learning in your class, it should happen that his persistent unpreparedness results in lower grades on your tests. That result should affect his pattern. The message might be simply, "I'll give you a pen now, but if you don't have one tomorrow, and you can't get the notes, don't come to me if you fail the test Friday." Then, the problem will have been handled simply as an education problem by grading. However, this problem does not usually present itself so simply. If you notice that in #5, we said, he has "neither pen nor pencil and proceeds <u>to ask other students</u> if he can borrow one." Now, he is disrupting the learning of other students; it is not just his own learning that is disrupted. If it were strictly the latter, it might simply be handled as an education problem.

But, since it is also disruptive to the learning of other students, then to call it a discipline problem would not be making a miscall. We will need to respond to these complex situations as education problems and as discipline problems. We will work on handling these later in the book. Meanwhile, let us notice here the skill required in properly identifying different kinds of problems and the responses appropriate to each.

6. Is the student who calls out a discipline problem? In terms of learning to distinguish discipline problems from miscalls, this is clearly a discipline problem. This is certainly a behavior we will need to work on to learn how to prevent and handle it. Calling out does disrupt the learning of the rest of the class and our role responsibilities as we attempt to teach. As a matter of fact, this clear and simple discipline problem will be a useful example that we will often refer back to as we work on preventing and handling discipline problems. For now, however, we are at least clearer about proper identification of such problems.

7. You may have the policy that students who come late to class with a late pass are not marked late. Or you may decide that persistent lateness, even with a late pass, is consistent unpreparedness. All of these considerations regard the latecomer as an appropriate education problem. However, again this situation is not a simple one. Although educationally your policy may be appropriate to his lateness, when he walks in front of you as you're teaching, he is also a discipline problem. His lateness, by disrupting your teaching and the learning of the rest of the class, makes him not only an education problem regarding his education but a discipline problem regarding the learning of the rest of the class. Let's say that you insist that latecomers enter the back door of the classroom (if you have one) and only give you their late pass at the end of the period. Then, you will have separated an education problem (late policy) from a discipline problem (disrupting your teaching). Such a separation would help you identify the different problems and act accordingly. If, however, you cannot make this separation in your classroom, at least making the distinction conceptually is helpful in learning how to properly identify and respond to these kinds of problems.

8. As we remarked previously, to respond to this grimace as if it were a discipline problem is to clearly make a miscall. This grimace does not disrupt the learning of the rest of the class. If the students are sitting in rows, usually no one will see this facial expression except you. Your role responsibilities as teacher are not being disrupted; you are being disrupted personally, as a "person." If the rest of the students are listening to you, and this one grimacing student is bored, you should control your personal ego reactions and be glad most of the students are with you. Obviously, to reprimand this student would be more disruptive to the rest of the class than the grimace. Also, such a reprimand would not relieve the student's boredom. Probably if you reprimanded the student, he or she would still be bored (perhaps act as if he or she weren't) and also be angry at you. You would have hit a screw with a hammer. But, you wonder, "What if fifteen students in the class all act bored, what then?" I think you then need to ask, "What is boring about my lesson?" However, this is an education problem, not a problem that warrants disciplinary action at fifteen students.

We can notice that our definitions of discipline problem and miscall do not tell us, by themselves, what a particular situation is and how it is best handled. We still need to carefully judge whether each situation comes under one definition or the other. But we now have guidelines for this determination. We can ask, for instance, "Is this behavior disruptive to our role responsibilities as teacher, or only to ourselves as 'person'?" Need it disrupt our ability to teach, determine fair grades, protect other students from injury, protect personal or school property, carry out fire drill procedures, take attendance?

No? Then, it's probably a personal disruption and a miscall if treated with disciplinary action. Is it a behavior or merely the expression of a feeling? Sometimes it may be difficult to decide, but this question is the guideline for the decision. Is the student only disrupting his own education or the education of others? If it is the latter, it is a discipline problem. If it is only the former, then it is probably handled best as an education problem. Generally, such education problems are best handled by either finding better ways to motivate the student or by showing the student how his or her behavior may result in poorer grades. If your tests are about what you teach in class, then grade evaluations are a way to handle the student who is not disrupting anyone else's education but his own. In this way, the student bears the responsibility of his actions without disrupting your teaching or the rest of the class.

Let's also notice that we need not consider the intention of the student in making these determinations. Students often are prone to try to manipulate their way out of trouble: "But I was only talking to Sue to get the homework." if teachers' decisions always involved them as judge and jury, especially about non-empirical matters, they would never be able to make clear decisions. The decision as to whether it is a discipline problem or not is determined by judging observable behavior. Is the student who talks to Sue disrupting the learning of the class and your teaching? Yes? Then, your response to this student must be something like, "I don't care why you were talking to Sue. When you talk to someone in the middle of my teaching, you disrupt the learning of those students around you, and my train of thought. Either don't be absent so you won't need to get the homework from Sue, or ask her before class, or after class, but not while I'm teaching."

(Of course, the definition of a discipline problem on the previous pages is generally for academic classrooms. A different setting would warrant a revision in what should count as "disruptive behavior" depending on the purpose of the setting. Thus, for example, students who are yelled at on a bus ride for talking to each of her would be a miscall but not if safety instructions were being given. Or cheering in a gym class might be O.K., but not in a study hall, etc.)

So where are we? There are many truly disruptive problems: students who call out; who talk during your lesson and interrupt your teaching; students who bother other students' learning, who throw things, pass notes, walk in front of the room, and make noise that disrupts your lesson, etc. We will discuss the prevention and handling of these kinds of problems in the rest of the book. Meanwhile, we have made important progress. One key way to prevent and handle discipline problems is not to create them. We create discipline problems by making miscalls. Miscalls are problems: education problems, guidance problems, teachers' personal hurt feelings, etc. But they are not discipline problems. If we can be more skillful at these determinations, we will eliminate one of the major sources of discipline problems in the classroom: miscalls.[22] Furthermore, making miscalls tends to deteriorate our relationship with our students. When students feel reprimanded inappropriately and they (rightfully) feel, "But I wasn't bothering anybody," they tend to look for ways to act out and retaliate. The maintenance of a good relationship with our students is the best way to prevent discipline problems.

Some of you may be wondering what to do if the administration of your school, your principal or supervisor, disagrees wish all of this and wants you to, e.g., go after that student in the fifth row who is falling asleep and wants you to do it right in the middle of your lesson. If so, please refer immediately to the end of section C below for some suggestions about handling administrators who would actually urge you to make what we have decided is a miscall.

B. Fifteen Typical Miscalls

Before we leave this problem of properly identifying discipline problems, it will be helpful to discuss different kinds of miscalls many teachers make.

---

[22] To reinforce this point about how not making miscalls prevents discipline problems, the research in Chapter 5 shows that kids rank this source as second highest in frequency!

1. The withdrawn student

If a student is withdrawn from your lesson but not disrupting either the learning of the rest of the class or you as teacher, to reprimand this student in front of the class would be a miscall. The student might have his head down on his desk in the back of the room, or be reading a book not related to your lesson, or looking out the window. If he draws attention to himself, and the other students become distracted, then he is a discipline problem. If however, he's not disrupting the learning of anyone else but his own, then he is either an education problem or a guidance problem, but not a discipline problem. As a matter of fact, if a student calls out, "Oh, look at Tommy, he's asleep back there," that student who called out is the discipline problem, not Tommy. In this case, it would be better to reprimand the student who called out and disrupted the learning of the rest of the class.

As an education problem, Tommy might best be handled through a private talk. He might be asked if he is feeling O.K., or you might remind him of an upcoming test. Or, if he's bored, you might try to discover ways to motivate him. You might say something like, "Are you O.K.? I hope you realize your education is your responsibility, and I can only help you if you help yourself. But if you choose to do poorly on the test, that's your choice; just don't disturb the other students or my teaching." As a guidance problem, Tommy might best be handled by your simply showing concern without embarrassing him in front of the class. If he's withdrawn because he's depressed or upset, then the first step might be to show him that you understand his feelings. In this case, usually questioning the student only makes him withdraw all the more. Try to share with him that you've felt similarly, at times, if you can. Whether Tommy is an education problem or a guidance problem, expressing your anger at him is usually not helpful here. Try not to take it personally that a student may be withdrawn from you.

2. The overreacted-to rule

A rule is obviously a restriction that has been generalized to cover many situations. However, many rules originate from one instance that is obviously appropriate and then are spread over too many instances inappropriately. That's why we often need to interject into a rule, "But, of course, if x is the case, then it's O.K. if you don't. . . ." These exceptions to our rules are made to correct our overreaction to, or exaggeration of, a rule. Sometimes the originating instance for making the rule is so intense we overgeneralize the rule's limits and lose sight of our original goal for the rule. In such cases, we then have an overreacted-to rule, the source of many miscalls.

One example of a commonly overreacted-to rule is the "no food" rule. Probably the rule originates appropriately with the child who begins to eat something like potato chips in class. Obviously, eating such food in class is noisy and, thereby, disruptive to the learning of the rest of the class and you as teacher. Such food is also prone to create jealousy and to be passed around the room. Objecting to the eating of potato chips in class is thus not a miscall. But, what about eating a sourball? Or, what about a cough drop? What if a student says, "It's medicine." Do we then revert to the rule, "No food except if you have a note from a doctor"? What about the student who is sucking loudly on a rubber band? When you yell at her, she then responds, "But I'm not eating any food!" To enforce the "no food" rule do we inspect every student's mouth at the beginning of each period? What if the student has no food in his mouth. but something that he's fooling with in his mouth is making a noise that's disturbing the class, and this something turns out to be his tongue!? We can't have him spit that out.

Obviously, if we proceed this way we are on the trail of an overreacted-to rule. The "no food" rule was designed so that eating food in class does not disrupt the learning of the class. What we really want is that students do not eat or suck on anything that disturbs the class. Then, whether they are sucking on medicine or not (even if they have three doctors' notes), making noise that disrupts the class means they are a discipline problem. We will learn how to deal with these noise-making students later in the book. Meanwhile, the miscall here involves our trying to enforce the "no food" rule to the point where our insistence on it becomes more disruptive than what's in students' mouths. Perhaps, what we want to enforce is something like, "Class, I'm not going to search your mouths in here every day to decide if you're eating food or a cough drop, etc. The main thing is that I will not tolerate any eating in class that disturbs our learning. You can eat a whole turkey if you choose, just don't let me or anyone hear you or see you and want some." That's the rule. This rule is more enforceable and is one that is less prone to miscalls.

Another example of a usually overreacted-to rule is the "no gum chewing" rule. What if a student is able to chew the gum silently, not tempt others with it, and not dirty property with it? We are prone to say, "I still would enforce this no gum chewing rule." But, if the student chews the gum such that no one hears it, or wants it, or notices it, and does not stick it to the desk—how would you ever even know about it to enforce it? Clearly, what we mean here is something like, "I can't stop you from chewing gum in here because I can't inspect everyone's mouth and distinguish gum from a rubber band, etc. But don't crack it, or blow bubbles, or do anything that distracts from our learning. Also, if I find it stuck to someone's desk, that person will have to clean it up. If you can't be responsible about gum chewing, I'll have to rescind the privilege." As we shall discuss later, this latter policy takes work to enforce, but the original "no gum chewing" rule often leads to impossible inspections, likely miscalls, and teachers' behavior that is more disruptive than any violation of this rule. (We will also have to discuss how we might handle rules passed on to you by the administration that you are not in full agreement with pp. 261–262.)

Another example of a usually overreacted-to rule is the "no writing in red" rule. Probably the rule originates appropriately when the teacher is unable to write clear feedback to a student when both the teacher's and the student's writing are the same color. Some teachers, therefore, will not tolerate students writing in red. But that's because most teachers mark papers in red. What if the student writes in reddish blue or bluish red? Is that O.K.? What if the student writes in green? Only blue or black is O.K.? Should students' pens that are red be confiscated? Should we make it illegal to sell red pens to minors? Do we feel that our authority is being threatened if students can use red? Our decisions here need to be based on whether or not what the student does interferes with our role responsibility as teacher: to grade and give feedback. The rule should not be about the color of pens. If all students wrote in red and we marked in low status pencil, we'd have all we need to grade and give feedback. Clearly, what we want to enforce is something like, "Class, I tend to mark your papers in (color) for you to see my feedback easily, so, please don't write in that color. If you do, I'm not going to go after you, or try to take your pen away or send you to the dean. You'll just be deprived of my feedback." This "punishment" fits the act. To view it as a <u>crime</u> is to make a miscall.

Another issue is that teachers do not tolerate students writing in pencil. Is that a miscall too? Does their writing in pencil disrupt your role as teacher because pencil smudges and can't be read? Or does it disrupt you as "person" because you feel personally insulted by being written to in pencil? But then pencil is more revisable than ink and thus could be a better educational tool. So, is objecting to writing in pencil a miscall? The answer obviously depends on your honestly judging whether a specific use of a pencil disrupts your grading or aids student learning.

3. The "I've got to win their feelings" need

This need is exemplified in example 8, above, by the student who grimaces because she is bored. Yes, it is true that this may be a sign that she needs to be motivated or that she is annoyed by you or your lesson. However, if she is not disrupting the learning of the rest of the class, she's not a discipline problem. As an education problem, you may wish to talk to her after class. Such a talk should be to show her your concern or to inquire if there's something wrong. The talk should not be with the attitude of "See me after class!" This attitude would be hitting a screw with a hammer. You probably feel insulted that she's bored with your lesson, but that's a feeling of being disrupted as "person," not as teacher. It's possible this student is angry about something that happened last period, or she's tired, or this lesson feels too easy for her, or she just thought of something her mother said. Try not to take her grimace personally.

You can't always win students' feelings. Sometimes you can only get them to take the notes or just not disturb the learning of the rest of the class. As people we like to have students smile when we're nice, answer our questions with the proper affect in their tone of voice, show excitement when we perform, and laugh at our jokes. As teachers, if we feel this need to win their feelings, we are prone to be angry at expressions of feeling that are not disruptive to the learning of the rest of the class or ourselves as teacher. It is then that we make this kind of miscall.

4. The "I need their attention" syndrome

You are writing notes on the front chalkboard as you explain something. The students are generally listening to you and copying the notes from the blackboard. At one point, you run out of room on the front chalkboard and walk over to continue your notes on the side chalkboard. All the students' heads turn as they follow you and your notes to the side chalkboard—except for Tommy. You immediately respond, "Tommy, look over here! I need your attention! Pay attention!" Tommy responds, "Hey, leave me alone. I'm not bothering anyone!" You're involved in a miscall. It is not true that, as teacher, we always need their attention. It's obvious in the above example that Tommy needed more to pay attention to the front chalkboard (he hadn't finished copying those notes) rather than to look at you and the side chalkboard. As people, we like to be looked at when we talk. Sometimes, however, students need to look at their notes, their pen, or think and look off to the side. Sometimes looking at their notes is more educational for them than looking at you. You may need their attention to point out to them a specific line on your chalkboard diagram or to illustrate a nonverbal point in your lesson, but it's not true that you, as teacher, always need their attention.

5. The "my ego is hurt" reaction

This miscall is just another form of 3 and 4. Sometimes we tend to reprimand a student not because she is disrupting the learning of the class or our lesson but because she has hurt our ego. An example of this is the student above, who is quietly doing her math homework in our Spanish class. Similarly, we may inadvertently reprimand a student who has not been laughing at our jokes.

Or we spend hours before class preparing our "great detective lesson" wherein students will be given ten clues to answer a wonderful math problem we've devised. At the very first clue, however, Tommy figures it all out and gives the answer (even properly raises his hand). Our entire great lesson is blown, our ego is shot down, and we're prone to be angry. If we allow our "person" to hit Tommy with a hammer, this miscall will probably discourage his participation or, worse, get him and the class angry at us.

6. "They're interfering with my getting my lesson done" reaction

You're a history teacher and you're up to the War of 1812, while the teacher next door has just begun teaching the causes of the Civil War in the 1850s. You're reading off your notes to the class on the War of 1812 as fast as you can, and the students are taking notes as fast as they can. Suddenly, Tommy raises his hand. You call on him and he says, "All this stuff reminds me of how fights can start at home, like because of jealousy and control, right?" You respond, "Tommy, we're not talking about home and families. We're discussing a war between Great Britain and the United States. Now, get back to your notes and stop digressing off the lesson!" You probably felt: off my lesson and have probably made a miscall.

Sometimes students will try to pull us off difficult learning problems because they feel uninterested or frustrated. However, sometimes they interject a question or comment because the lesson reminds them of their lives. Obviously, the latter reaction is educational. After all, we spend so much of our time and energy trying to make our subject matter relevant. We should feel glad if this relevance happens accidentally. Research has shown that learning that is not related to any significant affect in the learner's life is seldom remembered.[23] As teachers, we must be able to treat the associations students make to the content of our lessons as useful connections for learning. Of course we cannot go from the War of 1812 to discussing families for the next three periods. However, we can channel this relevant association, ask students to incorporate it into their notes, and use it to drive home a point in the curriculum.

What we must try to remember when we have the reaction "They're interfering with my getting my lesson done," is that its not our lesson that matters, its their learning. If we have only ten minutes left to the period, and we quickly dictate all the causes of World War II, and they get them down before the bell rings, we are fooling ourselves if we believe that now they've "got" the causes of World War II. Notes aren't learnings. If your train gets from New York to Chicago faster than the teacher's next door, but no one is on

[23] Weinstein and Fantini. *Toward Humanistic Education.* (Praeger, 1970): 23–29.

the train, you haven't accomplished anything. Sometimes you may have to go from New York to Philadelphia, and then to Chicago to pick up your passengers. Sometimes you may have to discuss Tommy's seeming digression about families to have students really understand wars. Tommy's digression isn't a digression, especially if many students' minds were also wandering in that direction.

Of course we must use our judgment here. Some students' questions are really digressions, remarks that are purposely off the subject. We must learn to ask ourselves, "Is this remark helpful to their learning? Or am I annoyed only because it's off my lesson plan, and I'm behind?" If the remark is helpful to learning, try to channel it. You can take notes on Tommy's remark on families; there's nothing wrong with teachers taking notes on the class discussion. Your taking notes will also help you keep track of what you taught in period five and perhaps prevent you from making this kind of miscall.

7. Displaced anger

Obviously, to get angry at a student who does not deserve your anger is to treat someone with disciplinary action inappropriately. This miscall occurs when we misplace our anger. It is usually easier and safer for us to get angry at children than it is to express our anger toward our boss or spouse. Therefore, students are apt to be the target of anger that has been displaced. You leave home angry at your spouse and take it out on this kid in row three. Or you're angry at your principal, so you walk into period three "ready to get someone." Or the last class got you angry about a point in your lesson, so as soon as the next class asks you about that point, you jump down their throats. Or this is the third time your chalk broke while you were writing on the chalkboard.

It is at these times that "screws" may appear as "nails needing the blow of a hammer." We need to be able to identify the source of our annoyance and not displace these irritations. Sometimes sharing your feelings with the class may help: "Class, I have a headache today and am annoyed about something that happened in the first period. It's got nothing to do with you. So if I sound irritable, I don't mean to take it out on you. I'd appreciate it if we all take it slow today. I just wanted to let you know how I'm feeling so we don't bug each other. O. K.?" This kind of openness may help you get rid of, or at least put aside, your anger and, by guarding against making this kind of miscall, promote a closer relationship between you and the class.

8. "I'm tired of trying to be understanding all the time" reaction

We all know this feeling. You're teaching English. A student in period one says that he still doesn't understand what a gerund is. You patiently reexplain it. In period two, a girl asks the same question. You explain it again, this time even clearer. In period three, a boy asks, "Isn't a gerund like a preposition?" That's it! You answer him sarcastically; he makes a wisecrack at your sarcasm, and it's war! This miscall occurs most when we're tired, or feel behind in our work, or when we're at the end of the day or year and beginning to run out of patience. Teaching is exhausting. It's not just the teaching that is so difficult, it's the listening, understanding, empathizing, being careful, being patient, etc., etc. However, if we can feel this miscall coming, we can prevent ourselves from creating discipline problems, which are more exhausting.[24]

9. The mirror effect

All of us are prone to overreact to certain students. We get more angry at them than is appropriate. Sometimes this kind of reaction has nothing to do with displaced anger or our ego. Instead, certain kids just bug us, like the kid who always tries to be cute. She doesn't really disrupt the class or your lesson, it's just her "trying to be cute all the time" that gets to you. Does she remind you of you, or how you used to be? If so, you are prone to get angry at her and commit this kind of miscall because of this "mirror effect." Usually, what we don't like about ourselves bugs us when we see it in other people. This may not happen often in our classrooms, but it can be the source of an inappropriate "hammer blow."

10. The "I need to control" reaction

We all need some control over our lives, our jobs, and our own reactions. Often when we can't seem to get control over our reactions, we revert to trying to control those things or people that make us so reactive. Certain little things just drive us crazy. Our reactions may be irrational, but we feel justified in trying to have things our own way anyway. Some teachers get upset when they see students who are not writing with sharp pencils. Or they are bugged by students who use small pencils. Or they can't stand students who won't sit up straight or fold their hands a certain way. Or some teachers have to stop their lessons if the seats in row four are not exactly straight.

We all have our little hang-ups. These are areas in which we need more control than is educationally necessary to do our jobs well. These reactions are personal hang-ups, not the result of disturbances that actually interfere with our role as teacher. We need to be aware of these irrational feelings and

---

[24] Of course, a student who challenges, "Do we really have to do this?!" is not calling on your patience with a real question. To stop such reluctant learners who disrupt your motivational methods is to correctly apply discipline action.

not coerce our students to accommodate to our unusual sensitivities. To use your power here to make yourself comfortable through an appropriate request is to make a miscall that can turn your students into enemies. If you cannot work out this sensitivity, at least talk to the student who is bugging you person to person, "Tommy, could you move your seat in a little? You're not doing anything wrong; it just bugs me when things are out of line. O.K.? Thank you." The miscall would sound something like this: "Tommy, would you sit that way in your house?! This is a school! We must have order! Move your seat in before I do it for you!" If this student were smart, he'd respond, "But I'm not disturbing the learning of the class or you as teacher." In other words, this is the miscall:

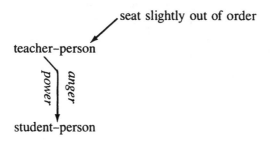

This way of handling it would avoid this kind of miscall:

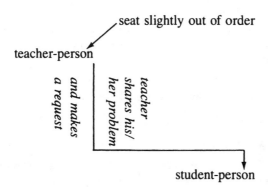

11. The "steam" for "smoke" mistake

If you've ever been driving on a city street and suddenly noticed what seems to be a fire on the road in front of you, you'll understand this miscall well. Usually, what looked like smoke pouring from beneath the street turns out to be only steam from an open steam pipe under the city streets. Sometimes we make an analogous mistake in our classrooms. We use our colored chalk, our role-playing techniques, or our ability for drama to rouse the interest of our students. If we are successful, students begin to participate: asking many questions, offering their comments, and generally getting excited. However, motivated students are less quiet than bored students. If you treat this excitement as if it is disruptive noise, you will have mistaken "steam" for "smoke." Steam is a form of energy. Smoke is usually a sign of fire. It's best to channel steam so it can do work. We may need to make sure that when students are highly motivated that they not call out and stay in their seats. We may even request that, "All of you who wish to speak must first write down your answer, or I won't call on you." It would be a miscall, however, to excite your class and then yell at students who show their excitement. A student who begins to pass notes to his neighbor might be exhibiting "smoke." This behavior may need to be extinguished before it becomes "fire," before his behavior disrupts the learning of others. However, we must be careful to distinguish "smoke" from "steam."

12. The venting for cursing mistake

The best way to explain this kind of miscall is by telling a true story told to me by a teacher years ago. It seems that this nine-old boy was in an art class in a parochial school. He was apparently painting a picture of his own yellow house with a blue sky in the background. The nun who was teaching the class began coming around to see each child's painting. The student (let's call him Tommy) began to get nervous and turned around to see if the nun was coming. As he turned around, he accidentally knocked over a jar of red paint all over his painting. When Tommy saw the paint spill, he blurted out, "Oh, shit!" The nun heard him. Tommy covered his mouth, but it was too late. The words had already come out. The nun grabbed Tommy by his collar and pulled him out of the class shouting, "How dare you talk that way in my classroom? I'll have you suspended for this!" She took Tommy to the principal's office and demanded that he call Tommy's mother immediately and inform her that Tommy would be kept after school for a suspension hearing. Apparently, the principal yielded to the nun's demand and called the mother. When the mother answered the phone, the principal said, "Sorry to bother you, Mrs. Smith, but I'm calling to tell you that we'll have to keep Tommy after school today because of what he did." The mother immediately responded, "Oh shit, what did he do?"

What Tommy actually did was only to vent his frustration and upset. The nun assumed that "Oh shit" was equivalent to cursing. She apparently took any expression of a "dirty" word as a personal curse at her. However, clearly, "Shit on you!" is not "Oh shit!" Cursing is different from venting. The former is at someone in order to hurt him, whereas the latter is usually an impulsive expression of some kind of anger. We must be careful not to mistake venting for cursing. Some children raised on the streets of large cities are not even aware of the transgression we see fit to reprimand: "Tommy, you cursed. You said a dirty word at me." "I didn't, Mrs. Jones, I didn't. Tell me. Tell me. What the f____ did I say? Tell me."

If a student accidentally says a word society has deemed "dirty" (after all, there are really no inherently dirty words—society deems them dirty), it might be best to let the expression slide. If the class responds, "Did you hear what Tommy said?!" it's because they want to see what you're going to do. The class isn't upset about this dirty word; they probably have heard that stuff hundreds of times. They react to embarrass you or push you to discipline Tommy. However, if we can realize all this, it's obvious that the disruptive behavior is the class's reaction to Tommy, not Tommy's venting. So if we're smart we can respond, "Now, class, just settle down. Tommy got frustrated, that's all. He didn't curse. I don't tolerate cursing at someone in here, nor your acting out with phony surprises every time someone says a four-letter word. So, settle down."

We acknowledge that this is a distinctly different problem in K–6. See Section D in this chapter for a further discussion of this issue in elementary school.

13. The prejudicial mistake

It is obvious that it is an extremely unprofessional miscall to reprimand a student simply because of his or her race, creed, skin color, or sex. However, we need to be reminded that prejudice often originates in anxiety turned to anger and generalized (Gordon Allport, *The Nature of Prejudice*, 1954). We are all raised with various kinds of prejudices that sometimes flare up in our unaware, biased judgments. The only safeguard against prejudice (until our society itself is cured) is awareness. We have the responsibility as helping professionals to continually ask ourselves, "Am I overreacting or judging wrong because of a prejudice I may have?" Along these same lines, we must take care that we are not playing favorites with those we are attracted to.

14. Holding a grudge

Similarly, we should not judge a student simply based on his past history or on the leftover anger we have with him from how he was yesterday. We must be careful that our decisions about whether to reprimand him are based on his current behavior.

15. The punishing the education problem mistake

Should you reprimand or punish Tommy in front of the class if he has not done his homework? We've already decided that if he's bored, or withdrawn, or even sleeping, he is probably an education problem, not a discipline problem. But, if he hasn't done his homework, isn't he then a discipline problem? Is his having not done his homework disruptive to anyone else but himself? Is he disrupting the learning of the class? Is this neglect of his work disruptive to your ability to teach? It seems that this behavior is only disruptive to the rest of the class if you call attention to it and spend class time on Tommy's neglect. If homework is not "busy work," but actually helps students learn, and if tests validly measure the learning you have taught and assigned for homework, then students who do not do their homework should do poorly on your tests. These poor grades can be a deterrent to neglecting homework.

"But," you reply, "what if they don't care about their grades?" Then, our reprimands or punishments will in no way cultivate their care. Such reprimands or punishments of an education problem (not a discipline problem) only produce coerced behavior, resentment, and further withdrawal. "But," you reply, "what if they can score high on my tests without doing their homework? What then?" Then, obviously, the students find that your homework is irrelevant to your tests. Then, it is the teacher who needs to go to work, not the students who need to be reprimanded for not doing homework.

In summary

What have we decided so far? There are real discipline problems, and then there are miscalls. The former are any behaviors that disrupt the learning of the class or the teacher as teacher. The latter are mishandled situations which become discipline problems. Therefore, one way to prevent discipline problems from occurring is by not making miscalls. Every time a teacher handles, for example, students who are merely withdrawn with disciplinary action, the relationship between these students and the teacher becomes more and more antagonistic. The greatest source of discipline problems is this antagonistic relationship between student and teacher. Students sense their rights, where our power is illegitimate, and what is unfair. By our not making miscalls, they will respect us more when our disciplinary action is legitimate and fair.

Of course, besides not making miscalls, we also have to take some real disciplinary action. After all, students who call out or interrupt you, who are withdrawn and noisy, who curse, etc., are real discipline problems, not miscalls. Even many of our education problems and guidance problems are discipline problems when they also disrupt the learning of others. So, we will not only need the skill of not making miscalls but many other skills as well to prevent and handle all these real disruptive behaviors. In the next few chapters, we will discuss he origins of these behaviors and how to prevent and handle them. However, before we do, it will be helpful to realize that as far as making miscalls, you are not alone.

C. What to Do Instead of Making Miscalls

"O.K.," you say, "these above 1–15 are miscalls, not discipline problems. But, if I don't discipline these situations, what do I do? I can't just ignore these problems! They are real problems you know!"

Yes, they are real problems, but they are not discipline problems. I never said that these kinds of problems should be ignored. All I am saying is: the correct way to handle these is not to discipline them. These situations should not be handled with anger or reprimands or any kind of scolding, especially in front of the class. They should not be approached with a kind of immediate assertive action to protect your lesson or the learning of the class. Why? Because these situations are not behaviors that are disruptive to the learning of the rest of the class or your responsibilities as teacher. Even if they frustrate you or anger you, you must resist this sort of "hammer blow" action, or you will make a miscall. Remember Mr. Blurt (p. 53). He reflexively responded by hitting a screw with a hammer and made things worse. Obviously, he should have taken his time and not responded with anger but with a screwdriver. That's what we need to do in these situations instead of making a miscall. Let's take each of the above fifteen typical miscalls and briefly discuss what you should do.

1. The withdrawn student

Since he is not disturbing your lesson or the students' learning, don't approach him or her with anger. Any kind of irritation in your tone would either make the student defensive, argue with you in front of the class, or have the student withdraw more; or he may "behave" now, but then not show up for the next class. Such action makes you into the most disruptive person in the class and/or doesn't help the student from not withdrawing. Instead, you need to do a slow, supportive, turn-around ("screwdriver") approach. During the class, just let the student withdraw. He is not disturbing anyone but you (personally). if you want to help him, don't call attention to him during the class. Perhaps, after the class (he'll probably be one of the last ones to leave) without an angry tone, ask him, "Tom, are you O. K.? I'm concerned about you. Do you think you'll be able to pass the test on Friday? I'm not angry with you. If I can help, let's talk during my prep period or after school." He'll probably say, "I'm fine." That's O.K. Keep laying out a "red carpet" for him. Share: "I sometimes feel lousy, too." Don't pull on him. If you pull on someone's tongue, they talk less, not more. Don't question him to death. Let hem be, but let him know you care. If he opens up and says anything, immediately say, "I understand." Don't argue with him, even if he says, "School is a waste." This is not the time for a lecture on future careers. His feelings need to be listened to and not judged. Try to share: "I also feel or felt that way sometimes." Hopefully, the student will begin to tell you the problem that has overwhelmed him or depressed him. Often, withdrawal and depression are the results of suppressed angers. Give him support to vent his angers.

If you discover in your talks with the student that you neither have the time nor the skill to handle his problem, then you may need to refer him for some professional help. "Referring" is a skill. It can be done wrong. Don't immediately say, "O.K., you need to see the school guidance counselor." The student usually will never go or will go with you once and never show up again. Such immediate referrals leave students feeling abandoned after you put out your "red carpet." Instead: (1) allow the student to depend on you for a while; (2) at the right time, after a few meetings, let the student know you want to help him but don't know what to do, or that he deserves more time than you have; (3) tell him you know someone personally who can help him better; (4) tell him he's not alone, that many students have these problems and also see your "friend" for help; (5) go to the first counselor meeting with the student and help him present his problem; (6) of course, prepare the counselor before you both arrive; (7) leave the first session only when the student feels comfortable; (8) encourage the student to go or come back to you; (9) let him see you if he feels uncomfortable with the counselor; and (10) hopefully, if the counselor is helpful, the student will leave you, not you leave him.

2. The overreacted-to rule

Obviously, just don't overreact. If the e.g., "food" problem interferes with your teaching or their learning, stop it. If it doesn't or doesn't spread, only comment that, e.g., the crackling of that paper is disruptive, and rule that out. Don't try to enforce "no food." How will you be able to inspect all bags or all mouths?! Just don't allow items that interfere with your lesson or the others' learning. For example, don't allow passing cough drops from student to student. Similarly, with gum, your emphasis should be on not cracking it, blowing bubbles, harming private property, etc., not on: "No gum in here." How can you inspect every mouth?

What about wearing sunglasses in class? Prohibit all sunglass wearing in class? Why? What about slightly tinted prescription glasses? Are you going to allow only a tint of 4.3 and inspect all for prescription lenses? Of course, this is absurd. The sunglasses are a form of hiding, or a form of withdrawal, or may be innocent. Since it doesn't disrupt your teaching or the class learning, such a reprimand would be a miscall. The student is either withdrawn (then follow 1 above) or needs to hide or will pass or fail your test on Friday. If he passes, you did the right thing not going after him. If he fails, you've handled it. If the whole class begins to wear sunglasses, what are you doing to turn off the whole class? (Consult Chapters 11 and 14 to diagnose yourself.)

3. The "I've got to win their feelings" need

You should reread no. 3 above on p. 64. Again, you can't always win students' feelings. Sometimes, you can only get them not to disturb the learning of other students. Your jurisdiction is their behavior. If you persist in not being satisfied with not winning their feelings, you will probably cause the confrontation to persist. The student who does not feel like you want her to feel is an education problem only, not a discipline problem, as in example 8 on p. 52. By "only" I don't want to diminish the problem. But it doesn't require a "hammer." You may wish to talk to her after class with concern, ask her if something is wrong, reason with her, etc. If she still hates, e.g., math, you may try again in your lessons to excite her interest, but if you can't, I know you'll feel bad (I understand). Try not to take her feelings personally, and be glad she's not also a discipline problem. Try not to take it personally.

4. The "I need their attention" syndrome

Just remind yourself that sometimes you don't need their attention or that sometimes you just can't get it, or something may be more important to them (their entire adolescence!) than what you're doing. As long as they are not disrupting your teaching or others' learning, just keep going. Hopefully, this inattentive student will pass your test on Friday. If not, then failing him is the best way to handle the inattention.

5. The "my ego is hurt" reaction

Simply recognize that that is what is bothering you, that it is not your teaching that is being disrupted—you can keep going—nor is the rest of the class disrupted. Let it slide or talk to a friend after school to repair yourself (or take it personally, get your pride involved too much, and go ahead and you be disruptive).

6. "They're interfering with my getting my lesson done" reaction

If a student's questions or comments are really <u>not</u> disruptive to the learning in the class, try to postpone your need to get your lesson done. As I said above, if you succeed in driving the train of your lesson from A to B, but no one's on the train, you haven't taught anything. Instead of getting angry and making this miscall, you can calmly, not angrily, tell the class your concern about their falling behind, that you're worried they may not do well on, e.g., the departmental final exam next week. You can say, "Let's talk about this that Tom just brought up, but then let's hurry and take down these notes before the bell rings." Or you can assign what you didn't get done in class for homework, not as a punishment, but as an option to be able to discuss what Tom mentioned (that the whole class does want to discuss and is educational).

7. Displaced anger

Simply recognize that your anger is really left over from elsewhere and that you are letting it out on the wrong people or student. Apologize, tell the class about the past angry event, that you don't mean to be angry at them, and get rid of the anger, hopefully, at the right person at the right time.

8. "I'm tired of trying to be understanding all the time"

Recognize that it's your patience that is drained and the student doesn't deserve your frustration, though someone asked the same question in periods 2, 3, 4, and 5. Apologize if you lose your patience, tell the student that it is a very fair question (if it is), and tell him or her, "sorry," you're just tired. Then muster more patience and try to get a well-deserved rest after school. (Teachers deserve more money, support, smaller classes, more respect, etc.)

9. The mirror effect

Try to notice that you are more angry at this one student than is called for. As explained above, she may remind you of you (or your friend or a family member, etc.). Instead, try to deliver only the reprimand that is appropriate to this situation at this time, according to the warnings you have delivered (we will discuss the appropriate "warnings" fully in Chapter 12, section A).

10. The "I need to control" reaction

Again, you only need to control in order to teach and protect the learning of the rest of the students and their well-being. Try to let slide what is not within this broad jurisdiction. You will find that your class may seem less controlled (by you) but heed more of the actual controls you really need to be a good teacher. (Reread the last paragraph on pp. 68–69.)

11. The "steam" for "smoke" mistake

As best you can, distinguish whether the student's behavior is "steam" or "smoke." If it's the former, you need to channel it. (Consult the methods in Chapter 14.) If it's "smoke," warn the student (and follow the guidelines for such warnings in Chapter 12, section A).

12. The venting for cursing mistake

Review the last paragraphs on p. 71 of no. 12. Try to follow my example there. Of course, punish real cursing; follow the guidelines for warning students about this by consulting Chapter 12, section A. For venting, allow it, as you explain the difference to the class. Of course, be on the lookout for abusers of the permission. Warn the abusers and follow through. You're the judge, not them. Of course, you have every right to teach them the best, or appropriate, language for venting, e.g., "damn!" may be better than "shit," or "shucks" even better yet, if you like. But respect that they may have a different cultural background. "Jesus!" may offend you and not be a curse to them.

A frequent example in gym class is when students "suck their teeth," a sound to show that they hate, e.g., being told that, "before we play basketball, we all have to do push-ups!" Of course, allow them to produce this sound of irritation. Sympathize with them that you also like basketball better than push-ups. Perhaps even say, "O.K., when I say go, everyone 'suck their teeth.' " The point is not to reprimand this venting, but understand it.

(Please see the K–6 section for a discussion of venting advised developmentally for the elementary school child.)

13. The prejudicial mistake

Recognize your prejudices and biases honestly. We all have them. I remember that I used to call on this cute kid very often, though others had their hand up first or deserved to be called on more. I realized it and modified my behavior accordingly. While changing your prejudices (that takes a long time), do the fair, appropriate, professional behavior.

14. Holding a grudge

If you have warned a student three times, and he violates your rule, follow through with what you warned. (See the guidelines in Chapter 12, section A.) If he starts the same disruptive behavior again tomorrow, don't punish him at the first infraction. Start out with a "clean slate." Your rule says, "three warnings"; follow it so you treat him as fairly as any student who violates the rule. If he has served his "first sentence" from Monday's three warnings and was punished, don't hold a grudge and go after him at the outset. Instead, start with warning #1.

15. The punishing the education problem mistake

A student who doesn't do his homework or who is withdrawn is now (according to our definition) <u>not</u> a discipline problem. These are education problems. With such, you need to inquire supportively about the causes, try to motivate with rewards, give high grades to the workers, less credit to less work, etc. Anger usually doesn't educate, though appropriate anger, warnings, boundaries, etc., do prevent and handle many discipline problems. (We will work on these appropriate warnings in Chapter 12, section A.)

(The reader is also referred to Chapter 11, section A, where there is more help available to prevent the making of miscalls.)

There still remains a problem for many of you: what if the administration, e.g., my supervisor, wants me to reprimand a withdrawn student right in the middle of my class? In other words, he pushes me to make what we have deemed a miscall. What then? My advice is to explain to him that the student is a problem, but you felt that to go after him like that in class would be more disruptive than speaking to him supportively after class. Your supervisor may counter with, "If you let him fall asleep, they'll all fall asleep!" Try and respond, "Of course, if this problem spreads and is potentially disruptive to the learning of the rest of the class [our definition], I'll do something about it." (Probably check Chapter 14 where there are 83 methods to enhance the delivery of your lesson plan so kids are less likely to turn off.) Or you can give a quiz tomorrow (and warn them about the quiz) on the lesson being taught.

D. Especially for Grades K–6

Here, the situation is somewhat different, especially in Kindergarten and even 1st grade. Here, there is less strictly cognitive, academic learning going on. Often, play, kids talking to each other, random comments, and physical fooling around are part of what the classroom is for. So, there needs to be a slight revision in the definition of a discipline problem. It is a discipline problem only when a student's behavior is disrupting or interfering with one of the above educational processes. Also, because a teacher's role responsibilities in the elementary school[25] extend beyond the classroom into the hall-ways, lunchroom, gym, and other specialty classrooms, we need to look at the definition of a miscall in these locations as well. The teacher's responsibilities outside the classroom in these locations focus less on the academic learning of the children and more on their social and behavioral learning. Also, the teacher's responsibilities focus on making sure that his/her class' presence in these areas does not disrupt the learning of other classes. Therefore, a discipline problem in these locations would be a behavior that interferes with this above social and behavioral learning (e.g., staying in line or listening to and following directions), or one that disrupts the learning of the other classes. A miscall in these locations would be a behavior that does not disrupt this kind of learning or the other classes, e.g., quiet talking among each other (when no directions are being given) while they stay in line with their partners. And, obviously, back in the classroom, the definition is more like the original definition. For example, children talking to each other while coloring is not a discipline problem, but a child pulling away a crayon from a child who is using it is a discipline problem. Or children talking while you read a story may not be a discipline problem. But a child who throws something at you or who yells twice while you are trying to give important instructions is a discipline problem.

Why do I say "twice"? Because, in Kindergarten, and even 1st grade, children often do not realize they are doing the wrong thing. They are first beginning to learn socialization, e.g., what is disruptive, what is fair, when to be quiet, etc. So, perhaps, the first or even second time a behavior occurs, it should not be reprimanded, but rather instructed. The kinds of discipline problems we have in Kindergarten and 1st grade are often: disruptions to procedures, kids fighting, not following instructions, and breaking various rules and routines that include social routines (getting in line, sharing, letting people have their fair turn) and management routines (going to the bathroom, getting a pencil sharpened, putting things away in their proper place, follow-ing instructions).

Sometimes, when "academics" is being taught, a discipline problem may be similar to the ones we discussed earlier in this chapter. For example (consult p. 52) in items 1–8, these would be miscalls: 1, 2, 5, 6, 8. However, regarding 5, the child needs instruction, perhaps even reward and punishments (these are different in K–6, and we will discuss them in Chapter 12, section A). Regarding 6, the same applies as in 5 (you should consult Chapter 12, section C.1 for help with instruction on this important routine). Item 3 is complex. If the student is doing an activity that the rest of the class is <u>not</u> doing, that may

---

[25] Generally, new suggestions for grades K–6 for this third edition were skillfully made by Ms. Mary-Ann L. Feller, P.S. 41, New York City.

be fine. S/he may need to avoid the task for a while, and you deem it's educationally O.K., as long as the avoidance is not too long that it develops into incompetence. Or the child may just need to be "alone" to recover from an emotional experience. Or the child may be rebelling. In such cases, you may decide to allow the child the anger or decide s/he needs to come back on track. Or you may decide this is a discipline problem because the violation may potentially encourage other kids not to heed your classroom routines. Item 4 refers to deception; again, if the deception is not harmful to others or the student involved, it may be best to let it slide or instruct rather than reprimand. And, in item 7, students who come in late are not a discipline problem in K–6 (see Chapter 12, section F).

A discipline problem more typical for K–6 is when a child brings a toy to class and was told that s/he cannot do so. This child violates a rule, and the toy is usually disruptive to your teaching, the classroom routines, and the learning of the rest of the class. (Either confiscate it, or enforce your rules and warnings [see Chapter 12, section A].)

Regarding "steam" vs. "smoke," in K–6 most of what looks like "smoke" (see pp. 70–71) is usually "steam." Kids in K–6 react, get excited, dramatize, emote, and make noise, simply as their way of expressing themselves. This is usually not noise made to disrupt the teacher, but to get attention and show their reactions. Such does not require immediate reprimands. Instead, you need to teach them how to channel this energy (sometimes they must raise their hands), and you need to instruct them when they are not following the prescribed routine. (See Chapter 12, section C, #1.)

K–6 teachers have an additional source of miscalls (this may also be the case in "immature" upper graders). When these children feel insecure or upset, they often cannot verbalize their feelings nor the cause(s) of them. Instead, they will communicate their distress by acting out. Elementary school teachers, in particular, need to be able to step back from a situation before reacting to it and ask themselves, "What is really going on here? Is this issue as straightforward as it appears? If there are possible causes not apparent on a surface level, what could they be?" This is not easy in classrooms that are overloaded with young children, all of whom seem to need something now, but by dealing with (hopefully) the real problem instead of the surface symptom, you can resolve the issue at hand rather than merely putting a temporary Band-Aid on it.

Regarding "venting" vs. "cursing," this is a good time to teach them how to express anger constructively. Usually, they are venting or just trying cursing to see if it's useful or gets them attention. You need to show them it's not as useful as other means of expressing anger, and you need to give cursing little attention to extinguish it.

It is also helpful to discuss the idea of language that may be appropriate or acceptable in one situation or location but not in another. Children of this age are still trying to define and make sense of their world. They do this by testing the boundaries of behavior, not to upset you or offend you personally, but to experiment with what reactions they will get based on different kinds of behavior. If you overreact to a situation in which a child is simply experimenting, you have sent the message that this behavior was a big deal and that the reaction to this behavior will be big, i.e., you have drawn battle lines on this issue. If, on the other hand, you can send the message that you recognize that the child was simply trying out a new vocabulary word, but that that word is not appropriate in the classroom, you are teaching the child to make responsible choices about his/her behavior.

E. Teachers Share Their Growing Pains[26]

"It is possible to be disrupted and it not be a discipline problem," said Professor Seeman.

What is he talking about? I soon began to realize that most of the so-called discipline problems in my classroom were miscalls or had begun as miscalls and snowballed into discipline problems.

I have tried to discipline students for looking out the window, not being on the correct page, sitting with one leg folded under, and doing math problems with a pen. I see now that the key to handling any situation successfully is to respond professionally rather than take events personally. I must ask myself, "Is that student bothering me or is he interfering with my teaching and with the learning taking place in my classroom?"

I have been, at times, the biggest problem in my classroom. Before realizing the difference between a miscall and a discipline problem, I ranted and raved over rolling eyes, raised eyebrows, yawns, snickering, gestures, facial expressions, drawings, forgotten gym suits, incomplete uniforms, and incomplete homework assignments. I ran the gamut of miscalls. I said things in response to a student's feelings. I often acted irrationally, my behavior becoming worse than the student's. I was the primary problem, and I was pushing the class away from me. The things that were irritating and distracting me were not, in fact, disturbing the class and should not have disrupted my teaching or the growth of the class.

I have to remember that what bothers me is not necessarily a discipline problem. I often cause the disruptive behavior by insisting on total attention, complete quiet, clean desks when I am teaching a lesson, etc. I get annoyed and disrupt the class.

• • •

I am still having difficulty in overreacting to discipline problems that are essentially miscalls. I am aware of the differences between the two, yet while

---

[26] What follows are comments compiled from teachers who have already gone though the training offered in this book.

an incident is occurring, I react first and then think about which kind of problem I am going to have to deal with. It takes a lot of self-control on my part to stifle my gut feeling that what is happening is only disrupting me as a person and not the class. I have found that in my daily teaching experiences, I have often been guilty of "jumping" at a situation that was not really a discipline problem in the first place. Miscalls is one area that I am most looking forward to working on in the fall because I can really see how I fell into that trap when my ego was hurt. When I think of how many times I had twenty of twenty-five students doing what I expected, and instead of carrying through with them, I stopped everything to work on the five who were quietly doing their own thing. Then I wondered why all of a sudden I had only seventeen kids with me. . . . I lost them reacting to something that I now know I will ignore until after class in a general passing remark. But if I slow down my instinctive reactions long enough to consider whether a real problem is at hand, I will hopefully avoid making a miscall because of my damaged feelings.

Anger is another area I feel that often gets me to make a miscall. Many times while I was steaming inside from some outside happening, I would literally explode at some minor little action of a kid who caught my attention. The next thing I know is that ME and the KID are involved in an ugly exchange of words because I lost control. In the future, if I am faced with the situation of going in front of a class in a pissed-off mood, I will approach the class honestly and ask them to please pardon my head because I am angry at something that happened beforehand. I must also mention that the anger side of miscalls is a two-way street. When a student walks into the room in an obviously angry state, I will now try my best to ignore his feelings as long as he is not disturbing the class.

Another type of inappropriate anger of which I have been guilty is reacting poorly when I feel kids are asking too much. The important thing to keep in mind here is that kids are usually only asking us to do our job—to help them. I have found that I exhibit this type of anger primarily when I am very tired.

During the past year, I feel I have made some progress in avoiding the pitfall of displacing my anger onto my pupils. Last year I was hassled a great deal by the school administration. This in turn led to my being easily "set off" by the slightest provocation, sometimes even a non-existent one. The theory that "we put our anger in the safest places" definitely rings true in a school. Before my troubles were made clear to me, I categorized nearly every classroom mishap as a discipline problem. If a child was playing with a box of crayons or leaning back in his chair, I would stop teaching immediately and make some remark—usually sarcastic—to the culprit. I took all these happenings as direct insults, assaults, and affronts on my <u>person</u>. More of my person reacted than did the teacher part of me—my ego suffered tremendously!

One that I found myself doing was the "I've got to win their feelings" situation. It bothered me when I felt that a student was disinterested, made a face, or even yawned loudly. I would often stop and ask the student if something was wrong or I would ask him if he had enough sleep or I might call on him and put him on the spot. Each of these actions were really counterproductive in that they would interrupt the lesson, draw class attention to the kid, and sometimes make the student feel hostile.

• • •

Last year, when I first began to teach, I made many miscalls. I thought that to be a good teacher I needed to follow every rule in the student's handbook. If a child was caught chewing gum, I would immediately make him/her take it out. If a child was eating a lollipop, I would get angry and start my "no eating" speech. But as the year went on, I began to realize how silly many of the rules really were. I started to ease up on many of the harsh/silly rules I implemented. For example, I explained to my students that I would allow them to chew gum as long as certain conditions were met. I would see no harm in gum chewing as long as they didn't blow bubbles and/or crack their gum. I also began to realize that the "no eating" rule in general goes perhaps too far. It's true that if students eat certain foods, such as potato chips or sunflower seeds, it can be disrupting to the teacher and class, but some foods are not. I began to realize there would be no harm if a student sat quietly and ate a lollipop, mint, or cough drop. Sometimes teachers carry some rules too far.

• • •

I also used to get angry if during a matching test a child placed lines to the correct answers instead of just corresponding letters. I learned that I used to get angry because he was making my job harder. However, I have come to realize that maybe, for some students, drawing lines instead of placing letters is easier.

• • •

I used to really get upset if a kid was not paying attention to me in class but still staying quiet. The dialogue would go something like, "John, why aren't you paying attention?"

"I wasn't doin' nothin'."

"John, you're supposed to be paying attention while I'm teaching."

"I was paying attention."

"No, you weren't. You were off in your own little dream world."

"Hey, man, why don't you leave me alone?"

"John, if you don't pay attention, I'm going to call the dean."

"I don't care who the . . . you call."

And so it would go. The point is, I created a discipline problem where there was no discipline problem. If I had asked John about this situation after class, there would not have been this confrontation. Also, it would not have developed into this ego thing where, in front of the class, I had no chance against John. I have found out through experience, that if a kid is not being disruptive, it is not worth having a confrontation in front of an entire class.

• • •

I have trouble with, "They're interfering with my getting the lesson done." If I get too much questioning, almost immediately I think "time," and this occurs more in regents classes. I am trying to disregard that regents or curriculum "fever" and evaluate questioning more carefully. Can the question be useful? I must make a decision, "What's best for the class?" not necessarily me and my speed, or that one student asking the question.

• • •

At times, students will say, "I'm bored," or "I hate math," and I will feel the need to win this student over to my side. Because I have a strong need to be liked and approved of I have extrasensitive feelers when it comes to students of this type. To insult my lesson or yawn on my message is to say that I am not worth listening to. I do like to be on the center of the stage and when I speak I want my students to listen. This is the ol' ego talking. My inner self is saying, "Hey kids! I'm fabulous, listen to what I have to say."

• • •

Displaced anger: I have on many occasions been guilty of this. Something in the hallways would upset me and I'd enter the class ready to kill anyone who so much as batted an eye. Now, I let my class know I'm upset and to be patient with me. In return, they are to let me know how they are feeling and I'll take it into consideration.

• • •

Tired of being helpful: How many times have I lost my patience when asked the same thing time and time again. Now I first reevaluate my explanations to make sure I'm being clear.

• • •

When I make miscalls, it is usually due to displaced anger. A picture of myself would look like this:

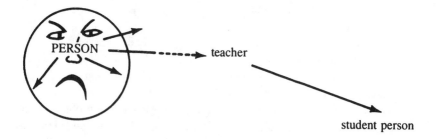

Any little thing got me pissed. It could be a student who just wasn't doing anything but looking out the window or someone who didn't do their homework. I blew everything out of proportion. At first, I did this very often because I had personal problems and blamed the students for them. Student teaching took up so much of my time (writing lesson plans, making up tests, grading tests, correcting homework, etc.) that I didn't have much time left to spend with my husband.

• • •

I often try to discipline the student who is not doing my work even though he/she is not disrupting the class. This kind of kid really bothers me for a few different reasons. I tend to take it as a personal insult when a kid is not paying attention. I want the kids to like me and what I'm doing and when one of them shows by his actions that he is indifferent or worse yet bored or disgusted with what I'm doing, I really feel put down.

When I feel rejected by my peers, I tend to withdraw—but in the teaching situation I feel I have more power. Under the self-righteous banner of "it's for her own good" or "he's just lazy" or "it's my job to teach them whether they like it or not," I go after the indifferent ones with guns blazing.

I can now see more clearly what kind of situations combined with my own lack of confidence can cause this miscall.

• • •

My ego is at stake: I would work out drills in my gym class that I thought were fantastic. I would get the class broken into groups, set them up and start them working. I'd go from one group to another and inevitably when I wasn't looking, one group would alter my drill. I felt they were robbing me of my authority and knew more than I did. I would stop them and force them to do it my way. I realize now their drill had just as much worth as mine (if not more) and I should have made it a positive experience. If it happens again, and if the drill is good (no, even if it's not), I'll have the class observe the drill and have them do it. Then they can also remark on it and try to make it better.

• • •

There isn't one day that goes by at school where I am not interrupted by an announcement over the P.A. I get so annoyed that I take it out on the class. I try to control myself by telling the class I am not annoyed with them but with the announcement. However, its not always easy and sometimes I take it out on them.

• • •

Michael had a habit of sitting on one foot with one arm on the back of his chair.

Throughout the school year I negatively reinforced this behavior by reprimanding him on a random schedule.

I can see now after taking this course that Michael's behavior was not a
discipline problem but became one because of my efforts. Not only was I
giving him attention but I was also taking away from class time.

I remember that all through my Catholic schooling I was required to sit
properly. Not adhering to this rule would have put me in detention. Of course,
I accepted this rule as a part of life but hated it just the same. I believe that
imposing this behavior on Michael was satisfying an earlier need in my life
to rebel. Knowing that this rule was unjust when administered to me, I found
it acceptable in my picture of the role as a teacher.

A deep-rooted part of my person took over and therefore forgot for a while
what it was like to be in the fourth grade. A soldier is what I had to be, so
Michael was also to become one.

• • •

As a substitute teacher, I am quite often faced with a great deal of disruptive
behavior. One reason why I perceived so much disruptive behavior was that
I termed all negative behavior disruptive. On many occasions, I disrupted the
class, as I scolded students for sitting in a certain manner.

After having taken this class, I have been led to the realization that many
of the actions that bothered me were those that my teachers never tolerated.
I am now quite amazed at myself, that I am able to continue with a lesson
without becoming upset.

Recently, I was working on "problem solving" in my math class, and I
finished showing the students how to do the work in the prescribed manner.
A girl in the class said that she had done it in an easier way. We got into a
discussion about the "better" approach. Because of my ego, I think that I
treated her self-expression as arrogance, and thus, it really did become a
discipline problem.

I often find myself having the most trouble with control and miscalls when
I am not feeling well, either because of lack of sleep or because I have caught
yet another childhood disease from someone in my class. I try to be open
with my second grade class when I am not feeling well. Usually, I try to start
the day normally, but by the end of our Morning Meeting, I will find myself
saying something like, "Guys, I know this isn't your fault, but I really don't
feel well today. Just like I try to take it easy on you when you have a headache,
I would appreciate it if you would be a little extra nice to me today." In
general, I find that this kind of honesty pays off since it helps to build a
relationship in which the children recognize that I am human too and we all
work together when someone needs a little extra help. I realized that they had
learned my "signals" even better than I had when one day I came in with my

glasses on not because I was sick, but because I had lost a contact. (I have very bad eyes and am a contact lens wearer. Only when my eyes are really tired or sore will I leave the house with my glasses on.) In the middle of Morning Meeting I heard a message being very quietly and discreetly passed around. I started to get angry that the children dared to not listen. Then I (barely) heard what they were saying. "Mrs. F has her glasses on. She must be feeling sick. Be nice to her today!" My anger turned to a smile to myself. I chose not to stop the meeting, since when I checked, everyone was paying attention before and after the message passed them. After the meeting was over, I explained that I was not feeling sick, but that I had merely lost a contact lens. I made a point, however, of thanking the class for their consideration and rewarded them with a marble in the marble jar. (See chapter 12, section F for a fuller explanation of the marble jar reinforcement technique.) It was a situation that could have blown way out of proportion. Instead, we all started the day in a little bit better mood than we had when we entered the room.

F. Training Exercises and Checklist for Chapter 4

Exercise One: Definition of a Discipline Problem

Can you write out the full definition of a discipline problem without consulting pages 53–54 for the answer?

Exercise Two: Making up Examples

- Can you give three examples of situations in which only one student's education is disrupted but not the rest of the class?
- Can you give three examples of situations in which only the teacher as "person" is disrupted but not the teacher as teacher?
- What are five examples of responsibilities that do fall under the role responsibilities of the teacher as teacher?

Exercise Three: Identifying Discipline Problems vs. Miscalls

Below you will find several descriptions of classroom situations. Read each carefully. If you think that the situation is definitely a discipline problem, place a D in the blank. If you think that the situation definitely is a miscall (if treated with disciplinary action), place an M in the blank. If you think that the situation depends on certain conditions, place a C in the blank. For each, underline the part of the description that most determined your answer.

_____ 1. A student is doodling in her notebook instead of copying your chalkboard notes.

_____ 2. A student comes in late and places his late pass on your desk while you are writing on the chalkboard. He then begins to explain why he was late.

_____ 3. A student in the back of your room waves to another student as she passes by your classroom.

_____ 4. You call on a student who has raised her hand. She responds, "I find this stuff boring."

_____ 5. You point to a sentence on the chalkboard. Instead, a student shakes his head to show his irritation and looks out the window.

_____ 6. A student in a front seat suddenly says, "Damn!" and looks at his pen and shakes it.

_____ 7. A student's wrist alarm goes off. The student laughs and shuts it off.

_____ 8. You ask a question that requires careful thought. Just as you finish the question, a student shoots up his hand and says, "I know, I know, I know."

_____ 9. A student laughs when, for the third time, your chalk breaks.

_____ 10. While you and the class wait until everyone has finished copying the notes on the chalkboard, one student mouths something to another student who lipreads it and nods in agreement back.

_____ 11. A student is rearranging his entire looseleaf notebook instead of opening his book to the page you asked the class to turn to.

_____ 12. A student gives you a doctor's note that says she has to suck on cough drops. You say, "O.K." She sits down and proceeds to spend about five minutes opening the cellophane package and then sucks loudly on the cough drop.

_____ 13. A student in the last seat of row five takes out a comb, combs her bangs to one side, and puts the comb away.

_____ 14. A student in the first row, first seat, takes out a comb, combs her pony tail a few times, and puts the comb away.

_____ 15. A student in a front seat falls asleep while you are showing a film.

_____ 16. During your lesson, you notice that a student has written on the corner of his notes, "This class sucks!"

_____ 17. A student in the back of the room sneaks a note to his neighbor while you are explaining something. They notice you saw them and make believe that they weren't doing anything.

_____ 18. For the third day in a row, when you ask the class to open their books, you notice the same student has forgotten to bring her book to class again.

_____ 19. A child in the third row, third seat, starts to suck her thumb while she copies notes from the chalkboard.

_____ 20. A student who is answering your question begins to slouch in his chair as he answers.

_____ 21. You put the homework on the chalkboard at the beginning of the period. You notice that two students begin to do their homework while the rest of the class listens to today's lesson.

_____ 22. A student puts his elbow on the desk of the student behind him.

_____ 23. You notice that a student is cheating during one of your tests.

_____ 24. You reprimand a student for calling out. He stops calling out, withdraws from listening to your lesson, but continues to murmur, "Big deal. So, I won't do anything. If that's the way she wants it. The hell with her! I try to do the work. . ."

_____ 25. A student puts on sunglasses in your class.

_____ 26. To illustrate a point, you tell the class an amusing story. At the end of it, a student raises his hand, and says, "Ah, that's not so funny!"

_____ 27. A child says to another child (in Kindergarten), "This story is silly; I know a better story," while you are reading to the class.

_____ 28. A child (in 1st grade) throws a ball of paper at the garbage can while you are explaining vowels and consonants.

_____ 29. Children sitting around a table (Kindergarten) all coloring start to tickle each other.

_____ 30. You are telling people to wait their turn, and John goes ahead of Tom who is before him (in Kindergarten).

_____ 31. John does the above again.

_____ 32. The class is working in their writing journals (grades 1–3). The same student gets up three times in fifteen minutes to sharpen her pencil.

_____ 33. Your school has a buddy system for trips to the bathroom in grades K–2. The same two boys ask to go to the bathroom together twice in a row.

_____ 34. A student in your class (grades K–3) is particularly clumsy. She stumbles in the hall and pushes another student into the wall.

_____ 35. A student in your class (grades K–3) knocks her lunchbox against the closed doors of other classrooms as your class walks down the hall.

_____ 36. The class is working on a math page (grade 2) illustrating the lesson you have just taught. You catch two students whispering to each other about how to tackle a certain problem.

_____ 37. The class is taking a math test (grade 3). You catch two students whispering to each other about how to solve a certain problem.

_____ 38. The class is broken up into groups working on culminating projects for your social studies theme unit (grades 2–6). Three students from the same group are off in the corner pretending to look at books for their research but are really discussing why they are having trouble working together.

_____ 39. The class is broken up into groups working on culminating projects for your social studies theme unit (grades 2–6). Three students from different groups are off in the corner pretending to look at books for their research but are really discussing a fight two of them had at lunch.

Exercise Four: Being Careful of the Mirror Effect

A. List the names of three students who really bug you a lot:

1. _____
2. _____
3. _____

B. For each student, list the characteristics of that student that really annoy you.

Student	Characteristics
1. _____	1. _____ _____ _____
2. _____	2. _____ _____ _____
3. _____	3. _____ _____ _____

C. Place a check next to any characteristic that describes (or described) you or describes someone else significant in your life. Do any of these checks explain the intensity of your annoyance?

Exercise Five: Being Careful about Cursing vs. Venting

Make a list of those "dirty" words a student might say that would cause you to reprimand and punish him or her in front of the class, even though the student might say the word accidentally and out of frustration.

Exercise Six: From Miscall to Education Problem

A. Write three descriptions of classroom situations where one student's learning has stopped, but that student's behavior is neither disrupting the teaming of the rest of the class nor you as teacher.

B. For each situation, write out how you might handle and help this student by either referring him to a counselor, or applying some kind of motivation technique, or by depriving him or her of credit.

Checklist

Listed below are the fifteen typical miscalls most teachers make. For each, place the letter in the blank beside the miscall that best describes you. Place an N in the blank of the one that is <u>never</u> a pitfall for you. Place an S in the blank if this is one you fall into only <u>seldomly.</u> Place an O in the <u>blank</u> if you often fall into that miscall.

_____ 1. The withdrawn student
_____ 2. The overreacted-to rule
_____ 3. The "I've got to win their feelings" need
_____ 4. The "I need their attention" syndrome
_____ 5. The "my ego is hurt" reaction
_____ 6. "They're interfering with my getting my lesson done" reaction
_____ 7. Displaced anger
_____ 8. "I'm tired of trying to be understanding all the time" reaction
_____ 9. The mirror effect
_____ 10. The "l need to control" reaction
_____ 11. The "steam" for "smoke" mistake
_____ 12. The venting for cursing mistake
_____ 13. The prejudicial mistake
_____ 14. Holding a grudge
_____ 15. The punishing the education problem mistake

A. Have you mistakenly reprimanded a withdrawn student who was not interfering with the learning of the rest of the class?
B. What encouraging, non-angry ways do you use to handle withdrawn students?
C. Do any of your rules go too far? Do any of these rules have overgeneralized limits that are unreasonable or non-enforceable?
D. Have you recently reprimanded a student merely because he or she felt a certain way?
E. Are you requiring students to look at you, though you really don't need that kind of attention to teach them?
F. Have you pressured students to get the notes down and to stop asking questions to "catch up"? Have you missed the opportunity to use some student comments and questions to teach the curriculum?
G. Have you taken out your irritation on a student when, in actuality, your annoyance is from another source?
H. Have you reprimanded a student inappropriately just because you're tired?
I. Have you found yourself irritated with a student while there seems to be no rational reason for this irritation? Does the student remind you of you or anyone you know?

J. Are you trying to control certain routines or students more than is really necessary to be a good teacher?

K. Have you accidentally reprimanded the class's enthusiasm?

L. Have you mistaken venting for cursing?

M. Have you reprimanded a student because of your prejudices?

N. Have you reprimanded a student simply based on his past behavior rather than on any behavior that he is currently doing?

O. Have you treated an individual education problem (that was not disrupting the learning of the class) with disciplinary action?

P. Have you reprimanded a child who violates a routine you just explained when the child simply didn't understand the routine (K–6)? Have you reprimanded a child (K–2) who talks to his neighbor when what you were teaching really didn't require concentrated listening?

Q. Have you yelled at your class (K–3) for behaving wildly when you gave too many directions for them to handle at once?

R. Have you thought about the outside factors that may be contributing to a child's behavior, especially when that child is suddenly behaving in a way that is not typical for that child?

CHAPTER 5: FROM THE HORSE'S MOUTH
"I like to bug Mr. Johnson because he always . . ."

We should not, as the previous chapter shows, interpret every initially disruptive incident as if it is surely a discipline problem. Some of these hasty reactions might be miscalls on our part. Thus, we have isolated at least one major source of discipline problems: miscalls. Thereby we can <u>prevent</u> some discipline problems from occurring. But, obviously, there are many other sources of real discipline problems. If we can identify these, perhaps we can do more in the way of prevention, <u>before</u> these problems rear their heads. To systematically diagnose the many other sources of discipline problems, let me call your attention to the following research.

Listed below you will find 176 reasons students gave for why they sometimes felt like acting out or being disruptive in certain classes with certain teachers. These descriptions were obtained from two sources:

1. From 195 college freshmen and sophomores (matriculated at Lehman College, New York City in 1985) who were asked about why they were sometimes disruptive when they were in junior or senior high school. This group, therefore, was describing fairly recent memories and describing these with a certain sophistication that their distance from these experiences gave them. Also, since they were college students, all who had at least an 80 average, and were generally "good" students, their past disruptiveness in school was rarer than students who, e.g., dropped out of high school. One might speculate that they were "good" in most classes but were "bad" (disruptive) only in some classes, for some reason or other. It is this "for some reason or other" that we should listen to as we read their descriptions. These are, perhaps, the students who were "good" in period three but disruptive in period four. Why would such a difference in behavior occur? Their personalities didn't change when the bell rang, nor did their home life change upon beginning period four. The source of their desire to be disruptive deserves much of our attention.

2. In addition, 227 students in grades K–4 and 7–12 were asked why they tend to (with some teachers, and in some classes) act out, misbehave, and be disruptive. These were students in the New York City public schools from 1978 to 1980 and 1990 to 1995. These descriptions follow the other descriptions from 1 above, and each of these is numbered in bold, to distinguish them from the others. They are not as sophisticated as the other descriptions, but these students are closer to the experiences they describe.

3. Also, I interviewed two third graders who are both doing well in school and asked them: "Why is it with some teachers you are good in class, and, then, some teachers do things that make you angry, and then you do <u>not</u> want to be good?"

4. Finally, I interviewed a nationally certified elementary school teacher, Mary-Ann L. Feller, who has been teaching since 1991 regarding salient comments made by her students when she asked them to explain why they had been disruptive.

None of these descriptions have been edited for grammar or spelling so that we may see these experiences as they actually appeared to the students.

Some further clarification of how these student comments were collected is appropriate. Regarding **1** described above: I asked classes of freshmen and sophomores to first remember certain classes and certain teachers in junior and senior high school who tended to incite in them the desire to be disruptive or to act out. Once they had fixed memories in mind, I gave them the following schema:[27]

Why I Sometimes Acted Out in Classes

6A. because of what was going on outside of school from just growing up

6B. because of what was going on at home, or due to my friends

6C. because of things going on right outside the classroom (halls, lunch room, etc.)

7. because of how this teacher's class was set up

8A. because he/she seemed to pick on me and others when we weren't doing anything

8B. because he/she was a phony, or "bullshitted," or I never really believed him/her

8C. because I believed he/she would never really do what he/she warned us about or would really do what he/she said

8D. because he/she would "put you down," make me look stupid, or feel inferior, or make me do insulting things

---

[27] This schema not only served to collect students' perceptions but became the rationale for the organization of Part II of this book.

8E. because his/her rules were unfair
9A. I felt he/she also didn't really care about what he/she was teaching
9B. there was no feeling put into what he/she did
9C. it felt like all taking notes and nothing else to do
9D. the lesson felt like it had no relation to my life
9E. I felt there was no way I could get his/her attention in order to participate in the lesson
9F. I never knew where he/she was going in the lesson, and I felt lost
9G. I never felt I could get called on, and felt: "why bother!"
9H. I just didn't understand what he/she was teaching, so I got frustrated and felt like just fooling around
10. for other reasons

I then asked them to check the item or items that fit their memory or memories. Then, they were asked to describe each of their memories on 3 × 5 cards and sort each description into the schema, with its appropriate number and letter, according to how they best saw fit. If their memory did not fit items (6A–9H), they assigned their memory to number (10) "for other reasons."

This schema was continually revised until it became exhaustive for the sources of discipline problems and then the basis for the systematic topic headings of Part II of this book: Prevention: Locating the Sources of Disruptive Behavior. The numbers and letters correspond exactly to the sources of disruptive behavior that will be described in Part II of this book, with one exception. The schema's reasons are Part II's chapter sections translated into how a student might express the source of disruption. For instance, Chapter 6: From Outside Your Classroom, section A "from childhood to adolescence," on the schema has been worded: (6A) "because of what was going on outside of school from just growing up." And any memory given a (10) "for other reasons" was either sorted by me into an already existing book section source category, or a new source category was created. Thereby, I believe, the source categories are exhaustive not only according to my judgment but also according to the perceptions of a total of 415 students.

Regarding **2** above, the collection of the comments of students who were still actually in grades 7–12, these comments were collected by their teachers who simply reassured them that their "reasons for being disruptive" would be collected anonymously (on 3 × 5 cards) and that they could write whatever they wanted to write. All the cards were shuffled by the students themselves and mixed with cards from other classes before they were collected by the teachers and given to me. Comments from students in grades K–4 were noted by their teacher and written down in an anecdotal record. I then sorted all of the student comments into what I felt was the appropriate source category.

Some disclaimers are now in order. In one sense we have listed below some useful phenomenological descriptions. However, in another sense, this is not completely rigorous phenomenological research, for many reasons:

(a) The source categories were not originally created from the students' perceptions and judgment.

(b) The memories of the freshmen and sophomores have been influenced, even construed, from their reading of the schema I gave them.

(c) The comments of the students in grades 7–12 may not be as truthful as we would hope, since these students may still not have felt safe writing out their reasons for being disruptive, no matter how much reassurance their teacher gave them.

(d) Ideally, these latter students should have self-sorted their own comments into the appropriate source category.

(e) Not all of the comments from all of the students are listed here. Many were unreadable, or redundant, or showed that they misunderstood what was asked of them.

For those interested in knowing which source categories received the highest frequency of response, the following is their frequency distribution from most named source of disruption to least: (6B, 8A, 6A, 8E, 8D, 9A, 9C, 9B, 8C, 8B, 9D, 9G, 9F, 9E, 7). Some hypotheses might be conjectured from an analysis of this distribution:

(a) That most of the sources (at least the ones remembered) are either from outside the classroom (Chapter 6) or from the interaction between the teacher and student (Chapter 8).

(b) That most sources come from the home or peers (6B) or from experiences where students feel "picked on" unfairly (8A and 8E).

(c) That the least named source of disruption (although so many books on discipline problems too often focus on it) is the physical environment of the classroom (7).

However, as I included responses for this chapter, I only included what I considered exemplary comments and paid little attention to the frequency distribution. Although the above hypotheses are interesting, we cannot put much scientific faith in them. We have no way of knowing if this is a truly representative sample. And it may be that students forget or don't see some frequent sources of disruption, whereas they remember or notice actually infrequent sources.

However, the reader should keep in mind that I have not written this book by collecting these data, analyzing them, forming hypotheses from the data, etc. The book has been written from my experiences mentioned above and by my having to design and redesign methods for training about 1,500 prospective and current teachers at Lehman College, New York City, and about 5,000 teachers and administrators in ten states across the country. These phenomenological descriptions, although not completely rigorous, are "from the horse's mouth," from actual students who truthfully describe why they sometimes were disruptive. We need to listen to their point of view. I present them so that we may increase our empathy, learn from them, and have some substance that is down to earth to supplement our often ivory tower abstract theories. These responses reinforce and validate what I have always suspected we need to work on and have given me new insights into what I might have neglected. The kids can teach us a lot!

To preserve the impact of the students' perceptions, the spelling and grammar of the following student responses are reproduced verbatim.

A. From Outside Your Classroom (Chapter 6)[28]

From childhood to adolescence

1. As a teenager in high school I was very distant. I was wrapped up in a world of personal insecurities. School work was something I did only because I had to.
2. Outside, a war was raging, a sexual revolution was simmering and the music was changing. Politically and socially my values were changing quickly.
3. Basically I felt lost, high school did not play an important role at that age. Also I was soul searching. I had just arrive to the U.S. And finding acceptance to specific group was easier with the kind of behavior I would display (negative).
4. I sometimes acted out in classes because of what was going on outside of school from just growing up. What I mean is that being a high school freshman during the early 70s.
5. I have ant's in my pants. And I were fruit of the looms.
6. **6.** Well, the reason why i act up in class is because some times i be mad when i came in to school.[29]

---

[28] The topic headings here correspond to the schema on page 94 given to the students, except in the schema the topic headings were in their language according to their point of view. We now translate these topic headings into more objective language for our professional use. Thus, "What was going on outside of school from just growing up has become "From childhood to adolescence." All other schema phrasing has been similarly recast. Numbering and order of the schema conform to Chapters 6–9, which constitute Part II of the book.

[29] Comments preceded by numbers in bold print are from students who were in grades K–4 and 7–12 at the time of the survey.

7. The reasons why I call out is because by that time of day something has annoyed me immensely and I cannot do anything about it. So to relieve some of the pressure bottled up inside me, I call out. Other times I wake up on the wrong side of the bed and my actions express my feelings.

8. Everytime I come into school I think about it. I found out that Stacey and Shaneklia, me best friends, was talking about me, and saying things behind my back. And it hurts! to think that someone you like as your best, turns on you. [with drawing of broken heart]

9. Sometimes I act out and it's not the teacher's fought, it's mine because I had a bad morning or woke up on the wrong side of the bed.

10. The news said that we were in a war and I'm afraid that someone is going to blow up my apartment. (Kindergartner during the Gulf War Conflict, during a discussion exploring why he was acting out and displaying verbal aggression.)

11. I hear fights and guns outside my window at night. Then I think that I have to be tough too to protect me and my mother. (Third grader in a gifted program explaining why he gets into fights.)

From home and peers

12. When I was in junior high school, my mother was very ill and I felt as if my being in school was very insignificant. I didn't know whether or not she was going to get better so l felt restless while I was in school. I didn't think anybody understood what I was feeling.

13. At home the emotional tensions were very high-energy and hysterical re: clothing, social & sexual attitudes & responsibilities, smoking, marijuana, drugs, clothing and sexual revolutions.

14. My father likes to drink and whenever he is drunk, he Will start to beat my mother and when this goes on, I get upset and when I arrive school, my attention will be divided.

15. Trying to fit in with friends and with family.

16. My friends were in other schools. When I moved I didn't feel welcomed by the teachers or students.

17. I act up in my classes because I have problems in my house with my brother and my mother, so what happens is that I let out all of my anger by getting somebody else mad. That is the teacher.

18. Why I misbehave in school is because when I come frome my house I did something bad in my house I take it out on my self by not doing my work in school.

19. I behave bad in my house. I fight with my brother I hit him. My mother tells me to not him my brother. His always bathering my mother says to not be bad with my brother. My mother gets me bad because she makes me clean the dishes and swip the floor and feed the baby. She make me give him milk and shange his dampers.

20. I think that they act bad in school, just to show there friends how bad they are and how tough they could be.

21. My brother always gets what he wants, but I don't.

22. The way people tease after school cause I got my hair cut. Me and my brother always argue. News that my mother told me. My mother hardens up on me because I getting older. I moved away from ail of my good and best friends. Because my mother finds out that her mother could still be alive after 38 years. My closet friend might have to move cause she is being terorized by some man.

23. When I can't go outside. When I can't watch T.V. When I have to go to the store on Saturdays. When I have to eat chick-hen.

24. The problem is at home. A lot of things happened that it was my father then it was my mother they did something to just stop. My mother did it because she got made because of my father that is why I didn't come to school. Everybody was crying, I cried but only once and it made my insides crumble. I think that is why act up sometime. I try to keep cool in school.

25. I like my friends to pay attention to me, so l tell jokes in class.

26. All my friends act up in class, it's cool!

27. My dad says that I should always fight back and if I hit him harder than he hit me then he won't hit me anymore. (Kindergartner explaining why he is always in a scuffle with other boys.)

28. My mom is in the hospital. When I think about it my mind goes crazy and I don't know what I'm doing. (Kindergartner explaining why he scratched another child in line.)

29. I don't get any attention at home, but when I act up in class everyone pays attention me.

30. Once I had an argument with my best friend and couldn't concentrate in my class.

31. Almost every day me and my brother and sister have a fight and I get upset.

32. When kids make fun of me or some of my friends. When nobody believes me when I say something that is true.

33. Kids act out in school because they use drugs like Pot and they don't know how to control it so they take it out on their friends and teachers.

34. The reason I act desruptive is my mother I feel she doesn't care about me. I feel she doesn't spen enough time with me. I get mad and take it out on somebody else.

35. What turns me off in school is boys. Because they call me names like brat, dumb, and crazy. And I hate that. I gets on my nerves. And it makes me mad.

36. I act up when my mother & father fight. And when I get in fights with my sister.

From right outside your classroom: hallways, cafeterias, and bad or loose school rules

37. Students were roaming the halls disrupting classes and plus my classroom was right by the cafeteria & the parking lot.

38. If I had seen a commotion or something happening outside the classrom, I would get involved in it by not paying attention in class.

39. When hangin' out, like in the halls or lunchroom, I seemed to be in a hyper type feeling, and it sometimes became difficult to settle down it the teacher's class room.

40. Why I tend to be disruptive or act up during class. Noises outside the classroom. When 5th or 4th grade go to the washroom and slam the doors. When seventh grade girls come to the washroom and open the door and the door squeaks.

41. My first period teacher is very strict & I take out my frustrations in 2nd period.

B. From the Environment of Your Classroom (Chapter 7)

42. The teacher is a man that's very sloppy and likes things done fast. The room was always messy and smelled like chalk dust. He would teach the subject at the beginning and end up talking about his dog or his family.

43. I didn't feel like a mess, but the desks were so much of a downer and the room a mess; it made you didn't give a dam.

44. The school was a big opened building. My class was situated in a corner. We were constantly interrupted by other things that were going on in the school. The teacher herself was disgusted with the physical setting.

45. This teacher's class was set up in such a way that it was ridiculous.

46. This teacher would have the students sitting too close together. The good students would be next to a bad student or to someone who is a clown. Thus, I would laugh at what the clown was doing or try to defend myself from bad students whom this teacher would over look.

C. From the Interactions Between You and Your Students (Chapter 8)

From making miscalls[30]

47. She became annoyed at something she shouldn't have become annoyed about. She should have explained it as many times as was necessary.
48. The teacher was the type of person that gave zero's if you raised your hand while he spoke, or if you had a closed newspaper on your desk. He wanted to be a dictator ordering you around.
49. Teachers tend to pick you when you're not paying attention. Well at least w/ me. Sometimes it was done to embrass you & when it would be I would make sure I would give her a piece of my mind.
50. The teacher would pick on me & criticize me for no reason. I would be doing my work.
51. I got in trouble by 5th grade teacher four using a fowl language in his class. The reason I use a fowl word in class because some boy called me a name and I didnt tell the teacher what he called me instead I called him a name back.
52. Last year, I would always be in the dean's office because of my Cosmetology teacher. She didn't allow us to wear street clothes under our uniforms.
53. English. I walk in the class feeling in a good mood feeling like talking not working. My teacher was very angry because everybody was talking. I didn't started talking yet because I didn't know whether he wanted us to right yet. When I walked in the class he said you look like you ready to start trouble for the class. I didn't say anything because when he's talking to me he say something so l can get mad so he could call my parent's.
54. It started out as a regular schoolday & my science teacher walked into the room. She was mad, because of the fact that some student slashed the two front tires on her car. She really hated me so the blame automatically got lowered on me.
55. What really bugs me, IS when the teacher accuses you of talking or something really unreasonable. For Example, Mr. X (Music) is very unreasonable. He made a boy play the drums with an arm cast. The boy had a rough time and dropped a drumstick. For dropping it he had 5 pts. taken off his mark. He is the most unreasonable teacher I have ever had.

---

[30] We obviously do not have enough information to know whether the following are, in fact, miscalls. But, as we recall the points made in Chapter 4, they certainly seem likely candidates.

56. I wasn't following along in Spanish so my teacher said to me get out and wait fore her in the office so she could call my mother to find out why I wasn't following along. I wasn't following along because I was very ill.

57. In Gym I had a roller in my hair, and she said go get dress. I didnt know what I had did until, then she said because you had a roller in your hair.

58. In my Social Studies class last term I didn't like my teacher. Every time it seemed that she had a problem or has a headache she always had a bad attitude. Sometimes she use to pick on me when I was so quiet as can be. Every time she use to embarrass me in front of the class.

59. I got in trouble for no reason. The teacher went off because I was reading before the class began.

From being incongruent[31]

60. She was a new teacher and arrived in the middle of a term. She wanted us to like her, but way inside her we felt she wasn't authentic.

61. He was into the role he played that drove us all wild.

62. The teacher acted as if he was going to have a heart-attack and teaching this class was like doing time. Even if someone made a funny remark, he'd half-ass smile like he was scared to show he could be human.

63. Not perceptive, he did not yield to a joke or a diversion from the lesson. He was too stiff, too rigid.

64. Very official; she was there for one reason, to teach. The teacher really didn't expose her personality.

65. We just try to crack him up, he was so teacherfaced.

66. One teacher I had for religion was so full of it. Instead of trying to be a good teacher and a nice person she tried to get on our student level, where she didn't belong.

67. Even his, "You're doing good" was bullshit.

68. The teacher played a strong role because he was chairman.

69. The personality of this teacher was one that was always straight faced. All right school is school, but once in a while you can fool around with your class.

70. The teacher started teaching the moment she took our names. She didn't sit down to get to know the class or let the class get to know her. She never smiled.

---

[31] This is Carl Roger's term for what students usually call phoniness"; we shall discuss it in detail in Part II, Chapter 8, section B.

71. When grownups lie they say they were covering up for someone. When you lie its big shit and you'd think they'd cut your lips off.

From not following through

72. He would always threaten to fail us or throw us out of his class if we werent behaving but he never did anymore than yell and pout.
73. Sometimes you tend to see how far a teacher would go, to get you in trouble.
74. I never believed her warning.
75. Just the fact that we could get away with it.
76. He just let people con him.
77. When she yelled or said things, we never believed her.
78. Weak, weak, he couldn't control anyone. At first you felt sorry for him, then you joined in with the rest of the class.
79. I felt that I could get away with anything when it came to this teacher. She was a very submissive person.
80. The teacher was very soft spoken and expected or assumed that we always did what she assigned. Everyone knew that we could get away with many things, so we use to bullshit in her class.
81. The teacher would tell the class to stop acting wild. But, nobody listened. If a student would say "O.K., shut up," everybody would listen. The teacher would still teach if a riot was going on.
82. Because if we see one person do it and he does not get in trouble.
83. If you would be a little firm you would have better control of the class.
84. When she acts like Miss Perfect, and wants everything her way.

From being inappropriate

85. Teacher "cut you down" at times, made fun of you if you gave a wrong answer.
86. Teacher didn't care about anything or motivating anyone. If the teacher constantly puts students down, it certainly does not help the students to succeed or reach their full potential.
87. ... she was tired and hated the students, the situation, and teaching altogether. She had an attitude that drove me up the wall. She talked to the class as if we were still in third grade. Asking questions any six year old could answer. Most of all she always saying "we" Now "we'll" do this won't "we", it just brought back the feeling I had in the third grade.
88. He had a habit of talking at you instead of to you.
89. When I was taking Biology in high school the teacher didn't care about the students. She used to sit and read a magazine while we read the

textbooks. She used to grade us by the way we behave while she was readings We used to eat ice cream, popcorn, play cards, etc. which bothered her very much, but she didn't realize that she was "cheating" on us. She didn't do her job as she was supposed to and as a consequence I have problems later on in higher grades.

90. He was prejudice. If something happened at home, he will blame it on us and would give us more class work or homework. He thought that we were all dummies, and he was the smart one.

91. Teacher didn't care about failing students. Everyone in the class (including myself was very poor in math. Teacher would always crack jokes about how lousy people did. Ex. When he handed tests back he'd say to a student, "You flunked again, Smith (whatever their last name was) "

92. He wrote on the board to show an example. If you didn't get it, he erased it, and wrote it over again—not saying a word—but smiling. After he was done he just said, "Get it now." If more explanation was needed he did it again.

93. This teacher used to pick on everybody. She used to scream at us. Called us stupid. She was always being sarcastic while she talked. If somebody hited the wrong key when playing the piano, she would have said that this person is a mentally retardic. Since it was a beginning class, I supposed that it was O.K. to make mistakes.

94. In the English class hour the profesor spent the time eating cake and drinking coffee and almost all the time she spread the coffe on the table and when that happen she she real hangry and she start bullshitted the students.

95. I remember an incident about a year ago that caused me to become very annoyed in class. Prior to my class, I went downstair to see the principal and inquire about my high school application to a particular program at Hillcrest. Under the instruction of both my teachers and my parents, I have done the same thing the day before. However, when I inquired about my application which was late already, again, the principal asked with impatience and annoyance, what my problem was. After she lectured me about my slowness in comprehension I went back to class and decided not to participate in class until I've calmed down.

96. Math Problems. In the class he tells us that this is just a learning experience since the majority of the class will not be passing the Regents. He then teaches as if we are 3rd graders and should be treated as such.

97. I have terrible handwriting and one in 4th grade my teacher embarassed me in front of the whole class because of my handwritting so in a fit of rage I yelled at him and stormed out of the room.

98. When the teacher has a pet and treats people unfair

99. When the teacher gets frustrated and then, gets mean to the kids and its not their fault

From being unfair

100. I was never a disruptive student, but I had to disagree that all the students in class had to pay for what one disruptive child did; therefore, making me angry with the teacher and hating to go into class.
101. It wasn't the lesson, it was her attitude! She didn't give a damn about Black kids. She thought most of them were from the ghettos and wasn't going to be anything anyway, so why bother!
102. I get mad when one student acts up in class and the teacher decides to let the whole class get punished for it. I then begin to think that if I am going to get punished I might as well create a real reason to deserve the punishment. In other words I act up in class to
103. Because some people talk or ask me question during a lesson and I get in trouble for talking or when someone starts talking.
104. She seemed to be prejudice and have only her favorite students picked out. She would only be nice to the prettiest girls or the handsomest boys in the class. Even if you where smart she wouldn't care.
105. When I get blamed for something another kid did.
106. Sometimes I may be obnoxious to a teacher when I don't think that the teacher is being fair about something and because they to the teacher—what they say goes. If a teacher says something offensive to someone that he/she shouldn't have said or something to me I sort of speak out of line and tell them off.

D. From the Delivery of Your Lesson Plan (Chapter 9)

From incongruent content

107. Yes, the teacher was more apathetic than the students.
108. He always acted like he was so into his subject when in essence he wasn't, and was a lousy teacher.
109. The way the lesson was presented. The teacher was not tuned in to our responsiveness. It seemed she was probably as disinterested as we were.
110. All I remember is, it was real bull. I'm sure if a different teacher taught the subject, I might have learned one.
111. She was talking like she did not care, it was just like she was there on schedule. Just to recieve her pay during the week had no feeling on the subject.

112. I was in a history class. The teacher taught the class in a very boring way. There was nothing about the way she taught that was captivating. The blackboard was filled with questions or something that had to be copied down before class began. The attitude of the teacher was that of an "I don t care"; and as I look back now I realize her attitude rubbed off on us.

113. You can sense when a teacher has no "gut" feeling to his teaching. How or why, is a student going to want to learn if the teacher doesn't feel for what he/she is teaching?

114. You could identify when a person was going through the motions without feelings.

From not being affective enough

115. She was teaching the class with no feeling, all by her self so the kids took advantage.

116. The guy knew his stuff, but he made the 11:00 news sound exciting.

117. He was repetitious, boring (because he spoke in a monotone voice) which made me restless; and at times I was very bored.

118. The teacher was boring, and she sounded like she's dead and they forgot to bury her.

119. The lesson was about as interesting as a dead frog, and it was so irrelevant to everything. My feeling was basically one of hopelessness, helplessness; and I usually felt like saying, "HELP! GET ME OUTA HERE!"

120. It was not so much the content of the lesson, than the way in which this teacher delivered the lesson.

121. I wasn't disruptive in the manner of being a trouble maker, but disruptive with the teacher as a person.

122. I talk in class to keep awake. If I listened to the teacher I would fall asleep.

From not being actional enough

123. The teacher might have been giving notes all class long, after a while it gets boring.

124. I went to class with all the things that were expected of me, but all we did was take notes and he just read from the book.

125. I was in a psychology class with a teacher who never allowed you to participate in his teaching. He gave notes and you wrote them down. You spent a better part of the class just writing.

126. Yes, because it was a kind of class that the teacher just spoke, and we had to write notes. Sometimes I just wanted to scream and ask him to keep quiet.
127. It was a class of continuous copying from the board and no real learning.
128. Very boring, since he just dictated his notes straight from the book.
129. When all you do is take notes, you feel useless because all there is to do is listen to someone else say their opinion on the subject.
130. I had one social studies teacher just wrote notes all class, we would come home with anywhere from 10–15 pages of notes, not ever knowing what we had just written about.
131. Most of time the students in high school are asked to take notes and nothing else to do.
132. Teachers no matter what the subject should implore more interaction w/ students instead of note taking.
133. I tend to act up in class Becuse I don't have anything to do or don't no what to do or what the teacher has for me.
134. School is boring, so it's fun to fool around and get in trouble.

From not being inductive enough

135. The teacher discussed about whatever she wanted to talk about and whatever pleased her. Her points of views were completely in the past and extremely unrealistic.
136. To me the teacher taught as though (she or he) had to. I always thought: 'why does a teacher teach without wanting to.?' There was nothing interesting about the lesson; it was straight from the book; and as far as I'm concerned at that time I couldn't relate to anything that comes from a book without comparing it to something similar that happened in the present time. I'm not disruptive but imagine those who are and how they felt.
137. I disagreed with the way the course was being handled. It was during the height of the Vietnamese conflict, and the teacher was discussing the Ming Dynasty.
138. The material being covered was not what I thought the course should cover. There was so much that should have been done considering the time in history and all the world problems and changing moralities, and Vietnam.
139. I felt having to attend a Spanish class was absolutely ridiculous when I didn't give a damn about the language or the people and I didn't think it was pertinent to my life.
140. In some classes like psychology my teacher's discuss She aspects of life and so on. But in other classes such as English, they should discuss

the aspects of life to the english they are teaching. So the class could be more interesting.

141. The lesson felt like it had no relation to my life—pure academic principle w/o social consciousness. Growing up in the suburbs I was sheltered from racism, prejudice yet . . . it came through right-wing ideology not so much in the teaching but the community & home life. . . . Teachers tended to feel politically alligned with bureaucracy & refrained from honestly dealing w/ Civil Rights and Peace Movement issues. It made no sense & I lost respect for Educators. There was a gutless sheep-like quality in them that I hated.

From not being interactive enough

142. Boring, no class participation. I felt that she was oblivious to the class being there.
143. Just because a few students understood the problem, he had the idea that all the students understood the problem also.
144. A teacher who never allowed you to participate.
145. He had an attitude that morning and was very rude to the class. He was very intolerant of a person who asked questions while he was teaching. He wanted you to wait until he finished his lesson. But by the time his lesson was finished, you had somehow lost the question you wanted to ask.
146. I might get in trouble in science because I get restless at the end of the eighth period. And to top it off I don't understand the way my teacher teach, like when I raise my hand to answer a question and no one else knows the answer. He'd say the answer hisself before calling on me.
147. When your about to answer a question and someone shouts the answer before you even get to open your mouth.

From a lack of a felt sense of order, reward, and momentum

148. You couldn't tell where the hell he was going or why.
149. The lessons were always too long, and he never stayed in one spot. He would jump from this century to the last century to no century; and then expected you to understand where he's coming from.
150. The teacher never seemed to have her lectures prepared in advance. Her thoughts were disconnected which made it difficult to follow her lectures.
151. He would never get to the point.
152. The teacher was running around the lab table like a chicken without his head; throwing facts around and leaving a lot of loose ends in the lesson.

153. The teacher moves around & skips many chapters. I never know what he is talking about. One moment he will be talking about the subject & the other minute he will be talking about something that doesn't pertain to the lesson.
154. Mr. J. would start the class discussing one topic, then jump to something that happen in his home and on to something new. We felt lost, lessons and class was lousy. He needed alot of organizational skills, maybe he should have taught garbage collectors.
155. He would jump from lesson to lesson and wouldn't even go over the lesson the day before or any homework we did. At the time of the test everyone was lost. Everyday he would talk about something different and he wouldn't even tell us when he was in the book.
156. He kept jumping from page to page. All of a sudden he would start a conversation that had nothing to do with the lesson.

From a mismanaged distribution of attention

157. There was no way to be good in that class.
158. The teacher ignores me whenever I raise my hand to ask a question.
159. When we tried to be good he would still bother us and give us bad grades. The way we figured is, why should we be good and do our work if we weren't going to get credit for it. Therefore we just played around and didn't pay him any mind.
160. I think kids act out because they want to be the center of <u>attention</u>. They want to be noticed.
161. You always sit next to him so he'll listen and not hit other people, so I thought if I talked a lot you would sit next to me.

From not being supportive enough or explained well

162. When I raise my hand, and she doesn't pick me for a long time
163. When you want to say something for a long time but she just ignores you
164. Sometimes teachers take for granted that everybody in the class knows what she/he is talking about. This brings a lot of daydreaming to the environment.
165. It was the teacher herself. If you didn't understand the lesson, she couldn't understand why.
166. He didn't have a lesson that was prepared for that day. When you asked him a question he didn't know the answer, so you said to yourself "why try."
167. The teacher's lesson was very unclear. She just kept on talking and talking and didn't look at the class's response.

168. Some teacher's discuss topics in a differcult way, this is not good to student or even the "A" student because it is hard to understand they don't even care, if student learns.
169. I act up in class because I don't understand what the teacher is saying.
170. You go to fast and you write to small.
171. The way the teacher writes to small. Also he goes to fast with the work. I don't understand what is going on.
172. He only writes on the board but doesn't explain any thing.
173. I want to misbehave when the teacher pushes me to do something, or try something when I'm not ready.
174. I know I can't get it right and I don't want to look stupid.
175. I don't know how to read yet and everybody knows it.
176. I turn-off when she starts making the class do things that makes us feel stupid.

However, we cannot just swallow these student comments whole. Now, we must make some difficult, professional decisions. Although the preceding are all from the "horse's mouth," we would be inept educators and parents if we accepted all these perceptions uncritically. Often students' (not just educators' and teachers') visions are skewed. Frequently students' anger and complaints of injustice have their source in a frustrated desire to always be nurtured and never weaned. Some, if they could, would always like to find the easy way out, not work, and try to run away from the unhealthy consequences of low self-esteem, debilitating dependence, and lack of growth. Since it is our responsibility as educators and parents to help children healthfully grow, we now must take these student perceptions and use them to make decisions that are best for them and best for our handling and preventing discipline problems, that also stop our children from learning and growing.

The best way to proceed is now to review systematically the sources of disruptive behavior (Part II of this book) and then later to concentrate on how to prevent and handle these sources of the problem (Part III of this book).

Beginning next with Chapter Six, we will concentrate on understanding those that come: From Outside Your Classroom. Before we do that, let's just review the systematic list of the sources of disruptive behavior that we have uncovered above. (They have been numbered according to the chapter numbers where each will be discussed in detail.) They are as follows:

- Chapter 6: From Outside Your Classroom
  A. from childhood to adolescence
  B. from home and peers
  C. from right outside your classroom
  D. especially for grades K–6
  E. training exercises and checklist

- Chapter 7: From the Environment of Your Classroom
  - A. disorder breeds disorder
  - B. from the physical environment
  - C. from the seating arrangement
  - D. from your procedures
  - E. from being poorly equipped
  - F. especially for grades K–6
  - G. training exercises and checklists
- Chapter 8: From the Interactions Between You and Your Students
  - A. from making miscalls
  - B. from being incongruent (inauthentic)
  - C. from not following through
  - D. from being inappropriate
  - E. from being unfair
  - F. especially for grades K–6
  - G. training exercises and checklists
- Chapter 9: From the Delivery of Your Lesson Plan
  - A. from incongruent content
  - B. from not being affective enough
  - C. from not being actional or experiential enough
  - D. from not being inductive enough
  - E. from not being interactive enough
  - F. from a lack of a felt sense of order, rewards, and momentum
  - G. from a mismanaged distribution of attention
  - H. from not being supportive enough, or explained well
  - I. especially for grades K–6
  - J. training exercises and checklist

PART II

*Prevention: Locating the Sources
of Disruptive Behavior*

CHAPTER 6: FROM OUTSIDE YOUR CLASSROOM

Let us first discuss the fact that a major source of discipline problems comes from outside of your classroom. Students are often already angry and frustrated before they even enter your classroom. They are prone to misbehave just from the difficult tasks of growing up, from their childhood through adolescence. Often, situations at home or among their peers have so upset them that they cannot behave appropriately no matter how well you conduct your class. Or all may even be fine, but disturbances right outside your classroom (in the halls, cafeteria, or school in general) rile them up.

All of these sources of discipline problems are pretty much beyond your control, or at least somewhat out of your hands. Yet, can we in some way understand them and deal with them better? I think we can. Let us first understand each of the sources more clearly.

A. From Childhood to Adolescence

Growing up (to state what we all remember) is often riddled with frustrations, angers, understandable reactions of revolt, and desires to act out. Children from childhood through adolescence often have it so rough, they cannot help taking their angers and frustrations out on other things, on other people, and in a variety of environments outside the home.

Getting through childhood has a lot of developmental tasks. In infancy, hopefully, a child experiences a secure environment where his/her needs are met so that the child learns to trust the world. Then, s/he must feel enough trust to be able to initiate and try things to be able to feel industrious and be able to make or do things to build a sense of ego and a sense of self. Even if this is accomplished, childhood is a fragile time when a child's sense of security must be constantly maintained by supportive relationships with family members and a consistency of routines at home. Elementary school children develop the ability to predict the outcomes of their actions then to anticipate them. Finally, they try to enforce consequences on themselves based on an understanding that their world has a predictable order. If they do not have the security that comes from this kind of consistency, the anxiety that this randomness produces can cause them to act out at home and at school. They are usually trying, through trial and error, to find a pattern of cause and effect that will allow them to make sense of their world. These must all be accomplished well enough so that, at adolescence, s/he can develop comfortable peer relationships yet have enough emotional strength to resist destructive peer pressures and make decisions about his/her independent future. During this time, the adolescent must build a sense of efficacy, a feeling of can do, and not feel isolated, or alone in his or her feelings.[32,33]

We can be more sensitive to the intensity of these developmental problems if we keep in mind that, apparently, just growing up is even more difficult than it used to be: "The rise in adolescent suicide has been dramatic since the 1960s. . . . In the U.S. in 1957, the adolescent suicide rate was 4.0 per 100,000 people; 10.9 . . . in 1974; 12.2 in 1982. These data indicate a significant increase of over 300 percent!" Teenage pregnancy and drunk driving are now epidemic among adolescents.[34] And, in the United States by 1993, it was reported that teenagers accounted for almost half of all arrests for property crimes; unwed teens gave birth to 650,000 infants; and a teenager committed suicide every 90 minutes![35] These problems are the tip of the iceberg effects of the turmoil of trying to manage one's behavior on the road to a mature and healthy life. Some completely fail before they even enter your classroom. Some enter while on this tumultuous road. And some fail after they've left you. This journey and its difficulties are not your fault. But, unfortunately (or fortunately), they "must" be there (compulsory education) during your class time. For instance:

You're in the middle of explaining the causes of the Civil War in your history class. The class is generally listening or copying notes from the chalkboard. Suddenly, about ten minutes into the period, Daryl bursts into your classroom late, dressed slovenly, wearing a weird red hat, and swinging his jacket. "Hi, teach!"

"Daryl, you're late."

"Yup, those are the breaks." The class laughs. Daryl tips his red hat and bows.

"Daryl, get to your seat!" you raise your voice.

---

[32] The above paragraph is a very brief summary of Erik Erikson's descriptions of psychosocial development.

[33] For a discussion on "Strengthening Students to Be Less Vulnerable to Peer Pressure," see Chapter 12, section E.

[34] Hart and Keidel. U.S. Division of Vital Statistics, 1979, and Annual Statistical Abstracts of the United States, Bureau of the Census, 1986.

[35] Hess, Markson and Stein. *Sociology,* 5th edition. New York: Allyn and Bacon. 1996: 155

"Woow! Hey, cool it, you're not my father." The class murmurs a laugh. Daryl slightly tips his hat again.

(You say to yourself: "I don't deserve this!" You're right.)

Or:

The students are putting their math homework on the chalkboard. All seems to be going well when suddenly Helen in the third row, third seat yells out.

"I did not call you!"

Fred laughs at her.

"Go ahead and laugh, you're too fat to date anyway!"

Fred gets furious and makes a fast move to hit Helen.

(You say to yourself: "I don't need this now!" You're right.)

Or:

You ask your students, "What do you think Frost means in his poem: 'Miles to go before I sleep'?" Many raise their hands, some look down. "Motivating them is work (you say to yourself), but at least they're somewhat with me." Then, suddenly, Tony comes in (twenty minutes late!) looking depressed and tired. You ask him, "Where are you coming from?" He makes a face at you, ignores you, walks past you in front of the room, and with his hand smears the line of the Frost poem you were discussing.

(You say to yourself: "I don't deserve this!" You're right.)

These three problems (Daryl, Helen, and Tony) are, according to our definition, real discipline problems, not miscalls. They do disrupt your teaching and the class's learning. But their sources do not seem to be from the physical environment of your classroom, nor from the interactions between you and your students, nor from the delivery of your lesson plan. Their source seems to be from outside your classroom. It is probable that the sources of these behaviors are complexly rooted in these students' development from childhood through their adolescence, over which you have no control. After all, let's remember some of the remarks from our students in Chapter 5: From the Horse's Mouth (pp. 97–98): ". . . I was very distant. I was wrapped up in a world of personal insecurities." "I sometimes acted out in class because of what was going on outside of school from just growing up." ". . . I act up in class . . . because some times i be mad when i come in to school." ". . . to relieve some of the pressure bottled up inside me, I call out." "I have ants in my pants." "I found out that Stacey and Shaneklia, me best friends, was talking about me . . . behind my back."

Growing up is besieged with specific developmental tasks and problems that produce frustration and anger, often vented hostilely. This is especially true with adolescents, the age group in which discipline problems are most prevalent.

What is the day like for our "Johnny," the adolescent of our secondary schools? He awakes at 7:00 A.M. and eats breakfast with a rushing family that has little time to care about his feelings. By 7:45 A.M., he is either on a crowded bus or subway train, either worried about the school day he is about to try to endure or worried about his friends or his future—and here has little chance to talk constructively with anyone. Somewhere about 8:15 A.M., he sits in his first period class forced to set his whole personality in gear (no matter what is happening to his personal life) to, i.e., the use of the gerund in English Composition, the death of Louis XIV, or the Pythagorean Theorem.

For about the next eight periods, at the sound of each bell, he must shift his emotional gears to get interested in whatever his next subject class demands, while he must retain control of whatever emotional feelings that press for expression. Each class is seldom interested in what he is being taught nor what he feels about his personal everyday life. Escaping from each period at the sound of each bell, the student has about five minutes to get to his next class, digest the information of the last class, shift gears for the next class, and find some friends he may be able to say hello to long enough to let out all the emotional reactions he may now have to his day and his teachers' battery of hours of facts about the world and life. If he has a study hall period, he must sit in an auditorium at least one seat apart from any other student, and he must study—which often becomes but a situation in which he is forbidden to express himself. And this will be his schedule in school for about seven hours a day, five days a week, for ten months of every year. At about 3:15 P.M., he takes the same crowded subway or bus home, with little chance to really express himself. From about 4:00 P.M. until about 10:30 P.M., his emotional life is in the hands of the kids on his block and his family. Here, his peers may just want to get high; his mother and father may just want to eat dinner and watch T.V.; and, anyway, he has about two hours of homework to do so that he can awake at 7:00 A.M., prepared for the school that is supposedly helping him with his life.

It is unimportant that the above, in some cases, may be an exaggeration. What is important is that we realize the adolescent is going through probably the most emotionally tense and chaotic period of his life; perhaps no other period finds him as emotionally burdened yet unprepared.

For instance, adolescents experience comparatively sudden weight and bodily changes with accompanying consequences that are difficult to adjust to. Such changes are made more difficult by the fact that they occur at unequal rates in different parts of the body and organs. Most emotional among these physical changes are the onset of puberty and changes in primary and secondary sex characteristics. For males, the testes enlarge, pubic hair appears, the penis doubles in size, facial hair grows, and the voice deepens. For females, hips begin to widen and round, breasts develop, pubic hair and facial hair (down, on upper lip) appear, and sex organs fully develop. Emotional and psychosocial, besides physical, adjustments to these changes are very difficult.[36] Adolescents experience motor awkwardness, difficulty in maintaining equilibrium under the pressure of new unconscious drives,[37] and a very self-conscious concern over their appearance to peers, while being pressured by the standards of parents and adults in general. They must accept their new physical self and attain emotional control over these new changes.[38] In a way, this new body becomes a "symbol of self"[39] that he or she must learn to consolidate. It is understandable that adolescents respond very emotionally to comparatively slight stimuli[40] and are often thrown into a state of emotional disturbance very easily,[41] which they often have no control over.

Among these bodily changes, probably the most difficult task is dealing with the new disconcerting internal impulses of sexuality within the pressures and mores of one's peers, parents, and society in general. Particularly demanding can be menstruation for females, whose average onset age now has fallen to 11–15 in this country. Such emotional and social adjustment is often more difficult when we consider the fact that the onset of menstruation usually is quite irregular at the beginning.[42] However, the major source of the anxiety, frustration, and feelings of rejection that occur is trying to understand, define, and adjust to one's sex role, both physically and societally. The latter is even more difficult today when society itself is undergoing a transition regarding sex-role responsibilities and expectations. Given this sex-role ambiguity, the adolescent must discover and adjust to sexual orientation, gain acceptance from those he or she is attracted to, and make difficult sexual decisions. The task is to negotiate internal sexual urges in the face of external demands and limits, handle one's self (a self yet to be formed), and gain some kind of acceptance and satisfaction without feeling guilt or loss of respect. Midst this struggle, the adolescent has probably begun to masturbate with its usual consequent feelings of anxiety, guilt, and ugliness.[43]

All of these new problems must be dealt with within the forming, chaotic arena of questioned self-identity. The adolescent is no longer the child who

---

[36] John E. Horrocks. *The Psychology of Adolescence.* Boston Houghton Mifflin. 1951: 261.

[37] Sigmund Freud. *The Basic Writings of Sigmund Freud.* New York: Modern Library. 1938: 137.

[38] Geraldine Lambert. *Adolescence.* California: Wadsworth. 1972: 15.

[39] Caroline B. Zachry. *Emotion and Conduct in Adolescence.* New York: Appleton-Century. 1940: 34.

[40] Phyllis Blanchard. "Adolescent Experiences in Relation to Personality and Behavior," in J. Hunt (Ed.), *Personality and the Behavior Disorders,* Vol. II. New York: Ronald Press. 1944: 692.

[41] Luella Cole. *Psychology of Adolescence.* New York: Rinehart. 1948: 17.

[42] Harold C. Stuart. "Physical Growth and Development," in Jerome M. Seedman (Ed.). *The Adolescent: A Book of Readings.* New York: Dryden. 1953: 104.

[43] Fred Brown and Rudolf T. Kempton. *Sex Questions and Answers.* New York: McGraw Hill. 1950: 90.

can be free from knowing who he/she is. School asks, vocational pressures ask, peers and family ask, "Who are you?" and "Who will you be?" He/she can no longer adequately just be a mimic of a model, or just, "son or daughter of my parents." The adolescent wants and needs independence from these sources of identity. But leaving these means a new struggle at forming a self. The adolescent is almost constantly preoccupied with the question, "Who am I?"[44] The central problem is to establish a "sense of identity," organize ideas about oneself in terms of society's definitions and rules of passage.[45] The childhood old self fades, and with this loss comes a security threat, loneliness, moodiness, and intractability.[46] No wonder the adolescent is self-conscious. Trust is a problem. How can s/he trust her/himself when the self is not secured? If not secure, how can s/he trust others, or even time? Thus, initiating relationships and planning become quite anxious. Often, the only solution is to find at least the unloneliness of sameness among one's peers. Peer conformity becomes a necessary defense for this identity confusion.[47] In this turbulent arena of forming a self, the adolescent must be on guard to protect her/himself from devaluation[48] and accept his/her uniqueness and ordinariness while trying to feel self-directed amidst pressures from peers and adults.[49] This situation may often be made more difficult when a vulnerable teen is bullied by other peers and/or is having to cope with a divorce between his parents. The struggle to mature must be mounted midst ongoing conflicts. Adolescents experience the "catch 22" of trying to gain self-feedback through some kind of intimacy with others, yet have an unprepared self by which to negotiate the necessary intimacy. No wonder s/he depends on models of famous people or is influenced by mass media's parading of, e.g., sports figures or its idea of attractiveness. Often males can only obtain their idea of self from vocational experiences, and females from establishing intimacy with others.[50] And, again, society's own confusion and limits during its self-role transition makes the task also more difficult. We can only appreciate the upsets involved in the task if we can remember this identity struggle. To refresh our

---

[44] Bruno Bettelheim. *Symbolic Wounds: Puberty Rites and the Envious Male.* Illinois: Free Press.1954: 21.

[45] Erik H. Erikson. *Childhood and Society.* New York: Norton. 1950: 228.

[46] Gardner Murphy. *Personality: A Biosocial Approach to Origins and Structure.* New York: Harper. 1947: p. 508.

[47] Erik H Erikson. *Identity: Youth and Crisis.* New York: W.W.Norton. 1968: 120–121.

[48] James C Coleman. *Abnormal Psychology and Modern Life.* Chicago: Scott, Foresman. 1956: 86.

[49] Carl Binger. "The Concept of Maturity" in Sidonic Gruenberg (Ed.). *Our Children Today.* New York: Viking. 1952: 208.

[50] David Elkind. *A Sympathetic Understanding of the Child.* Boston: 1974: 154.

memories, let's listen to what it's like (first from Anne Frank and then from Barry Stevens):

> If I talk, everyone thinks I'm showing off; when I'm silent they think I'm ridiculous; rude if I answer back, sly if I get a good idea, lazy if I'm tired. . . .[51]
>
> In the beginning, I was one person, knowing nothing but my own experience. . . .
>
> Then there were two of I. One "I" always doing something that the other "I" disapproved of. . . .
>
> In the beginning was "I" and "I" was good. Then came in other I, Outside authority. This was confusing. And then other I became very confused because there were so many different outside authorities. . . .
>
> Sit nicely. Leave the room to blow your nose. Don't do that, that's silly. . . .
>
> The most important thing is to have a career. The most important thing is to get married. . . . The most important thing is sex. . . . The most important thing is to have everyone like you. . . . The most important thing is to love your parents. The most important thing is to be independent. . . .
>
> Out of all the other "I" 's some are chosen as a pattern that is me. But there are all the other possibilities of patterns within what all the others say which come into me and become other "I" which is not myself, and sometimes these take over. Then who am "I"? . . .
>
> Smile, and you will be rewarded. . . .
>
> Why am I so hollow and the hollowness filled with emptiness?[52]

To make matters worse, the adolescent is the child who has matured to the realization that life (his or her life) doesn't last forever. Mortality becomes a more conscious background to the present. Children believe they will live forever, or more accurately, don't need to feel "forever," for they are not aware that their lives will end. On the other hand, the adolescent has now probably seen either his/her pet die or his/her grandparents pass away. They are pressured about their future career, with the implication: "you haven't got forever." Thus, adolescence is the onset of the life anxiety (the being-in-the-world with the preconscious awareness of one's death[53]) that will exist as a motivator, amd sometimes defeater, for the rest of their lives. With this realization comes realizations of limits and the end of once comforting myths. Daddy's money isn't always there. There's no Santa Claus. He/she cannot just scribble any longer; he/she must now draw, or make products, work, be practical, and not just play.[54] The red pen of the teacher can be bought in

---

[51] Anne Frank. *The Diary of a Young Girl.* New York: Modern Library. 1965: 57.

[52] Carl Rogers and Barry Stevens. *Person to Person: The Problem of Being Human.* Utah: Real People Press. 1969: 184–186.

[53] Martin Heidegger. *Being and Time.* New York: Harper and Row. 1962: 293–296.

[54] John J. Small. "Why a Core Based on Adolescent Needs?" *Educational Administration and Supervision.* Vol. 43, No. 112. 1957: 34.

stationery stores, and the teacher is just a finite person like his/her mother—who also was (and sometimes is) just a little girl. Anxiety created by these realizations motivates often a desperate need to feel control. But the inability to control everything brings on feelings of inferiority, depression, and more anxiety. The awareness that one must prepare for the future (since one doesn't have forever) brings about the stress of occupational identity, a major adolescent worry.[55] Adolescents experience a sense of time diffusion amd urgency, and often, to deal with these stresses they act as if time were not important.[56]

With this anxiety about the future, the desire to understand, to predict, to control, leads to a need for developing a system of ideas. If things are systematic, they are less chaotic and threatening. If the fear of change can be put into ideas (idealized), they can be held still and manipulated. Adolescents begin to build systems and theories to deal with the fears of possibility.[57] They need to develop am ethical framework as they begin to dissociate ideas about right conduct from authoritarian sanctions.[58] They question the existence of God, become introspective,[59] and experience the insecurity of not feeling a confident personal point of view.[60] This insecurity is compounded with the frustration of often being unable to put their feelings into words.[61]

All of the problematic feelings of adolescence must go somewhere. Often, they are taken out on others: parents, adults, and certainly those they have transient relationships with, teachers. Or students try to cover up their upset feelings of adolescence[62] (their "season of shames"[63]) and escape, abuse drugs, or just become truant.

If you could see into Daryl, Helen, and Tony's lives [the students who came into your classroom (above) already disruptive], you would realize that:

Daryl "has to" make wise guy remarks and bow as he comes in late. From 9 to 14, Daryl felt awkward about his too fast growing body. He was embarrassed about his penis and his sexual feelings. Now, at sixteen, he has covered these non-integrated feelings with a "macho style." Daryl's father, an alcoholic, died when he was nine, and since then Daryl knows he doesn't want to be like his father. But he's not sure who he wants to be like, or is. His mother, needing the money, has put vocational (identity) pressures on

[55] Erik Erikson. *Childhood and Society.* New York: Norton. 1950: 228.
[56] Erik Erikson. *Identity, Youth and Crisis.* New York: Norton. 1968: 169.
[57] B. Inhelder and J. Piaget. *The Growth of Logical Thinking.* New York: Basic Books. 1958: 187.
[58] J. C. Flugel. *The Psycho-Analytic Study of Family.* London: Hogarth. 1931: 45.
[59] Mollie S. Smart. *Adolescents.* New York: Macmillan. 1973: 70–71.
[60] Jean Piaget. *The Psychology of Intelligence.* New York: Harcourt Brace. 1947: 148.
[61] Irene Josselyn. *The Happy Child.* New York: Random House. 1955: 314.
[62] Laurence F. Shaffer. *The Psychology of Adjustment.* Boston: Houghton Mifflin. 1936: 166.
[63] Norman Kiell. *The Adolescent Through Fiction.* New York: International Universities Press. 1970: 13.

him, and he feels he can no longer be the self that was his mother's child. Daryl often feels alone and depressed but covers these feelings. So Daryl tries to feel "cool" that he has found an identity in his red hat that he bows with to his peers. They like him for this little revolt that makes them all feel unalone. Getting his peers' acceptance helps Daryl feel a unique identity and deal with his feelings of really going nowhere. Daryl tries not to let time or the future bother him. He tries to let these slide off his back. That's why he's late, says, "Those are the breaks," "You're not my father," and tips his hat. If he didn't, he'd have to feel all the pains of where his life is.

Helen yells out, "I did not call you!" to defend herself. She is not just defending herself from Fred's laugh at her. She is also trying to defend herself from the upset of some very difficult feelings. In the past few years, Helen's breasts have not grown much, while her friends' have. She feels flat-chested and ugly. At night she often looks in the mirror and fears she has too much facial hair. She hates the cramps of her period, while its irregularity causes her fears she will never be a "real woman." She feels sexual desires but feels she's supposed to say "no" or she'll lose respect. But, she's not sure what to say "no" to, or when, or to whom. She's told to be assertive, that it's O.K. to call Fred. But she worries Fred will think she's too forward, that he likes the traditional passive girls. Helen is not sure who she should be. She is often self-conscious. No wonder she got upset and yelled out, "I did not call you!" when Fred whispered with a smirk on his face, "Did you want me when you called last night?" Helen needs to say Fred is "fat" so she can reject him before she gets rejected.

Tony is late because he's had trouble sleeping for weeks. His best friend died last year, and his favorite uncle, a priest, died when he was ten. Tony spends many hours alone in his room watching T.V. Actually, he doesn't really watch it, he just looks at it while he keeps asking himself things like: "If God is good, why did he let my friend die?" "If I hate God, will I go to hell?" Tony wonders if reincarnation is true. Then, "Who was I?" "Maybe all religions are myths; my uncle wasn't saved by the religion he preached!" "It doesn't pay to live or work for anything." And, Tony can't put these feelings into words; he's too depressed. So, he just walks in late and smears the sentence that reminds him of all this that he sees on your blackboard: "And miles to go before I sleep."

B. From Home and Peers

Another major source of discipline problems comes from the home, also pretty much out of your hands. Again, let's recall some of the remarks from Chapter 5: <u>From the Horse's Mouth</u> (p. 100): ". . . my mother was very ill . . . so I felt restless while I was in school." ". . . my father likes to drink and whenever he is drunk, he will start to beat my mother and when this goes on, I get upset; and when I arrive at school, my attention will be divided." "I act up in my classes because I have problems in my house with my brother . . . , so I let out all of my anger [on] . . . the teacher." "I don't get attention at home, but when I act up in class everyone pays attention to me."

The students in your class are attempting to wean themselves psychologically from their family. To attain a healthy identity, they must abandon the incestuous aim, replace family infantile objects, and find their own personality differentiated from their once idealized parents[64] all while they still need their families. Their parents' anxiety may push each adolescent to say "no" to sex and imply that masturbation is ugly, even sinful. The adolescent, pressured by internal impulses and peers, often finds these frustrating sexual conflicts turning into anger at those who apply the pressure, viz., parents. But his/her parents demand that, "You shouldn't talk that way to your mother." So, the anger is repressed, ready to be spilled out in school.

Daryl's mother is "on his case." She's constantly criticizing him for not thinking about a career or being lazy. He can't talk to her about his feeling lost, or depressed from the death of his father because his mother is still angry that her husband was an alcoholic and irresponsible. So, she is worried her son may end up like him. So, Daryl comes into your class late with the upset from his mother that he couldn't let out there.

Helen's father is always away on business trips. Her mother always watches T.V. Helen's mother feels that her life got lost after she had Helen when only eighteen years old. She keeps telling Helen to forget boys and her looks (and sex) and, "make something of yourself!" Helen can't tell her mother that she feels unattractive, so she comes to school very vulnerable that she may be whispered about.

Tony's father lost his oldest protective brother, the uncle and priest who died that Tony so admired. Tony's father believes bad feelings will just go away by not discussing them. He also will not argue with his son about religion or ethics. When he grew up, you just listened to your parents, that's it. "If you're my son and you argue with me, then you don't respect me!" Tony feels that sometimes he is so distant from his opinionated (sometimes depressed) father, that he is losing his father too. But he can't tell him, so he just feels like giving up sometimes—as he comes in late and wipes his hand on ". . . miles to go before I sleep."

And your students' peers are also a source of discipline problems that is often out of your control. Again, Chapter 5: "I don't feel welcomed by [the other] . . . students." ". . . people tease [me] after school cause I got my hair

[64] Bruno Bettelheim. *Symbolic Wounds: Puberty Rites and the Envious Male.* Illinois: Free Press. 1954: 21.

cut." ". . . I had an argument with my best friend and couldn't concentrate in class." ". . . kids make fun of me."

How can your students listen to their parents and you when their security in the group is so vital[65] and may conflict? They need their peers to feel unalone with all these upsets that they feel no one seems to understand. They need their peers as a place to rehearse for adulthood.[66] Daryl needs the approval of his peers, since you or his mother don't give it to him. Helen is even teased by her girlfriends, who are enjoying feeling sexy. She can't hold in her reactions to Fred. And Tony's peers think Tony is weird when he looks up books on religion rather than goes to rock concerts.

Finally, to make matters worse for these students, Daryl, Helen, and Tony are living in a society in which the breakdown of family solidarity is rampant.[67] The divorce rate in this country through the 1990s is now projected at fifty percent, and one out of four children will not be living with both parents.[68] And adolescents are even more burdened with economic-vocational pressures than they used to be: "The percentage of high school students who work part-time increased from four percent to twenty-seven percent for males and one percent to twenty-seven percent for females just from 1940–1970."[69] These societal pressures are experienced by students facing the specter of possible nuclear war, compounded by media proliferation of violence and all sorts of acting out behavior.[70]

I am not advocating we just understand these kids. No matter how much we can feel for the Daryls, Helens, and Tonys, we cannot just empathize with them as they enter our classrooms. They are still disruptive to the class's learning and your job as a teacher. Our job is to protect the learning of the other students from these real discipline problems, even if these problems are not your doing and come from outside your classroom. We still must deal with these problems that enter from the outside. Although the sources of these behaviors are somewhat out of your hands, we must find ways to curtail their destructiveness to others, reduce their intensity, and find ways that at least prevent these behaviors from having a ripple effect on the rest of your class. We shall discuss these methods that stem these disruptions in Chapter 10: Dealing with Those That Are Somewhat out of Your Hands.

[65] Irene Josselyn. *The Happy Child: A Psychoanalytic Guide to Emotional Growth.* New York: Random House. 1955: 147.
[66] Peter Stein, Hess and Markson. *Sociology* New York: Macmillan. 1985: 119–120.
[67] Elizabeth Hurlock. "American Adolescents Today," in *Adolescence.* 1 (1966): 8.
[68] Hess, Markson, and Stein. *Sociology.* New York: Macmillan. 1994.
[69] Mary Ann Lamanna and A. Reidman. *Marriages and Families.* New York: Macmillan. 1985: 456.
[70] Allen Curwin and Richard Mendler. *Taking Charge in the Classroom.* Virginia: Reston. 1983: 5–6.

C. From Right Outside Your Classroom

Another major source of discipline problems comes from right outside your classroom: hallways, cafeterias, and bad or loose school rules. The students know this (again, from Chapter 5, p. 100): "Students were roaming the halls disrupting classes, plus my classroom was right by the cafeteria . . ." "If I had seen a commotion or something happening outside the classroom, I would get involved in it. . . ."

Often the hallways are not monitored by the school staff, and students will hang out in the halls after classes have begun, make noise, and disrupt even the best teachers. Or students can't hang up their coats and hats prior to your class and bring in clothing that can disrupt your teaching. Or students wave or communicate to your class through the door window to your classroom. Or students come into your class still eating a candy bar from their lunch. Or students just come in two minutes late, five minutes late, etc. Or staff or mothers pushing a bake sale barge into your room in the middle of your lesson. Or the jukebox in the cafeteria two doors down is too loud. Or the school staff is not enforcing rules like: no smoking, no hats in class, etc.

Many of these sources of disruption are somewhat, or seem completely, out of your control. Yet we can reduce their frequency and/or stem their flow into your classroom. We will discuss how to curtail these and handle them in Chapter 10: Dealing with Those That Are Somewhat out of Your Hands, section B. We shall also discuss in Chapter 10 how to deal with problems that come from just growing up, and from home and peers that also enter from outside your classroom.

D. Especially for Grades K–6

Here, you encounter problems from kids just growing up, or from home and peers, and outside your classroom that are somewhat different from those described above. Children who did not learn sufficient trust in early childhood may be withdrawn or resistant (out of anxiety) to following classroom routines. They may be unable to adequately relate to their peers and, thus, may be picked on by other children. They may have a low frustration tolerance and, thus, cannot endure long tasks or accomplish either academic or fun (art) projects. As a result, they may throw temper tantrums or try to manipulate (even be "bad") for extra attention. Children who suffer these problems may have a lot of difficulties with separation from their parents and wish transitioning from one activity to another. As a result, they may need that you "mommy" them more. Or they may sulk when they don't get what they want. Or they may just refuse to move from one activity to another. (In such cases, give little attention to sulking and provide attractive rewards in the next activity.) Those children often do not bear up to any kind of competition with their peers, or compete angrily, or have difficulty waiting their turn or sharing. (They need nurturance, little attention for not following routines, and much approval for following routines.) Often, something as simple as a smile and/ or a hug to every child as s/he enters the room will help avoid many potential discipline situations. This bit of reassurance to a child that may be out of sorts or may be entering the room with emotional baggage from elsewhere may be just what is needed to put out the "smoke before the fire."

The biggest outside-the-classroom source of behavior problems in early childhood, though, stems from the lack of self-control that comes from inconsistency in the home (or anywhere in a child's environment.) "I had a second grade student who did anything that came into his head. He was rude, disruptive, and often violent. He had no self-control and sometimes appeared as if he just had no sense of right and wrong. His responses to his peers were way out of proportion."

"What I eventually discovered was that he was living with his mother and his grandmother. It turned out that his grandmother watched him after school every day. She would basically ignore him, letting him do anything he wanted until he got on her nerves, and then she would, without sense or warning, hit him. Watching television was fine, until she suddenly decided it was time to do his homework. Then, he would get hit by his mother for watching TV when he came home. At home, running around yelling was OK until his mother got a headache and then he would get hit for being too noisy. Eating a snack of whatever he could find was OK until she decided he shouldn't have any more cookies. Then he got hit for eating junk food!"[71]

What this child had learned about life was that there was no consequence to his actions. There was no cause and effect in his world. There was no way to predict when or why he would get hit, so he just followed any impulse he had. This behavior naturally carried over into his life at school. Although this is an extreme case, it was also a real child, and he is not alone in his situation.

If elementary school-age children cannot find a predictable order to their world, if there is no consistency, then they have no guidelines to help decide their actions. They will act out, not out of malice, but because they have no understanding that their actions cause consequences, that they can predict these consequences, and that they can therefore decide in advance whether to do what they are thinking of doing.

Regarding disturbances that can come from the physical space outside your classroom, you will find that unattended kids will not be looking in the window of your door—at least it is less than it happens in grades 7–12 where students

---

[71] Mary-Ann Feller, elementary school teacher, N.Y.C.

change classes each period. But you may encounter at least two problems that are unique to K–6.

1. Your classroom is unfortunately located near the playground, or your students can see the playground from your classroom.
2. You find that parents want to talk to you at all different times during your class day, especially at "drop off" in the morning. And these parents seem to drop in at any time and disturb your class.

We shall discuss how to prevent and handle these in Chapter 10, section E.

E. Training Exercises and Checklist for Chapter 6

Exercise One: Noticing Sources of Discipline Problems That Are Coming from Outside Your Classroom

To become more sensitized to the fact that many angers and frustrations have nothing to do with you, that they're not your fault, plan one day to arrive at your classroom before the students. Then, just carefully observe each student's bodily and facial expressions as he or she arrives. Mentally give each student a +1 if s/he looks content, or a +2 if s/he looks in a very good mood. A student who looks kind of neutral, give a 0. A student who appears somewhat depressed, give a −1. And a student who looks frustrated or angry, give a −2. Try to do this for at least the first ten arriving students. You can often tell how someone is generally feeling just by looking at them carefully. You will probably notice that many of your students are already either depressed or withdrawn (usually a sign of repressed anger or loss) or outwardly frustrated and angry upon arrival. About what percentage arrives already upset?

Exercise Two: Noticing the Problems Associated with Puberty

Immediately after one of your classes (perhaps the last class of your day), sit down and make a list of students who in that class seem to be physically awkward or who seem self-conscious about their body and appearance. Which ones seem to move or present themselves as if they are trying to hide parts of their body or the way they look? Are any of them wearing a hat to conceal acne or clothes that intentionally hide their breasts? These students may be struggling with the changes in their body we discussed above. Write these students' names down. To resensitize you to these problems (that are not your fault), look at this list and try to feel what these students might be feeling from this observational standpoint.

Exercise Three: Noticing the Problems Associated with Sexuality

When you have some time, walk through the halls during a change of class and notice how much is going on with your students that has to do with just dealing with sexual attraction. Do the girls cluster in a gossip session watching a particular boy? Do some of the girls just call out remarks in the halls to get another student to notice them? Do either the girls or the boys walk by each of her with a kind of walk that hopefully will make them look good? Do some of the boys seem nervous when they pass a cluster of girls, or certain girls when they pass a cluster of boys? How many students, after they walk by each other, turn to sneak a glance at how the other looks from behind? Of course, the more you are noticed by the students, the more these reactions will be hidden. However, if you see some of these reactions, their intensity is probably much greater. These probable sexual attractions and reactions are also present in your classroom. The only thing is that there they are repressed underneath the lesson you are trying to teach. Try to remember the power and upset of sexuality (especially for adolescents) so that when it sometimes bursts through the surface of your lesson you can remember this is often beyond your control.

Exercise Four: Noticing the Problems Associated with Self-Concept

During a class discussion try to observe how many students' answers seem to be motivated by just trying to look good to their peers or how many seem reticent simply because they are afraid to look bad to their peers. How many students seem to answer questions by including their own reactions often mixed up into the factual answer? Or how many tend to talk in a distancing way: e.g., "You know, when you go to school, you sometimes feel nervous; like when one tends to . . ."? Such speaking in the third person often is a way of speaking about one's self, but in a hiding, distant way. All of the above students are likely to be experiencing worries and awkwardness with their sense of self. Try to remember that these reactions may be the effects of their struggling introspective attempt to form an identity that is acceptable to themselves, their peers, and only sometimes acceptable to you.

Exercise Five: Noticing the Problems Associated with Anxiety

Start a discussion in your class that either has to do with the future, or endings, or mortality. For instance, in a history class, draw a time line and have the students locate past events on the line, their own birth, and then have them project events for about the next seventy years on the line (past their probable life span). Or, in an English class, have them write about their future, their hoped-for career, or goals. Or have them write about endings: the loss of friends when they moved or the death of a pet. Or, in a science class, discuss the inability to understand, predict, or control things. Or discuss the vastness of the universe or the infinite complexity of the human body. Then, ask them to relate to these discussions personally. Many may only be able to share their reactions by talking in the third person: e.g., "you tend to feel . . . ," or "that reminds one of. . . ." Some students may just joke off their reactions to these subjects. Others may just seem to withdraw. These reactions may be the awareness of finitude that has newly entered their adolescent worlds. Often these awarenesses produce feelings of anxiety or powerlessness. If these feelings are not handled, they often can turn into anger at the frustration over the inability to control such realities. How many of your students seem to fly into a rage just because things are not controllable? Who in your classes goes into a rage when his pencil breaks or his pen won't write? Or who gets very upset if his or her sense of order or answer is disturbed or not perfect? These reactions are not your fault, nor can you prevent these uncomfortable reactions to the brute facts of human finitude now first intruding on their vulnerable worlds. It's understandable that the anxieties associated with these new knowledges sometimes will appear in the form of disruptive behavior.

Exercise Six: Noticing the Problems That Stem from Home or Peer Relations

At an appropriate time, have your students draw their own sociogram (a social map of their life) either as a homework assignment or in class. This is easily done by asking them to draw a little square in the center of a blank page that they label: "me." Then ask them to place the males (indicated by triangles) and females (indicated by circles) on the page around them (their "me") either close to them, or distant from them the way these people <u>feel</u> in their lives. Close friends will be drawn close to them, or touching their "me," distant ones far away. Have them fill in the person's name (or initial) in each circle or triangle. Then ask them to darken the circles or triangles that are the most important to them. A sociogram of their peer life might look like this:

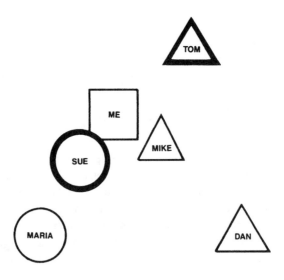

Then, ask them to do a sociogram of their family. It might look like this:

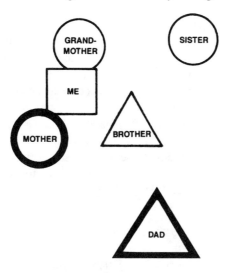

You may notice that in their peer relations, e.g., Sue is closest and most important, whereas Tom is very important but, maybe, too far away for the needs desired to be fulfilled, or that Mike is too close and maybe bothersome, since he's not so important. Or notice the sex of the people. Are sexual tensions present?

Or, in their family, their mother is closest and most important. And the father is very important, even needed badly, but too absent. Or their less important grandmother is around too much for comfort. Or they don't like their sister and feel fine that she is not close. You might even ask them to draw arrows at their "me" that indicate pressures on them:

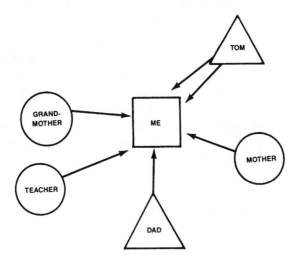

You should collect these sociograms and study them after school. Notice the problems each student has from the pressures in their peer and family network. You may wish to discuss these maps in a general way in class by asking, e.g., "Do you notice power struggles in teenage lives?" Keep your questions general and only allow personal discussion of these if the class can handle it. Protect students from the ridicule of others. Or share your own sociogram to help them feel unalone. Or incorporate these maps into a discussion of examples of other power or social maps, e.g., political power in the United States, or Congress, or during the Civil War. Or have them draw the sociogram of the characters in a piece of literature, e.g., Hamlet or Animal Farm. (If you choose to discuss these personal sociograms to make curricula material relate more to them, follow the guidelines for teaching emotional education I give in Chapter 12D, p. 317.)

Exercise Seven: Noticing the Problems That Come from Right Outside Your Classroom

Is this area a major source of disruption for you? Place an x next to each item below that seems to happen too often.

A. Students hang out in the halls outside your classroom.
B. Students bring, e.g., coats and hats into your room, which should have been put in their proper place before arriving to your class.
C. Students communicate to your class through the front door or front door window.
D. Intruders (deans, mothers, other teachers) come into your class in the middle of your lesson.
E. Noise from another part of the school is bothering you or your class.
F. Unenforced school rules are intruding on your ability to teach.

Checklist

_____ 1. Have you wrongly assumed that all the disturbances at the beginning of your class are at you, because of you?

_____ 2. Are you getting overly angry at a student who may be feeling self-conscious or physically awkward?

_____ 3. Are you reprimanding a student in such a way that it makes him or her very uncomfortable in front of peers, especially the opposite sex, or a girlfriend or boyfriend?

_____ 4. Have you gotten overly annoyed with students' answers that seem to be too much about themselves?

_____ 5. Have you yelled too much at a student who has flared up over a worry or anxiety about the next period or the future?

_____ 6. You have just punished this student. Do you know where he or she stands with their peers or what the home life is like? It may still have been best to do what you needed to do. However, this sociogram observation may make you smarter at handling his or her next disruptive behavior.

_____ 7. Are you being interrupted by things going on in the halls, by intruders to your classroom, loose or bad school rules?

_____ 8. Are there students in your class who act out because they are anxious and distrustful?

_____ 9. Are there students who get angry and balk at activities because they have a low frustration tolerance?

_____ 10. Are there students who annoy you because they need you to play their "parent" too much?

CHAPTER 7: FROM THE ENVIRONMENT OF YOUR CLASSROOM

A. Disorder Breeds Disorder

Besides the sources of disruptive behavior that come from outside your classroom, an important source of disruptive behavior also comes from the environment of your classroom. Here, disorder will breed disorderly behavior. You can probably remember what happened to you when you suddenly entered a very clean, very well kept wall-to-wall carpeted home with everything in its place and a place for everything. Perhaps it was a home that seemed to have systems all around you, e.g., for how you should enter or a place where coats should be put, and where you're supposed to put your umbrella, or where you're supposed to wait for your host. Such places make you feel "*mores*-bound": that there are subtle rules, *mores,* here that you need to follow or need to adapt to, or you will feel like a misfit, like not belonging, or even being rejected. You wonder at these places: "Maybe I should take my shoes off before I enter, and enter quietly."

On the other hand, you've all gone from such tidy, almost too well kept living rooms to, e.g., the downstairs basement playroom. There, papers are strewn on a no-rug floor, games thrown around, pillow chairs used for furniture, and a big sloppy dog is playing with an old torn rag doll. Here, you feel you don't have to watch your step, you can speak louder, throw your coat over a chair, and not have to watch your behavior as carefully.

Environments push us into specific psychological sets; they tell us the range and kinds of behavior appropriate for where we are. The classroom environment can, in a way, tell students to care or not care about their behavior, or even suggest disruptive behavior. By "the classroom environment" we mean here more than just the physical environment, the room itself. We also mean: the seating arrangement of the class; the procedures of that room, your procedures; and the equipment used by you in the classroom. All of these can be individual environmental sources of disruptive behavior. After all, let's recall what the students said here from Chapter 5: From the Horse's Mouth (p. 100): "The room was always messy." ". . . the desks were so much of a downer and

135

the room a mess; it made you didn't give a damn." "This teacher would have the students sitting too close together."

We need to examine specific potentiating catalysts of disruptive behavior that may come from these environmental factors: the physical environment, the seating arrangement, your procedures, the lack of proper equipment.

B. From the Physical Environment

The physical classroom in which you teach may be a source of disruptive behavior if any of the following are the case:

1. The room is not the same classroom for each subject class period you teach. You already do not usually have enough control over the physical setting of your work as a teacher. But, if each period you must move to another room, you have even less control over where the room is located, its lighting, physical arrangement of seats and equipment, and the chalkboards and bulletin boards.
2. The room is located too far away for you to get there before most of the students get there.
3. The room is located too near noisy areas, e.g., too near a music class, auditorium, gym class, cafeteria, industrial arts class.
4. The windows face a football or baseball field, a playground, or a very interesting, distracting street.
5. The lighting is bad, or one light is not out but flickering.
6. The floor is noisy to walk on, e.g., it is tiled badly, or is concrete, and the room has an echo.
7. There are papers all over the floor.
8. The room is too warm. A warm room makes students lethargic, inattentive, bored, and disruptive.
9. There are no shades to block out glaring sunlight that may shine on you or the students.
10. The room has only one entrance door, and it's in the front of your classroom, where the chalkboard is. It's the only way latecomers can enter your room, right in front of your lesson.
11. The front entramce door has a large window in it where students in the halls cam distract students in your class.
12. There is no place in your classroom, away from the rest of the class, where you can have a private conversation, give a private reprimand to an individual student, or where students can work in solitude or in small groups.
13. There is no chalkboard. Or there's a chalkboard but there's no chalk or eraser. Or all of the latter are there, but the chalkboard is filled with another teacher's work or students' graffiti when you arrive.

14. There are no bulletin boards in the room.
15. Or there are bulletin boards, but they're a mess, filled with old papers, torn work, or with thumbtacked old announcements, signs, etc.
16. Or the bulletin boards are full of too colorful, distracting pictures or notices.
17. There is no garbage can; or it's there, but it's in "basketball range" for the students to attempt great hook shots with papers.
18. The pencil sharpener is in grinding noise range and in front of the class.
19. There aren't enough chairs and desks (plus one or two extra) for the number of students in your classes.
20. The desks or chairs squeak or are broken and/or filthy.
21. The room is cluttered with useless or non-essential furnishings.

C. From the Seating Arrangement

Are any of the following the case?

22. The room is too small for the number of students in your class to work well without either tripping over each other or being completely imprisoned in their seats.
23. All the seats are in neat rows, but this tidy arrangement does not allow the students to respond to each other's questions and answers well; each student can only see the back of the others' heads (and you). Class participation thus ebbs, and the pressure is on you to motivate them, without the advantage of their ability to interact much. Then, you have to police them so that no one turns around too much to see who is responding to your questions or who has a question.
24. All the seats are such that you're on one side of the room and they're on the other; it's you against them, in a way.
25. All the seats are arranged such that the only way students can get attention is through you or from others but then only by being disruptive.
26. The seats are arranged such that you are not easily visible to the students and/or you are too far away from them.
27. The students are so close to each other in such a way that innocent moves by students distract other students.
28. The seats are such that there is a poor traffic pattern, e.g., to come to the chalkboard or to enter and leave the room.
29. The seats face too much toward the windows or the entrance door to the class.
30. The seats are in a circle or a horseshoe, and each student too often watches each student, not you; there's too much interaction.
31. The seats are nailed to the floor, and there's nothing you can do about it.

32. The students keep choosing their seats, and differently every time. You can't seem to keep a seating plan for taking attendance or for learning their names.

33. There's no empty chair either in the back of the room (near the back door) nor in the front of the room (near the front door) that a latecomer could sit in after s/he enters the room.

D. From Your Procedures

Are any of the following the case?

34. The seating arrangement is not congruent with your teaching style, e.g., the desks are in groups, but you teach by lecturing, or, conversely, you use cooperative learning methods, but the desks are in rows facing the front of the room.

35. You have not given them any task or sheet that requires them, e.g., "to fill out" or "fill in blanks" at the start of the learning period.

36. You have not posted rules or routines in some visible permanent place in your classroom.

37. You don't do things in routines, in an order, such that your style has almost its own predictable way about it.

38. You don't demarcate places or time in your procedures: e.g., there's no calendar, nor list of topics that you have already taught, nor any clear sign of where you are going.

39. You have not planned a lesson plan with a sense of order that not only you know but the students can feel.

40. You tend to teach while you are handing out papers or materials. Or you want their attention when what you're giving out or doing attracts their attention away from you.

41. Your handouts have unclear directions, or immediately request too much work, or, right at the start, seem too difficult.

42. You don't have a clear policy for latecomers.

43. You don't have a clear homework policy.

44. You don't have a clear grading system.

45. You don't have a clear policy about going to the bathroom.

E. From Being Poorly Equipped

Are any of the following the case?

46. You don't carry with you (or have readily available) a piece of chalk or an eraser (or a rag) just in case there's none in the classroom you're going to.

47. You don't have or carry any colored chalk, e.g., yellow, besides regular white chalk.

48. You have no way to save either your notes for the class, or their work, or anything you wrote on the chalkboard for, e.g., the next meeting of that class. For instance, you don't have or use: newsprint pads, 5 × 8 cards posted, a portable chalkboard, etc.

49. You don't have or use a large calendar that the class can see that shows, e.g., the curriculum topics date by date.

50. You don't carry or use:
    —a few rubber bands
    —a "3M post-it pad"
    —a mechanical lead pencil
    —press-on white labels
    —a black ink ball point pen
    —a few 3 × 5 cards
    —a yellow high-lighter pen
    —a red pen
    —looseleaf reinforcements
    —a "wash 'n dri"
    —a single-edged razor blade[72]
    —aspirin
    —paper clips, large and small
    —a piece of carbon paper
    —a magic marker
    These can be "little tools of survival" and can all be carried in a small pencil case.

51. You don't have or carry an appointment book (or "day-timer").

52. You don't carry a couple of quarters with you for possibly needed pay phone calls, or you also don't have a phone credit card.

53. You don't use or have a "Delaney book" (or something similar).

54. You have not prepared any manipulatives, etc. (Manipulatives are materials that students physically manipulate to better understand a concept: e.g., pattern blocks, cuisenaire rods, unifix cubes, and bean counters) or other materials in advance so that they are easily distributed when needed (e.g., multiple sheets should be stapled together in packets and math manipulatives should be in easy-to-carry bins).

55. You don't have access to a computer to help you design educational materials, download free shareware for your classes, nor easy ways to contact other educators for a wealth of resources. Or, you have a computer

---

[72]As a tool to cut paper with that can be carried in a slot of your wallet instead of looking for, or carrying, a bulky pair of scissors.

with a modem, but you don't know how or where to look for these resources.

The above must seem very numerous. That's true; there are many environmental and procedural factors that can be the sources of disruptive behavior. Rest assured we will discuss how to handle, correct, and/or obtain all of the above in Chapter 10, section C: "Working on the Environment of Your Classroom." Some of these you may already be able to do something about from just reading the above list, from being more sensitive now to these potentiating environmental factors. The training exercises and checklists below will be helpful in increasing this awareness until we can work at solving and curtailing these environmental sources in Chapter 10, section C.

One more point before we go on. Some readers may be getting the feeling from the above list, and from this chapter onward, that I will be suggesting that we become teachers who are a kind of a controlling dictator. I am not. But I am suggesting that a good teacher needs to be systematic, well planned, assertive about limits, very organized, and good at keeping track of things. Yes, a good teacher needs to be able to control things: systems, plans, limits, organization, and recorded and retrieved information. But it is a popular misconception to believe that to be systematic means to be non-creative, cold, and dictatorial. As a matter of fact, it is usually the reverse. Only teachers who have first gotten some control over what they are doing and the class can be creative, can form warm relationships with students, allow student input, and be flexible. There is no contradiction in being firm, even stern, and being creative, even loved as a teacher. For one thing, children find security in limit-setting and respect such ability, and, for another thing, structure is the prerequisite for creativity. Lack of structure is not flexibility. Flexibility is the ability to change within a framework. Pure change is chaos. And creativity means the spontaneity of creation within structure. "Pure creativity" without control or a mapped-out framework, has no context to be interpreted in, has no language, and can't be communicated. "Creativity" not communicated is nonsense. That's why jazz is not haphazard notes, but trained creative techniques. So, do not feel guilty as you get more control over things while you try these recommendations. You can also be creative, you will also be creative, if you master some of these problems. As a matter of fact, in Chapters 8, 9, 11, 12, and 14 our focus will be on how to be a teacher students feel good with and how to deliver creative, interesting subject matter that allows students more (not less) participation. So rest assured you will not grow rigid as you, e.g., tackle your environment with the exercises you try below.

F. Especially for Grades K–6

Although most of what has been said in the rest of this chapter applies to grades K–6, it is important to emphasize the role of the classroom environment in these grades. "The learning environment can be a powerful teaching instrument at the disposal of the teacher, or it can be an undirected and unrecognized influence on the behaviors of both teachers and children." (Loughlin & Suina, *The Learning Environment,* Teachers College Press, 1982) As an aside, I strongly recommend this book for teachers in the elementary grades. Although the classroom environment is not by any means the primary cause of discipline problems in the elementary classroom, it cannot be underestimated as a source of unnecessary yet easily fixed disruptions.

Any of the above items 1–55 may be a source of disruptive behavior for you that comes from the environment of your classroom, but in K–6 other special sources also need to be located:

56. There is no sense in your classroom that the classroom is a little "world" of its own; each thing does not seem to have its own place; there doesn't seem to be a way one "does things" in your room, and you can't see past and present (and even future) activities by just looking around.
57. The physical environment is not organized into work areas or activity areas, e.g., art center, science center, etc.
58. It is difficult to find materials in your classroom. They are not clearly labeled and organized to promote student independence.
59. The kids can't easily see where they belong or sit or how to function in each work area.
60. The seating arrangement doesn't allow the kids to work alongside each other and yet give them room enough for their own individual work.
61. The seating arrangement doesn't give the kids enough access to your attention.
62. The procedures for each activity are unclear. One does not know, from a kid's point of view, "how to be good" in your classroom.
63. The students are not sure what happens if they are "bad."
64. The routines for each activity (how one uses supplies, cleans up, goes to the bathroom, etc.) are not clear.
65. The walls and bulletin boards are not used well to give students recognition or to demarcate progress, time, past projects, etc.
66. You do not have ample art supplies, or paper, or sharpened pencils ready "to borrow." And you have not kept these organized for easy access by you and your students.

67. You have not posted an outline of the day in a visible location so that the students can predict the schedule as they move from one activity to another.

(We will discuss some help with the above in Chapter 10, especially section E.)

G. Training Exercises and Checklist for Chapter 7

Exercise One: Does Your Room Look Disorderly?

One day get to school about fifteen minutes earlier than you usually get there. After you've checked in, go to your classroom(s) before anyone has arrived. Go with paper and pencil in hand to take a few notes. Before you enter your classroom(s), try to make believe you're a student and a student who is arriving at this room for the first time. Now enter and look at the room from this point of view. Does the room look, overall, orderly? What looks disorderly? The walls? The chalkboard? The floor? The seats? Is the room in a noisy place? Does it smell funny? How's the lighting? Does it look like a room that has some procedures and routines? Answer these questions to yourself and note any areas that need improvement. Then, place a checkmark next to the ones you can do something about fairly soon. Decide when you'll do these. Then place an "X" next to those that seem out of your hands. Then, place a "?" next to those you're not sure what you should do about. If you feel there's a lot of sources of disruption from just this environment, and you feel this area needs help now, skip to Chapter 10, section C now.

Exercise Two: Diagnosing Specific Environmental Sources of Disruptive Behavior

Another way to assess these environmental factors is to go back to the beginning of this chapter to section B where the list of specific sources starts from #1 and ends at source #55 (or #66, if you teach K–6) above. Go down the list with a pencil marking the following alongside each in the left column: O—if it's never for you, or not the case; 1—seldom; 2—often; 3—always. Take a look at your overall score. Is it high? (If you marked more than about ten items with at least a "2" that's high.) Is this a major area you need to work on? What areas did you score the highest: the physical environment, the seating arrangement, your procedures, equipment? Begin to work on those areas with the highest score, or all those items you gave yourself a "3"—as soon as you can. If you feel this is an immediate first-aid area for you, skip to Chapter 10, section C now.

Exercise Three: Assessing Whether Changing Any of These Is within Your Power

It may be the case that even after reading some of our suggestions in Chapter 10, section C: "Working on the Environment of Your Classroom," you find that you are still frustrated in this area. You feel that many of these items are out of your hands completely. Sometimes, that may be true. But, sometimes it just initially feels that way. Let's assess the situation before we tackle the problem. With pencil in hand, go down the above list 1–55 (1–66, if you teach K–6) and place a checkmark next to the item you feel you can do something about if you put in the time and the effort. Place two checkmarks next to the ones that seem easy to fix fairly quickly. Place a "?" next to ones you're not sure you can remedy. Place an "X" next to those that feel unchangeable, seemingly beyond your power. How many ✔s, or ✔✔ s, or ?s, or Xs do you have on your list? Make a contract with yourself to work on the ✔✔ s now, and later the ✔ s. After we discuss Chapter 10, section C, I think you will find more ✔✔, more "can fix." (Why have you not fixed the ✔✔ until now? Answer yourself.)

Exercise Four: Seeing the Room as a Student

Especially if you are an elementary school teacher, make sure that you know the impact of your room from your students' perspective. Sit down on the floor (yes, really!) and look at the room from the height of your students. Are things posted at an adult's eye level or a student's? Are there things that are distracting from this perspective that you don't see as an adult? Are there important posters or work hung up so high that they are difficult for a child to focus on? Can your students see the parts of the room you want them to see, e.g., the bulletin board, wherever you stand to teach most of the time? Are materials clearly labeled and are the labels visible from this height? Often, we set up great classrooms that look wonderful to adults who walk in, but we forget that the room is really there for the students, and that it is their perspective that counts.

Checklist

In the first column on the next page, list all the numbers of the items you gave only a #3 to in Exercise Two (as "always" a problem for you) and those you also gave ✔✔ in Exercise Three (as "easy to fix fairly quickly"). For example, if #34 (no "do-now" on chalkboard) you gave a #3 and ✔✔ put #34 in the first column. Next, write exactly your plan of action for that item in the next column: "plan of action." Then, decide when and about what time you will put this plan into action. Finally, if "done," check it off. Do this for as many items as you can that you gave: #3 ✔✔. Then do it for items: #3 ✔, #2 ✔✔, #2 ✔, etc. We will discuss in Chapter 10, section C how to tackle the #3's and #2's to which you gave a "?" or "X."

Item to be Worked on	Plan of Action	Date & Time	Done
A. 34	Put on chalkboard: "Do exercise 4 on p. 98 of your text, <u>now</u>."	Monday, 1st period	
B.			
C.			
D.			
E.			
F.			
G.			

CHAPTER 8: FROM THE INTERACTIONS BETWEEN YOU AND YOUR STUDENTS

Another major source of disruptive behavior is one that has received too little attention in the literature and is within your control: the interactions between you and your students. Here, we are not talking about disruptions that originate from outside the classroom (just from growing up or from home or peers) or from the environment of your classroom. How you interact with the students can often incite disruption, prevent it, or curtail it. That's why it can be that Johnny is disruptive in period three, but usually not so in period four—even though the teachers have similar rules and teaching methods. Nothing happened to Johnny's personality when the bell rang at the end of period three. What happened was he went to a teacher in period four who has a different personality. The teacher in period four "comes off" differently regarding: what s/he calls a "discipline problem" (miscalls); how s/he presents her/himself how s/he says what s/he says; whether s/he consistently follows up lessons, promises, and warnings; his/her attitude toward the students professionally; fairness; and the way s/he generally delivers the lesson plan (not what s/he puts down in the written lesson plan).

Again, the most important and influential factor in dealing with or preventing discipline problems that is within your power is your personality, how you interact with, or react to, students. Yet, because educators either do not fully realize this, or don't know how to work on it, or feel this area is too sensitive (verges on therapy), it is one of the most neglected of the key sources of disruptive behavior: "the [education] courses said almost nothing about a teacher's most important resource—himself. The problem of simply being a person with the children was completely overlooked."[73] What we are pointing out here is that probably one of the major sources of disruption is a bad relationship between you and your students. Students "go after" teachers they feel are "the enemy." Preventing the formation of this enemy relationship is one of the most important things we can do to prevent discipline problems. When students are not generally angry with a

[73]Carolyn Mirthes. *Can't You Hear Me Talking to You?* New York: Bantam. 1971: 129.

145

teacher, when they feel that the teacher is on their side, is working for them (even if the teacher doesn't do well all the time), they do not want to "go after" the teacher. As one study showed, teachers who had more discipline problems differed not so much with regard to their lessons, but with regard to their understanding of students, attitude toward students, and their own emotional adjustment.[74] In other words, these differences in personality characteristics make some teachers interact with students in a way that potentiates a bad relationship with them and, thereby, discipline problems. Our students are being perceptive when they say that they were often disruptive (Chapter 5: From the Horse's Mouth, pp. 101–102 just because: "The teacher was the type of person . . .," "she always had a bad attitude," "we felt she wasn't authentic," "he was into the role he played," "he was too stiff, too rigid," "the personality of this teacher was. . . ."

We need to analyze those aspects of the interaction of the teacher's personality with the students that cause a poor teacher-student relationship and, thereby, disruptive behavior. We shall particularly study these disruptive sources in the following:

A. From Making Miscalls

We have already discussed in Chapter 4 how calling a situation a discipline problem when it is not (making a miscall) can cause disruptive behavior. Our students may be sensing these miscalls when they say (from our Chapter 5, pp. 101–102): "She became annoyed at something she shouldn't have become annoyed about"; ". . . when the teacher accuses you of talking or something really unreasonable"; "the teacher would pick on me and criticize me for no reason. I would be doing my work"; "sometimes she used to pick on me when I was so quiet as can be"; "the teacher went off because I was reading before the class began." Making a miscall is not merely an action of misidentification due to a mere cognitive mistake. Clarifying the definition of a discipline problem and understanding typical miscalls (as we have done in Chapter 4) is only half the job. Many typical miscalls are made by teachers because of who they are, their personalities, their needs and feelings. So, a source of disruptive behavior may be those needs and feelings of the teacher that generate the tendency (sometimes accidentally) to make typical miscalls.

Let us review (from Chapter 4) some typical miscalls, but now let's try to uncover what may be going on inside the teacher, the teacher as person, that may be the source of these miscalls.

---

[74]Richard L. Turner. "Teacher Characteristics and Classroom Behavior" *ERIC Clearing House Report*. ED 015-886. February, 1966.

1. *Disciplining the withdrawn student* (from p. 62). You need the student's attention because your ego is hurt that he is not listening to your great lesson (though he's not really bothering your teaching or the other students' learning). Or you are frustrated that this student is "going under," and that you can't save him. Or you are upset that the student is not using his potential and are frustrated with yourself that you feel not able to tap into it. So, you want to try even if it disrupts your own lesson. Or he reminds you of you, when you withdraw; and he (you) shouldn't do that.

2. *Overreacting to a rule* (from pp. 62–63). You're so angry at, e.g., gum chewing, you just lose your temper and make a generalized, overreactive statement you feel you must then stick to. Or you feel so anxious and upset you just lose control and feel like, "I've got to just CONTROL! everything," so you lay down (unreasonable) RULES.

3. *You feel you've got to win their feelings* (from pp. 64–65). You can't stand to be disliked. You sometimes feel lonely in your personal life or not liked in general. Or how the kids feel about you and your lesson means so much (too much) because it's the main thing in your life (you have little else in your life that feels meaningful).

4. *You feel you need their attention* (from p. 65). Even when you don't really need their attention for educational purposes: you just need attention. So, if a student is not looking at you (and your performance), you feel insulted or hurt (even when it's better educationally that he look at the chalkboard notes he's copying that you gave him).

5. *You discipline when your ego is hurt* (from pp. 65–66), even though the student's action is not educationally disruptive.

6. *You discipline when you feel, "they're interfering with my getting my lesson done"* (from p. 66). You feel competitive with how far Mr. Johnson, next door, is in his teaching, and you're only up to World War I! You feel unaccomplished and falsely believe if you can get through all these notes by the time the bell rings, you will have accomplished a lot, as if you've then taught a lot, forgetting that the point is that they learn a lot.

7. *You displace your anger* (from p. 67). You have a lot of frustrating, angry situations going on in your life, in and outside your job. You also feel you can't tell the people who deserve your anger that you're angry. They'll be too hurt, or dislike you, or punish you in some way. So you (accidentally) let out your anger (or its stored up intensity) on your students or the wrong students.

8. You wrongly discipline a student because *you're tired of trying to be understanding all the time* (from pp. 67–68). You're just out of patience. You got little rest last night. You can't remember when you had fun last. You're tired of the same questions and topics. You need a vacation, or you are just plain needy. So, you're just "out" of giving for others' needs.

9. You get angry at a student because of *the mirror effect* (from p. 68). The student reminds you of the parts of you that you don't like or wish you could change or of someone significant in your life you don't like.

10. *You feel like exercising control* (from pp. 68–69) though such control is not needed educationally. You may be obsessive about doing things certain ways or how things "must" be. Why? "Just because!" Perhaps, because you feel generally worried and anxious and feel if you can't feel control and "together" inside, controlling things outside will calm you down.

11. *You discipline steam, thinking it's "smoke"* (from pp. 69–70). Actually, you probably fear (not think) it's "smoke," so you jump on it. The noise of class participation or the students' excitement suddenly makes you worried that the class is getting out of control. So, rather than trying to find a way to channel this energy, you just yell at it and cut it off (and also some of your relationship with your students!).

12. *You get angry at venting as if it were cursing* (from pp. 70–71). Actually, you get personally insulted when you hear a four-letter word, as if this word is at you, when it's really an expression of frustration, maybe even a student's anger at himself, not you. You feel insecure about whether you are respected, and any "dirty" word feels like an example of a word that your parents would never tolerate when you were a kid. So, you won't tolerate this in your "home," the classroom. The trouble is that you have forgotten that the context here is not your "home," but the context of a frustrating situation vented in the form of a blurted out angry word. Seen in its proper context, the word probably has nothing to do with you or your self-respect.

13. You overly reprimand a student because you make *a prejudicial mistake* (from p. 71). Some particular student has previously angered you or gotten you quite anxious. To protect yourself from any future anger or anxiety you have unconsciously made a generalization: to be leery of "this kind of kid." You have begun the stereotyping process. You generalize about this kid or about those who seem similar. We all do this when we have bought a particular brand of car that turns out to be a "lemon" and decide we'll never buy that brand again. However, we are destructively prone to also stereotyping people with regard to race, creed, gender, skin color, sexual orientation, etc. Some of us just immediately dislike fat people. These negative generalizations are also often reinforced by our prejudiced society. Thus, our teacher reprimands may be impulsively reactive in a prejudicial way.

14. You reprimand a student because you are still *holding a grudge* (from p. 71). The student is, currently, not being disruptive. But you are still angry from how s/he was yesterday, and you are hanging on to the hurt or insult you still feel, with a vengeance.

15. *You punish an education problem as if it is a discipline problem* (from p. 72). Is this individual student who is doing poorly disrupting your teaching or his/her learning? If not, your reprimand will probably be disruptive to the rest of the class's concentration on your lesson, and your anger will usually not help this particular student's education problem. Sure, you feel, "How dare he not do the homework," or "He's going down the drain; wake up you idiot!" or "Not in my classroom!" your ego says. So you make this miscall; now you are a source of disruption.

We need to work on all these teacher needs and feelings that make us prone to making these miscalls, an important source of disruption that comes from the interactions between you and your students. We shall, in Chapter 11: Repairing Your Student-Teacher Interactions, section A, "Not Making Miscalls."

B. From Being Incongruent (Inauthentic)

Another very important and neglected source of disruptive behavior that comes from how teachers interact with their students is from teachers being incongruent. Carl Rogers uses the term "congruence" to describe a situation in which one's words, gestures, and behavior accurately reflect or correspond to what one is actually feeling.[75] If a speaker's words, gestures, and behavior do not correspond to what s/he is really feeling, then they are being "incongru-ent." What Rogers calls being incongruent our students often call being phony, or "bullshitting." Students, like most people, and especially adolescents, hate phonies. Let's recall what they said in Chapter 5 (p. 102): we were disruptive because "we felt she wasn't authentic." "He was into the role he played. . . ." "he was scared to show he could be human." ". . . he was so teacherfaced." "One teacher . . . was so full of it." "Even his, 'You're doing good' was bullshit." I would venture to say that being congruent is the prerequisite skill for all the other skills for preventing discipline problems. Or, conversely, even if you don't make miscalls, have a good lesson delivery, follow through on all your rules and warnings, etc., but are incongruent—you will still suffer many discipline problems. In other words, the necessary backing that will make your lessons and rules effective is your ability to be congruent.

---

[75]Carl Rogers. *On Encounter Groups.* New York: Harper and Row. 1970: 118.

Let's take a closer look at exactly what this ability, being congruent, is for a teacher. If we assume that all communicated messages (subject matter lectures, teacher's descriptions, questions to the class, etc.) have a cognitive content delivered with an underlying emotional feeling, they, in a way, look like this:

$$\frac{\text{cognitive content}}{\text{feeling}} \longrightarrow \text{MESSAGE}$$

For example, if a teacher says in a Social Studies class: "Now class, we must look at the causes of this war." The MESSAGE looks something like this:

$$\frac{\text{``Now class, we must look at the causes of this war.''}}{\text{This is important; I need you to understand and notice what I'm about to discuss.}} \longrightarrow \text{MESSAGE}$$

When the message's top and bottom parts back each other up, or correspond, the message is congruent. When the bottom of the message does not back up or correspond to the top, the message is incongruent. For instance, in, "I'm not angry with you" we have:

$$\frac{\text{``I'm not angry with you!''}}{\text{Boy, are you annoying!}} \longrightarrow \text{MESSAGE}$$

The above is clearly an incongruent message. Teachers may often deliver subject content, descriptions, rules, etc. incongruently. Students may notice at times that teachers are not really "behind" what they are saying. For example, a teacher who says in a monotone while yawning, "This lesson is very important; the first important point is . . ." appears incongruent. Another way to explain an incongruent teacher message, where the teacher, as person, doesn't seem to be behind what he's saying is to picture it like this:

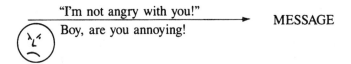

teacher / person

Here, the teacher's role is up front and the teacher as <u>person</u> is behind a mask, or a defensive posture. What the teacher says doesn't seem to be related to how he really feels as a person. The above teacher probably comes off incongruently to his students, whereas this teacher:

teacherperson

comes off congruently. This teacher is not trying to play the role of a teacher, but instead, is teaching how he teaches, his style; he is being himself while teaching such that who he is as a person is related directly to how he is as a teacher. He is not only not hiding his personality as he teaches but uses it to reinforce his job as teacher. This teacher is congruent.

One more way to picture congruence and incongruence might be to say that:

- A congruent teacher speaks from the heart.

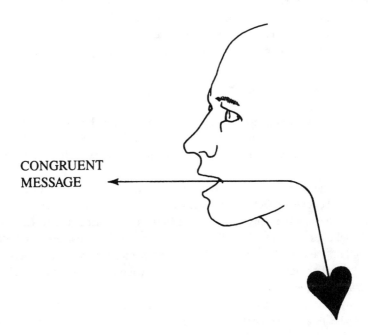

CONGRUENT
MESSAGE

- An incongruent teacher formulates messages from what he thinks will look good, or sound good, or from his or her image of what a teacher should look like or do.

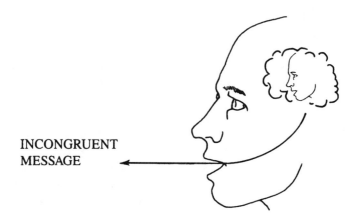

INCONGRUENT
MESSAGE

In summary, being incongruent looks phony to students, annoys them, destroys any ally relationship they feel with you and becomes a potential source of, even motivation for, disruptive behavior. In Chapter 11, section B we will work on how not to be incongruent regarding your rules and warnings, your lesson delivery, and your general interaction with your students.

C. From Not Following Through

Another source of disruptive behavior that comes from how teachers interact with the students is from teachers being inconsistent, from not following through on what they say. Let us not confuse inconsistency with incongruence. A teacher may say what s/he really feels (be congruent), yet not do what s/he said s/he'd do (be inconsistent). Or a teacher may say what s/he does not really believe or feel (be incongruent), yet follow through and actually do what s/he said (be consistent). An example of the former is a teacher who really believes it is time to call a student's mother, but just doesn't follow through on the call. An example of the latter is a teacher who overreacts and says, "No class party on Friday because John called out!" and then sticks to his or her guns and has no party on Friday (though the class and John were very good the rest of the week). We shall see that being congruent helps a teacher be more consistent. But, though they affect one another, they are different skills.

So, we are saying here that being inconsistent, not following through on your rules and warnings, on your messages generally, will be a source of discipline problems. Our students also know this. They said, in Chapter 5: From the Horse's Mouth (pp. 95–96): "I never believe her warning.' "He would always threaten . . . but he never did anymore than yell and pout." "When she yelled . . . we never believed her." We shall work on how to be more consistent and follow through in Chapter 11, section C.

D. From Being Inappropriate

Another source of disruptive behavior that comes from how teachers interact with their students is from teachers being inappropriate. By "inappropriate," we mean that they act counter to what is expected of them professionally according to their job responsibilities. In short, teachers are inappropriate when their behavior is "unprofessional:" But, what does this too often brandished word mean? Well, since we can safely say that a teacher's job is to nurture and be responsible for students' education and growth, we can say that a teacher whose behavior is not in line with this responsibility is unprofessional, inappropriate. A good teacher watches his or her behavior and at least implicitly always asks: "By my doing this, whose needs are being served?" If the teacher can say: "the students," then that teacher is acting appropriately, being professional. On the other hand, if the answer is "my needs, not the students," then that teacher is acting inappropriately, being unprofessional.

I know a teacher who used to hand out large maps and sets of crayons to the class and, in the guise of teaching geography, just begin the class period with: "Class, color in Asia this period." Then, she'd sit back, put on her makeup, and read the *New York Times* for the rest of the period! She was being inappropriate; she was meeting her needs, not the students'. You decide to tell the class a joke that takes ten minutes. Inappropriate? Well, is this joke for their sake, will it help them learn what you're teaching? Maybe it'll at least help improve your relationship with them so you can be a better teacher for them. No? You want to tell the joke because you just want the attention and approval? Well, then the joke is inappropriate. Is the verbal, maybe sarcastic, remark you are about to say to a student self-serving, even a harmful "put down"? Then, you are about to be inappropriate. You give a punishment assignment to a disruptive child. Does the assignment, besides attempting to change behavior, in any way serve to educate the student or the rest of the class? Have you punished him or her by asking that s/he wash your car? Then, you're being inappropriate.

Mr. Johnson says to Susan, "You are looking very attractive this week." If Mr. Johnson is her Health or Physical Education teacher, etc., and has been helping her with her diet because Susan has had a weight problem, the statement may be appropriate. The statement is then a support for her willpower at having stuck to the diet and lost ten pounds. However, if Mr. Johnson is none of the above and is just attracted to Susan, he is being inappropriate, unprofessional.

Again, as teachers we should try to make all our statements and behaviors serve the growth and education of our students. That's not easy. But that's what we're being paid for. And also importantly, when you are inappropriate, self-serving and not for them, students know it and begin to hate you for it. Their hate can motivate them to disruptive behavior. Students will even accept a punishment assignment with less anger if they can see that you have their interests (their education) at heart and that the assignment has educational value. Let's listen to students sensing this inappropriateness (Chapter 5, pp. 103–104): I misbehaved because: "She used to sit and read a magazine while we read the textbooks . . . , she didn't realize that she was cheating on us. She didn't do her job as she was supposed to." "The teacher would always crack jokes about how lousy people did." "She . . . called us stupid. She was always being sarcastic. If somebody hited the wrong key when playing the piano, she . . . said this person is a mentally retardic." "In the English class hour the professor spent the time eating cake and drinking coffee." "I have terrible handwriting and . . . in 4th grade my teacher embarrassed me in front of the whole class because of my handwriting. . . ."

Again, we must not confuse this professional obligation and skill of being appropriate with congruence and consistency. Teachers can easily be congruent (say and do what they really feel), be consistent (follow through and actually do what they said they'd do), but what they say or do can still be very inappropriate (serve only the teacher's needs). Such inappropriateness angers students and, thereby, is an important source of discipline problems. We shall work on not being inappropriate in Chapter 11, section D.

E. From Being Unfair

Another source of disruptive behavior that comes from how teachers interact with their students is from teachers being unfair. A teacher is unfair if s/he does any of the following:

1. Applies rules or warnings, or evaluative standards unjustly, with partiality or bias. If the rule is, "if you call out three times you see me after class" and you enforce this with some "call-outers" and not others, then you're being unfair. If you have decided that the grade for the marking period is decided by only one's test scores averaged, but you give a lower grade to a latecomer regardless of his average, you're being unfair. In other words, you're being unfair if you apply any rule, warning, or standard inconsistently.[76]

---

[76]From our previous understanding of "consistency" (pp. 152–153), this would also mean that a teacher is unfair if s/he didn't do what s/he said s/he'd do. But, usually we call this "unfair" when what s/he said s/he'd do was a promise of reward. Sure, then if s/he doesn't give the reward promised, s/he is seen as being unfair.

2. Punishes the wrong student
3. Applies a punishment that seems overreactive, too harsh, one that does not seem to fit the intensity of the "crime"
4. Punishes the whole class for one student's behavior when this kind of punishment has no value other than to: try to manipulate the class to get this one student or show the class the intensity of the teacher's anger and frustration
5. Punishes or applies standards without any just rationale

From the above, we can also see that being prejudicial is obviously unfair (as we discussed in "typical miscall" no. 13). And, often, we also use the term unfair for what we called "inappropriate" when a teacher neglects or hurts students in the service of his/her own self-serving whims or needs. And, just in case there is any confusion about our terms, a teacher can be unfair congru-ently (s/he truly feels prejudiced) and consistently (follow through with the unjust punishment).

Our students hate unfair teachers. Unfairly applied rules or standards leave them with an anger that swears, "I'll get you back for this." Remember that especially for adolescents who are struggling to assemble a sense of order in the world and their own values—being unfair is a particularly sensitive issue for them. Let's listen to how angry they get (and their tendency to be disruptive) when they sense that a teacher is being unfair (Chapter 5, p. 105): "I get mad when one student acts up in class and the teacher decides to let the whole class get punished for it." "Unfairness on marks . . . bug me and anger me, and causes me to act up." "She would only be nice to . . . the handsomest boys in class." "When I get blamed for something another kid did." "I got a zero in Spanish class and she won't even tell me why. I think she's a great teacher . . . but I wish she wouldn't give me a zero for no reason."

Of course, often we cannot find the time to explain our rationales. We may look unfair, but we're being as fair as we can. Not being unfair to the students all the time is a very complex skill of both perception and system. We will work on "not being unfair" in Chapter 11, section E.

F. Especially for Grades K–6

Although the above areas may be a source of disruptive behavior in your K–6 classroom, an elementary school teacher (especially teaching K–2) will experience other unique sources of discipline problems. These also come from the unique interactions between you and your students.

First, the dynamics are very different here in several ways. In the elementary grades, kids, especially the younger ones, often need the substitute parental affections, attention, and approval of the teacher. Often, the teacher's attention, recognition, and approval are more important, or as important, to a student than a student's peers. (In junior and senior high school the reverse is more likely: peer pressure is often the greater influence than teacher approval.) Also, since there is no departmental schedule (kids do not change periods every 43 minutes to go to a different subject teacher), the influence of the personal interaction of the teacher on his/her students is intensified.

As a result, it is even more true in the lower grades that the teacher's personality is the most influential tool educationally in the classroom. It is still true that a source of disruptive behavior is incongruence on the part of the teacher in grades K–6. But, since it is possible to occasionally fake the needed dramatic emotion (act) to fit the lesson, when it comes to working with young kids, "congruence" can sometimes be faked: "Class! Oh, Boy! We're going to study the great, wonderful multiplication tables!" But even this pollyanna charade wears thin, and kids won't believe such a teacher for long. Instead, a more frequent source of withdrawal and discipline problems is the teacher's inabilities to express feelings, to emote, to give approving attention, to listen attentively with a show of concern, and to be nurturant. A teacher who is unable to show the proper emotion for the appropriate activity, give attention according to shaping the correct behavior, listen attentively, "be there emotionally," and notice and nurture appropriate needs will have more discipline problems than one who can. Again, one may be able to fake the above responses for a while with some valuable results. But the best teacher in K–6 is one who naturally feels this way—is open emotionally, naturally expresses his/her feelings, truly cares about and is attentive with kids. Consistency is even more crucial in the elementary school classroom than in the upper grades. Consistency teaches the ability to predict. Young children need to be able to predict their world to make sense out of it. If they can't predict that you will follow through with your rewards and punishments, you are guaranteed to have discipline problems.

Regarding the other sources of disruptive behavior mentioned in the general text, miscalls, of course, need to be avoided. In K–6 especially, the teacher who cannot tolerate a general ongoing harmless din of noise will probably make more miscalls. Of course, as we just explained, s/he must follow through regarding warnings and promises, especially to young children. An inability to keep track of what you said you'd do, or will do, will become a source of disruptive behavior. Also, inappropriateness on the part of the teacher will engender hurt, if not anger, with students. And "fairness" is crucial. Since young children have vulnerable, often competitive, egos and are first learning what is and how to be "fair," they are particularly sensitive to and become angry with "unfair" teachers or teachers who seem to be playing "favorites."

Finally, another factor that is very influential in the elementary grades (not the upper grades) is the personality of the teacher-assistant or aide (paraprofessional) usually hired to assist teachers in grades K–1 or 2. Here, all of the inabilities of the teacher described above also apply to the assistant. An assistant who, e.g., cannot express feelings or be fair, will contribute to creating discipline problems or will not help curtail them. Although s/he has less influence on the students, his/her effort is influential, especially if the teacher and the assistant are not in sync or are inconsistent with each other.

All in all, K–6 teachers have an exhausting job because their influence in their interactions with students is often more foundationally important. We will discuss how to handle these specific sources of disruptive behavior in Chapter 11, especially section F.

G. Training Exercises and Checklist for Chapter 8

Exercise One: Recognizing Your Feelings and Needs That May Cause You to Make Miscalls

(a) Below you will find the list of typical miscalls explained in Chapter 4, section B. Go down the list and place a check only next to those kinds of miscalls you are prone to make.

_____ 1. The withdrawn student
_____ 2. The overreacted-to rule
_____ 3. The "I've got to win their feelings" need
_____ 4. The "I need their attention" syndrome
_____ 5. The "my ego is hurt" reaction
_____ 6. "They're interfering with my getting my lesson done" reaction
_____ 7. Displaced anger
_____ 8. "I'm tired of trying to be understanding all the time" reaction
_____ 9. The mirror effect
_____ 10. The "I need to control" reaction
_____ 11. The "steam" for "smoke" mistake
_____ 12. The venting for cursing mistake
_____ 13. The prejudicial mistake
_____ 14. Holding a grudge
_____ 15. The punishing the education problem mistake

(b) Now, for each one you are prone to make look up the feelings and needs that are associated with each one you checked. (These feelings and needs are described above in section A, on page 157; there you can locate each miscall by its number.)

My Feelings	My Needs—that may lead me to make miscalls
1.	
2.	
3.	
4.	
5.	
6.	

(c) What do you notice? Write a short paragraph here that describes what you notice about your personality regarding this tendency.

_____

_____

_____

_____

_____

_____

Exercise Two: Recognizing Your Incongruent Messages

(a) Below, make a list of the rules you try to enforce in your classroom.
Rules

1.
2.
3.
4.
5.
6.
7.
8.

(b) Now make a list of the usual reprimands or punishments you apply when these rules are broken.
Reprimands or Punishments

1.
2.
3.
4.
5.

6.
7.
8.

(c) Now, list about ten specific subject matter topics you will be teaching, or have taught, in your class.

1.
2.
3.
4.
5.
6.
7.
8.
9.
10.

(d) Are you congruent with regard to all these rules, warnings, or reprimands, and topics you teach? Do you really believe in all of these? Are these really you? Is your "heart" in them? Are you "behind" them? Do you truthfully feel what you are saying to your class?

(e) Place an A next to the ones you feel a definite "yes" to. Place a B next to those you feel, "I somewhat believe in this." Place a C next to ones you have mixed feelings about. Place a D next to those which you feel like you are just mouthing what "teachers are supposed to say." Place an F next to the ones you don't really feel, nor care about, nor believe in.

(f) How did you do? Where are you most incongruent? Write out what you noticed in a small paragraph here.

Exercise Three: Recognizing Your Incongruent Interactions

If your students were to watch you outside of school, e.g., in a pizza parlor, what would they notice is different about the way you are compared with how you are in school?

- Is your language, the words you use, very different?
- Do you have very different gestures?
- Would you feel exposed if they saw how you act and dress "in your natural habitat"?
- Are you somewhat phony in front of your students?
- Have you ever said to yourself, "What would my students think if they could see me right now?!" What were you doing at that moment and why would it have surprised your students?

Exercise Four: Recognizing How Much Your Person Is Behind Your Teacher

A. A congruent teacher looks like this:

teacherperson

B. An incongruent teacher looks like this:

teacher/person

C. A congruent teacher-counselor might look like this:

personteacher

D. A congruent, but yet private, teacher might look like this:

teacher person

E. Which diagram is most like how you are?

F. Now, draw your own diagram that best represents you here. (If you are different for different classes, draw one for each class and write a quick note that explains why you think you act differently for that class.)

Exercise Five: Recognizing Your Inconsistency

Look back at your list of reprimands or punishments you listed for Exercise Two above. These are probably preceded by warnings you give the class, e.g., "If you _____ , then _____ ." Do you follow through on these? For each reprimand or punishment you listed, give a 4 to those you always follow through on; a 3 if the answer is usually; a 2 if sometimes; a 1 if seldom; a 0 if you never follow through on what you said you'd do. Which ones received 4's, which 3's, 2's, 1's, 0's? Do you believe in these warnings and their punishments? Do you just lack the nerve? Do you just need support? Are you sometimes lazy? Add up your score amd figure out your average.

A. An average of "4" means you're excellent regarding consistency.

B. An average of "3" is good regarding your follow-through.

C. An average of "2" means your rules will probably fall apart.

D. An average of "one" means your class is probably a "zoo."

E. (If you averaged a "0" you're probably on sick leave or gave up teaching.)

Exercise Six: Recognizing Your Inappropriateness

(a) Below, make a list of your evaluative, or judgmental remarks, e.g., "That's good!" "You're not right," "That's not true," or "That's illogical," etc. There's nothing wrong with being evaluative or judging. Part of your job is to judge things such as: statements of fact, appropriate grammar, and writing and computation ability. But some of your remarks may be both evaluative and "put-downs," sarcastic. List some of your typical evaluative remarks that you tend to make, as honestly as you can.

Evaluative Remarks

1.

2.

3.

4.

5.

6.

7.

8.

Which of these remarks do serve to nurture and help educate your students? Give these a checkmark. Which ones are just your vocabulary and you're not sure if they help the students? Give these a "?" Which ones may be expressions of your frustration and actually may be a disservice, a "put-down" to the students, one that lowers their sense of self-esteem? Give these an "X."

These latter ones may actually sap your students' motivation to learn, and be damaging your relationship with them.

(b) Below make a list of your typical classroom procedures.

Procedures

1.
2.
3.
4.
5.
6.
7.
8.

Which of these procedures help to educate or manage your class? Give them a checkmark. Which ones mostly serve you and only somewhat serve the class? Give these a "?" Which only serve you? Give these an "X."

(c) Again, look at your list of reprimands and punishments you listed in Exercise Two. Which ones have educational value? Give them a checkmark. Which ones are not educational but do teach socially appropriate behavior? Give these a "?" Which are neither educational nor teach socially appropriate behavior? These latter may only be "pure punishments." Give these an "X." These latter ones may only be generating vengeful anger at you.

Exercise Seven: Recognizing Your Unfairness

Do students often say, "You're unfair!" or "That's not fair!"? Well, this may mean that you should look at this area. But, it may only mean that they perceive you as unfair, or are trying to con you. If it's the former, you may need to take some time in class and explain your rationale for what seems unfair, but is actually as fair as possible. If it's the latter, trust your sense of fairness and don't be duped!

(a) Let's look back at your rules, Exercise Two above. Can you orally recite a rationale for each rule that justifies it as a fair rule? You can? Well, stop now and make a little speech, as if to the class, about the rationale of each one.

(b) How'd you do? Are you convinced? Would they be convinced? Do you need to practice your speech? Or is it that your rationale is hazy because you are not totally convinced the rule is fair either?

Now, try the same questions on yourself with your marking system, e.g., when you give zeros, credit, penalize, etc. How fair are your evaluative procedures?

Checklist

Listed below are a series of statements that hopefully you can mark with a check as meaning "I don't . . . ," or "that's not me." If the statement may sometimes describe you, place a "?" next to it. If you do fall into the description being admonished, place an "X" next to it. Hopefully you have many Vs and very few Xs. Each check indicates you're probably O.K. with regard to accidentally initiating sources of disruption from the way you interact with your students.

Miscalls

_____ 1. I don't need attention so much that, if a student is not looking at me, I get insulted.

_____ 2. I don't feel upset at my powerlessness when I can't seem to "save" all these students.

_____ 3. I don't feel constantly anxious and thus always need control.

_____ 4. I don't mind being disliked by the students sometimes, as long as they learn and follow rules for the sake of others.

_____ 5. I don't feel that the meaning I get from teaching is the crucial and only meaning in my life.

_____ 6. I don't find that I worry about my ego so much in front of the class.

_____ 7. I don't feel competitive with the other instructors.

_____ 8. I don't believe that if they just get the notes quickly that "they've learned."

_____ 9. I don't take my anger out on the wrong people.

_____ 10. I don't often run out of patience about having to explain things a lot.

_____ 11. I don't find that I get angry at students because they remind me of me or someone else.

_____ 12. I don't cut off class excitement mistakenly worried that it is a growing disruption.

_____ 13. I don't get insulted if a student accidentally says a four-letter word just out of frustration.

_____ 14. I don't think I have psychological biases around race, creed, color, gender, sexual orientation, fat people, skinny people, etc.

_____ 15. I don't hold grudges. When it's over, it's over.

_____ 16. I don't tend to get angry at a student who is just having an "education problem" and not bothering anyone else.

Incongruent

_____ 17. I don't act phony in front of my class.

_____ 18. I don't think: "some of my rules are a little ridiculous."

_____ 19. I don't think: "some of my reprimands are a little overboard."

_____ 20. I don't usually say to myself: "this subject matter is generally boring and not very important."

Inconsistent

_____ 21. I don't get lazy and not follow through on my warnings.

_____ 22. I don't feel nervous about following through.

_____ 23. I don't say: "Why bother! It won't help anyway."

Inappropriate

_____ 24. I don't have rules only for my sake.

_____ 25. I don't have classroom procedures only for my sake.

_____ 26. I don't tell jokes or stories I like that have little to do with their education.

_____ 27. I don't give pure punishment assignments; my assignments are educational.

Unfair

_____ 28. I don't come down harder on some students than others.

_____ 29. I don't apply my rules differently for different students without a clear rationale.

_____ 30. I don't believe in: "Just because I said so!" I have rationales for what I do, that they understand.

_____ 31. I don't overreact; my punishments usually fit the "crime."

_____ 32. I don't believe it's a good idea to punish the whole class to get one student.

For Grades K–6

_____ 33. I don't get angry at the general, harmless din of noise in the room.

_____ 34. I'm not unfair and try not to choose "favorites."

_____ 35. I don't mind giving a lot of attention or expressing supportive emotions.

_____ 36. I don't forget when I promised a student (or the class) a punishment or a reward.

_____ 37. I don't give too many warnings so that I never get to the punishment.

_____ 38. I don't apply the rules to some students and not to others (without a very rational, fair reason).

_____ 39. I don't feel that my students are strangers to me. I'm not afraid of getting close enough to them to be able to know them and to nurture them.

CHAPTER 9: FROM THE DELIVERY OF YOUR LESSON PLAN

Many of us have probably had at least some instruction about making up a good lesson plan. We are told, for instance, to take some paper and write out, e.g., our <u>Aim</u>, our Objectives, the specific topics of the Subject <u>Matter</u>, and the <u>Methods</u> we'll use to get these across. We might even plan (write down) some good <u>questions</u> we can use to get the class to participate. All this is well and good, but it is far from sufficient. There is a big difference between what you plan on paper and how you deliver this lesson plan. And just writing down the <u>Methods</u> you'll use is not sufficient for guiding you through all the complex subtleties of a good <u>delivery</u>. We all know that writers write for comedians. Some good comedy writers are not able to be good comedians. Some comedians with the same material are funny; some are boring. It's all (or much of it is) in <u>the delivery</u>. We shall attempt here to analyze the subtleties of a good lesson plan <u>delivery</u> into its varying competencies. Some teachers do not come off to a class with the competencies that make for a good delivery. A lesson plan delivery that comes off lacking one of these competencies becomes a source of disruptive behavior. What are the sources of disruptive behavior that come from the delivery of your lesson plan?

A. From Incongruent Content

From our previous discussions on incongruence (Chapter 8, section 8), we need only review here what it means to say that sometimes a lesson plan delivery espouses content (subject matter) that seems incongruent. A teacher who says in a tone with little affect, almost yawning, "This is important," is delivering a message that looks like this:

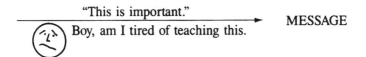

165

Or his "heart" is not really in what he's saying; he's just doing what he's supposed to do, as if it's a tape in his head. He looks like this:

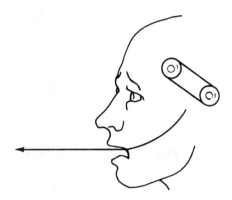

He doesn't look like this:

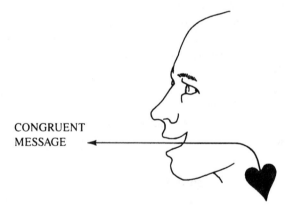

Or what he is teaching, as a teacher, he doesn't in any way relate to as a person. He resembles this:

teacher/person

He is the opposite of this representation:

Teacher ← person

In short, his subject matter delivery comes off incongruent, with no flair or charisma, and is not moving (motivational). Students find such deliveries boring and, if carried to an extreme, a sign that the teacher "doesn't care about what he wants us to care about." The reaction is, "he's got some nerve," "the phony," and the results are anger and the beginnings of disruptive behavior. Here are some of the ways our students put it (from Chapter 5, p. 102): "It seemed she was probably as disinterested as we were." "It was real bull. . . ." "She was talking like she did not care." You can sense when a teacher has no 'gut' feeling to his teaching. How . . . is a student going to learn if the teacher doesn't feel for what he/she is teaching?"

I know that some of my readers are asking, "But what do you do if they make you teach this stuff?!" "I can't revise the whole curriculum!" "It's not my fault I'm teaching out of subject, out of my license." I understand. But, we need to work on this area or students have a right to "turn off" to us. The problem here is complex, but we will tackle it in Chapter 14, section A.

B. From Not Being Affective Enough

By "affective" we mean as opposed to merely cognitive. Of course, no curriculum is purely cognitive; some philosophers of language even argue that it is the necessary involvement of ideation in a concernful network (one that is intrinsically about care, feelings, affect) that makes ideas have any meaning.[77] A purely cognitive proposition would not relate any sense. And affect, emotion, to mean anything must be transferable out of its private language, or it is not language.

For teachers, this means that the more one teaches only ideas, the less meaningful they become. Or notes aren't learnings for students, no matter how much they take them down, or you put them on the blackboard. Content taught, if it is to have interest for students, must evoke, have, or relate to some emotion or affect. Emotion moves—moves students to be more attentive, to be more motivated to learn. As Kelley put it: "how a person feels is sometimes more important than what he knows, because feelings control behavior; and knowledge is used in behavior and decisions; but how it is used

[77]Martin Heidegger. *Being and Time.* New York: Harper and Row. 1962: 107–114.

depends on values and feelings."[78] In short, if your lesson is not affective, it is not effective. Or mere labels aren't learnings. In a way a "learning" looks like this:

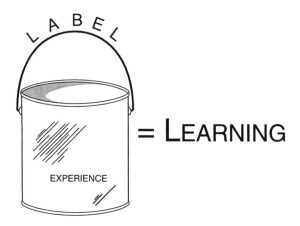

= LEARNING

For instance, to teach a student what "imperialism" is, by giving him a definition, is to give him only the main label, "imperialism," with other labels (words of the definition) that he can hopefully understand or has the required experiential knowledge of. But labels aren't learnings, even if you give a student many of them. A student has learned what "imperialism" is when he has a "feel" for the term and can imagine the experience to which it refers. Only then can he grab the "handle" of the bucket in the diagram and carry away what he has learned. No wonder students throw their notes away after exams and seem to remember little of what we thought they learned. Their notes were full of only "handles," labels, and little of the "feel" for the subjects taught.

When lessons are not affective enough, our students "turn off." Since there's little emotion in the lesson, they feel little emotion, and cease their motion. Some students are unable to wait until you finish the unit on, e.g., World War 1, a month from now when you finally say, "Now, let's take a few minutes to see how this relates to you today." Some, in their struggle to relate their feelings to the lesson, may even bring up what seems to be "digressions off the curriculum." Then, we apply coercion to get them back into the ideational framework we need to teach. We must remember that it's not our teaching that's the focus, it's their learning. And for them to learn they must feel a

[78]Earl C. Kelley. "The Place of Affective Learning." *Educational Leadership.* Vol. XXI. (1965): 455.

relation, even emotionally, to the lesson. Coercion, rewards, punishments, etc. are not the answer here. These only make them into tentatively cooperative, bored enemies of your task. Lessons that are not affective enough become the seeds of disruptive behavior. This is what happens to our students (from Chapter 5, p. 106): I started to act up because "she was teaching the class with no feeling. . . ." "The guy knew his stuff, but he made the 11:00 news sound exciting." ". . . she sounded like she's dead." "The lesson was about as interesting as a dead frog, and it was so irrelevant to everything." We will work on making our lesson deliveries more affective in Chapter 14, section B.

C. From Not Being Actional or Experiential Enough

Similarly, actions speak louder than words, than just dictating notes to students, than their just listening, sitting there, being mostly passive, and louder than their just talking, answering your questions, asking questions, talking, notes, talking, notes, talking, etc. Boring! Students, especially adolescents, need to be moving, doing, acting. They need to not just use their head and mouth and writing hand. They need to use their body, act on their feelings and thoughts, and meld their bodily movements, thoughts, and feelings into action. Actions put words, feelings, and ideas into their bloodstream. We remember most what is not just in our heads, nor even in our hearts, but what is in our being. Learning, and being, and knowing are "ing" words—anything we can do that unlocks students from behind their passive desks, passive copying of notes, makes our lesson delivery actional. These kids are flowing, churning, growing, and steaming with bodily, self-concept, value, social, and sexual changes. To ask them to bottle all that up and sit there and just take notes is not just difficult for them, it's a waste of their energy, and a waste of the ingredient that makes learning stick. We've got to get them doing things: role playing, simulating, reversing roles, turning verbal messages into nonverbal ones, illustrating learning by drawing, imitating, playing music, voting, dancing, etc. We've got to think more "ing." Students, who are fenced in to a lesson delivery that coerces them to be mainly passive, either "turn off" or feel frustrated. Both become sources of disruptive behavior.

We must also remember that different students learn in different ways, and very few of them can learn passively. To have content "stick," we need to acknowledge and use the learning styles of as many of the students as possible. In Howard Gardner's work on multiple intelligences, he identifies seven main groups into which intelligence strengths can be divided: verbal-linguistic, logical-mathematical, interpersonal, intrapersonal, bodily-kinesthetic, musical, and spatial. Knowing these areas of strength and how they influence the students' learning helps teachers to tap into the different ways students access knowledge. Some students learn better through discussions, some through manipulatives, some through movement, etc. [For a more detailed discussion of the impact of learning styles and strengths, I suggest reading Mr. Gardner's book, *Frames of Mind*, (1983 Harper Collins.)]

From Chapter 5, pp. 106–107: I got disruptive when "all we did was take notes and he just read from the book." "You spent a better part of the class just writing." "It was a class of continuous copying from the board and no real learning." ". . . you feel useless because all there is to do is listen." "I tend to act up in class because I don't have anything to do." We will work on making our lessons more actional in Chapter 14, section C.

D. From Not Being Inductive Enough

Related to these points, a lesson that is taught inductively is also bound to be more affective and related to students' actions. When is a lesson delivery inductive, as opposed to deductive? A deductive lesson first teaches a knowledge-generalization and then relates it to specific here and now events. An inductive lesson begins with here and now events and builds toward, develops from the ground up, the knowledge-generalization. For instance, you can teach the causes of World War I, and then ask, "How does this relate to your life now?" That's deductive. Or you can have students list various reasons for conflicts they are experiencing right now (on their block, at home), put these on the chalkboard, and have them induce generalizations about causes of conflict that also existed in 1914. That's inductive. An inductive lesson obviously is more affective and actional because it begins with the events students are involved in, actions they are doing, and pulls these into and up developmentally to build the generalization.

It is easier to teach deductively. You simply ask them to follow your deductions down to, hopefully, the relevance to their lives. It is more difficult to teach inductively. Then, you must follow them as they give you the initial data that you must channel toward the generalization. In the deductive lesson, they take notes. In the inductive lesson, you must take note, even notes—since each class period may build toward their learning differently. But, in the deductive lesson, by the time you get down to their lives, they may not "be there" anymore. In the inductive lesson, they're in it from the start. Every lesson can't be inductive, but even deductive, traditional lessons, can be more inductive than they are usually delivered. When they are not inductive enough, your students have to wait too long to catch the relation of your point to life. Again, they either "turn off," or get frustrated—seeds of disruption. As they put it (Chapter 5, pp. 107–108): I felt the urge to act out when "I couldn't relate to anything . . . to something similar that happened in the present time." "The lesson felt like it had no relation to my life." We will work on making our lessons more inductive in Chapter 14, section D.

E. From Not Being Interactive Enough

By "not interactive enough," we mean that the lesson delivery does not provide enough opportunities for the students to interact with you and each other. As a matter of fact, the lesson should not just "provide the opportunity" for such interaction, it should urge, even make, the students interact more with you and each other. And, that they interact with each other is often more important than their interaction with you. In other words, it is important that students have ways in your lesson to participate, that they are urged to participate, even made to do so. To do this, we can provide them with opting in our explanations, rewards for their participation, and techniques that necessarily involve them in the delivery of the content of the lesson.

Students "turn off" less, get less frustrated, have a chance to vent frustration, feel less alone and less your "enemy" in class when they can interact more with you and each other. Also, simultaneously, the lesson then becomes more affective, actional, and inductive. They can interact with their feelings in an actional exercise from their experience. Interaction allows them to be unlocked from their passive note-taking and use their (adolescent) energy. You need to talk less and ask more questions. Or let them try to explain things (even if they know less). You need to reward them for their comments and questions more, put their (not just your) ideas and notes on the chalkboard. You need to know their names and talk back and forth to them, not just teach them. Also, they need to be allowed, even urged and made, to talk to each other, trade papers, listen to each other, question each other, argue, plan, devise, brainstorm, challenge, etc. each other. To do this, you need to stay out of it more; you need to shut up longer and let them talk to each other.

"Hold on," you say. "This will create chaos! An interactive class, the way you're describing it, will be even more disruptive!" I understand your fear. However, we must take the chance and allow more interaction, because lack of participation is an important source of disinterest, frustration, and acting out. When students have nothing to act into, they act out; their energy must go somewhere. But not to have this participation turn into chaos, we will have to learn how to give proper openings for their participation and rewards and techniques to channel their interaction. Right now we are silencing them out of our fear that too much interaction will cause discipline problems. However, in actuality, our silencing lesson plan delivery feels like a restraint by someone over them that they hope will slip up, or ease up, so they can burst out.

This is how one teacher described what we sometimes, unfortunately, are doing:

> There is a game played by students and teachers everywhere. The game goes like this: the teacher tries to find out what students don't know so that he can

correct those deficiencies; concerned with grades and slippery images they try to hide their ignorance in every way they can. So it is that students seldom ask pertinent questions or participate. So it is that teachers assume that students possess knowledge which, in fact, they often don't.[79]

A class that is made to be mainly a passive receiver of your notes never has much opportunity to let you know how they are doing. You don't want to know at the test; then, it's too late.

Making students more participatory is not easy. First, we will have to help you allow it more. You will need to look at how you accidentally (besides purposely) cut off their interaction. Then, we need to channel this Interaction so it is productive and enlivens, without it being disruptive. Handling energy is exciting and anxious, especially when <u>interactive</u> energy is with adolescents whose ambiguous, vulnerable selves interact with other ambiguous, vulnerable selves—and all under peer pressure! But to hold it all back and lecture at them while you try to keep them "cooperative" is worse, a delivery style that is an important source of discipline problems. Let's listen to our students (from Chapter 5, p. 108): I tended to act out because the class was "Boring, no class participation." "He was very intolerant of a person who asked questions. . . ." ". . . I raise my hand to answer a question and no one else knows the answer. He'd say the answer hisself before calling on me." What gets me is "a teacher who never allowed you to participate."

We will work on how to provide a lesson that is more interactive and participation techniques that channel and spark this kind of energy without causing disruption to your teaching and their learning in Chapter 14, section E.

F. From a Lack of a Felt Sense of Order, Rewards, and Momentum

We are about to talk about what philosophers call "phenomenology." A phenomenological description of something is not a description of how a thing is, but how it appears or feels subjectively.

Your written lesson plan, and even your lesson plan delivery, may seem to you to be orderly, have rewards and a momentum, a sense of movement, a flow with impetus. But does it, as you deliver it, appear this way, feel this way, to your students? In other words, phenomenologically, does it have a sense of order, rewards, and momentum? You may write all of these aspects into your lesson plan and intend these, but does the <u>delivery</u> display these enough for the students to feel these?

[79]Jaime M. O'Neil. "No Allusions in the Classroom." *Newsweek,* 14 (Sept. 23, 1985).

Let's start with "a felt sense of order." Does the delivery of your lesson plan evoke in your students a felt sense of the order of your lesson? I know you wrote down: "Aim," and "Topic 1., A., B., C.," and then "Topic 2., A., B., C.," etc. But when you talk to the class in your lesson, can they feel this order? Can they sense where you were, are, and are going? Remember, you sense this easier than the students; you know the subject well, had courses on this, you wrote up the lesson plan, have even taught it in this order before. But, for them, this is their first time. They don't know the subject and have never seen your lesson plan. Also, their heads may be in their weekend, or their worry about what's at home. What seems perfectly logical to you, and orderly, may feel "lost" to them. We need to find more ways to make our delivery, not just the written lesson plan, evoke a sense of order. Students need to keep feeling where you were, are, and are going. Otherwise, they will "turn off," get frustrated, and become disruptive.

Regarding "a felt sense of rewards," they also need to feel that the lesson has a meaning, purpose, that there is something rewarding about following all this you are saying. In a way, students are always saying to themselves, "Why the hell should I be learning all this stuff?" (and sometimes they say it out loud). They have a right to ask this, as they are bound to compulsory education. We have an obligation to make the answer as apparent as possible, if we are to be good teachers. A lesson should seem either (a) intrinsically interesting and rewarding or, at least, (b) symbolically rewarding or, if need be, (c) extrinsically rewarding. If we're lucky (a), the content seems to be rewarding in and of itself, e.g., it's about teenage problems. Or it is (b) a means to future rewards, e.g., it's about how to obtain skills That will get you a good job or a better lifestyle. Or it is (c) knowledge that will give you credit in school, e.g., if you know this, you'll pass this course. Certainly we often motivate students with (c), or at least (b), and try to develop (a), just a love for learning itself. But students must feel (a), (b), or (c), or they won't feel why they should learn all this stuff. You know why they should learn it. You're aware of (c), or (b), even feel (a). But just because you feel these and wrote them into your lesson plan, doesn't mean they feel them. When they don't, they "turn off," get frustrated, and become disruptive. We will need to work on how to make your lesson plan delivery feel rewarding.

Finally, the delivery also needs to have a felt sense of momentum. In a way, your job is to drive a train on an orderly track, with a surge of fuel (make it feel motivationally rewarding), and keep it moving. As with a train, if you slow down, people look out the window ("turn off") and look around and wonder, "Is there a cow on the tracks?" "Why are we slowing down here?" If you stop the train of your lesson, people not only look out the window, they get off (start doing other things). Pretty soon people are looking out the window to see why people are looking out the window. You have to stop to have them get their heads in, which makes even more people look out, and get off the train (off your lesson).

We need to keep our lessons moving. We accidentally slow down or stop for the wrong reasons or at the wrong times. As a result, we satisfy one student's question and lose momentum and many of the other passengers. We will need to work on how to keep the lesson moving, yet not stifle participation, a complex skill.

Here's how our students feel when a lesson delivery lacks a felt sense of order, rewards, and momentum (from Chapter 5, pp. 108–109): "You couldn't tell where the hell he was going or why." "He would jump from this century to the last century, to no century; and then expected you to understand where he's coming from." "He would never get to the point." "We felt lost. . . ."

We will work on a lesson delivery that gives a felt sense of order, rewards, and momentum in Chapter 14, section F.

G. From a Mismanaged Distribution of Attention

We all need attention. Some of us can wait longer for it than others or get it in other forms. Elementary school children crave attention. They are often motivated solely by how to get their teacher's attention. Junior high school students want the teacher's attention and their peers' attention, or things that will get them attention. High school students begin to care less about the teacher's attention and more about getting attention from their peers, or getting things that give them attention, e.g., a car, or a job that makes money that they can use to get more attention ("be somebody!").

Elementary school teachers often have a simpler job (though exhausting) of managing the distribution of attention to the students. Since the students want the attention mostly from the teacher, the teacher is the major feeder of this attention.

But the job is more complex (and still exhausting) for junior and senior high school teachers. They still must be at least one of the feeders of attention and also facilitate the attention students want from each other, while also managing the distribution of those things (incentives) that are means to attention. And they must manage this complex distribution of attention without having kids climb all over the teacher and each other for it.

The answer is not to stop them from getting the attention from each other and just make them get it from you. That won't work. They don't want it from just you, and your coercion to stop them from getting it from each other will develop holes, with bursts of disruption. Also, if you try to be the major feeder of all the approval and attention, you will suffer burnout if you do it or anger when you can't.

The answer is to stop trying to be the major feeder of attention and to develop methods whereby students can give each other attention within the lesson, in a channeled non-disruptive fashion. Attention sometimes is all the reward they need to stay with the lesson. But you alone do not have to be the major distributor of attention and rewards. You can't do it all. When you try, you miss some, reward the wrong ones accidentally (the "caller-outers"), and leave the class feeling, "I don't know how to be good in here." Here's how they feel it (from Chapter 5, p. 109): "I think kids act out because they want to be the center of attention. They want to be noticed." "The way we figured is, why should we be good and do our work if we weren't going to get credit for it." "There was no way to be good in that class."

We need to work on how to manage the distribution of attention (and rewards) so that students don't "starve" for it, or feel there's no clear way to get it; otherwise, they will become disruptive. We will work on these skills in Chapter 14, section G.

H. From Not Being Supportive, or Explained Well Enough

Of course, if your lesson delivery is incongruent, not affective enough, not actional, not inductive enough, nor interactive, and there's little felt sense of order, rewards, or momentum, and students feel frustrated about getting attention—you have little feedback from them about how well they understand your lesson, since there's probably chaos in the room, or they're all "turned off"! When students don't understand, they get anxious and frustrated. If they have weak egos (and they will if they keep feeling like they don't understand) and can't tell you, they just give up. If they feel you're phony anyway (incongruent), can't feel any emotion (affect) about the lesson, can't find a way to participate, and don't know where you're going or why, they keep their feeling, "I must be dumb," to themselves.

Without their ability to give you this feedback, no wonder you often don't explain things well enough, push students who are not ready, and make them feel more inadequate in front of the class. No wonder they have turned off. Then you find out, too late, when you give them a test. We need to provide ways in our lesson delivery for our students to continually let us know if we have explained things well enough. Then, we can also, more easily, try ways to re-explain things we didn't know they didn't know. We also need to make our lessons more supportive, so that we are not inadvertently making our students feel anxious, inadequate, and uncomfortable in front of their peers. Students who feel dumb, can't follow you, and feel difficulty in letting you know this "turn off," get frustrated, feel alone, and become disruptive. Here's how they put it (from Chapter 5, p. 109): "Sometimes teachers take for granted that everybody in the class knows what s/he is talking about." "She just kept on talking and talking and didn't look at the class's response." "I act up in class because I don't understand what the teacher is saying." "She makes me do things that I don't feel ready, . . . make me feel stupid."

We will work on this in Chapter 14, section H.

I. Especially for Grades K–6

Although the above areas will also be sources of disruptive behavior in grades K–6, there can be special deficiencies in the delivery of lessons in the elementary grades. First of all, because the lessons are often social-emotional, affect, and how the class is involved, are even more important than in the upper grades. Although the content needs to be delivered congruently, it especially needs to be delivered with emotion, even dramatically. A lesson that lacks emotional content will land on deaf or, at least, closing ears. This is also true if the lesson (or just a procedure explained) does not seem to be nurturant for the attention and approval needs of the students. Of course, if the lesson is dramatized and experienced, all the better. But, if it has no "emotional life," it will die. The class will often move where the attention is being given out, like chickens after feed. A lesson that doesn't feed attention, in an organized way, will be a source of disruptive behavior. Activities that go on too long, beyond attention spans, will lose students. Directions with too many steps (especially in the early childhood grades) will cause kids to shut down before they ever start an activity; they will feel that, if they can't even get the directions, the lesson is obviously too hard for them. Unclear, complex explanations, in too long intervals, will turn kids off. If students can't feel where they are in simple, clear steps, they will get lost and "leave."

Also, it is all too common for teachers in elementary school to underestimate or overestimate the developmental readiness of their students. Because elementary school teachers generally have more flexibility in choosing the topics for their units and their lessons, they are often tempted to teach a lesson that is "neat" but for which their students may not be ready.

Finally, the lessons need to give students access to the teacher as substitute parent, even if this access is by way of first having them relate to each other, wait turns, get gold stars or points or grades, and then be approved of by you, the teacher (besides their peers). We will work on improving the delivery of your lesson especially for grades K–6 in Chapter 14, especially section J.

J. Training Exercises and Checklist for Chapter 9

Exercise One: Recognizing Sources of Disruption That Come from the Lesson Plan Delivery

Ask a friend or colleague to observe you teaching a lesson. Or observe a colleague teaching a lesson. Or, if you're in an education workshop or class, each one of you can volunteer to teach the first ten minutes of a lesson. Now, with the framework below, answer these questions, 1–17, on the line next to each question, "yes" or "no," as best you can. If this lesson is <u>perfect,</u> your answers should be the answers at the bottom of the next page.

_____ 1. Does the teacher seem to care about the topic(s) s/he is teaching?
_____ 2. Does the lesson delivery seem to be impersonally coming from just memorized notes or just his or her head?
_____ 3. Is the lesson too cognitive? Does it lack emotional content?
_____ 4. Does the content have any, even implicit, relation to the present that is, at least, somewhat apparent?
_____ 5. Does the lesson only call for the students to listen, question, comment, and take notes?
_____ 6. Does the lesson keep going from a stated generalization (item in the curriculum) and then, only much later, to a relation to experience?
_____ 7. Or does the lesson sometimes begin with students' experiences and then move toward a curriculum learning?
_____ 8. Are the students allowed, in the lesson, for the sake of the lesson, to interact with each other?
_____ 9. Or are they pushed to relate mainly to the teacher and reprimanded when they interact with each other, even when it relates to the lesson?
_____ 10. Can you <u>feel</u> the order of this lesson?
_____ 11. Do you know where the teacher is going?
_____ 12. Can you feel why s/he's going there?
_____ 13. Does the lesson have momentum?
_____ 14. Does s/he slow down or stop too much?
_____ 15. If you were a student with this teacher; would you be able to get enough attention from the teacher and your fellow students?
_____ 16. Do you understand the lesson well enough so that, when the teacher moves on, you don't feel left behind?
_____ 17. If you didn't understand something, could you easily find a way to let the teacher know this?

				17. yes	16. yes	15. yes
14. no	13. yes	12. yes	11. yes	10. yes	9. no	8. yes
7. yes	6. no	5. no	4. yes	3. no	2. no	1. yes

Where you had different answers, you can now locate the area that needs work and skip to Chapter 13 for the area you want to improve.

1 and 2 were about incongruent content.
3 and 4 were about lacking affect.
5 is about not being actional enough.
6 and 7 were about being inductive enough.
8 and 9 were about being interactive enough.
10–14 were about a felt sense of order, reward, and momentum.
15 was about the managed distribution of attention.
16 and 17 were about whether the lesson was explained well enough and also about, in a way, all of the above.

Exercise Two: Recognizing Your Incongruence Regarding the Subject Matter You Teach

Hand either lesson plan or a copy of the textbook that you use to teach to a colleague or friend. Ask them to call out topics at random in the lesson plan or file text (try about five topics). For each topic they call out to you answer, "Why the hell should I learn this?" as if a student were to ask it as a challenge. Give an immediate answer as best and as honest as you can.

How'd you do? Do you have an answer right away? Was your friend convinced by your rationale? Were you being sincere in your answer? How much do you really believe in the meaning and value of the subjects you teach?

Exercise Three: Recognizing the Lack of Affect in Your Lesson Plan Delivery

Tape one of your lessons. Then, don't listen to it for at least a week.[80] When you do listen to it, with pencil and paper in hand, answer the following questions:

_____ 1. Did you start the lesson's introduction to the class with some statement of how you feel about this topic?

_____ 2. Does your voice tone express some real care and feeling for the subject?

_____ 3. Did you actually say many emotional or valuational words, e.g., "valuable," "significant," "beautiful," etc.?

_____ 4. Did you support students' emotional reactions (not just their cognitive statements) about the subject maker?

---

[80]If you listen to it right away, you will read into it what you would like to think your lesson said.

(If you are able, you might allow a friend or colleague to observe your lesson and evaluate you on the above questions. Or, if you're in an education workshop or class, you can take turns and do this for each other.)

Exercise Four: Recognizing How Actional Your Lessons Are

Either tape one of your lessons or allow a friend or colleague to observe one of your lessons. Or, if you're in an education workshop or class, do the following for each other:

Place a check here each time:

_____ 1. Students in your lesson are directed to take notes.
_____ 2. Students ask you questions.
_____ 3. Students comment on the lesson.
_____ 4. Students explain or re-explain a part of the lesson.
_____ 5. Students are asked to draw something, e.g., a diagram, chart, picture.
_____ 6. Students are asked to do something that requires them to get out of their seat, e.g., to go to the chalkboard.
_____ 7. Students are asked to vote on something.
_____ 8. Students are asked to role play or simulate something.

The items above have been arranged from passive to most actional. Are students asked to spend most of their time in your class doing things like (1, 2, or 3)? Or do they spend more time doing things like (6, 7, or 8)? How actional are your lessons?

Exercise Five: Recognizing How Inductive Your Lessons Are

Either tape one of your lessons or allow a friend or colleague to observe one of your lessons. Or, if you're in an education class or workshop, do the following for each other:

_____ 1. Place a check here each time you make a point in your lesson by starting out with a generalization and then relating it to the students.
_____ 2. Place a check here each time you make a point by going from your students' reactions and experiences to a generalization.

The latter style (2) is inductive. The former style (1) is deductive. How inductive are your lessons? (If you often do neither, your students probably "turn off" because they seldom feel any way to relate to the lesson.)

Exercise Six: Recognizing How Interactive Your Lessons Are

Either tape one of your lessons or allow a friend or colleague to observe one of your lessons. Or, if you're in an education class or workshop, do the following for each other:

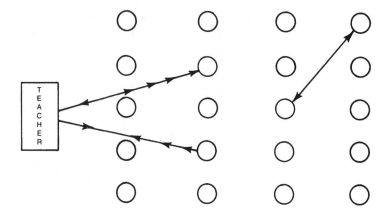

Each time in the lesson students interact with the teacher, draw a line between the teacher and the student, as in the above diagram. If the interaction is mostly <u>teacher to student</u>, put the arrows mostly toward the student. If the other way, then put arrows the other way. Each time the students interact with each other, draw a line between student and student.

After marking the above diagram throughout the whole lesson, notice if (a) most arrows go between the students? (b) most arrows go from students to teacher? (c) most arrows go from teacher to students?

The more that (a) or (b) are the case, the more interactive is the lesson. If the lesson is almost all (c), students probably feel little chance to respond.

Exercise Seven: Recognizing If Your Lessons Have a Felt Sense of Order

In the middle of teaching your lesson, stop and ask a student to please summarize briefly where we are and where s/he thinks we are going. Do this once or twice each period for at least four or five periods. How often do students sense where you are and where you are going? Do your lesson deliveries have a felt sense of order?

Exercise Eight: Recognizing Whether Your Lessons Have a Felt Sense of Meaning or Reward

In the middle of teaching your lesson, stop and ask a student to please summarize briefly why this topic is important. Do this once or twice each period for at least four or five periods. If the students can't say why, ask them if they are just following you for the, e.g., sake of passing the upcoming test.

How many students seem to feel the significance of the topic? How many are with you only for extrinsic rewards? How many are not with you because they feel neither?

Exercise Nine: Recognizing Whether Your Lesson Loses Momentum

Either tape one of your lessons or allow a friend or colleague to observe one of your lessons. Or, if you're in an education class or workshop, do the following for each other:

Place a check next to each of the following each time one of these things happens:

_____ 1. You stop the (train of your) lesson for a comment or question.
_____ 2. You follow "a side point" you want to bring in for a minute.
_____ 3. You explain something more than twice.
_____ 4. You reprimand a student using class time often, instead of handling it, e.g., after class.

If you do many of these things often, students probably "turn off," look out the window, or get off the train of your lesson often.

Exercise Ten: Recognizing How You Feed Attention in Your Lesson

Either tape one of your lessons or allow a friend or colleague to observe one of your lessons. Or, if you're in an education class or workshop, do the following for each other: Draw an arrow: (a) from teacher to student each time the teacher gives attention; (b) from student to student, each time a student gives attention to another student as part of the lesson, e.g., students show each other their work, comment on each other's comments, etc.

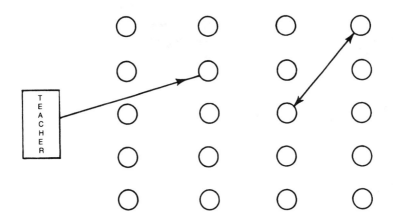

Are you the major feeder of attention? Do you allow, and even provide, ways for students to give each other attention? Are you afraid of the latter? Are you exhausted at always trying to be the major feeder?

Exercise Eleven: Recognizing If Your Lessons Are Explained Well Enough

In the middle of teaching your lesson, stop and ask, "How many students follow what I'm saying, understand this point? Raise your hand." Then ask, "How many are not sure?" and "How many are a little lost?"

Notice how many seem to feel they <u>understand</u>, are <u>not sure</u>, <u>don't follow your points</u>. Also, notice how many do not raise their hands for any of these. These latter students must be feeling one of these, yet are not comfortable enough to give you feedback. That's significant. Now, ask the ones <u>who understand</u> (get a volunteer) to explain to one (get a volunteer) who felt <u>not sure</u>, or one who <u>felt lost</u>. Listen to your students re-explaining what they think you said about this topic. Are they hearing you correctly? Are your lessons generally explained well enough? Do students feel free to give you feedback when they're lost?

Checklist

_____ 1. Do you believe in the importance or value of the topic(s) you are teaching?

_____ 2. Do you tell your students how you feel about the topic(s)?

_____ 3. Do you provide ways for students to share their <u>feelings</u> about the subject matter?

_____ 4. Do you provide ways in your lesson for students to do more than take notes, comment, and ask questions?

_____ 5. Do you allow, even urge, students to respond to each other?

_____ 6. Do you provide either verbal or other signs in your lesson that give your lesson a sense of order?

_____ 7. Do you provide clear ways for students to feel the meaning of the lesson, or at least, to get reward or credit for their work or class participation during the lesson?

_____ 8. Do you slow down, or stop too often, or digress too often in your lesson?

_____ 9. Do you give all the attention, or do you also provide ways for students to give each other attention, e.g., show and tell each other?

_____ 10. Does your class feel free to give you feedback?

K–6

_____ 11. Do you give emotional content to your delivery?

_____ 12. Are your explanations in simple small steps?

_____ 13. Are your explanations or planned activities too long?

_____ 14. Is your content appropriate to your students' developmental level and learning style?

We are now ready to work on preventing and handling these sources and problems. Before we do this in detail, let's survey Part III. Following is an outline of how we shall proceed.

Chapter 10: Dealing with Those That Are Somewhat Out of Your Hands

A. School Violence
B. Learning How to "Duck"
C. Dealing with Disturbances Right Outside Your Classroom
D. Working on the Environment of Your Classroom
E. Being Well-Equipped (Survival Tools)
F. Especially for Grades K–6
G. Teachers Share Their Growing Pains
H. Training Exercises and Checklists

Chapter 11: Repairing Your Student-Teacher Interactions

A. Not Making Miscalls
B. Being Congruent (Authentic)
C. Following Through
D. Being Appropriate
E. Being Fair
F. Especially for Grades K–6
G. Teachers Share Their Growing Pains
H. Training Exercises and Checklist for Chapter 11

Chapter 12: Preventing Your Rules from Falling Apart, and Saving Kids

A. Twenty-one Guidelines for Effective Rules and Warnings
   1. Sample: School Rules of a Typical Urban High School
   2. Sample: A Typical "Student Referral Form"
B. The Debates about: "What's Most Effective"?
   1. Warnings and punishments
   2. Corporal punishment
   3. Rewards
   4. Inappropriate rewards and punishments
   5. Rules
   6. Suspensions

C. Systematic Rewards, Instead of Punishments: 43 Suggestions
  1. For Grades K–6
  2. For the Upper Grades
D. Conflict Resolution (CR) Training
  1. Setting Up a School Violence Prevention Code
  2. Training School Staff in CR
  3. Training Students for a CR Court
  4. Teaching Students a CR Curriculum
E. Strengthening Students to Be Less Vulnerable to Peer Pressure
  1. What Kind of Child Is More Vulnerable?
  2. What Kind of Child Is Less Vulnerable?
  3. What Parents Can Do
  4. What Teachers Can Do
F. Warding off Bullies
G. Working on Asserting Yourself and Taking Stands
H. Especially for Grades K–6
I. Teachers Share Their Growing Pains
J. Training Exercises and Checklist for Chapter 12

Chapter 13: Specifics

A. How to Handle the: "See me after class!"
B. How to Handle Students Who:
  1. Call out
  2. Fight
  3. Cheat
  4. Come in late
  5. Don't do the homework
  6. Have crushes on you
  7. Wear hats
  8. Bring personal stereos to class
  9. Have beepers
  10. Criticize, "dis" each other
  11. Are "high" or dealing drugs
  12. Carry weapons
    a. Extent of the Problem
    b. Kinds of "Weapons"
    c. What a School Can Do
    d. A Sample Policy Statement
    e. What a Teacher Should Do
    f. Resources

C. Especially for Grades K–6
D. Training Exercises and Checklist for Chapter 13

Chapter 14: Repairing the Delivery of Your Lesson Plan (89 Methods)

A. Delivering the Subject Matter Congruently
B. Making the Lesson Affective
C. Making the Lesson Actional and Experiential
D. Making the Lesson More Inductive
E. Involving the Students: Participation Methods
F. Creating Lessons That Feel Orderly and Have Rewards and Momentum
G. Managing the Distribution of Attention
H. Making the Lesson Supportive, and Explained Well
I. Especially for Grades K–6
J. Teachers Share Their Growing Pains
K. Training Exercises and Checklist for Chapter 14

Chapter 15: Helping the Substitute Teacher

A. Securing Your Place
B. Some Helpful Techniques
C. Some Useful "Task Sheets"
D. Especially for Grades K–6
E. Training Exercises and Checklist for Chapter 15

PART III

Preventing and Handling the Sources of
Disruptive Behavior

Introduction to Part III: Four Guiding Caveats

Up to this point we have only accomplished two things, though two very important things: (a) we have diagnosed the sources of disruptive behavior and (b) we have distinguished a discipline from a miscall and have suggested that mistakes regarding this distinction are a major source of disruptive behavior.

But we have not yet decided what to do about all those problems that are not miscalls, namely, actual discipline problems. We have suggested, or implied, two strategies: (a) try not to make miscalls; (b) be sure of all the sources of disruptive behavior discussed in Part II. These two strategies may help our awareness of the problem, even help us not to be, ourselves, a source of discipline problems. But even acute awareness is far from sufficient here. "Fine, I understand, but now what do I actually, specifically do to prevent and handle the discipline problems?" you ask.

We are about to offer specific suggestions that will in many cases prevent these discipline problems from surfacing. Some suggestions, while they can't prevent their happening, will help you handle them and/or curtail their ripple-effect spread. So you will now be working on more than just becoming more intelligently aware.

However, before you proceed to study these suggestions in Part III, Chapters 10–13, I must caution you to keep four guiding caveats in mind as you listen to these suggestions:

1. If you try many of these suggestions that follow, expect that at first your job as teacher will get more difficult, not easier. What will be suggested will require study, understanding, some practice and training, and then application over and over again of new ideas and techniques, that are not your old natural style, until you feel a sense of mastery. This will take work. However, I promise that if you work hard now, e.g., in September, you'll not only make it to June without having to take "mental health days," but you'll also find that by October or November your job will be easier: you'll have far fewer discipline problems. You'll also enjoy your students more, they'll feel better about you, and you'll like your job more. Other teachers take it easy in September: they don't plan much, nor follow through on warnings, nor heed many of the ideas suggested here in Part III. They have less work in September but are angry by November, hate their students and their job by March, and are calling in sick by May! That's the choice that Part III's suggestions give you.

2. Don't swallow whole any suggestion that you don't feel congruent with. If it's not "you," if it's not your style, if you can't do it with your "heart in it," or put your person "behind" it, don't do it! No matter how effective the suggestion, it will be ineffective if it's not "you," how you are, what you believe in. Again, as we said in Chapter 8, section B, the requisite for prevention of discipline problems is being congruent.

3. However, I now must make one important disclaimer about the above: certainly don't do the suggestion if it's not "you," but you can't decide, "that's not me" from just listening to the suggestion or just trying it once. You'll have to give it more than just listening and one simple attempt to decide whether it's congruent with you. Why? Because all new learnings and skills, at first, feel non-natural to you. This feeling alone cannot be the judge of whether it will fit "you," that it is "you," a new and better "you." For instance, long ago, when you first swung a baseball bat, you probably swung it sloppily, awkwardly, and seldom got a hit. Then, one day, if you were lucky, someone coached you and said, "Stand like this. Swing level. No, don't look down, keep your eye on the ball." Your first reaction was probably, "This feels uncomfortable. I feel self-conscious and awkward. This is not the way I naturally swing. This isn't me." But, if you had a good coach, and practiced, and practiced, the new swing began to feel more natural, and you started to hit the ball better. Today, now, that learned swing is "you." So try these suggestions. More than once. Practice them. You'll, at first, feel self-conscious and awkward. However, if you practice enough, some of these suggestions will eventually feel more natural to you and will be congruent for you. However, if after really trying them out, they're not "you," don't use them. (Also, certainly don't change your style in a certain area if it works for you; "don't fix it if it's not broken.")

4. Don't fret if you find that you cannot apply all these suggestions. No single inapplicability will collapse your total ability to better deal with discipline problems. Just keep in mind that the more suggestions you can apply, the more you will have eliminated and better handled the sources of disruptive behavior.

In summary, keep these caveats in mind as you read Part III: (1) at first, this will be more work; (2) do what's congruent for you; (3) really give each suggestion a good try before you abandon it; (4) apply as many as you can, and don't fret if you can't apply particular ones.

CHAPTER 10: DEALING WITH THOSE THAT ARE SOMEWHAT OUT OF YOUR HANDS

In this chapter we will work on preventing and handling discipline problems that you often have little control over:

(a) You cannot prevent the kindling of those problems that happen from just growing up, or from home, or relationships with peers. However, you can prevent their ripple effect onto the rest of your class as these upset students enter your classroom, and you can work on handling these upset students better.

(b) You often cannot control what happens in the whole school, its rules, or in the halls right outside your door. However, there are ways to repair school rules and deal with external disturbances more effectively.

(c) You often have little control over the environment of your classroom. However, there are some things you <u>can</u> do to better the environment.

The first point about handling external factors is to develop the kind of relationship with your students such that you are not the only "policeman" of discipline problems. If you work on not making miscalls, being congruent, consistent, appropriate, fair, and effective in your lesson delivery, your students will like you better, and they'll feel good about coming to your class and learning. Then, if Daryl comes in late and makes cute remarks at you that disrupt your lesson, you still won't be able to control this disturbance whose source may be external to your class, but Daryl will get less support from his fellow students. Your students might even say, "Hey, cool it! She's trying to teach us something." There will be little ripple effect from Daryl's problem, and you won't be the only disciplinarian; your students will be too. So, if you work on what follows, even the ones somewhat out of your control will also be handled along with the other sources.

A. School Violence

Violent behavior is behavior that obviously goes far beyond merely disruptive behavior and can refer to illegal or criminal behavior. Such behavior is often out of your hands. [However, it is still true that (a), (b), (c) above <u>can</u>, at least, stop the spread of such behavior into your classroom.] Although violence in our schools (and in our whole society) is beyond the scope of a book on "discipline problems," let us try, at least, to give a brief overview of the problem.

1. The problem

Violent behavior is on the increase in our schools and threatens to destroy the very fabric of our educational system. Eighty-nine percent of respondents in 700 cities and towns surveyed by the National League of Cities in 1994 said that school violence is a problem in their community. The trouble is that the problem is societal; it cannot be remedied by working on just one particular field, e.g., education, or on any one segment of our society. Researchers have identified several major causes for the increase in violent behavior: poverty; racism; unemployment; substance abuse; the effects of how violence is portrayed in our T.V. programs, and movies; destructive home life communication (or non-communication) styles; inadequate gun control laws; our too lenient court system, etc. are all major contributing factors to violent behavior in children.[81]

Strategies

a. Stronger Regulations

Some educators and lawmakers feel that what we need is stronger laws, and regulations. Many have suggested, e.g., stricter school suspension policies; more efficient juvenile courts with consistent penalties imposed; financial restitution by juveniles to their victims of their violent crimes; compulsory "boot camps"[82]; and alternative schools for violent juvenile offenders.[83]

However, some groups, who are concerned about protecting students' rights, have demanded more "due process procedures" (see S.F. 3) that have sometimes hampered schools' abilities to take stronger action.[84] But recently, schools are getting more legal power to counter the destructive influence of, e.g., gangs. Law enforcement officials in California got a ruling from the State's

---

[81]From: ED379786 Mar 95 School Violence Prevention. *ERIC Digest,* Number 94. Author: Walker, Dean. ERIC Clearinghouse on Educational Management, Eugene, Oregon.
[82]"We Must Act Now To Make Our Schools Safe," Danny l. Coe. *National Association of Secondary School Principals Bulletin,* Oct., 1994, pp. 108–110.
[83]In March of 1997, New York City's School's Chancellor, Rudy Crew, proposed that students who carry weapons, drugs, or commit physical acts of violence to students or school staff be placed in alternative SOS schools ("Second Opportunity Schools") or be expelled. And the city's mayor backed the plan with about eight million dollars from the city's budget.
[84]Toby, Jackson. "Everyday School Violence: How Disorder Fuels It." *American Educator,* vol. 17, no.4, Winter 1993/94, pp. 4–9.

Supreme Court (Jan. 31, 1996) that allows cities to prohibit suspected gang members from standing together on streets, wearing beepers, etc. These legal limits on gang members (although undergoing A.C.L.U. debate) may soon translate into more power for schools' policies to fight potential violence.[85]

b. Prevention

Most educators would rather focus on prevention, not greater regulation. One area for prevention is to improve the operations and climate of the school, per se. Research indicates that it would be helpful to break through the anonymous, impersonal atmosphere of jumbo high schools. Students who feel recognized and appreciated by at least one adult at school are less likely to act out against the school's ethos of nonviolence (H. Walker).

It would also help to get students involved with beautifying the school building and grounds, which would give the students a sense of ownership and motivate, perhaps, some protective care of their own school (Sandra R. Sabo, 1993). It seems that it would also be helpful if there were smaller schools that can create a sense of community: where teachers know students' names; where nurturance and inclusiveness can be promoted[81] (wearing school uniforms that create a sense of belonging, and counteract gang membership); where codes of conduct can more easily be enforced, etc. As dysfunctional families contribute to juvenile delinquency, a dysfunctional school, one of disorder, where students are not held responsible for their behavior, contributes to violence in that school.[84]

Also, the research shows that students usually bring weapons into for protection, not for aggression. Therefore, if students felt safer in schools, fewer weapons might be carried into schools.[86] (For a detailed discussion of this strategy see Chapter 13 B12).

It seems that we would also go a long way toward prevention if we could teach students nonviolent conflict resolution and "character education," e.g.:

- ways to counteract how students learn how to handle anger and conflict from watching adults (e.g., their parents) who communicate destructively
- ways to use compromise to settle disputes
- how to listen empathetically
- how to give constructive feedback

(For a complete discussion of the above strategy, see Chapter 12D.)

The administrators of a school, e.g., the principal, can also make useful input here. S/he can help establish school norms of nonviolence and community

[85]*The New York Times,* Feb. 1, 1997, p.6.

[86]Wood, Craig, and Mark Chestnut. "Violence in U.S. School; The Problem and Some Responses." *West's Education Law Quarterly,* v. 4, no.3, p. 414, 416, Jul., 1995.

by developing sincere, caring relationships with groups of students and individuals. By maintaining a high profile, walking the halls, visiting classrooms, and being accessible to students and staff, the principal reduces the likelihood of antisocial behavior (Stephanie Kadel and Joseph Follman, 1993). S/he should take advantage of federal breakfast and lunch programs, institute antiracism programs, speak out against all harassment, and make social services available to students who need them (Curio and First). Also, the principal can encourage a sense of ownership of school programs and policies by sharing power with the staff and parent organizations. Shared power makes it more likely that discipline plans and academic goals are supported (Aleem, Moles, and others).[81]

c. It Takes a Village

However, principals, teachers, schools, even our lawmakers, cannot make inroads into this crisis acting alone and separately. As Hillary Rodham Clinton has urged: "It takes a village!" For example, if high school degrees were actually tied to students' abilities to secure jobs, such that employers were tied to the schools more, such tactics would rearm the schools with the ability to offer students real rewards.[84] Though ambitious goals, we need to reach out to children who face poverty or abuse or other problems that ultimately foster violent behavior. Schools need to collaborate closely with community social service agencies to provide children and their families with timely and affordable access to counseling, financial assistance, and protection. Parent education courses should be offered at schools for families of children who are in trouble. (Stephanie Kadel and Joseph Follman, 1993). We need to provide school/community work programs and more after school use of school buildings for youth programs.[82] We need to also make sure that we share information with police, and we plan antigang interventions with the whole school community (Robert P. Cantrell and Mary Lynn Cantrell, 1993).[81]

It does take an entire village. But, fortunately, our village is beginning to place this awareness into priority:

> Character education must be taught in our schools. We must teach our children to be good citizens. And we must continue to promote order and discipline, supporting communities that introduce school uniforms, impose curfews, enforce truancy laws, remove disruptive students from the classroom, and have zero tolerance for guns and drugs. (President Clinton's *State of the Union Address*, Feb. 4, 1997)

*The reader should refer to the following sections of this book for more detailed discussions related to school violence:

- some of the causes of violent behavior that originate from outside the classroom: Chapter 6: From Outside Your Classroom:
  A. From Childhood to Adolescence
- ways to make school rules more effective
  Chapter 12: A. Twenty-one Guidelines for Effective Rules and Warnings
  1. Sample: "School Rules of a Typical Urban High School"
  2. Sample: A Typical "Student Referral Form"
- school suspension policies
  Chapter 12: B. 6. Suspensions
- using positive reinforcement:
  Chapter 12: C. Systematic Rewards, Instead of Punishments:
- character education: counteracting the effects of the media and destructive family communication styles
  Chapter 12: D. Conflict Resolution Training
  E. Strengthening Students to Be Less Vulnerable to Peer Pressure
  F. Warding off Bullies
- how to handle students who
  Chapter 13: B. 2. Fight; 11. Are "high" or dealing drugs; 12. Carry weapons.
- what are the current legal parameters?
  Appendix C.

Resources

1. If students feel unsafe, there are now national hotline numbers that students can call: 1-800-552-4867 or 1-800-467-7719 where they can talk to either a counselor or police officer with complete confidentiality.
2. The National School Safety Center (NSSC)
   4165 Thousand Oaks Blvd., Suite 290
   Westlake Village, CA 91362
3. The National Report on School Violence, (800) 274-6737, at: http://www.bpinews.com or e-mail at: bpinews@bpinews.com (includes information on innovative programs, contact persons, phone numbers, etc.
4. "Violent Schools-Safe Schools," National Institute of Education, 1978.
5. Basian, Lisa D. "School Crime: A National Crime Victimization Survey Report," Washington: Bureau of Justice Statistics, 1991.
6. "Preventing Crime and Promoting Responsibility: 50 Programs That Help Communities Help Their Youth." 1996. *President's Crime Prevention Council* (202) 395-5555 or e-mail: PCPC @A1.eop.gov or write: Crime Prevention Council, 736 Jackson Place NW, Washington, D.C. 20503
7. Hayes, Diane Williams. "Reading, Writing, and Arithmetic—An Education in Violence." *Crisis,* vol. 100, no. 4, pp. 8–10 April-May, 1993.

8. John Eddowes. "Violence: A Crisis in Homes and Schools." *Childhood Education,* vol. 67, pp. 4–7, Fall 1990.
9. The National Council on Crime Prevention at: http://www.weprevent.org
10. blackbird.iss.indiana.edu
   Offers both text and multimedia files providing information on school violence: films, videos, etc.
11. From: www.ed.gov/ (US Dept of Education):

As part of a new initiative to encourage local communities to put a new focus on the development of effective truancy programs, Secretary Riley will send a Manual to Combat Truancy to every school district in the nation.

For other relevant resources, also see Chapter 13 B. 12: Resources.

We hope that what you are usually dealing with is disruptive behavior, not violent behavior. Disruptive behavior is usually more localized, and its sources more specifiable than societal violent behavior. We will now focus on preventing and handling many kinds of disruptive behaviors (Chapters 10–16). Yet, even disruptive behaviors whose sources are societal, which are somewhat out of your hands, can be decreased by the interventions we shall now discuss.

B. Learning How to "Duck"

The warning bell rings for the start of the third period. You must get to your class (room 210) in four minutes when the bell will ring signaling the start of the third period. You're in a hurry. As you walk quickly down the second floor, a student comes almost running up to you and quickly says, "Hey, where the hell is room 208?" You're a bit caught off guard. (You say to yourself: "What's this, 'Hey' stuff! I'm a teacher here; I worked too hard to get my license to be called, 'Hey.' And, what's this 'hell' stuff! I wish these kids would learn respect and not curse all the time; he's asking me for help and mad at me? Some nerve! Who the hell does he think he is?!") So you say, "Wait a minute! What's your name? Where's your program card? And my name is Mr. Saunders, not 'Hey.' Don't you learn manners at home? And, if you want my help, don't curse. And stop being so angry. You'll get along better in this world if you. . . ." The student gets angrier, "Hey, you're not my f—ing father! You teachers are all . . . !"

The above, in many situations, may not even be an exaggeration. What has happened here? You're insulted. You demand respect on the spot. You even attempt to teach this kid something, right there in the hall. And, before you know it, you have a full blown confrontation on your hands. Now you're really late for your third period, which will mean more discipline problems when you get there.

How advisable is the above reaction? Does it accomplish anything that is worth the fallout? Have your remarks gotten you respect? If you're lucky, this student will go passive and feel guilty, repress his frustration, and feign respect. But that's not respect. And his repression does him no good either. If you're not lucky, this student is aggressive, and <u>your</u> demanding anger makes him fight back. That's not respect either. No, respect means a feeling for <u>whom</u> a person is. This student doesn't know who you are; and do you want to spend time teaching him who you are? Maybe you want him to respect your "office," your "status": teacher. Then, if it's not personal respect you want, why did you take his upset personally? Does your lecture about manners at home and how to handle the world really fix up his home life and teach him how to be in the world? In thirty seconds?! You're not a genius preacher. And, since this student is in a hurry and upset, he probably can't even listen well, certainly not learn now. But maybe you have taught him not to curse? But was he cursing or just venting? (Remember "the venting for cursing mistake," p. 77.) Even you used "hell" above when you felt angry. Should he be punished because you said your frustration to yourself while he said it out loud?

What's happened here? This student is late for class. He's lost, frustrated, and angry. He can't find room 208. He sees you, and you look like someone who may know. He's worried about time, maybe his grades, or his friends' opinions as he comes late, that his mother and father are angry at him, etc. So this student is, in a way, flailing his arms and fists in frustration and anxiety. You're also late and upset so you are caught off guard and take this whole situation <u>personally</u>. In a way, you've stuck your jaw in front of his wildly swinging-in-the-air fists. Now, you're really hit and have a fight on your hands.

Why do I say, "you've stuck your jaw in front of his wildly swinging-in-the-air fists"? Because this student's anger is anger all over the place; it's displaced and really not at you. The intensity of his anger and its frustration may be the result of frustrations about his body, his friends, career worries, his parents, etc. He's not angry with you; he doesn't even know you. He might be angry at his father who has pressured him about responsibilities. He then might be angry with all society's pressures and authority figures who remind him that he feels inadequate. Thus, he may see you as one of these and impulsively lays his anger on you. But, again, he's really not angry at you. You have taken his generalized anger that is displaced and taken it personally. You've hit him in his flying fist with your jaw.

Students have weak ego strength. Thus, they have less impulse control. Since they often feel inadequate, they seldom feel safe. When they feel unsafe, they hold in their angers a lot for fear of the consequences. However, if they feel safer, or their anger gets stronger than their control, it escapes and gets displaced on the nearest victim. This displaced anger is not really at its misplaced target.

Of course, since we are also human and vulnerable, we seldom realize all this on the spot and often get into "no-win" battles with people's displaced anger. We can't win because it's like fighting with a ghost that is not really there nor able to be exorcised in a brief encounter.

What might be a better reaction? Let's play the scene over again and try a different tack: The student comes running up to you and says, "Hey, where the hell is room 208?" (You realize he's really not angry at you; he's late and anxious like you are. You decide he's not angry at you nor disrespects you because he doesn't know you. So . . .) You just point to room 208 and say, "Over there."

Have you really lost respect or a great opportunity to teach this kid by pointing and saying just this? I don't think so. For sure you'll be less late for your class. And this student might even surprisingly react to your pointing, "Over there," with, "Thanks." He might even feel helped and understood by an adult who he generally feels "doesn't understand." You may have, for an instant, broken his stereotype, calmed him, and allowed him the brief safety of venting his frustration.

I'm not saying that you should ignore all student angers and cursing in all situations. But I am saying there are many student angers, seeming cursing, in some situations, where you should learn to duck, learn not to always take all these angers, seemingly coming at you, personally.

When should you learn to duck? I think when any of the following are the case:

1. If you simply sense that the anger coming at you is not really at you; it's just displaced, that its cause or even intensity does not seem to fit your interaction with the student. You sense that the student is either overreacting or was already angry before you and s/he had this incident.
2. If you find that the student's anger or misbehavior is out of your jurisdiction. For instance, the student is yelling at another teacher in the hallway, apparently in a disrespectful way. Or you see a student in the library throw a book on the floor, behind the librarian's back.
3. If the behavior or "curse word" seems to be venting, not a cursing at someone. Or it is a cursing at someone, but, again, out of your jurisdiction, e.g., the student is cursing at another student, "Fu—you!" in the hallway or cafeteria.
4. If it seems that the anger is due to transference to a generalized authority figure, and really not at the person in the uniform or role.
5. If it seems as if the anger or disruptive behavior is going to be short-lived. Interceding to stop it might make for a longer disruption than letting it quickly blow over.

6. If it seems as if the anger is merely the result of frustration at trying to do something, e.g., a math problem. Or it seems to be the reaction the student is having from being weaned, left to try something on his or her own.
7. If it seems as if you are suddenly trying to earn respect (a long-term feeling) in a very short-term immediate situation. If you are getting into trying to preach respect into this kid.
8. If you are trying to win a feeling from the kid and trying to get more than the extinction of his disruptive behavior that is bothering your teaching or the class's learning. For instance, you tell the student to stop tapping his pencil. The student stops but makes a very "disrespectful" face at you. So you now go after trying to change his face (trying to win his feeling, not just his behavior) because you take his facial expression of anger as <u>personally</u> disrespectful.
9. If you think that the anger or behavior is none of the above, but you discover as you try to confront this student, that s/he is too upset to hear you now. Then, for now, duck, and wait, and deal with the student when s/he is calmer and more able to hear you. (That's assuming that during the "wait" s/he won't be destructive to his or her self, or others, or property. Otherwise, try to get him or her out of your room, duck the confrontation and punishment application now, and see him or her, e.g., in the dean's office.)

Thus, these situations would be good examples of when you should duck:

1. The hall situation described above.
2. You are walking down the hall and you overhear a student cursing who has just discovered that his locker has been broken into.
3. You begin to do a "coverage" or substitute for a regular teacher, and you hear a student curse in the back of the room as you walk in.
4. You overhear a student in the back of the cafeteria talking to another: "Mr. Rodriguez is a bastard!"

Now, when I suggest that you should duck if any of the above are the case, there are many forms of "ducking":

(a) You might say nothing, and just let the anger and behavior go by. (That's if it is not seen by other students as, "S/he's easy. You can get away with things with this teacher.") This kind of ducking might be best for 1, 5, and 8, above.

(b) You might just say something like, "I understand you're angry, your manner bothers me, or others . . ." and then just ask that it be expressed later, or with someone else, or elsewhere (again, if other students don't see this as making you look like a pushover) for 1, 3, 4, 5, 6, 7, and 9.

(c) You might just say something like, "John, I think you're upset and I don't really deserve your anger. Are you upset about something else? Let's talk later," for 1, 3, 4, 5, and 6.

(d) You might just decide not to confront the student at this time and place and refer the problem to someone else who has better jurisdiction over it, for 2, 3, and 9.

(e) You might just demand a non-disruptive behavior and decide to work on his or her feelings with you at a private time. There you and s/he can respectfully listen to each other's gripes, and you can respect his or her complaints so s/he can respect yours for 7 and 8.

Study the above. Let its attitude of ducking digest inside of you. Then, remember our four caveats: (1) this will take work to implement; (2) don't do any of these if they are not congruent for you; (3) but give this, "sometimes: duck!" attitude a good try before you decide you can't do this, that it isn't you; (4) no need to fret if you can't always do this suggestion.

Just remember the main suggestion here: Don't necessarily take every student anger and all behaviors personally.

However, don't duck all angers and behaviors. Only duck if they seem to be in the bounds of 1–9. For instance, if the anger is at you (not displaced), is disrupting your teaching or the class's learning, is in your jurisdiction, e.g., your classroom, is a cursing and not merely a venting, is not short-lived, etc., then don't duck. In such cases, we'll need to handle it with the skills of our next chapters. However, some ducking will at least better handle those sources of disruption that are somewhat out of your hands: from just growing up, home, peers, those outside your classroom. But there is much more to be handled, so if you understand how ducking can be useful sometimes, let's move on.

C. Dealing with Disturbances Right Outside Your Classroom

Though you have almost no control over sources of disruption that come from just growing up, or from home and peers (Chapter 6, sections A and B), you do have some control over those disturbances that come from right outside your classroom. Still, since these sources of disruptions are not in your classroom, you sometimes may only be able to limit them, prevent their ripple effect onto your class, but seldom eradicate them completely.

How can you better deal with students hanging outside your door, waving to their friends in your class, or staff who enter midclass, or the cafeteria juke box that is too loud, or students who enter eating food, etc.? If you consider the four caveats we discussed, try these suggestions.

1. For students who hang out outside your door

(a) Before the bell rings for the start of your class period, stand outside your classroom door sternly, arms folded, as if you're a guard. You should have a "do-now!" assignment on the chalkboard for your entering students.

This stance, when seen by potential "hanger-outers," may discourage them from choosing your doorstep as the best place to hang out.

(b) If you see any potential "hanger-outers" not going to their class, start to question them: "Are you supposed to be going to class now?" or, "You two, please get to class; your teacher will miss you."

(c) Usher your hanging-out students into your class: "Come on, John, let's go, there's an assignment on the board." (Make sure you link the "do-now!" assignment to some kind of reward or penalty if not done on time when you collect it, e.g., five minutes after the bell.)

(d) If these only solve a few disturbances, then try to notice if the "hanger-outers" tend to be the same student(s). If so, then:

1. Notice where he's supposed to be going and get the name of his destination-teacher. Find that teacher, e.g., during lunch time, and ask this teacher's help regarding this student. S/he can reprimand him or her, if you can't.
2. Or try to find out this student's homeroom teacher's name, and tell her or him about this problem.
3. Or make a point to locate, now or later, the person on hall duty and ask that he or she patrol near your classroom that period.

2. For students in the halls who wave at students in your class

(a) Don't stop your lesson and try to go after the wavers. Instead, reprimand your students who wave back or give attention to the wavers. The students in your class, the audience for these wavers, you can reprimand. Look toward your class, or keep teaching, or reprimand responders in your class. But don't turn toward the wavers by your door. This will only promote negative attention and make the door window more of a stage for performers and your class more an audience to react to them.

(b) Place a piece of cardboard over the window of the door. This will cut off communication midlesson between the hallway and your class.

(c) Or place a piece of cardboard almost over the whole window, leaving a small opening at the bottom as shown in illustration:

Most passersby will not go through the trouble of stooping down to look in, especially if this behavior calls more attention to a hall-duty teacher.

(d) Or with a little work, cut out slats of cardboard about 2 inches wide and about 2 inches longer than window's height [illustration (a)] and then bend bottom of slat, and top, each 1 inch [illustration (b)]. Now glue the slats into the window, so window looks like illustration (c). These vertical blinds will allow you (since you're in front of the room) to see out, but make it very difficult for the hallway students to see your class, or your class to see out.

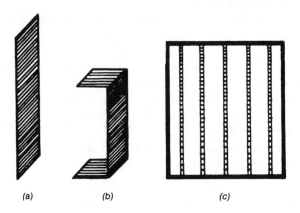

(a)   (b)   (c)

(e) Similar to (c) above, place cardboard over the window so only the top space is visible. Passersby will have to call attention to themselves by standing on tiptoe or will be too short to see in.

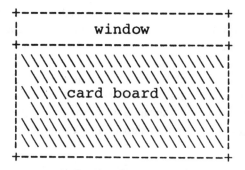

3. From loose school rules

(a) A school can cut down on hallway problems, food eating in classrooms, etc. by holding useful staff meetings. Try to consult with your felllow teachers about these problems, and try to raise these issues as a "staff concern" not just your concern, as "suggestions for agenda" for a staff meeting. Don't raise your concerns as demands, but as concerns. Try to describe your feelings of frustration, irritation, upset, not describe the administration's negligent behavior. Suggest that the best school rules that will be most enforceable will be those owned by all faculty, voted on by faculty, rather than those dictated to the faculty by the principal. Allow the administration to tell you the complexity of what their job is. Listen. You both need to be empathetic toward the difficulties of both of your jobs.[87]

(b) At such meetings you might suggest that hall-duty teachers not be stationed at a post on a particular floor, but patrol the entire floor.

(c) Or you might suggest that no parents or other staff enter a classroom once the period has started, unless it's an emergency.

(d) Or you might suggest that all teachers can lock their front door once ten minutes or so into the period.

(e) Or you might suggest that cafeteria monitors not permit any student to leave the cafeteria with food, on the way to a class.

(f) Or you might suggest that teachers stop issuing passes so liberally, which only creates too much hall traffic. Hall-duty personnel might even keep a tally of which teachers tend to be issuing too many passes.

(g) Or you might suggest that there be "hall sweeps": that hall-duty teachers "sweep" the halls ten minutes after the bell and bring any "hanger-outers" to the dean's office. If the same student ends up there, e.g., twice, call (or send a letter to) his or her parent.

(h) Or you might suggest that there be some place in school (the cafeteria, or a student lounge, or yard) made available for students' interaction and

---

[87]A new Part 100 regulation calling for New York State districts to work out a discipline plan—with teacher consultation required—is a result of the N.Y. United Teachers' persuading the Regents of the tremendous importance of this issue.

Part IUO.2(1) of the new regulations states that by Jan. 1. 1956, every N.Y. school district must adopt and implement a written policy on school conduct and discipline (in New York City, each community school district. as well as the central board of education, must have such a policy). This policy must be "developed locally in consultation with teachers, administrators, other school service professionals, students and parents"

The policy must include: "a bill of rights and responsibilities of students which focuses upon positive student behavior and which shall be publicized and explained to all students on an annual basis; a discipline code for student behavior setting forth prohibited student conduct and the range of penalties which may be imposed for violation. . . ." Disciplinary measures set forth are to be appropriate to the seriousness of the offense and to students' previous records. The code must be explained to students, sent in writing to all parents annually, and must describe the roles of teachers, administrators, board of education members, and parents.

The code must set fixed procecures for the enforcement of public order on school properly, must involve all segments of the school community in identifying and resolving discipline problems, provide alternative programs appropriate for individual students needs, and must provide guidelines and programs for inservice education for all district staff members to ensure effective implementation of these policies. Boards of education are to review the policy on an annual basis and file it in all buildings. It is public information, "available for review by any individual."

venting. After all, students hang out in halls talking to their friends or waving at their friends in your class because it's difficult to hold in all their reactions to growing up, home, peers, and new school lessons all day, especially when they only have four minutes to talk to their friends and get to class between bells.

For any of these suggestions to work, you and your faculty and administration will need to work on feeling like a team. You may need to meet often at first. And you all must follow through. Also, keep the four caveats in mind: (1) this will take work; (2) only do what's congruent; (3) give each a good try before abandoning it; (4) don't fret if you can't apply all of them.

D. Working on the Environment of Your Classroom

Now, the environment of your classroom is more in your control. Of course, you don't have all the power you'd like to have over its environment, but you can usually make some improvements in (a) the physical setting itself; (b) the seating arrangement; (c) your procedures; and (d) the equipment you have. Let's work on improving each of these one at a time.

a. The physical setting

The Room Itself
1. The first and most helpful thing you can do is to try to get the same room for all the subject-class periods that you teach. If ideal, the homeroom (or section class) will also be the same room, so you never have to move. Then, the classroom can be pretty much your room to have more control over the seating arrangement, procedures, equipment, walls, furniture, etc. Or, at least try to get the same room for, e.g., periods 1–4 and another room for periods 5–8. The fewer the rooms you have to use the better. And, if you have to go to two or even three rooms, at least get them as near to each other as possible. If you can do this, you will also be able to arrive at the classroom(s) before some of the students and thus will be more able to head off discipline problems before they start.

How to Get the Same Room
2. Locate the person in your school who is in charge of assigning rooms that coordinate with teachers' schedules. This is usually not the principal or assistant principal. The job may even be given to a secretary who is asked to simply reserve rooms for a class schedule she is given that has been made up by someone else or a committee. Approach this person before school starts, or at least between semesters or marking periods. These assignments are

usually decided in September, even before the first staff meeting. Tell this person your problems when you have several rooms. Try to state your frustrated, even anxious, feelings. Don't demand; ask for help and be appreciative of how much juggling their job demands. Start out asking for the same room for all teaching periods. Leave it at that for a while. Come back after a while, or a day later, and ask if you got that. If not, express your upset (not anger) and ask to be at least in only two rooms, but near each other. Proceed in this fashion. It is inadvisable to try to go over this person's head. That usually just causes anger and may even give you more rooms, just from spite. Try just to ask this person as a personal favor and keep this request confidential. If you get your request met, don't publicize it. Their job is hard enough without everyone asking for the same favor. Make sure you thank them, or return the favor.

The Kind of Room

3. When you go to this person to request the same room, or nearby rooms, try to have a few specific rooms in mind. Make a list of rooms (two or three) with your ideal preference on top, e.g., Room 203. Try to get a classroom that has as many of the following characteristics as possible (a) if more than one room, that they are very near each other; (b) that is not near a gym, music room, auditorium, cafeteria, industrial arts class, or a smelly chemistry lab; (c) that doesn't have windows that face a sports field or interesting or busy street, or face a usually sunlit southerly direction; (d) that doesn't have broken or flickering lights; (e) that has a carpet; (f) that has window shades in good condition; (g) that has a back door as well as a front door, and the back door can be locked; (h) that has a front door with no window, or a window shade, or you can put paper or shade over it to limit passerby wavings; (i) that has a non-noisy working heating unit or air conditioner that you can regulate to keep the room cool; (j) that has windows that can be slightly opened from the top and/or bottom; (k) that has a desk with a drawer that can be locked; (l) that has a closet that can be locked; (m) that has some corner of the room (even behind a divider) where you can have a private place to reprimand a student without an audience reaction; (n) that is not the last room on the custodian's schedule to be cleaned.

Its Walls

4. Have green (non-glaring) chalkboards instead of blackboards

5. Have bulletin boards

6. Are thick, not sliding walls, or partitioned walls

7. Are free of graffiti

Its Furnishings

8. There are two garbage cans, one near the front door, one near the back door; however, make sure both are either close enough or far enough from students not to tempt them into trying "basketball shots."

9. The room either doesn't have a pencil sharpener, or has one at least in the back, rather than the front, of the room; but you may want to remove it.

10. It has enough desk-chairs for your largest class, plus at least one extra you can leave empty near the front door, or back door (if you have one).

11. Hopefully, it has moveable, non-screwed down, fairly clean desk-chairs that are in good, non-squeaky condition.

12. It has only the essential furniture you want; try to get rid of anything in the room that will just be clutter for you.

b. The seating arrangement

Kinds of Patterns (Grades K–6)

13. If you are working in grades K–6, you probably have the same students and same room all day. You also teach them all subjects, and usually the desks are small tables that have separate chairs that are all moveable. In this case, you should just rearrange your room according to each learning activity. If at a particular time you want students to work together in small groups, arrange the chairs and desks in several small circles or horseshoes. You might want to set aside an area for individual work, or a private place where you can reprimand a student without an audience reaction; probably the best place is the back corner of the room away from the back door. You may sometimes want to put the seating arrangement in rows (for lecture-type lessons), in horseshoes (for class participation lessons that can still be teacher-centered) or in a circle (for full class discussion, sharing, or "show-and-tell"). You can review the advantages and disadvantages of these configurations below in 14–17. However, since you'll usually be with the same students all the time, you'll easily learn their names and need not necessarily use the seating pattern that best helps you learn names or take attendance.

Kinds of Patterns (Grades 7–12 and College Classes, Workshops, etc.)

14. If you are working in grades 7–12, you probably have departmental change of subject-class periods every forty minutes or so. Thus, unlike in K–6, you cannot change the seating arrangements during each period to fit a change of learning activity halfway into the period. You will have to choose one seating arrangement that is generally best for you. All of them have their pros and cons. I discuss them here with the highest recommended (that takes the most work) first, and with my least recommended (that is the easiest) last.

In a Circle

15. The Pros: A circle seating arrangement provides the most opportunity for class participation. Instead of stifling the peer-group energy (as sitting in rows does), it can use it. Students can share ideas with each other better, listen to each other more, ask each other questions, etc. The teacher need not keep repeating answers given by students, nor repeat a student's question for the class to answer. The teacher need not be the major feeder of attention, an exhausting job that is difficult to carry out with consistent fairness when students compete for attention. Students can learn each others' names easier. Students can then sometimes call on each other, instead of the teacher running the risk of being accused of "playing favorites," e.g., "you always call on John." Lessons can be more inductive and more motivational since students can more easily contribute their experiences. Fewer students are likely to turn off, because, in a circle, it's difficult to hide and there's more stimulation. The teacher will not have to go after as many withdrawn students. There will be less authority-transfer problems at the teacher because the teacher can sit in the circle as a member. This will also lessen the "class vs. teacher" feeling, an important source of discipline problems.

The Cons: The seating arrangement takes the most work and skill to carry out so that it will help teaching more than hinder it. It generates energy that, unless channeled by the teacher's very organized lesson, assertiveness, and follow-through rules, can merely become noisy and cause disruptive behavior. It requires that the teacher control the interaction of the circle with facilitative skills that (a) stop useless digressions; (b) stop students who disrespect others' values or feelings; (c) enable the teacher to share his or her feelings, besides teach facts; (d) necessitate the teaming of students' names; (e) require the teacher to be a gatekeeper who decides when it's time to shift topics and move on, lecture, or allow the class to react to each other and the topic just presented.

Tips on Setting up a Circle: If you have the same room for all your periods, putting the chairs in a circle (if they're not screwed down) will be easier. However, you may still want to meet the first few classes in traditional rows. Then, when you feel they're ready, explain the circle-seating to them. Then, as quietly as possible, have them (maybe five at a time) place the seats in a circle. Don't then immediately start to teach. Wait. Just let the class get used to this circle arrangement for a while. Ask them to discuss how it feels. Only after they're used to it, start a very organized (even note-taking) lesson. Control their responses by only calling on hand-raisers. And only let them talk to each other when you have so directed them to discuss a topic you've just explained. If the room is too small for all to fit in a circle, let some sit in an outside circle, so you have two concentric circles. Arrange the circle so your desk is beside your seat in the circle and you have access to it.

If you are not in the same room, you can try the following: (a) Appoint a good student or students as chair monitor(s) who arrive(s) at your room quickly because their prior class is nearby. Try to get a volunteer or volunteers and ask them to place the chairs in a circle for you when they arrive. Remember (or write down) their names and thank them each time, at least for the first few days. (b) Ask the previous period's teacher if s/he can ask a student or students to do this for you. Thank these students and teacher. (c) Ask the next period class teacher and students if they wouldn't mind putting back the class as the next teacher sees fit. (d) Have your whole class put the chairs in a circle when they arrive, then do a "do-now" assignment as soon as they arrive. And stop one minute before the end of the period and have the class put the chairs back in rows, quietly (five at a time). (e) Warn the teacher next door that the noise of the chairs at the beginning and end will be brief and under your control. (f) Tell the class, if they do not behave themselves, they will lose this privileged arrangement and have to go back to rows. (As far as handling knowing their names, and attendance in a circle, we will discuss this just below in section c., p. 212, "Your Procedures") As far as learning the facilitative skills for teaching in a circle, we will discuss them in Chapter 13, section E.

In a Horseshoe

16. The Pros: The horseshoe seating arrangement has almost all the advantages of the circle and takes less work and skill to manage.

The Cons: There is somewhat less chance for class participation than the circle because the arrangement is less student-centered and more teacher-centered. They will probably share, listen, and question each other less than if they were in a circle because they are pushed by the seating arrangement to give their attention more to you. You may have to repeat each student's questions and answers to the whole class more than if they were in a circle. You will now also bear more of the job of being a fairly major feeder of attention, a difficult job to do consistently well. You will have to apply more work to motivate the class because they will share less with each other. Therefore, it will be more difficult to make your lessons inductive. It will be easier for students to hide, and some may withdraw because of diminished stimulation from each other. There may be some authority-transfer effect and "class vs. teacher" feeling that may be a source of some discipline problems.

The horseshoe also requires many of the facilitative skills of the circle to teach well while using it. And, it also has most of the same difficulties regarding learning students' names and taking attendance as the circle. So, for Tips on Setting up Horseshoe, follow those Tips on Setting up a Circle, above. However, for many, the horseshoe, rather than the circle, is the best compromise. It has many more advantages than rows and requires less work and skill than sitting in a circle.

In Rows

17. The Pros: By using a Delaney book, or other similar record keeper, you can easily learn names and take attendance. You will have less interactive noise, comments between students, or digressions to control. You will have more of their attention. You will have no problem with arranging the class in rows because usually the teachers before and after your class also use rows. The students won't have to get used to the arrangement. You can collect and hand out things easily by rows. It requires less work and skills than the circle or horseshoe. It works well for teaching that is mainly delivering one-way factual information and note-taking.

The Cons: The class will not be prone to participate much in your lesson. Since they only see the backs of each others' heads and you, you and only you must find ways to encourage participation against the tide of the seating arrangement. Also, if they do look at each other to participate, they will have to turn their heads and bodies to look at each other. This may seem like a "discipline problem" for you, since they're turning away from you. So miscalls will be difficult to identify. You will be prone to reprimand students for the wrong reason, which will cause resentment that may cause more discipline problems. Also, students will seldom share ideas or feelings with each other about the lesson and won't listen to each other so much. You'll often be forced to repeat students' comments, questions, and answers to the whole class. You'll have to be the major feeder of attention to each student. You'll be in a "baseball umpire" position and called unfair by some people almost all the time. It will be difficult to teach inductively because students will be reluctant to give you their experiences to start the inductive process. More students can easily hide behind each other and withdraw. All the weight of stimulating them will fall on you. There will be strong authority-transfer, and feelings of "class vs. teacher," which will be a constant source of disruptive behavior that you'll have to work hard to keep canceling out. You will have to stifle the peer energy and interaction they feel and need for their natural psychological development.

Tips for Setting Up Rows: You will need little help here. If you decide to use rows, just keep them neat and orderly. As far as taking attendance and learning names, the procedures for these are easy. We will discuss these below.

Which Arrangement to Choose
18. Decide by reviewing the four caveats we discussed on pp. 186–187. Also, decide by the fact that circles (if done well) generate fewer discipline problems than horseshoes, and rows generate the most problems but require less work and skill. You may decide to go through the trouble of changing the seating arrangement for different learning activities: rows for lectures, horseshoes for lectures with student interaction, circles for total discussion. For instance, on Monday you may give a factual lesson on the American Civil War in rows. On Tuesday, you may put the class in a circle, or horseshoe, and have them share their reactions to Mondays lesson. For tests, you might go back to rows to eliminate cheating. However, I must warn you that too much change creates anxiety in youngsters, which can turn into disruptive behavior. Sameness, stability, a class that feels like its own consistent "world" will calm your students. Also, consider the arrangement that causes you fewer problems with your administration. You may not wish to put in the energy and negotiation to do the arrangement that is not typical for your school. If you do decide to try a seating arrangement not typical for your school, either talk to or write your principal, beforehand. Don't argue. Just list your reasons for your desire (use the "Pros" l listed above) and express your negative feelings in the context of your concerns (use the "Cons" I listed above).[88]

Other Tips on Seating Arrangements
19. No matter which arrangement(s) you use, make sure you can easily be seen by your students.

20. Make sure that the seats are not on top of each other. If they are too close to each other, students will be disruptive accidentally for want of their own sense of space.

21. Make sure you are near enough to them to be able to touch them, e.g., give them an approving pat on the shoulder, etc. Or just walk around a lot to be near them.

22. Try to have as few seats face the windows as possible.

23. Leave a good traffic pattern no matter which seating arrangement you choose.

---

[88]For further thoughts on these seating arrangement decisions consult: S. Axelrod et al. "Comparison of Two Common Classroom Seating Arrangements," *Academic Therapy* (Sept. 23–31, 1979).

24. Leave an empty chair near the back entrance door (if you have one), or near the front door, for latecomers.

c. Your procedures

The procedures suggested here are only those that shape the "world" of your classroom: its environment.[89] These are procedures that set up how students enter your classroom, how attendance is taken, and how the environment is used.

How Students Enter Your Classroom

25. From our discussion in (b) above, you should have arranged for the seating arrangement of your choice to be in order prior to student arrival. Again, you might leave an empty chair near the front or back door for latecomers, who then do not have to walk in front of the room or around the room to get settled.

26. You might allow them to take any seats they wish. Then, you can use this privilege as a reward or punishment. A student who disturbs the class loses his or her seat (near a friend). Or, for the convenience of learning names and taking attendance, each student enters and must take his/her assigned seat.

27. Have a "do-now!" assignment already on the chalkboard that they must do immediately in their notebook for that day and period. The best "do-now!" is short (and takes about five minutes while you take attendance). It may be either about the last class, the homework or a warm-up for today's lesson. Also, the best "do-now!" does not ask them to do too much. Instead, it asks that they: "write a sentence for each . . ." or "fill in these blanks," or "match these," or "place in correct order," or "find the mistake," etc. These little exercises should also start with the easiest and maybe even with an example of the correct answer. To ask them to do too much, with difficulties, is to run the risk that they will get overwhelmed and turn off in the first five minutes of the period.[90]

28. if your classroom is not the same room each period, you will find it difficult to get a "do-now!" onto the chalkboard in time. Then, prepare a "hand-out" that you give each student as s/he enters your room. Hand it to each student, look at them directly, and say something like, "This is for right now!" Or write "Do task-sheet no. 3 Now." on the chalkboard. You can number these "do-now!" task sheets, title them with the name of the task, and have

---

[89]For specific procedures that safeguard your rules, handle calling out, latecomers, homework, fighting, cheating, etc., see Chapter 13.
[90]See Chapter 15, section C for good examples of "do-nows!" in the form of "task sheets."

simple directions written boldly at the top. These task sheets should follow the guidelines I gave in the previous paragraph (no. 27), or simply say things like: "Place an X next to the items in your homework you had trouble with; place a checkmark next to those that were easy; place a ? next to ones you have questions about."[91]

Taking Attendance and Learning Names

29. If you decide to use rows as your seating arrangement and assigned seats, you have decided on the simplest way of taking attendance and learning names. Use a Delaney book with cards set up for each period you teach. (Any chairperson or fellow teacher can show you how it's used.)

30. If you use a horseshoe, or circle, instruct the students to print their names in bold letters on the top of their "do-now!" sheet. Then, walk around the room during the "do-now!" and check off the attendance of each student in a Delaney book or on a list with columns for each attendance day. Or you may wish to make your own Delaney book with slots in a circle or horseshoe for the Delaney cards.

31. If you do not want to assign seats (but allow them to choose seats that can then be used as reward or punishment) or just really want them and you to learn each student's name (for full circle and horseshoe participation), then you might want to try the following: (a) Right after the "do-now!" ask a student to volunteer an answer from the "do-now!" or from the homework (or simply ask an opinion question, or feeling question that has no correct answer, but warms up today's lesson). (b) Then ask that volunteered student's name, and thank him or her. (c) Then, ask for a volunteer (for another answer, opinion, or feeling) sitting next to the last volunteer. This student not only gives his or her answer, opinion, or feeling, but also has to name the previous student's name and his or her own name. (d) The next person in the row, or horseshoe, or circle then gives his or her response and the previous names of the other students and his or her own name. (e) This is done all around the entire room until the last person gives his or her response and repeats all the names of all the previous students in the class.

This procedure might take (for the first week or so) half the period. But, by the second week, it will take only ten minutes, and you may only wish to do it once a week. It doesn't waste time. Students help each other learn names. They use their peer energy to answer your question about a fact, an opinion, or feeling about the lesson. You and they learn each others' names. And you now have a class that will participate more, be called on easily, and feel warmer to each other. The system is designed such that it forces listening and

---

[91]For more ideas and examples of "task sheets," see Chapter 15, section C.

learning by repetition. Then, once you have done this system for about a month, you are free to have them sit in rows, horseshoes, or circles according to your needs for the lesson without problems about learning names or taking attendance.

How the Environment Is Used

32. Post or write on the chalkboard or bulletin board such things as: (a) your general rules; (b) homework assignments; (c) the "do-now!" assignment; (d) the topics to be covered today. If you move from room to room, you'll have to reserve a space in each room for your (a), but you can write up (b), (c), and (d) onto newsprint and tape them onto the chalkboard each period you move to a different room.

33. If you have the same room, or only a few rooms to go to, post their work, or the past topics or past "do-nows!" on the side bulletin boards to remind them of where the class has been. Use the bulletin boards to build a sense of "their world": tradition, remembrances, uniformity.

34. Don't use thumbtacks on the bulletin board. Instead, post things by opening up the stapler and stapling things onto the bulletin board. Students tend to pull out thumbtacks, and use them to post items you have no control over or remove items you want left up. With staples, since they're harder to remove, the bulletin boards will stay more in your control.

35. Don't post anything that is either too distracting or requires a lot of attention to be understood.

36. There should be both a clock and a large calendar that are easily visible somewhere in the front of the room. You should cross out past dates or circle upcoming important dates. Make it a practice to demarcate where you were, are, and are going with your lessons.

The Bathroom Pass

37. Either forbid any bathroom going midclass, which is my preference (they must learn to go before or after), or place one bathroom pass by the door. Set rules for its use. For example: (a) You can only use it once during the period; (b) you can only use it once a week; (c) you must leave your name by the small table where the pass is before you use it. Do not use a sign-out book. Students will then take too long signing it and getting attention in front of the room. Instead, if they wish to use the pass, they write their name down on a small piece of paper (with the time, period, and date) at their seat. When the pass becomes available, they take the pass and leave this paper (already written) by the pass. You can collect these little bathroom-pass papers at the end of the period to check if anyone has violated, e.g., rule (b) above. Don't keep the pass on your desk. Leave it near the door so bathroom goers are less in front of the room. And instruct students to go around the back of the class, instead of passing in front of you. For students who violate the rules, rescind the privilege. If bathroom going becomes a problem, rescind the whole procedure and tell them they must go before or after the period.

The Pencil Sharpener

38. Don't have one. (For grades K–6, however, you'll need one. But you can still eliminate the problem here. See p. 215, "Survival Tools," #49.) If there's one in the room, unscrew it and give it away to another teacher. Require that students bring a pen and two sharpened pencils. If they don't have these, or can't write, they may wish to be in a situation of always having to borrow a pencil or a pen. But warn them that if they become a discipline problem (a disruption to others or your teaching), they will be punished. Or, if they don't become disruptive borrowers, but just sit there unprepared, they may <u>not</u> borrow from you, they may not get the homework, or they fail today's quiz. Thereby, they may just fail the whole marking period if unprepared often. Recommend to those whose pencils need sharpening, they buy a mechanical pencil. Today they are very inexpensive (about $1.30), hold extra leads, and last a long time. If you choose to have a pencil sharpener in your room, be prepared to enforce elaborate rules that eliminate its noise and it becoming a stage for just fooling around.

Miscellaneous

39. Keep a garbage pail by the back door, or one also by the front door, but not next to your desk. Do not allow students to throw paper away during the class period. They can throw away paper as they enter or when they leave the class at the end of the period. They must (and you should) hold onto it during the period. This will stop the garbage pail from becoming a scene of disruptive stagings of basketball shots into the pail near your desk.

40. Leave custodians notes if you are having problems with lighting, heat, windows, etc. Follow these up and thank them.

41. It's probably always best to leave the windows slightly open (at the top) so the room is cool rather than too warm and lethargic.

42. Learn where the sun comes in during what periods and note this to yourself as a reminder, e.g., to pull down the back shade for the third period.

43. Arrange the furnishings such that there is some private place in the room where you can, e.g., reprimand a student without an audience reaction while the class works on an assignment. Or see the student after class.[92]

---

[92]We shall discuss how to handle the: "See me after class!" in Chapter 13, section A.

E. Being Well Equipped

Your environment is also shaped by the equipment you have. Often little tools of the trade bring your classroom more under your control. You may not be able to obtain all of the items below, but your job will be easier and have fewer disruptions if you can get and do some of the following:

"Survival Tools" You Can Carry with You in a Pencil Case

Item	Its Use
44. a piece of chalk	**44.** just in case the room you're going to has none
45. an eraser (or small rag)	**45.** just in case the room you're going to has none
46. perhaps a piece of colored chalk	**46.** in case you wish to <u>underscore</u> something you wrote last period or will write today
47. a few rubber bands	**47.** in case you need to band some things together
48. a "3M post-it pad"	**48.** in case you wish to stick a note onto your or a student's book, paper, etc. They are self-sticking.
49. a mechanical lead pencil	**49.** they are always sharp; no need to find a pencil sharpener; and such pencil notes are always fine, clear, and erasable
50. press-on white labels	**50.** with either address label size or one-line width labels, you can "white-out" anything or label anything
51. a black ink ballpoint pen	**51.** such a pen can be used best for clear carbon copies, for writing down things more reproducible by a copier than a blue ink pen
52. a few 3 × 5 cards	**52.** They can be used for participation exercises,[93] notes that you can make to yourself that can be sorted, for passes, etc.

---

[93]We will discuss many participation exercises in Chapter 14, section E.

53. a yellow hi-liter pen

53. to hi-lite points in your lesson plan for yourself that you skipped, went over, need to review, etc.

54. a red pen

54. if you choose to use it for evaluation notes to students on tests, homework, etc.

55. some looseleaf reinforcements

55. to keep loose pages from falling out of your lesson plan looseleaf book

56. a "wash'n dri"

56. for handy cleanups when no water is available

57. a single-edged razor blade

57. instead of bulky scissors for cutting out articles, pictures, etc. from magazines for your class; they usually come with a protective cardboard over the single-edged blade

58. a small tin of aspirin

58. in case of a headache

59. some large and small paper clips

59. to clip homework or test papers together from a particular class period

60. a piece of carbon paper

60. in case you wish to have a copy of any note you write home or give a student

61. a see-through plastic pencil case that zippers closed

61. to carry all the items above (44–60)

62. an appointment book

62. to keep track of your weekly appointments, things "to do," etc.

63. a couple of dimes or quarters or a phone credit card

63. to be able to easily make a phone call to a parent, friend, or home, or to the garage where your car is being fixed, etc.

Things That Should Be Readily Accessible in Your Desk Drawer or Closet

Item	Its Use
64. a Delaney book	**64.** for taking attendance, checking homework, giving credit for class participation

65. a newsprint pad

65. so you can note things on newsprint with a magic marker, tape it up, or take it down for items you want to save (instead of being erasable on the chalkboard)

66. a magic marker, or two

66. for use with #65

67. 5 × 8 cards

67. can also be used as in #65 above

68. a portable chalkboard

68. you can write on and wheel or carry into the next class to use as in #65 above

69. a stapler

69. For posting items on the bulletin board or putting papers together so you don't have to worry that paper clips may fall off

70. cardboard to place over entrance door window

70. to cut down on hallway distractions

71. a small can of machine oil

71. in case you discover a squeaky seat that students like to use to distract the class

72. E. Lement's *Teacher's Guide to Free Curriculum Materials.* Write: Progress Services, Inc., 214 Center St., Randolph, WI 53956

72. tells you where to write for free posters, maps, charts, pictures, etc., for Social Studies, Language Arts, Guidance, Science, and other curriculum curriculum subjects. It's updated every year.

Computer Resources

- *NetLearning: Why Teachers Use the Internet* **by Serim and Koch (Songline Studios Inc., Calif., 1996).** [1-800-998-9938] Their website: **http://www.songline.com/teachers** also has a list of additional education sites, some of which have been listed here.
- *World Wide Web for Teachers* by Ray Cafolla (Allyn & Bacon, Boston) 1996.

- **T.H.E. technological horizons in education Journal** at:
  http://www.thejournal.com/   for: coolsites
  roadmap/cool.html
  substitute: **roadmap/resources.html**   for: education resources
  substitute: **roadmap/socsci.html**   for: social sciences
  substitute: **roadmap/history.html**   for: history
  substitute: **roadmap/math.html**   for: math
  substitute: **roadmap/cultures.html**   for: cultures
  substitute: **roadmap/states.html**   for: state education departments
  substitute: **roadmap/govinfo.html**   for: government information
  substitute: **roadmap/grants.html**   for: grants and funding
  substitute: **roadmap/tools.html**   for: educational tools
  substitute: **roadmap/orgs.html**   for: education organizations
  substitute: **roadmap/hardsci.html**   for: science
  substitute: **roadmap/langarts.html**   for: language arts
  substitute: **roadmap/reference.html**   for: reference materials
  substitute: **roadmap/starter.html**   for: ways to get started online
  substitute: **roadmap/search.html**   for: search engines

Getting your school on-line

73. Getting U.S. Teachers On-line http://quest.arc.nasa.gov/online/ table.html
NASA provides this excellent resource, a list of education on-line service providers organized by state. This listing provides contact names and information about the service for educators looking to connect themselves and their schools. This is a great place to start if you are searching for an Internet connection.

74. Co-NECT http://co-nect.bbn.com/WWW/co-nect.html
Co-NECT (Cooperative Networked Educational Community for Tomorrow) is a school restructuring design created by a team of educators at Bolt, Beranek, and Newman, Inc., that works with schools to plan and implement restructuring. Districts pay Co-NECT for the whole-school framework and design brought to the school. Co-NECT schools group students in small clusters taught by a cross-disciplinary teaching team. Students remain in the same clusters with the same teachers for at least two years. The curriculum revolves around real-world projects that give every student an opportunity to acquire critical skills and academic understanding. The schools are also equipped with LANs, WANs, and desktop connectivity to the Internet.

75. NetTeach News http://www.chaos.com/netteach/
This is one of the longest running publications on networking and K–12

education and covers what is happening in and out of the classroom with K–12 networking.

76. Teaching with Technology http://www.wam.umd.edu/~mlhall/ teaching.html
A collection of links related to using electronic technologies in the classroom.

77. U.S. Department of Education http://www.ed.gov
From Goals 2000 to upcoming grants, the Department of Education provides a collection of resources for teachers, parents, and researchers. In addition to statistics, research results, calendars of events, and links to other educational resources, users can search Department of Education documents and request them to be sent via postal mail.

Education information

78. SurfWatch http://www.surfwatch.com/
SurfWatch blocks sexually explicit materials from reaching any individual computer.

79. AskERIC http://ericir.sunsite.syr.edu
Here you'll find a variety of lesson plans, including the curriculum for the "Newton's Apple" series that appears on PBS. The ERIC database, with the assistance of a searchable index and AskERIC's responsive staff, provides information on curriculum, instructional practices, and many other related educational issues.

80. The American Federation of Teachers http://www.aft.org (1-800-936-7100)

81. The National Association of Secondary School Principals http:// www.NASSP.org

82. EdWeb http://k12cnidr.org:90/resource.cntnts.html
If you're searching for some thoughts on education, reform, and technology, make a stop at EdWeb. You'll also find catalogs of mailing lists, newsgroups, and Web sites for education. Some good, thought-provoking articles about the use of the Web in K–12 education are located here.

83. Education Week http://www.edweek.org
Nothing short of being the place on the World Wide Web for people interested in education reform, schools, and the policies that guide them: education

archives, weekly education news, teacher magazines, special reports, education searches, etc.

84. PBS Online http://www.pbs.org/

PBS provides many resources for K–12 education. Educators in search of PBS schedules with videotaping rights will find them here, along with teacher guides and information about educational services available from their local PBS affiliate. This site also contains curriculum materials in a variety of disciplines (art, math, and social studies) that complement its programming and electronic field trips. Another PBS resource is PBS PREVIEWS, a free weekly on-line newsletter offering the latest information about PBS on-line and upcoming prime-time public television.

85. Teacher Talk http://www.mightymedia.com/talk/working.htm

A "Teacher's Lounge" on the Web where teachers can exchange ideas and find support from other educators struggling with the same questions.

86. Scholastic Network http://www.scholastic.com

Provides the publisher's services in general, including *The Magic SchoolBus*.

87. Global SchoolNet Foundation http://www.gsn.org/

Here you'll find a wealth of innovative on-line projects and supporting software, such as CU-SeeMe, available via FTP. SCHLNet Newsgroups are also worth a look. Global SchoolNet Foundation hosts many special on-line events for K–12 education. They also provide a project registry where you can advertise your own projects and find out about other resources.

88. Video Placement Worldwide http://www.vpw.com

Free sponsored videos and other education materials by requesting titles and grade level.

On-line field trips

89. The Birmingham Zoo http://www.bhm.tisnet/zoo/

90. Electronic Zoo http://netvet.wustl.edu............................

The Electronic Zoo is a comprehensive reference to animal resources located on the Internet. The Zoo's massive collection is, nevertheless, easy to navigate, with links grouped by both subject (animals, veterinary) and resource type (mailing lists, Gopher and Web sites). Sponsored by NetVet, the Zoo is a well-maintained site with a search facility, what's new list, and continual updates. This is a great place to go to visit and learn about animals without removing them from their natural habitat.

91. The Field Museum: http://www.bvis/uic/edu/museum/Dna_To_ Dinosaurs.html

92. ArtsEdge http://arsedge,kennedy-center.org
Here you'll find an electronic magazine covering the arts and the ArtsEdge Information Gallery, a collection of professional development resources, program information, and research on the arts and education. ArtsEdge also highlights the arts at work in classrooms. The goal of this site is to support the integration of the arts in the K–12 curriculum.

Language arts

93. Human Language Page http://www.willamette.edu/~tjones/Language-Page.html
This rich resource offers a variety of materials for students studying almost any language. You'll find lessons, dictionaries, phrases and words for travelers, audio clips, and various alphabets. The site also links to a variety of other resources addressing language and culture.

94. The Complete Works of William Shakespeare http://the-tech.mit.edu/ Shakespeare/works.html
Read Shakespeare texts on-line, download them, or search all of Shakespeare's works in a variety of ways, including for the occurrence of specified words.

95. Children's Literature Web Guide http://www.ucalgary.ca/~dkbrown/
The Children's Literature Web Guide contains a rich resource from on-line books to children's creations. In the Information about Authors section, you'll find listings for Lewis Carroll, Madeleine L'Engle, and Dr. Seuss, among many others. Resources for parents, teachers, and storytellers are also included.

96. National Council of Teachers of English http://www.NCTE.org
The National Council of Teachers of English, the world's largest subject matter educational association, is devoted to improving the teaching of English and the language arts at all levels of education. NCTE publishes a member newspaper, "The Council Chronicle," plus three monthly journals: *Language Arts, English Journal,* and *College English;* and ten quarterlies. Each year, NCTE publishes fifteen to twenty new books for teachers of English and the language arts at the elementary, secondary, and college levels. These books deal with current issues and problems in teaching, research findings and their application to classrooms, ideas for teaching all aspects of English, and other topics.

Math and science

97. Geometry Center http://www.geom.umn.edu
Courtesy of the Science and Technology Center at the University of Minnesota, you can manipulate geometric figures based on a variety of real-world questions and applications. Students can see how geometry relates to the world around them. You'll also find curriculum ideas and workshop information sponsored by the Center.

98. The Math Forum (formerly known as the Geometry Forum) http://forum.swarthmore.edu/
Ask Dr. Math (a.k.a. the SWAT team) is a group of students and world-famous mathematicians ready to answer K–12 students' math questions. Students can also test their mathematics skills by answering the Problems of the Week. This forum contains a searchable database of mathematics resources.

99. MegaMath http://www.c3.lanl.gov/mega-math
Explore infinity and beyond with elementary students through hands-on activities provided by the MegaMath project, led by Los Alamos Labs

100. NASA's Spacelink http://spacelink.msfc.nasa.gov/
Travel throughout the galaxy with information and images from NASA's Spacelink. This site offers a wide range of materials (computer text files, software, and graphics) related to the space program. Its target audience is teachers, administrators, and students. Documents on the system include science, math, engineering and technology education lesson plans, historical information related to the space program, current status reports on NASA projects, news releases, information on NASA educational programs, NASA educational publications, and other materials chosen for their educational value and relevance to the space program. Materials on the system are organized and kept current by professional educators with experience in computer software applications and communications. Images such as Olympus Mons, the largest volcano in our solar system, are available from this site.

Social studies

101. K–12 History on the Internet: A Resource Guide http://www.xs4all,nl/ ~swanson/history/home.html
This is a narrative collection of existing online projects and a number of Internet-based resources for history and social studies teachers.

Where students can publish on the net

**102.   BushScene   http://www.bushnet.qld.edu.au/schools/herberton_
secondary/bushscen/index.htm**
An international teen magazine completely written and created by the students
of Herberton State School Secondary Department in Far North Queensland,
Australia. They invite students to contribute content and have many resources
that other teens may find fun or useful. Check out the Problem Page, where you
can seek advice from the sage staff, or the Rage Page, the ultimate graffiti area
where anyone can leave a comment. This is a great example of what students
can do on the Web.

**103.   Children's   Voice   gopher??vmsgopher.cua.edu.:70/or3719639416
gopher_root_eric_ae%3a%5b_edres.feb%5d9502.txt%3b5**
Children's Voice is a mailing list dedicated to sharing the writing of children
from kindergarten through grade eight. Writing is submitted via e-mail. All
submissions are sent to all subscribers, who are invited to print out copies of
works that interest them and share them with their students. Teachers and
students are also encouraged to e-mail young authors with their feedback.
Children's Voice is a Canadian mailing list, but languages other than English
or French are welcome.

104. KidPub http://engarde.com/kidpub/intro.html
KidPub is an open forum for children of all ages to publish their writing on
the World Wide Web. Anyone is welcome to submit poetry, stories, and news
about their schools and towns via e-mail for publication or to contribute a
paragraph to the current collaborative writing project. KidPub is a free service
offered by En-Garde Technical Communication. MidLink Magazine is a bi-
monthly on-line magazine, created by and for children ages 10–15, to link
middle schools around the world. Each issue features student writing and
electronic artwork organized around a theme, and readers are encouraged to
submit their own work for publication. This magazine also sponsors a variety
of on-line educational projects in which all schools are invited to participate.
MidLink Magazine is a collaborative project created by several middle schools
and hosted by the University of Central Florida.

Search engines

105. Yahoo http://www.yahoo.com
Yahoo features a hierarchically organized subject tree of information resources
that have registered. It offers limited search options but is often a useful
starting place because of its large database of authoritative sources.

106. WebCrawler http://webcrawler.com
WebCrawler is lightning fast and returns a weighty list of links. It analyzes the full text of documents, allowing the searcher to locate keywords that may have been buried deep within a document's text.

107. Lycos htto://lycos.cs.cmu.edu/
Lycos is named after a quick and agile ground spider. It searches document titles, headings, links, and keywords and returns the first fifty words of each page it indexes for your search. Its search engine is more configurable than WebCrawler.

108. Excite http//www.excite.com
Excite currently contains searches of 1.5 million Web pages and two weeks of Usenet news articles and classified ads as well as links to current news, weather, etc. It presents results with a detailed summary to provide you with an annotated selection.

Periodicals

109. Netteach News netteach@chaos.com in print and online.

110. Classroom Connect Newsletter connect@wentworth.com or 1-800-638-1639, in print and on-line.

Behavior problems

111. Preventing Classroom Discipline Problems http://www.panix.com/ ~pro-ed
A training video for teachers and prospective educators and a comprehensive handbook (with training exercises) for the diagnoses, prevention, and handling of classroom disruptive behavior (without the necessity of revamping a school's entire program.)

112. Solving Discipline Problems: Methods and... http://www.abacon. com:80/books/ab_0205165699.html
Because no one model can work successfully for all children at all times, the task is to show teachers how to draw from the various models and employ a variety of techniques. This book not only examines the various approaches or models but it uses The Teacher Behavior Continuum, which enables teachers to evaluate the power inherent in the various approaches.

In summary, if you can try some of these suggestions and find some control over: (a) the physical setting itself; (b) the seating arrangement; (c) your procedures; (d) the equipment you have, you will have eliminated many sources of discipline problems. Again, if some of these environmental controls require negotiation with your administration, don't demand or criticize. State your concerns, feelings, and needs. Listen to the administrators' difficulties, and try not to act alone; try to round up a few teachers who also have the same concerns and work as a team. Also, remember the four caveats: (1) implementation of any of these suggestions above will, at first, require more work; (2) only do what's congruent for you; (3) don't abandon a suggestion as incongruent until you really give it a good try; (4) don't fret if you can't apply many of these suggestions.

F. Especially for Grades K–6

Some of the above suggestions may also be helpful for grades K–6. But the elementary grades often require specific, unique preparations to ward off early childhood kinds of disruptive behaviors.

a. Learning how to duck

Of course, as in the above suggestions, if you are on a break, or just walking through the cafeteria, and you hear a child down the hall or at lunch "curse," don't go after it if it comes under criteria 1–9 on pp. 198–199. But, more often, you should also try to duck if "venting" happens in your own class (after all, you'll be with the same kids for almost six hours). Here, however, besides ducking, you may want to stop and instruct a child about a better use of language or a better way for him/her to handle their anger and frustration, especially if other children have heard the improper reaction and may be prone to imitate it.

b. Dealing with disturbances right outside your classroom

Some of the above may already be helpful, especially the suggestion on p. 202 (e). In addition, you may need some help with: (1) being too near the playground and (2) parents who seem to just drop by all the time and disturb your class because they need to "talk to you for a minute," especially at "drop off" in the morning.

1. Of course, you can try to ask for a classroom that is <u>not</u> near the playground. If kids can see the playground, they will "always" want to go there or

watch what's happening there. If necessary, close the blinds or pull down the shades of windows that look that way. Or turn seats away from that area.

2. Give every parent a sheet that lists many ways to talk to you or see you—to ward off their tendency to bother you at the wrong times. You can list any or all of the following:

- Give your home phone number and an hour that is good for you to talk.
- Give the phone number in the teacher's lounge where you are during your "prep" period and the times you usually will be there.
- Give the times and phone number of your aide (paraprofessional) who can be reached (Sometimes, the parent only needs to give a simple message that the aide can handle.) (Be sure to check this policy with your administration. Many schools have the policy that only teachers can talk to parents to avoid confusion about school policies, etc.)
- Send notes with your children. You can read these in your prep period and call the parents or answer the notes that need it. Often, parent comments are merely informative, e.g., "Johnny is going home with Billy today." Have a box or envelope in your classroom where students can place these notes. You can also place an envelope outside your classroom door where parents can drop off notes themselves. (It's a good idea to put blank paper and a pen with it so they don't disrupt your class to ask for them.)
- Ask that parents not come to the classroom at all in the beginning of the day four days a week. In exchange, offer a fifteen minute "open house" one day a week, when they can come in the room at the beginning of the day, see their child's work, talk to you, play a game, or read a book with their child, etc. This is also good because it promotes independence and responsibility in your students, i.e., they have to hang up their own coats and lunchboxes, turn in their own homework, etc.
- You can talk briefly to parents as they pick up their child at recess, e.g., in the school yard.

  You can also place an envelope on your door where parents can leave you notes with their phone number (if necessary) and a good time when you can call them, after you've read their note.

All of the above, with the reminder, "Please do not talk to me at 'drop off' or during class," will deter the problem.

c. Working on the environment of your classroom

1. The Physical Setting

The first thing to work on here is the seating arrangements and work spaces or activity centers. The students need to see clearly where they belong and what they do in each area. The room arrangement also should allow them to interact with each other, yet have enough individual work space at their table or desk, and also allow them easy access to your anention and approval. You'll need to decide where bookcases, student desk/tables, work areas, and your desk should go. These should not only allow for interaction among the kids, individual work space, and access to you but also be arranged in a good traffic pattern. Many elementary education texts have much good detailed suggestions on these physical arrangements. The author suggests *The Learning Environment,* Loughlin & Suina (Teachers College Press, 1982.) or *Getting Started in the New York City Public Schools* [phone: (718) 935-3320] as one of the best in this area. Some floor plans (suggested by *Getting Started in the New.York City Public Schools,* N.Y.C. Board of Education, 1992, pp. 61–63) are shown here:

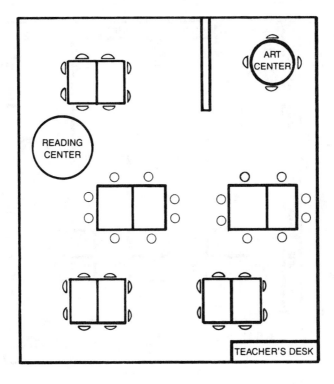

In your floor plan, you may also want to arrange a specific area to use "time out." Often, in Kindergarten, a child may be punished by removing him

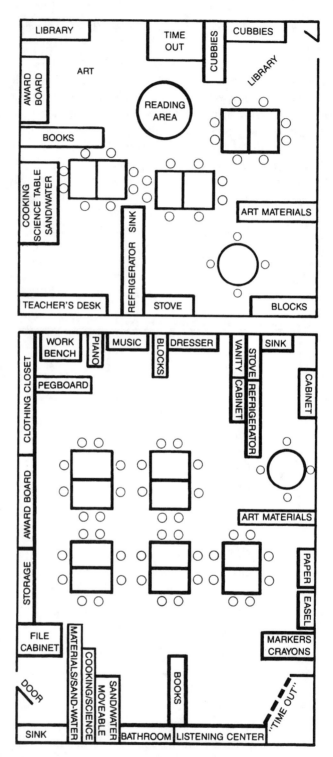

or her from the activity, you, and all the other students for a "cooling down" time ("time out") where the disruptive child must sit and get no attention for a specific period of time. Obviously, this space needs to be a private area where a child can sit safely, facing away from other kids, and have little or no access to toys, games, or fun of any kind.

Be careful of planning to change your seating arrangement too often, however. It is more advisable to find a seating arrangement that is congruent with your style of teaching and stick with it than to change the seats constantly. Take some time to experiment to find out which arangements you like, but once you have them, don't plan on changing your room during the day or even daily. It takes young children a long time to help you move furniture and you may end up moving furniture more than you teach! They also need predictability and consistency in their environment as much as they do in your teaching. In elementary classrooms, it is often possible to arrange the room so that you have many types of spaces at once. You may arrange the desks in groups for seat work and cooperative learning and then have a large rug in the front of the room for a meeting area or whole class discussions. Then you can rearrange the chairs into a horseshoe at the end of the month when you have finished your unit of study and the children are doing presentations for each other. When you move the desks back to the small groups, take advantage of the fact that you are moving furniture anyway to mix up the people at each table group. When you are considering how to arrange your room, ask colleagues for advice, and take a minute to glance back through *The Learning Environment* by Loughlin & Souina (Teachers College Press, 1982).

Regarding the walls and environs of your room, you need to be able to display student's work, signs, calendars, the alphabet, etc. Some teachers also hang clotheslines across the room to hang small projects, art work, photos, etc. On bulletin boards, you may wish to post calendars, "who lost a tooth," a weather chart, numbers, a morning message, "word of the week," who will do "the pledge" today, rules, etc. On the chalkboard you should post the outline or schedule of the day and a "Problem of the Day" or "Daily Challenge" type of assignment. The main thing is to use your physical space to give children recognition and to create a sense of a "world" in your classroom. You should post an outline of the day in a clearly visible location so that the students can predict the schedule as they move from one activity to another.

All materials in your classroom should have a clearly defined location where they belong. These locations should be clearly labeled so that you and the students know where they are and the students can find them and use them on their own. Make sure that you prepare any manipulatives (Manipulatives refer to materials that students physically manipulate to better understand a concept, e.g., pattern blocks, cuisenaire rods, unifix cubes, and bean counters etc.) or other materials in advance so that they are easily distributed when needed. Multiple sheets should be stapled together in packets; math manipulatives should be in easy-to-carry bins, etc.

2. Your Procedures

Procedures need to be very clear and easily understood in grades K–6. Children need to know clearly "how to be good" in your classroom. Routines need to be spelled out, followed in the same way each day to form a tradition in your classroom, or "how we do things" in here. You may wish the class to participate in the formation of the rules. This philosophy has its pros and cons. (See p. 27, J. my review of Keating's *A Guide to Positive Discipline.*) Again, there are many texts that suggest procedures for grades K–6, but below is a list of the procedures you need to prepare for, with a brief guideline (in parentheses) after each one:

(a) Have a sign on your door where your class is when you need to take them somewhere else, e.g., the playground. (These places can be on 3 × 5 cards so you can just tack up the appropriate one from the set in an envelope on the door.)

(b) Explain how students should come in and put their things away each morning they enter the classroom. (You should have individual "cubbies" for each child.)

(c) Have clear ways you start and transition to activities. (You may use an "attention signal" where the lights go on and off to give them directions. Call them by rows or tables. Leave time for cleanup.)

(d) Especially for grades 2–6, you may wish to start the class with a "do-now." (See Chapter 15C.)

(e) Have clear procedures for taking attendance. (Assign seats or let them choose but have a "seating chart" or a place where they turn over their name or photo (K–1) when they arrive; or use a "roll book," or have them write their names on an attendance sheet.)

(f) Have a clear procedure for lateness. (Students who enter can place "late passes" in a designated folder you can read and record later. This may not be necessary for K–1; see Chapter 12, section F.)

(g) Appoint monitors. (They can volunteer or be chosen by you for special recognition. The "jobs" should be clear, perhaps posted on a bulletin board each day. In K–1 this may be easier when the bathroom is in the classroom.)

(h) Decide how materials are given out and handled. (You may wish to use monitors for this, and only certain students each week are allowed to get the materials from "supply stations." Demonstrate how the materials and/or equipment are to be properly used.)

(i) Instruct and monitor cleanup procedures. (Give recognition and approval to desks that have been cleaned up well. Do not allow students to be able to go on to the next activity until they have cleaned up.)

(j) Explain fire drill procedures. (You may want to role play them with the class in slow motion. Decide, e.g., who will turn off the lights. Post and explain a map of the exits.)

(k) Explain and monitor bathroom procedures. (Use a "bathroom pass" and a sign out/in book. Decide limits to the frequency of using the pass and the length of time one can be excused to go. In K–1 this may be easier when the bathroom is in the classroom.)

3. Survival Tools

Although all of the listed tools on pp. 215–225 and all the computer resources listed are useful, a teacher of grades K–6 may also want to have these:

115. an ample supply of pens, pencils, washable markers, and paper for children "to borrow" This will also help you with the traffic to the pencil sharpener. (See #128 below.)
116. crayons, colored chalk
117. rulers
118. safe scissors
119. a teacher-only stapler
120. glue
121. a yard stick
122. a room clock
123. erasers
124. self-stick blank labels
125. storage boxes (clear ones are best)
126. forms [prepared beforehand, handmade for your specific needs, where you or a child can easily fill in the blank(s)]
127. a hammer, screw driver, pliers, some screws, and nails
128. a pencil sharpener (for teacher's use only: have a supply of sharpened pencils on hand. If a student's pencil point breaks by accident, give him one of your sharpened pencils, instead of having kids always going to the pencil sharpener.)

G. Teachers Share Their Growing Pains[94]

Ducking

I learned to duck about a year ago, when I realized that it helps to minimize the amount of confrontations I have with my students. There was a time, however, when I would take things students said and did very personally.

---

[94]These are comments from teachers who have already gone through the training offered in this book.

When a student cursed, I got very upset. When I first started teaching, I thought that students just didn't respect me when they cursed. I finally realized that cursing is part of their vocabulary, and it has nothing to do with respect. I feel much better now that I do not take things personally.

• • •

In retrospect, I realize that I should have let a lot of things slide. I took things too personally, which is not to say that many of the students' comments weren't blatantly disrespectful, but, as discussed, one cannot force respect.

• • •

I once had an experience that, now that I look back, I should have ducked. There is a student in my class that I find obnoxious. This student left my class to sit in another teacher's office and read yearbooks. When I confronted this student, I told her that this was inappropriate and that she would receive no credit for participating. This student then smirked at me, which drove me crazy (I think if it was from any other student I would have let it slide by). I told her to wipe the smirk off her face. Of course, this only led to a verbal match in which there was no winner.

Disturbances Right Outside Your Classroom

Over the past year I have taught in many different classrooms. Some of the resident teachers have put paper over their classroom windows, an extremely effective solution to a difficult problem but also an extremely gloomy one.

The methods that were discussed in class that I have been using are waiting outside the door until the bell rings and telling the class not to react to wavers outside the door. Both of these methods have worked well for me, and I intend to continue using them. Waiting outside is especially good because the students are encouraged to come into the room before the bell rings and to start their work immediately. Usually, I do not have to tell students to ignore wavers. I simply ignore the waver, give a stern look at the student waving back, and the waver goes away.

• • •

Because my classes are in the same room I'm able to put assignments on the board early. I also assign students to put assignments, especially the "do-now" assignment, on the board. When my students enter the classroom, they have work to start on. This gives me the freedom to stand at my classroom door and usher my students in and keep strangers out. I also lock the rear door, which prevents students from entering from the rear of the class. When the bell rings to start class, I lock the front door. This prevents students who walk the hallways from opening the door, looking in your class for friends, and calling out.

• • •

There is a monthly meeting of the executive committee of the union chapter and the principal in which we discuss issues that concern the teachers. Discipline is one of the things we talk about. We make suggestions like: all teachers should ban Walkmen in their classrooms. In fact, there is a rule in the school that these instruments of disruption should not be allowed in the school. We've suggested there be assistant principals patrolling the halls especially in between classes and help keep student noise and hyperactivity down to a minimum. We've requested that security guards patrol the halls during class changes. These suggestions are circulated to the faculty and sometimes discussed at faculty meetings. We've had a number of faculty meetings concerned with discipline, and, in fact, small committees have come up with many suggestions. For the cafeteria, we've suggested that there be security guards to keep a calm atmosphere (there are already plenty of teachers there, and they find the job an onerous one).

Seating Arrangement

In reference to the seating arrangement, I found it a useful threat to promise to change a seat if talkative behavior continues. Usually it works, and at the most, all I need to do is shoot a threatening glance in a certain direction and a potential disruption is warded off.

• • •

I use the circle and horseshoe form from time to time. For example, to discuss prevention of suicide, teenage pregnancy and if I have to use visual aids, those will be very useful.

• • •

I prefer circles or a horseshoe—more student interaction, less pulling teeth. The students can learn from each other—also social interaction. Suddenly, fellow students become human, and they also have feelings. Also, I can sit down more of the time and see their faces. It's hard to hide in a circle.

Procedures

When we spoke about lateness previously, keeping an empty chair by the door was one of the procedures for dealing with late students. I have been keeping an empty seat for those who come late, and I like the effects. First, the students make almost no disturbance when they are late, and secondly, they are punished because they cannot sit in their regular seat. They really hate the "late seat." Last week a girl came a few seconds late and took the late seat. About ten minutes later I saw tears down her face. I gave the class something to do and asked her if she wanted to tell me why she was crying. I was shocked when she said it was because she had to sit in the late seat. I was especially shocked because her reaction almost did not fit her "image," but her feelings were genuine. I have found that even in my eighth period class, students who were problems get there on time so that they can sit in their regular seats. The procedure has been very effective.

Another procedure is keeping the bathroom pass by the door, and the students exchange the pass for a paper with their name and date for the pass. I find that I am no longer annoyed with requests to use the bathroom. I always found it disruptive when a student asks to go to the bathroom and I called on the student because I expected a good answer to a question. On Friday, I spend about ten minutes going through the papers and marking B for bathroom on the front of their Delaney cards. By marking the Delaney cards I can check who has been using the pass too often as I take the attendance on Monday. I feel that this is also going to work out very well.

As far as items for the classroom, I have put up a calendar in each room. (It was not easy to get calendars for free.) In the three days that the calendars have been up, I must have used them a dozen times.

Equipment

In all honesty the information rendered concerning tools overwhelmed me. I realized that I was like a plumber going to work without his tools. There have been numerous times when I was unprepared to staple some tests together, mark a paper in red ink, or remember an appointment because I was not equipped.

I generally carry a plastic bag with some of the materials you mentioned. Sometimes I find the chalk falls out of a box and I'm left with crumbs. Maybe a zippered bag would make a difference. I'll try. The magic markers or special pens, which I use for writing on transparencies or even the ordinary pens, sometimes leak and I have a mess with which to deal. I've never heard of 3M Postem Pads, but they look as though they might be useful. I like the idea of a mechanical pencil and press-on labels, hand-wipes, and an appointment book a little bigger than my U.F.T. one. It never occurred to me to have in the drawer some machine oil.

H. Training Exercises and Checklists for Chapter 10

Exercise One: Learning How to "Duck" Ones Not Meant at You

Below, briefly describe five incidents this past week where you got very angry at some students right on the spot.

1. _____
   _____
   _____

2. _____
   _____
   _____

3. _____
   _____
   _____

4. _____
   _____
   _____

5. _____
   _____
   _____

It is possible that you overreacted or took one of these incidents personally when you should have ducked or at least "gone with the punch" and not have taken it so personally. To learn how to do this better and to decide if you fall into a pitfall, ask yourself these questions for each incident you described above:

A. Is it possible that the student's anger was displaced, not really meant for you, but you got it or took it personally?

B. Was the incident really out of your jurisdiction?

C. Is it possible that the "curse words" used by the student were really only venting a previous frustration rather than hostility directed at you?

D. Is it possible that this student is generally angry at authority figures?

E. Might the incident only have been short-lived, just a burst of anger and over with, had you not gotten so involved?

F. Were you trying to earn the student's respect on the spot, by verbal preaching, rather than over a long period?

G. Were you not only trying to get the student to behave but also trying to extract a feeling from him or her on the spot?

H. Is it possible that you chose the wrong place and time for your reprimand; the student couldn't really "hear" you at this time?

If you have answered "yes" to any of these for the above incident, it might have been better (at least at the time) to have ducked, or you probably took the incident too personally and overreacted.

Check the letter or letters above (A–H) that you need to watch out for as your "sensitive spot" or tendency for poor judgment or bad timing.

Exercise Two: Practicing Ducking

If you are in an education class or workshop, try this exercise. (a) Each person in the class thinks of a particular student in their imagination who is particularly angry. (b) Then, each person imagines where this student is in school and what's happening. (c) Now, each person imagines that this student comes across a teacher during the angry incident. (d) Get one person in the class to volunteer to role play "the teacher" in the imagined incident and one person to volunteer to role play the student in their imagined incident. (e) Before you begin the role play, prepare the person who will role play "the teacher" by describing the incident to "the teacher" you are about to role play with. (f) When you both understand the incident, begin the role play by the person playing the angry "<u>student</u>" speaking first.

The whole class watches the role play and notices how the "teacher" handled it. Did the teacher duck? Was this a ducking situation? (You can decide by reviewing questions A–H above in Exercise One.) How well did the "teacher" do?

Get a few volunteers to play "teachers" for a few volunteered imagined "students." You'll be able to practice your decisions about whether to duck or not and practice your ability to duck when appropriate.

Exercise Three: Dealing with "Hanger-Outers"

A. Notice whether the students who hang out and disturb your, e.g., third period class are sometimes the same students. Write down their names here.

B. Now write down either the name of these students' destination teacher, or homeroom teacher, or the name of the person who is on hall duty that period. Take your time. It may take a couple of days to fill in these names.

Name of Hanger-Outers	Destination Teacher	Homeroom Teacher	On Hall Duty
1.			
2.			
3.			
4.			
5.			

C. Now, write a note to or talk to one of these teachers (or all three). Follow up your warning to these hanger-outers. Thank the teacher(s) who help(s) you. If you don't feel like going through all this bother, note this to yourself, that you've decided to bear the disturbances rather than bother to do the above.

Exercise Four: Dealing with Students in the Halls Who Distract Students in Your Class

A. You need to practice going deaf, dumb, and blind to the students in the halls who try to get an audience reaction from you and your class. Instead, reprimand the students in your class who give the outsiders attention. What will you say to your students in your class about giving attention to outsiders? Write out your little speech here:

_____

_____

_____

_____

_____

B. What warning of punishment or loss of privilege will you apply to those in your class who feed attention to the outsiders?

_____

_____

_____

C. Have you slipped and given attention to these outsiders, e.g., by reprimanding them? Have you tried a window covering as discussed on pages 201–202?

Exercise Five: Choosing a Seating Arrangement

A. Review Chapter 10, section C, b., **13–18.** Use the chart below to decide your seating arrangement. Place a checkmark in the Pros or Cons column for each characteristic that is significant to you for each kind of arrangement.

Arrangement	Pros	Cons
1. in a circle		
2. in a horseshoe		
3. in rows		

B. Also, each time you see that that arrangement takes work (as described in the chapter) place an "X" in the Pros column along with your checks there. After you have scored yourself, you should probably consider the arrangement that has the most ✔s in the Pros column (the least in the Cons) and the fewest Xs. Or you may decide to sometimes shift arrangements.

Checklists

1. Ducking

You should be able to answer "No" to as many of these as possible.

_____ 1. Have you overly reprimanded a student who was just displacing his or her anger?

_____ 2. Have you gone after a student out of your jurisdiction just because you took his or her actions personally?

_____ 3. Have you taken a vented angry statement personally?

_____ 4. Have you taken personally anger which is really general, e.g., toward all authority figures?

_____ 5. Have you wrongly gone after an incident that would have quickly blown over had you not jumped in?

_____ 6. Have you reprimanded a student who was just showing frustration? You took their frustration personally?

_____ 7. Did you try "to preach" respect into a student today?

_____ 8. Did you try to win a feeling from a student today: the behavior wasn't enough?

_____ 9. Did you try to scold a student at an inappropriate time?

2. Disturbances Right Outside Your Classroom
   You should be able to answer "Yes" to as many of these as possible.

_____ 1. Did you put a "do-now!" on the chalkboard (or use a task sheet)?

_____ 2. Did you stand outside the door sternly and usher students in?

_____ 3. Did you note the names of students who repeatedly hang out?

_____ 4. Did you find out who their destination teacher is, or homeroom teacher is, or tell the person on hall duty?

_____ 5. Have you tried a covering or shade for your front door window?

_____ 6. Have you spoken to other teachers about similar concerns about, e.g., bad or loose school rules?

_____ 7. Have you spoken to the administration about these concerns?

_____ 8. Are you expressing your concerns in concert with others?

_____ 9. Have you described these matters in terms of "needs" and "concerns (rather than criticized the administration)?

_____ 10. Have you listened to the administration's problems around these concerns?

_____ 11. Do hall duty staff walk around the hall (rather than remain stationary)?

_____ 12. Have you suggested the rule that staff and parents not enter a classroom in progress, except for an emergency?

_____ 13. Have you suggested the rule that no food be allowed beyond the cafeteria?

_____ 14. Have you suggested that teachers stop being so liberal about issuing passes?

_____ 15. Will someone keep track of these too-often-issued passes?

_____ 16. Have you suggested "hall-sweeps" (Chapter 10, section B. 3[g])?

_____ 17. Have you suggested a place in the school where students may be allowed to have "time out" to just talk and vent?

3. The Environment of Your Classroom
You should be able to answer "Yes" to as many of these as possible.

_____ 1. Have you tried to secure the same room for each class period?
_____ 2. Have you tried to get rooms near each other?
_____ 3. Have you checked that your room(s) is not near a gym, music room, cafeteria, industrial arts class, chemistry lab, auditorium?
_____ 4. Have you checked that the room windows don't look out on a distraction?
_____ 5. Are the lights O.K.?
_____ 6. Is the floor quiet enough?
_____ 7. Are the window shades O.K.?
_____ 8. Does it also have a back door, with a lock?
_____ 9. Is the heater or air conditioning O.K.?
_____ 10. Can the windows be opened?
_____ 11. Does your desk have a drawer that can be locked?
_____ 12. Does the room have a closet that can be locked?
_____ 13. Is there a private place in the room where you can reprimand a student?
_____ 14. Are the bulletin boards and chalk boards O.K.?
_____ 15. Are the walls of the room O.K.?
_____ 16. Does the room have garbage cans?
_____ 17. Is there no pencil sharpener, or can you remove it?
_____ 18. Do you have enough chairs and desks, plus one or two?
_____ 19. Are they non-squeaky?
_____ 20. Does the room contain only the essential furniture?
_____ 21. Have you decided on a seating arrangement carefully? Have you carefully decided on a seating arrangement that is congruent with your teaching style?
_____ 22. Are you working on applying the "tips" for handling the seating arrangement of your choice (pp. 206–211)?
_____ 23. Can your students be seen by you and they see you easily?
_____ 24. Have you made sure that the seats are not too close together?
_____ 25. Have you tried to have them face away from the windows as much as possible?
_____ 26. Have you left a good traffic pattern in your seating arrangement?
_____ 27. Have you left an empty seat near the door for latecomers?
_____ 28. Do you put a "do-now!" on the chalkboard (or use task sheets)?
_____ 29. Are your "do-nows!" short, e.g., "fill in the blank"?
_____ 30. Do you use a Delaney book?
_____ 31. Have you tried the learning names exercise on p. 212?
_____ 32. Do you list the topics covered and to be covered on the chalkboard?

_____ 33. Do you use staples on the bulletin boards?
_____ 34. Do you have a large calendar and clock in the room?
_____ 35. Have you tried the "bathroom pass" strategies on p. 213?
_____ 36. Have you tried the "garbage pail" strategies, p. 214?
_____ 37. Do you communicate well with the custodians?
_____ 38. Do you keep the room cool?
_____ 39. Do you know where the sun comes in and have a shade for this glare?
_____ 40. Have you arranged the furnishings for a possible private place to talk to a student (K–6)?
_____ 41. Have you provided a place where parents can leave you notes (K–6)?
_____ 42. Have you found a way to keep children's attention away from looking out at the playground (K–6)?

4. Your Equipment

Hopefully you can obtain items **44–72** (**113–118** for K–6 teachers) listed in Chapter 10, section D (and section E for grades K–6). Check off each one. Circle the item number you want to get but don't have. Go after these items. (Place the date that you'll try to get it next to each circled item.) The list appears on pages 215–217 and 231.

CHAPTER 11: REPAIRING YOUR STUDENT-TEACHER INTERACTIONS

In this chapter we will work on preventing the sources of disruptive behavior that come from the way you interact with your students. Specifically, we will work on: (a) not making miscalls; (b) being congruent; (c) following through; (d) being appropriate; (e) being fair.

We will be looking at how you react to students in certain situations and how to repair some of your reactions that may incite an "enemy" relationship with students. Building a "non-enemy," ally relationship with students is the most significant thing you can do to prevent discipline problems.

A. Not Making Miscalls

In Chapter 4 we clarified the definition of a miscall vs. a discipline problem, and in Chapter 8, section A we described those needs and feelings a teacher may have that often lead to fifteen typical miscalls. Now we can move beyond recognition of this disruptive tendency and suggest ways that may help extinguish this tendency.

Let's review (from Chapter 8, pp. 147–149) the fifteen typical miscalls and the needs and feelings that may potentiate each one:

Typical Miscall	Teacher's Needs and Feelings
1. You discipline the withdrawn student.	1. Your ego is hurt, you feel powerless that a student is "going under," s/he reminds you of you.
2. You overreact about a rule.	2. You have a need for control, anger, loss of temper, a nonreasoned generalization made impulsively.
3. You've got to win their feelings.	3. You have trouble being disliked, you feel lonely, not liked in your personal life, nor much sense of meaning outside of school.

241

4. You need their attention.

4. You need attention.

5. You discipline when your ego is hurt.

5. You have a sensitive ego or easily hurt self-esteem.

6. You discipline when you feel "they're interfering with my getting my lesson done."

6. You feel competitive, unaccomplished, that quantity of notes dictated equals learning; you feel pressure from external standards.

7. You displace your anger.

7. You often feel frustrations, angers, and often powerless to tell those with whom these feelings belong; you feel worried that if you express these feelings, others will get hurt, or dislike you, or punish you in some way; so you store these feelings away that come out when you let go.

8. You're tired of trying to be understanding all the time.

8. You feel out of patience, you need a rest, you need to be replenished.

9. The mirror effect

9. The student reminds you of you, or of the parts of you that you don't like, or someone significant to you that you don't like.

10. You feel like exercising control.

10. You feel obsessive about doing things certain ways; you feel generally worried and anxious; you feel your life isn't "together" and/or that it is out of control.

11. You discipline "steam" thinking it's "smoke."

11. You fear the class is getting out of control; you don't know how to channel the energy of the class.

12. You get angry at venting as if it's cursing.

12. You feel personally insulted, disrespected; the four-letter word violates the values of your upbringing, "your home."

13. You discipline because of a prejudicial mistake

13. You feel the influence of some previous teaching on you, or the anxiety and anger of some previous event(s); to protect yourself, you generalize and stereotype.

14. You discipline from holding a grudge.

14. You are not over the past irritation, or hurt, and still feel that an injustice needs to be righted.

15. You punish an education problem.

15. You feel frustrated that (s)he's not doing well, that such reflects on your abilities; you feel his or her poor work is a personal insult to your ability.

From a review of the above feelings and needs that potentiate the tendency to make miscalls, we can locate some similar or related emotions. Miscalls 1, 5, 6, 12, and 15 all refer to a person with a sensitive ego, someone who, perhaps, doesn't feel much sense of self-pride or accomplishment. This person's sense of self-respect is easily insulted. With these related emotions now precipitated, we can make some suggestions about how such a person might remedy those miscalls incited by these kinds of emotions. First, such a teacher sometimes needs only to recognize that he or she feels this way: that they are easily sensitive about their sense of self-pride, sense of accomplishment, and self-respect. Sometimes just this intelligent awareness is sufficient as a monitor that guards against making miscalls. Such a teacher might say to him/herself: "That incident just got to me. I'm prone to overreact here because this one gets to my pride. The student might feel like a real problem, but in reality it's probably my vulnerability here that's getting me. So, calm down. Try to go on and not take this personally and disrupt the class with a personal confrontation." However, more can be done besides calling on a monitoring recognition of these feelings. This kind of teacher can notice that s/he is making these kinds of miscalls because s/he is taking what is really an educationally non-disruptive (thus a miscalled) action on the part of the student as if it is aimed at the person teaching. This miscall appears as in this illustration:

(1) is an action on the part of the student (e.g., withdrawing) not really intended for the person who is the teacher (not meant personally for the

teacher). But the teacher who is vulnerable here feels it personally (2), reacts not from his/her understanding as teacher (e.g., knowing a miscall from a discipline problem) but as a <u>person</u> (3), and takes it personally. Then, the <u>person</u> of the teacher strikes back at the student (3) (who also has a weak ego) who takes this (3) personally as (4), and strikes back at the person who is only now incidentally the teacher, with (5). And the war is on. Teachers who suffer these reactions need to recognize and be on the alert for (1) and (2). Then (3), (4), and (5) can be headed off. Also, a teacher who is sensitive about his/her self-pride can remedy this miscall tendency by just working on their sense of self-pride. This can be done in and out of the classroom. Such a teacher should try to work very hard at creating some great lessons for, let's say, a week or so. These should be lessons that the teacher places extra effort into, lessons that s/he can take pride in. The teacher should make a "to do" list to be accomplished this week and work extra hard to cross out and do some of the items on the list. The list can include responsibilities outside of school as well. The teacher should also choose to do a particular accomplishment that week that would make him/ her feel proud, or do something that s/he feels deserves respect. All of these tacks will make the teacher feel a stronger ego, sense of self-respect and, thereby, less vulnerable to those feelings that potentiate miscalls 1, 5, 6, 12, and 15. To support these efforts, I recommend that such teachers find a friend and tell him/her what they are working on or trying to do. Share with this friend. You'll need and deserve encouragement here. Finally, in some cases, the vulnerability to lack of self-respect may be historical, from some upsetting psychological events, e.g., with one's parents, while growing up. In these cases, it would be helpful for such a teacher (who is not alone with this kind of problem) to seek a counselor to help expurgate this inculcated vulnerability.

Miscalls 1, 2, 7, 10, and 11 are all sparked by feelings of powerlessness; this person feels a dire need for control, and gets very anxious (to the point of making miscalls) when things feel like they may go out of control. What suggestions can we make to this person who feels this while teaching? Again, sometimes just intelligent awareness of these miscalls and these feelings is enough monitor to guard against this tendency. You might say to yourself: "This student who is withdrawn, I can talk to him later; it's O.K. if I don't have the power to do everything right now." Or: "I'm stating an unreasonable rule." Or: "I'm displacing my anger." Or: "I think my anxiety is causing me to be a little obsessive here; it's O.K. if things are not perfectly orderly. They're excited and participating." Sometimes just recognizing that you are very sensitive to any loss of power or control will be enough not to make the miscall. You might also review the illustration of a miscall and just realize that this is what happens to you. On the other hand, you can also work on gaining more control and sense of power. Perhaps you should stop teaching one period, or part of a period, and just go over rules and proper routines with your class. Review your warnings, rewards, and punishments with them.[95] Write these rules, warnings, rewards, etc., on the chalkboard or on a handout sheet. Now, keep track of your warnings and follow through. You may wish to stay after school, or come to school early, to spend some time at getting organized. Make "to do" lists, a list of reminders, etc., whatever will help you feel more control. Do the same at home and in your personal life. Do you feel behind with responsibilities and overwhelmed? Take some time to get some of these things in order. This is time well spent and will calm you and help you feel more in control. Try to tackle a particular task you've been neglecting that has made you feel weak or unable. Again, it's always best to tell a friend what you're working on. Share with them your frustrations; ask for the encouragement you need and deserve. Finally, in some cases, this feeling of powerlessness may not just be situational, but, instead, characterological. You may generally feel this way because of past psychological, historical factors. Then, it would be helpful for such a teacher (who is not alone with these feelings) to seek some counseling to work on shoring up one's sense of personal power and effectiveness.

Miscalls 2, 7, 8, 13, and 14 are sparked by feelings of volatile anger; this person is often angry, stores up past angers, and loses his/her temper easily. Again, a teacher's intelligent awareness of being generally angry can often go a long way to prevent these miscalls. S/he can say to him/herself: "I'm overreacting about a rule here because I'm angry and losing my temper. I'm probably displacing my anger from a lot of other irritations that are bothering me. I need a rest; it's (or s/he's) not as bad as it (s/he) seems." Sometimes just the recognition that you arrived at school already angry, or angry from the last period, or that you tend to lose your temper can help. Reviewing the illustration of a miscall might be helpful. Also, if you have worked on the above feelings of low self-esteem and feelings of powerlessness, you will find that you will be less prone to frustrations and angers. However, the best way to solve generalized, stored-up angers and a bad temper is not to learn to control your angers more. Instead, you need more constructive outlets for these feelings of irritation and frustration. People who try to control their tempers lose their tempers a lot. This kind of fallacious attempt only yields a vicious circle of stored angers and lost tempers. Such people need to find friends who will listen to their irritations, people who allow you to get things

---

[95] If this area is particularly in need and in trouble for you, you might want to skip ahead to Chapter 12 for immediate help on "preventing your rules from falling apart." Then, you can come back to where you left off here later.

off your chest without being judgmental. If you are irritated often, meet friends at school for lunch or for dinner; call them up, listen to their gripes, and ask them to listen to yours. Also, get as much strenuous exercise as you can. Swim, jog, play tennis, racquetball, or work out after school and take a warm shower. Try hitting a pillow or writing an angry letter (you would never send) to the person(s) you're angry with. Find aggressive pleasures, not passive ones, so you have outlets. But you may also need a rest, a change of environment, or need to treat yourself. Finally, if you can't seem to let go of your angers nor find a safe place for their venting (you're not alone with this problem), you might find it helpful to speak to a counselor about your frustrations and angers.

Miscalls 3, 4, and 7 are often sparked by feelings of loneliness and a sense of lack of meaning in one's life; this person has few supportive relationships with others and, thus, seldom feels liked or gets much attention. Because his/her life is hollow, others' reactions (e.g., students' reactions) mean very much to them, too much. Such teachers can remedy their tendencies to make these related miscalls by sometimes just recognizing that they tend inappropriately to need to win students feelings. They tend to demand attention out of their own personal needs and/or displace stored anger from fear of being disliked. Sometimes just an awareness of these feelings of loneliness or emptiness can be a check on the tendency to be inappropriate. However, such teachers need to work on making friends and probably need to repair many of their human relations skills: to be able to trust, express feelings more openly, listen well, give and take nondefensively, etc. If these teachers had more supportive relationships, they would feel more liked, get more attention, and, through sharing, find more meaning. Then, they would experience less vulnerability to make miscalls 3, 4, and 7. If you can relate to this set of problems, begin now. Make a commitment to call people up, see people, try to be open to them, and listen (really listen) to them. We often forget how much having caring relationships gives us the strengths and abilities to handle our lives. However, sometimes if we have been too hurt, or are too upset, we can't trust or open up, or listen to others. In such cases (you're not alone), the first person you trust, open up to, and learn to listen with might be a counselor. S/he can be your bridge to other supportive relationships.

Miscalls 1 and 9 can be sparked by a student reminding you of yourself or someone significant to you. When this happens, we overreact. If the student reminds us of a part of ourselves we dislike or disliked, or someone else we dislike or disliked, we are prone to get overly angry. If the student reminds us of a part of ourselves we care or cared about, or someone else we care or cared about, we are prone to feel upset if we can't help or "save" them. This tendency of people reminding us of ourselves and others is quite usual. What is not usual is to be conscious that this is the factor that is intensifying our feelings. In a way, self irritations or important old irritations are sometimes pulled to the surface by present similar events or people. Or old cares or unmet wishes are rekindled by present reminders. For example, you feel overly angry with this clowning student because he reminds you of the brother you hated when he was like that. Or you feel you have to save this sad student because she reminds you of you when you were sad, and no one helped you when you were little. There is nothing wrong with these reactions in and by themselves. But they can lead to inappropriate, mistimed, misjudged behavior on the part of the teacher. All one can do here is recognize one's overreactions: "I seem to feel stronger about this than usual or stronger than makes sense, or I can find reason for." Of course, it's possible that your anger or love is not a psychological myth of reminders. But it's worth checking this out before you go after a withdrawn student in front of the class, or cruelly get enraged at this kid who makes this little grimace you go nuts over. Again, the best you can do here is to try to cultivate an intelligent awareness that checks these kinds of miscalls.

The same attitude is recommended to check miscalls 13 and 14. Generalized anxiety or anger turned into a defensive, generalized stereotype makes us prejudge—as long as these reactions are unconscious. Similarly, we attack a student (who is being good) today for the reprimand we already gave him yesterday but are still not over because we are holding onto a grudge—usually unconsciously. We need to know more often when we are angry, the cause, and to whom the anger rightfully belongs. We need to be able to do this identification even if we can't always do anything about our irritations. The identification gives an awareness that can teach us why we are acting a certain way, and can help us monitor our tendency to be inappropriate.

Similarly, miscall 12 can be monitored by an intelligent awareness. No word, in and by itself, is "dirty." Is "framis" dirty? Is "puta" dirty? They both are nonsense words I just made up. However, the latter can feel dirty if someone places it in a, e.g., Hispanic context and gives it a "dirty" connotation. Words can be expressions of venting or curse words, depending on the context or situation. To drop a set of dishes and say, "Shit!" is not the same as "You are shit!" Teachers often come from value systems and upbringings different from those of their students. Your classroom is not "your home." You may wish to teach them new values; fine. Until then, it is not true that every four-letter word is inherently "dirty," a personal insult to you, or a curse at someone. You may wish to teach them better ways to express their angers[96] or change

---

[96] However, verbal anger is already much better than physically destructive hostility. Usually, the instruction. "Don't say things like that!" does not impede destructive behavior. As a matter of fact, such instruction usually suppresses the angry feeling that then does become the stored-up spark of the unwanted destructive behavior.

their values. But meanwhile, try to be aware of your overreactions to mere venting or to words "my mother would never tolerate."

Finally, regarding miscalls 6 and 11, we need to work on handling educational issues better. We often find out too late that just because students have copied all the notes, they still haven't learned much. To make use of this understanding, that "notes aren't learnings," we need to make better use of class time and homework assignments. Class time should be mostly used to reinforce cognitive learning, not for copying down or recording cognitive material. By "reinforce" I mean: give it affect or emotional value, give it an experiential significance, organize it for retrieval, study its use, share its significance, manipulate and use it, etc. Homework, reading, books, handouts can be used for the initial collection and recording of facts, whereas the classroom should be the laboratory for the participation in those recorded facts. Try to divide up the curriculum you must teach into learnings that just need to be recorded vs. those that need to be processed or engaged in. Create assignments that do the former, and try to leave your class time for the latter, or for at least the reinforcement of the former, if you feel pressure from external sources, e.g., your chairperson, explain your strategy here and that you are trying not to make miscall 6 (explain it to him or her). If you do leave more time in class for, e.g., participation in learning, you may then worry that you see "smoke" when it's actually "steam" (miscall 11). Don't panic and just go back to dictating notes. You'll now need to learn some participation techniques that can channel this "steam" and that can use the energy you have now allowed for learning. This tack will stop you from making miscalls but leave you with the job of learning new participation techniques. (We will discuss these in Chapter 13, section E.)

It is impossible for all teachers to work on all these feelings and needs in order not to make all these miscalls. However, just recognition of some of these tendencies and potentiating feelings can often eliminate much of this major source of discipline problems. Again, keep in mind the four caveats as you work on remedying this area: (1) at first the above suggestions will take more work before they then make your job easier; (2) only do what is congruent for you; (3) but don't abandon a suggestion until you give it a good try; (4) don't fret if you can't apply all of the suggestions.

B. Being Congruent (Authentic)

In Chapter 8 we discussed one of the important sources of disruptive behavior: being incongruent. To curtail this source, we now need to work on how a teacher goes about being congruent. Here, we focus on the major tool that the teacher has to prevent discipline problems: his or her personality. This is the factor that often decides what kind of relationship you have with your students. An ally, or at least a non-enemy relationship, not only prevents discipline problems but also often enlists the class as a team with you to help you deal with individual disrupters: "Cool it, John, can't you see she's trying to teach us something!"

Let us review (from Chapter 8, section B) our understanding of incongruence and congruence so that we can focus on the skills involved in the latter. In a way, all teacher-messages look like this:

$$\frac{\text{cognitive content}}{\text{feeling}} \longrightarrow \quad \textbf{MESSAGE}$$

An incongruent message is one in which the bottom part of the message does <u>not</u> match or support the top part, as in:

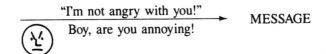

$$\longrightarrow \quad \textbf{MESSAGE}$$

A congruent message is one in which the bottom does match or support the top, as in:

$$\frac{\text{"Now class, we must look at the causes of this war."}}{\substack{\text{This is important; I need you to understand and} \\ \text{notice what I'm about to discuss.}}} \longrightarrow \quad \textbf{MESSAGE}$$

Or an incongruent teacher is a person who separates or puts his or her real personality aside or hides his or her real self as s/he teaches:

In contrast, a congruent teacher puts his or her real self into his or her teaching, uses his or her personality, and shows who he or she really is in their teaching:

teacherperson

Or an incongruent teacher formulates messages from what s/he thinks will look good, or sound good, or from his or her image of what a teacher should look like or do:

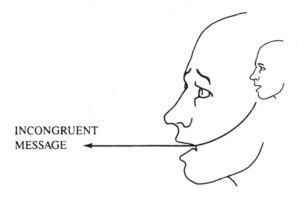

INCONGRUENT
MESSAGE

A congruent teacher delivers messages from who s/he really is, how s/he really feels, "from the heart":

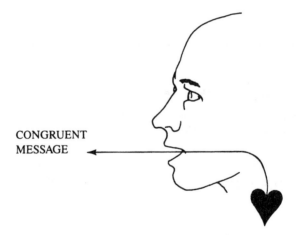

CONGRUENT
MESSAGE

Being congruent is the prerequisite skill to preventing discipline problems. To not make miscalls, to be appropriate, follow through, be fair, and deliver effective lessons, a teacher must first be congruent. Incongruent teachers make more miscalls, act inappropriately, have trouble following through, are more unfair, and deliver ineffective (not believable) lessons. Because being congruent is so crucial, it is the major reason why there can be no "cookbook" recipes for what a particular teacher should do when Johnny does X. Teachers can't just give each other blanket advice, because such advice only works to the extent that these teachers feel similarly or have similar personalities. This is also why it is so difficult to train student teachers to handle discipline problems, and why so many books that try to help teachers fall short of remedies. You cannot just transfer one technique from one teacher to another, or tell another teacher to just say what I say.

But you can teach teachers to be more congruent. It is a learnable skill. And once understood and mastered, a congruent teacher can be helped to discover what to do or say, what works for him or her in the classroom. So, what we shall work on is understanding how to be more congruent, and how to master this skill. And then we shall work on how to locate your congruent self as teacher in your general interactions with your students, your designing classroom rules, and your delivering lessons.

How can you become a more congruent teacher? Well, the first thing is not to misinterpret how one becomes congruent. Looking back on our illustrations of incongruence and congruence, it would be wrong to think that you go about being congruent by just choosing the top part of a message (the content) and then just backing it up with a supportive bottom (feeling). That's not being congruent, that's acting. Actors take scripts written by others and then try to reinforce these lines with directed feelings. Sometimes they are effective with an audience, sometimes not. They are effective when their messages seem as if they are being congruent. But congruent teachers are not good actors. Instead, they first figure out how or what they feel (the bottom part of the message) and then articulate (the content) what truly matches or supports what they feel. Learning to be congruent requires the ability to figure out or know your feelings and then to formulate a content statement that comes out of how you really feel. Or, to look at our other illustration, being congruent is not trying to be the kind of person a teacher is supposed to be. Instead, to be a congruent teacher is to be yourself while teaching, or not to hide yourself while teaching, or to put yourself into your teaching. Or, to look at our last illustration, being congruent is not saying what you think you should say or what a teacher should say. Instead, being congruent is to say what you really feel as you responsibly teach.

The best way to work at being congruent is to keep trying to be yourself while teaching. Don't try to be "the teacher." To be yourself, you need to know yourself. You need to know how you feel about things. You are yourself at a party when someone asks you, "Do you want a drink?" and you answer how you really feel. If you answer how you should answer, or how one should be, you've lost your congruence. To generally interact congruently with the class, you need to feel who you are and be comfortable being who you are spontaneously. To design and reinforce congruent rules in your classroom, you need to figure out how you feel about these rules and be able to say that. To deliver congruent, effective lessons, you need to figure out how you feel about your subject matter and say that effectively. You cannot interact, design rules, or deliver lessons from cues on how you should be, or what you should say, manipulated from "ought-to" instructions in your head. You can't keep trying to act out the proper feeling for what you just said or did to get the students to believe you. Dramatizing the subject matter is not the answer. Instead, when you can put your real feelings into the subject matter you really care about and believe in, your delivery will be dramatic.[97]

So being congruent is knowing your feelings first, how you feel, and being and saying and formulating messages in line with those true feelings. That means you need to keep checking with yourself (as often as you need to remain who you really are) by asking, e.g., "Am I angry?" "Do I really feel that was funny?" "Do I really feel he's being disruptive?" "Do I really believe in this rule?" "How do I feel about this subject matter?" In other words, if you're angry, say so. If you think what this student just said is really funny, laugh. If he is again funny, but you're losing some patience, laugh again (to the extent you feel it), but also show the student that you're starting to lose your patience. If he cracks a joke again that is now feeling not so funny, but annoying, say and show that. Don't worry so much about being consistent. If you feel that it's funny and then later not so funny, fine. Be congruent, not consistent by rules in your head that say you must be this because you said that. Congruent statements (being real to students) feel consistent to students. They know your feelings change for different things, at different times. Then, if you monitor your appropriateness and fairness, you will be consistent and real and honest enough for the students to feel good with you. Also, unless you're insane or have pathological multiple personalities, by being congruent you will be fairly consistent. Your personality (who you really are) does not change much from day to day. So don't give out unfelt rules and doggedly stick to them (when you don't believe in them). Decide on the rules you feel congruent with, and these rules will be naturally, generally consistent.

Why is it so difficult to be congruent? First, most of us do not bother to learn what it is we feel about things. We generally say we feel "O.K.," or "Fair," or "Not so good." But we seldom take time out to find out if we are feeling angry, guilty, sad, excited, bored, hypocritical about a rule, not sure why this particular thing is important, etc. We sometimes take time to study our feelings when: we write a diary, see a counselor, we try to figure out whether to have a baby or whether we should marry someone, etc. We feel these situations require a careful understanding of our feelings. Well, to be a responsible good teacher also requires a careful understanding of our feelings.

---

[97] Of course, some of you see a problem here: what if you don't care or believe in the subject matter? This is a real problem for you (and your students) that we will address soon in the next few pages: 263–265.

Some of us decide to "skip over" a look at our feelings as we decide to marry or have a baby, etc. Many pay a high price for neglecting this study of feelings. Teachers also, who neglect finding out how they really feel about, e.g., late homework, students not having a pencil, teaching the Civil War, etc., also pay a price. In this case, the price is inattentive, disruptive students. So it's difficult to be congruent because we often don't want to go through the task of discovering how we feel about things. Instead, we just blurt out rules, or lectures, or laugh or don't laugh according to what "they" would say or do.

There are other reasons why it's not easy to be congruent. Sometimes we are aware of our feelings, but we either don't like what it is we really feel or worry that others won't like what we feel and really want to say. In these situations, we are prone to be incongruent. Or we "distance" our statements, we talk in the third person, or ask indirect questions. For instance, "Tom, we really shouldn't be talking now, should we?" Or, "Sometimes when you don't understand something you feel embarrassed. Right, Tom?" In the former statement, the teacher probably really feels, "I'm annoyed. Your talking is really out of order, so stop it, or I'll . . ." But the teacher may not like expressing anger or is afraid to assert him/herself. In the latter, the teacher could say, "Tom, when I don't understand something, I also sometimes get embarrassed." But then the teacher would have to talk directly and show some of him/herself. In such instances, to develop your ability to be congruent is to work on asserting yourself[98] and/or to work on liking yourself more or changing what you don't like about yourself. The more you like who you are, the more you will feel the trust to let yourself say and be what you spontaneously feel. You need to find the courage to be honest with yourself, analyze why you feel the way you do, and learn to accept yourself. Or remain in hiding and incongruent and often in trouble as a teacher with students. For instance, before you say, "We don't do that in here," you'd better figure out: why you feel this way, and if you really feel O.K. about this rule; then, you need to find the courage to say how you really feel about the rule to the students and be able to say it in a "non-distant" way.

We also have trouble being congruent because we tend to teach the way we were taught, especially when we're anxious or don't know what to do. "I'll just be like Mr. Johnson, my old Social Studies teacher." Or, "I'll say what he would say here." Or, "I'll use the rules 'they' gave me when I was a student." The problem here is that you have a different personality than, e.g., Mr. Johnson. What worked for him, what seemed real and honest when he did it, won't necessarily be so for you. And, if it's not congruent with you, it won't be effective.

---

[98] We will work on this in Chapter 12, section G.

Anxiety makes us blind and more dependent. When we are anxious, we can't bother to see or can't see what we really feel about, e.g., a rule. We, instead, want someone to save us. So we quote, e.g., some strong person in our head. Be careful, you will most often be incongruent when you're anxious, worried, or nervous. At these times, slow down, resist trying to act like "the teacher." Instead, try to tell the students of your moment of doubt, "Class, I'm not sure . . . ," take a moment to figure out how you really feel, and then honestly tell them how you feel, mixed feelings and all. A complicated rule or statement is better than an anxiously made up simple rule or cliché that seems unfair or phony.

Anger is also a cause for incongruence. When we are very angry, we tend to blurt out the first thing that pops into our heads. "John, if you call out, you're suspended for a month, or I'll flunk you for the whole course!" You don't really believe that that's fair, but you can't really bother (or haven't bothered) to figure out what you really feel is a fair punishment for such calling out. So, since you don't know how you really feel or what you really feel like doing about such calling out, you blurt out the rage of your frustration. You could, of course, try to follow through with this outrageous punishment to be consistent. But, then, you'd be more incongruent. You'd know it, and they'd "smell it." No, the best way out of this is to stop and figure out what you now feel. Then, say that, even if it means cancellation of the blurted warning with an institution of a new warning that you now really believe in and can follow through.

It is worthwhile to try to ward off incongruence or work on being congruent. Congruent teachers have fewer discipline problems. Being congruent creates the components of rapport with your class. The class feels you say what you mean, mean what you say; they believe you and believe in you more. Thus, they are not busy trying to tear the mask off of you to reveal a phony, or show you up, or find error. Therefore, you need to apply less coercive power to protect your weak spots from "the enemy." Instead, they can be more allied with you and even be your support as you need to discipline students who come in already disruptive to their class. Since you aren't playing the inauthentic role of "being the teacher," you are more *teacherperson*; they don't relate to you as: "Hey, teach." They also relate more as *studentperson* and are more open to you, even share their feelings, which you can incorporate into lessons. And, when you need to push them, or demand from them, e.g., more work, or to go through a boring topic cooperatively, you'll have more of a relationship with them to "bank on." Also, congruent messages from a congruent teacher are more definite, clear, and impactful, even charismatic. Since you really feel and believe what you say, you are more able to naturally follow through. You will be consistent, naturally. You'll be able to give reasons for rules and assignments because your known feelings are behind what you ask for. And by having your feelings related to your subject matter delivery, your lessons are automatically more affective. You'll also need to yell less. Teachers who are incongruent tend to yell to compensate for the lack of impact that incongruent messages have. You will also be more assertive and more able to take stands, since your demands will come from your heart, and you will be on your two feet when pushed by a challenge. Finally, since you'll be fighting less with their low motivation, and challenges, and your own inauthenticity, you'll suffer less "burnout."

But, it's not easy to be congruent. Let's work on being congruent more specifically by discussing being congruent with regard to: (1) your general interaction (How much of a real person can I be with my students?); (2) your rules; (3) your subject matter delivery.

1. How much of a real person can I be with my students?

A congruent teacher is one who generally interacts with students as a *teacherperson*. Such a teacher tries to be his/herself while teaching. S/he teaches with his/her own language, own style, and with his/her own gestures. If the teacher is teaching math, s/he may only be talking about equations, but his/her "person" is still felt as present, if only more distant: *teacher person* If the teacher is teaching social studies, then the facts may be presented with his/herself more in the descriptions: *teacherperson* If the teacher is counseling, the personal response may be more up front than the teaching: *personteacher* However, if you're congruent, you are (and the class can feel) attached, flowing out of who you are as you teach.

One clearer way to understand what I'm suggesting here can be illustrated by what I call "the pizza test." I think all teachers should have to pass "the pizza test." What is this? A teacher should have to teach for at least one full week. Then, let's say on a Friday after school, s/he must go to a pizza parlor and eat a large oily slice of pizza (with only one thin napkin) in front of a picture-window on the ground floor facing the street. About halfway through eating the slice, this teacher's class will be paraded by the window to see this teacher eating this sloppy slice. Some teachers would be prone to hide; some teachers would just naturally keep on eating, and wave "hello." The former teachers fail the "pizza test"; the latter pass and are probably congruent teachers in class because they are pretty much "themselves" in and out of the classroom.

But how much of a real person can I be with my students? The answer is different for different *teacherpersons*; You need to decide how you shall and how much you can attach your "person" to your "teacher." You need to answer such questions as:

1. If students ask me any of the following, should I tell them?
   - my age
   - marital status
   - my first name
   - where I live
   - my phone number
   - where my accent is from
2. If I feel irritated or depressed about something outside of school, should I tell them?
3. Should I tell them (at least) what mood I'm in?
4. Should I tell them why?
5. Should I talk in my own language, the way I talk?
6. Should I ever tell them that sometimes I worry about my job or work?
7. Should I ever let them call me by my first name?
8. Should I sometimes mention how I'm feeling about some things?
9. Should I ever just chitchat with them, e.g., about the Yankees, after school or in the cafeteria?
10. Should I dress in my kind of clothes, my style?
11. Should I ever tell a student that I particularly like or dislike him or her?
12. Should I ever do things with my students after school, e.g., play basketball with them?
13. Should I ever visit a student at his or her home or let a student stop by my home?
14. Should I ever eat lunch with a student?
15. Should I continue my talk with a student after class in, e.g., the faculty cafeteria?
16. Should I tell the students jokes or listen to theirs? In class or only after class?
17. If I feel a student is funny, should I laugh?
18. Should I let the students know that I won't be in tomorrow and that they'll be having a substitute?
19. Should I tell them how I really feel about my rules or the school's rules?
20. Should I tell them the real reason I wasn't able to correct and give back the tests?
21. If it's my first time teaching, should I let them know that?
22. If I'm teaching "out of license" and feel a bit unsure about the subject matter, should I let them know this?
23. If I make a mistake on the chalkboard, or on an exam, or in a lecture, should I let them know?

24. If I feel nervous about whether something I'm trying will work, should I let them know that I'm feeling this?
25. Should I admit that I don't know the answer?

There are no "correct" answers to these questions, only congruent answers. You need to ask these questions of yourself now, not respond from the top of your head on the spot when suddenly asked by a student. Many of these answers depend on the student who is asking and on the situation. Fine. You do feel less open with some students and in some situations. For instance, you might feel like it's O.K. to hear a student's joke and laugh, if it's relevant, or won't detract too much from the lesson. But, if all your answers to these questions are generally "no" or "very seldom," you may not be putting enough of your "person" into your "teacher." You need to answer "yes" as much as possible to attach your "person" to your "teacher."

Here are some suggestions on how you can do this:

- Joke with them sometimes.
- Admit some mistakes, or problems.
- Use your own words, at least sometimes.
- Tell them sometimes how you feel about some rules and topics in the lesson.
- Call them by their first names.
- Sometimes tell them how you're feeling as you start the lesson or how you feel from the last class.
- Pat them on the back or shoulder, if you feel it as they are near you sometimes.
- Don't be afraid to smile, or wave "hello" in the hall, or after school.
- Share a personal story (especially if it relates to the lesson) at least once in a while.

I am recommending you allow them to see at least some of your feelings not only because congruence is effective and a preventative to disruption but also because their "radar" can tell how you are feeling anyway (they are better than adults at this)! So you might as well show them.

There are some difficulties that must be managed if you are to be more open with students. It is not just being congruent that is difficult. It is also often a delicate matter to manage the implications of such a policy. If a student asks you how you personally feel about some, e.g., historical or political fact in your social studies class, by sharing your personal feeling you might influence him or her too much. Or you might cut off their own responsibility for learning critical thinking or their own value clarification. In such cases, you might simply say, "I have a particular feeling about this. I'll tell you after class, but what do you think?" Or, "I feel uncomfortable telling you my bias, because it may bias you. What's your thought on this?" Sometimes saying it feels "uncomfortable," or "this is too private" is accurately how you feel, thus, congruent. If a student asks you how you feel about another teacher or the principal, you may feel that this kind of "openness" would be unethical or is "none of their business." If you feel that, say that. However, there are also advantages for teachers who follow this policy of congruence. For instance, though it may be a miscall to reprimand venting as if it's cursing, you can <u>personally</u> ask a student not to say "those" words from your "person." (You shouldn't reprimand him or her from your "teacher.") You can say, "John, I know you're frustrated, and I'm not going to be angry at you like some authority figure. But that word really bothers me personally. Could you please try not to use it, for me." If you have been congruent generally, your rapport (rather than power) will be a better influence and with less backlash.

Before we go on to discuss being congruent about your rules, let me clarify what it is I am not saying about your general interaction with your students. Though being congruent is being a *teacherperson*, I am not saying that being congruent is always being "a nice guy." If you feel like being a nice guy, fine, be this way. If a student irritates you (and it's not a miscall), don't be a nice guy. Instead, express your appropriate irritation. You can also be congruent, a "nice guy" (if they're not misbehaving) <u>and be stern, systematic, even controlling.</u> Sometimes students want to retreat from the work that helps them learn and grow. You can be open and warm, <u>and stern,</u> if you really feel that's the only way they'll learn, and you do care about them. (They'll feel that, and will, begrudgingly, respect you.) Also, a congruent teacher is not a "goody-goody." Don't give, unless you feel it. If you're appropriately withholding, because you feel that's best for them to grow, that's congruent. Some supervisors advise: "Don't let them know they got to you." I disagree. Let them know. Express your anger, and enforce the removal of a reward, or privilege, or punishment, if you have really thought it through congruently. Students like "to get to" those teachers who don't express their anger or follow it up. These are the teachers they "play with." But don't go the other way either and "act as if you're really angry." That's incongruent (and "bullshit" to the students, who can spot it well and will "nail you" for it). Also, being congruent is not always being open about how you feel. As I illustrated above, you may congruently feel that telling them your feelings is unethical, or none of their business, or will influence them too much. Fine, say that; that's being congruent. The skill is to know how you feel, to bother to identify your feelings accurately, and not to speak in the third person. You need to find the courage to say more how you feel, not be "the teacher," but be yourself as you teach.

2. Your rules

It is important to be congruent regarding the rules you lay down and follow through. Rules that are not how you really feel will not only fall apart but also will be difficult to remember, enforce, and follow through. And, since students can "smell" when you don't really mean it, these rules won't come off credibly. The rules you decide to enforce need to be your rules, not rules suggested by another teacher, or out of a book, nor dictated by the administration.[99] If they are from any of these latter sources, you'll need to decide if you can own these "as is," or with slight revisions, or not at all. To the extent you can "get behind" the rules you specify, to that extent will they be felt as yours and carry weight. You need to think out how you feel about, e.g., "calling out." Is it a discipline problem? Does it disrupt your teaching or their learning? Yes? Then, you believe in "no calling out." But do you feel "calling out" once is O.K.? Twice? Three times? What is your rule for a "caller-outer" who only does it once? A student who does it twice, three times? And you can't say, "If you call out three times, I'll, I'll, you'll see . . . !" A congruent rule is a rule that is clear, comes from your clarified feeling about the severity of the infraction. You can't imply, "You'll see . . . !" If you feel that: a student who calls out three times (after the first time, just a look, then a verbal warning) should get an extra assignment—you must specify that in your rule.

Yes, you need to think out how you feel, what you will do, and can do, for each discipline problem, and beforehand, not on the spot. For instance, for the following situations, would you say "yes," "no," or "maybe":

1. "Can't I go to the bathroom during the period?"
2. "Can I go twice, three times?"
3. "Would you penalize me if I don't do the homework?"
4. "If I call out once, will you give me a homework assignment?"
5. "Twice? Three times?"
6. "Or just see me after class?"
7. "If I throw garbage across the room, will you punish me?"
8. "Would you lend me a nickel, dime, a dollar?"
9. "Can I talk to my friends for a second while you're teaching?"
10. "How about ten seconds?"
11. "If I don't have a pen or pencil, would you lend me one?"
12. "Two days in a row?"
13. "Can I borrow one from another student?"
14. "Even if it disrupts your lesson?"
15. "Two days in a row?"
16. "Can I get out of my seat?"
17. "Can I tell a joke in class?"
18. "Can I wave at a friend in the hall?"

---

[99] There are obvious difficulties here that we shall address just ahead on pp. 261–262.

You need to decide. If some of your answers were "maybe," you need to decide, "if what?" What are your conditions? For instance, the student maybe can call out, if it's an accident? If it's not more than twice? Maybe s/he can go to the bathroom, if s/he's back in five minutes? Students don't ask all of these questions all the time, but eventually you'll have to respond to these, and respond congruently. And, in a way, they do ask these; they test teachers all the time.

I wish it were the case that I could simply give you twelve or twenty rules that work. I can't. Your rules need to be out of how you feel about each infraction from who you are, how you feel about it, and what you believe is an appropriate reprimand. All I can do is urge you to think them out now. I can (and will in Chapter 12, section A, pp. 285–294) give you guidelines for your rules. One of the first guidelines is: "Make sure you are congruent with the rule and with your warning about its infraction." (I'll give you other guidelines in Chapter 12, section A.) But you must first decide what you really believe in before you can apply any other guidelines.

Stop here and ask yourself: how do you feel about each of the following, and what would be your specific warning or reprimand?

1. absences
2. fighting in classes[100]
3. arguments among students
4. going to the bathroom
5. bus passes
6. cheating
7. chewing gum
8. being high in class
9. personal stereos with earphones
10. eating in class
11. poor handwriting
12. students who don't do the homework[100]
13. coming to class late[100]
14. name calling
15. note passing
16. spitting
17. whistles
18. talking to another student while you're teaching
19. calling out[100]

---

[100] Fighting, missed homework, lateness, and calling out will be dealt with specifically in Chapter 13, section B.

20. throwing things
21. running
22. jokes

Keep in mind that, as you decide your rules and warnings for these, that you may have <u>mixed feelings</u> about, e.g., late homework, or note passing. If you do, say your mixed feelings in just a more complex rule. For instance, "I don't want late homework. I'll penalize you one point on your report card for each late homework. But you can make up the homework, but only for that week. If you want to make up homework back two weeks, at the end of the marking period, it's too late!" Or, "Don't pass notes. If I don't see it, fine. But, if I do, you'll see me after class. If it happens again, you'll do an extra homework assignment." In other words, don't state a simple rule, if you don't feel simply one way about it. But don't avoid figuring out the complex rule you feel congruent with because you have complex feelings about it. It's work to figure these out, but it'll pay off because your rules will be less apt to fall apart.

Now, what if the principal puts a directive in all the teachers' mailboxes that says, "Follow this rule: If a student curses in your class, the student should receive an extra homework assignment and be sent to my office where his/her parent will be called."? What if you don't feel congruent about this rule nor its punishment? What should you do? I must say that if you read this rule to your class, and make believe you feel this way, and say you'll enforce it (when you really don't feel this way), the rule will fall apart. Also, your relationship with your students will begin to fall apart. So this faking your belief and advocation of the rule will, eventually, not solve any discipline problems and may even create more. Well, the administration of your school certainly doesn't want that to happen. So, if they are smart, they would not dictate such a directive without gaining a sense of ownership from the staff. The best rules from the administration are those that come out of the administration's survey of the staff's problems and from the staff's design of what might be best to enforce. But, what if your administration is short-sighted here? What do you do then? You feel that not all four-letter-word users should receive an extra assignment. They certainly should not be sent to the principal. And to call their parents certainly seems overreactive to you. So what should you do? Follow your boss's order and be good, but then be a bad teacher who delivers incongruent messages to his or her class? You know the class will "smell" that you don't really believe what you're reading to them. If you push a non-credible rule on them, they'll wonder about the credibility of what you say in general. Some student might even ask you, "Are you really going to do that?"!

My suggestion here is: when you are caught between the administration's rules and your own congruence, <u>don't lie to the students</u>. Your lie will be "smelled," the rule won't stick, and their anger with you will cause even more discipline problems. Also, your acting as if you will uphold this rule will eat away at any congruent credibility you have built up for all of your other rules and promises. Instead, you can read them the rule. "Class, I just got this in the mail. Quote: 'If a student curses. . . .' Now, class, let me tell you how I feel about this. If you use a four-letter word in here, but you weren't cursing at someone, but were only frustrated and said it accidentally. . . ." Then, you should tell them what you believe the punishment should be and what you will do. In other words, you should deliver your congruent revision of the rule. Most administrators would feel O.K. about this tack because what they want is to curtail discipline problems. Well, if they understand your care about congruence here, they would see that your approach will curtail discipline problems. So, by doing the above suggestion, you will be using different means toward similar ends. Of course, I also recommend that you tell your principal (e.g., at a faculty meeting) your suggested revision, even explain how important you feel about congruence. Certainly, survey other teachers about how they feel about this rule or whether they also agree with the importance of congruence. Also, suggest (if your administration doesn't already) that the staff, as a team, create the school's rules so that all can own them better (feel more congruent with them) and, thus, enforce them better. Again, the key to enforceable, effective rules is congruence. Work for this for yourself, for your students, and for and with your administration.

3. Your subject matter delivery

It is important that you are also congruent regarding your subject matter delivery. Students who feel that even the teacher doesn't care about the lesson being taught not only turn off to that lesson but also resent that teacher. We must work on being congruent with the subject we teach, or our incongruent delivery of the lesson will be another major source of discipline problems.

Hopefully, you really do care about the subject you teach. Hopefully, you chose this subject as your major in college because you believe in its value. If you chose your major because you just liked Mr. Johnson in the eighth grade (who just happened to teach math), but you really don't care for math, you're in trouble. You can't motivate a class about something you yourself are not motivated about. You can, maybe, fake it for a while. But, eventually you'll either burn out from faking your enthusiasm all day, all year, or the students will sense your inauthenticity eventually and turn off and go after you. Hopefully, at least eighty percent of the subject matter you do care about, do feel is valuable, but not some twenty percent. For instance, you do believe in studying math but don't value doing quadratic equations. Or you do believe in studying social studies but don't value knowing, for example, the lineage of all the British kings. Fine. You are generally congruent with the curriculum you must motivate. You can honestly keep saying or implying each lesson, each day, "Class, this is important," congruently. If you come to quadratic equations or the lineage of British kings, you can say to them, "Class, this stuff you may not find so exciting or valuable. Maybe you will. I hope so. But we've got to learn it. It's required. Stay with me, O.K.?" If you have been congruent, this congruent statement can often bring them with you as you bank on your previous authenticity with them.

But, what if you don't care about fifty percent of the subject, or seventy-five percent of it?! You cannot keep admitting to the class that most of this stuff you don't care about either. They'll feel, "Why the hell then are you teaching this?!" And they're right. Why are you spending every day, every year teaching students that they have to care about, work on, sacrifice time for (midst all their own problems) something you yourself don't care about? You need the money? Go out and get a job where you become a teller, painter, messenger, etc. for a salary per hour! You are imprisoning youngsters in compulsory education through your disservice to them. They will not be motivated, will have trouble learning the subject—even hate learning—from your attitude. You will also (you already?) hate your job, be bored with the subject, discover the kids dislike you, constantly be having discipline problems, etc. Be good to yourself and to them and work on either teaching what you care about or finding another job. The money can't be worth it.

About ten years ago, I was supervising a young student teacher who was teaching the Renaissance in a social studies high school class (I'll call him Fred). I observed him teaching the class. Fred was teaching the rise of towns, increased trade, the invention of the printing press, etc. He spoke well, wrote notes on the chalkboard, gave assignments, and had rules about disruptive behavior, etc. But, for some reason, the class was always bored, non-participatory, and then eventually disruptive. About halfway through each period, though Fred warned, coerced, and argued with them about paying attention, the class would turn off, and class clowns and wise guys would appear all over the room. I even felt bored with Fred's lesson (and I do care about history, the Renaissance, and social studies). After the class, I gave Fred my perceptions of his class as constructively as I could. Then I asked, "Fred, do you care about the Renaissance?" "Of course I do," he jumped. "No, Fred, calm down, it's O.K. Maybe you don't care about it so much." "Well," he said, "I don't find it a very exciting topic." "Very exciting?" "Well, to tell you the truth I feel it's a bit boring sometimes." "Well Fred, the class can sense that." "They can?" "Of course." He looked a little upset. I asked, "Do you care about the causes of World War I or II, or religious history, or how geography affects history?" "Well, not very much." "Why are you teaching social studies?" I asked a little incredulously. "Because I'm a social studies major." "But, how did that happen?" "Well, I liked my history teacher in seventh grade. . . ."

Fred was in trouble. To make a long story short, I found out from some more questions that he did love Renaissance art and did find it exciting how creativity was enlivened in the arts during the Renaissance. Fred even painted a lot and wrote short stories, even did some sculpting, after school. I asked him to design a lesson plan about this aspect of the Renaissance. And I asked him to create this lesson from his heart. On February 20, a Friday, Fred taught this lesson. He again used the chalkboard, the same methods as before, and the same rules and warnings. But on that day this man glowed! I never was very interested in the details of Renaissance art, but on that day I was enamored as I listened to Fred. He was excited, caring, very there, looser, and even charismatic. The class was glued to his words, wanting to feel that way (the way Fred felt) too: caring, alive, concerned. There were no discipline problems that day and not even any need for any threats to the class. No class clowns appeared nor wise guys. Fred was the best performer and much the wiser. I later learned that two years later, after Fred had graduated, that he quit trying to be a teacher and was now editing for a small magazine, selling paintings, and doing part-time work as a guide in an art museum. Fred thanked me. Students should thank him too.

You must understand that every minute of every class, every day, students are always in a way asking: "Why the hell should we learn this stuff?" Sometimes they even ask it out loud. We are obligated to give them an authentic answer, sometimes explicitly, always at least implicitly, as we teach. They have a right to feel that this stuff matters, especially during the turmoil of the other things that so matter during their adolescence. I myself am a bad math teacher mainly because I just don't "dig" math. I can't feel for much of it: "why the hell learn a lot of it." I should never teach math. However, I know a math teacher who loves math. When she teaches it, I care to learn it.

It is crucial that we get as congruent with our subject matter as we can, or teach another subject, or don't teach. Again, if you only feel bored with twenty percent of your subject, you can be honest and carry your class pretty well. What you need to do is to ask what your class is asking: "Why learn this stuff?" For example, if you're a social studies teacher, "Why learn the causes of World War 1?" "Because it's important, you say. "Well, why?" "Because it teaches you how conflicts start." "Well, why learn that?" "Because if you learn about how conflicts start, maybe you, we, can prevent them." "Why learn that?" "Because conflicts hurt people, destroy lives." Now that makes sense. I recommend that now that you have traced where your real concern is regarding teaching World War 1, you teach from that concern. Perhaps your opening to your class is: "Class, list three conflicts you've seen lately." Or "Class, how do you prevent a conflict?" "Why do they start?" By connecting yourself and the class to this authentic care you really feel, you will deliver the lesson on World War I more congruently. You need to sit down and look at the topics you will teach this week. Ask yourself "Why are they important?" Because of X? "Well, why learn X?" Because of Y. "Why learn Y?" And so on, until you meet your "heart." If you take the time to do this, you will teach with your heart more in your subject. And the class will feel it. Don't be afraid to use the subject matter to teach your real concern, or what you believe in, value, or gets to you. Or teach what they feel, are concerned about, believe in or value, through the subject matter. Use the subject matter as a vehicle for cares, not just as an end in itself. A congruently delivered lesson prevents many discipline problems from arising.

In summary, you need to work on being congruent with regard to: (1) your general interaction with your students; (2) your rules; (3) your delivery of your subject matter. It's work, but it will be worth it. You'll have more rapport with your class. You'll need to threaten them less about being disruptive. You'll have more credibility and influence with them. They'll be more motivated and you'll be less exhausted as a teacher. But remember the four caveats: (1) At first, this skill of being congruent will take more work, before things get better and easier. (2) Only do what's congruent for you. (3) But, remember, at first try, the new suggestions won't feel like you. Give each a good try and practice them. They may become naturally you and, thus, congruent. Don't abandon a suggestion too quickly. (4) Don't fret if you can't do all of what is suggested.

C. Following Through

In Chapter 8, section C we discussed another important source of discipline problems: not following through. Obviously, to curtail this source you need to follow through with what you warn or say you will do. If you say, "We'll have a spelling bee on Friday," you need to do that Friday. If you say, "I'll give back your tests Thursday," you should mark them and have them ready for Thursday. If you say, "If you call out again, you'll do an extra assignment," you need to have such an assignment ready, give it when s/he calls out again, and remember to check it. This takes remembering your promises and warnings, often some record keeping, and bothering to follow through. You may not want to bother to keep records, or follow through, or you can't seem to remember. Your job has too much to do as is. So you don't follow through.

However, not following through will make your job initially easy (when you let the warning or promise slide) but eventually much more difficult. The follow-through you do on your promises and rewards is the backing to your words and rules, as gold is the backing to paper currency. Every time you don't follow through on what you said, your words and rules lose their backing; they mean less, get inflated, until the students think you are just "hot air." You must realize that if you don't bother to carry out one rule or promise, it doesn't just bring lack of credibility to just that rule. One lack of follow-through infects all your rules and words with a feeling, "S/he really doesn't mean what she says." As a result, students listen to you less, believe in your motivations less, in your rules less, in your warnings less, in you less. I understand that you said to Tom: "If you throw another piece of paper, I'll call your parents," this morning. I understand the day is over now, it's three o'clock, and you don't really want to bother to find the phone number and call. I understand. But, if you don't call, you will be weakening not just your rules with Tom, but with the whole class, who will check to see if you meant it. You will be weakening all of your rules.

To follow through, you can't blurt out the first warning that just pops into your head. For instance, when John calls out again, you can't just say in a fit of anger, "John, if you call out again, you'll have to stay after school until 5:00 P.M.!" That may not be possible for you or John. You must decide now not only what you believe in for typical infractions but also what you can and are willing to do. Decide now what you can and will do if: a student calls out for the third time, interrupts you with a wisecrack twice, throws paper, keeps whistling, etc. Decide now, so you'll blurt less what you can't nor feel willing to follow through.

If you keep the above in mind, you may be more able and motivated to follow through. As far as remembering to follow through, if you work on checking out your congruence with your promises and warnings, you'll automatically remember more to follow through. If you believe in what you said, believe this infraction is serious, that it warrants calling a parent, or an extra assignment—you'll remember. Teachers tend to forget to follow through when the promise, rule, or warning is not theirs. When it's your promise or rule, if it's violated, you feel it violated as yours. Your "person" will help you remember because you are personally attached to it, congruent with it. So, if you're congruent, you'll tend to follow through. If you still tend to forget but are congruent about your promises and warnings, do more record keeping. Have a page in your lesson plan book or Delaney book for each period you teach. If you promise or warn someone in, e.g., period three, clip a reminder note to that page about it. At the end of the day, remove all reminder notes, take them home, and work on following through on each one. These suggestions, if kept in mind, should help most teachers follow through.[101]

---

[101] Some teachers may still not follow through because they're just not "assertive." We shall discuss this problem in Chapter 12, section G: "Working on Asserting Yourself and Taking Stands."

Then, remember the four caveats here: (1) At first this will be more work, but eventually, you'll build a reputation of "S/he means it!" which will ultimately make your job easier. (2) Only do what's congruent for you. (3) Give each a good try before you abandon it. (4) Don't fret if you can't follow through on everything you say. Just work toward building as much credibility as you can for what you say. The more credible your words, the less you'll have to yell to compensate for your lack of credibility.

D. Being Appropriate

In Chapter 8 we discussed another important source of discipline problems: being inappropriate. To curtail this source teachers must do and say appropriate things. That means (to review Chapter 8, section D) they must act professionally and deliver messages that are in line with their job responsibilities. And since a teacher's responsibilities are the education and growth of their students, they must check if it is the case that what they are doing is in the best interests of students. Or is what you are doing or saying for your sake, or for the students' sake? If it is the latter, you're being appropriate.

One clarification here, if it's good for the students, e.g., that they learn to correct each others' papers, and good for you (gives you less marking to do) that's still appropriate, professional. But, if what you ask or say is only satisfying your needs, it's inappropriate. On pages 153–154, we gave examples of inappropriateness. We need only to remind you to check on your appropriateness. Your inappropriateness will eventually create an "enemy" relationship between you and your students, and thus lead to disruptive behavior.

You need to check whether you are being appropriate for your students with regard to: your general interactions with them, your rules, and your lessons. Are you playing favorites? Are you being sarcastic, "putting kids down"? Are you being racist, sexist? Are your rules for their sake, or at least, also for their sake? Are the topics and stories and jokes you are discussing or telling for their sake?

Remember, as we said in Chapter 8, be careful; you can be congruent and inappropriate. You can congruently be racist, or love your irrelevant jokes, or flirt with a student. But, if your behavior is not good for them, you're inappropriate, no matter how congruent you are. You must be congruent and appropriate.

E. Being Fair

In Chapter 8, section E we discussed another important source of discipline problems: being unfair. Students hate unfair teachers. They go after, and are disruptive with, unfair teachers. However, being fair is a difficult and complex skill. It is difficult because you will be confused by students who see you as unfair, when you're not. And, even when they see you as fair, they may try to con you into feeling unfair to make you feel guilty, to get out of whatever they don't want to be responsible for. So, since student perceptions are often short-sighted and are sometimes motivated by the desire to have less responsibility, you must be the judge of your fairness. You must still consider their reactions as feedback, but practice judging your judgers, and be the final judge. Your license gives you that authority. If you are called "unfair," consider it, it may be true. But, also consider all the facts you know that they don't know, decide if you're being conned, or if they are just being resistant to work or responsibility. Trust your judgment after you consider these pressures on you. If you still feel that you are being fair, stick to your guns. Often, you will not be able to give them a rationale for your action or decision. That's sad, but reality. Sure, try to find time to explain your rationale if a student wants to know "Why?" But, if you can't, but you do believe in a rationale you have thought through professionally, stick by your decision. Also, be careful here. A student who sincerely asks "Why?" is different from a student who challenges "Why?!" You may try to answer the former, but you have every right (if you believe in your fairness) not to "arm-wrestle" with the latter. If you tend to bother to be fair and think out your warnings and rules, you'll trust yourself. And, because you bother to be fair, the class will tend to trust you also.

To help you with this complex skill and judgment, here are some questions to help you decide whether your rules and warnings are fair:

(a) Are you going after a "miscall" (Chapters 4 and 11, section A)?

(b) Are you going after an incident that is a ducking situation (Chapter 10, section A)?

(c) Are you going after a student because you weren't "appropriate" (Chapter 11, section D)?

(d) Are you applying your rules, or warnings, or evaluative standards unjustly with partiality or bias?

(e) Do you let some students "get by" with some rules, warnings, or standards, and not others, for solely subjective reasons?

(f) Do you go after the wrong student because the "right one" is more difficult for you, confronting this one scares you more, takes more work?

(g) Do you sometimes overreact from your own personal feelings, and don't either apologize or correct these responses?

(h) Have you punished the whole class because of one student, having no value except to show them the power of your anger?

(i) Have you given a punishment that doesn't fit the "crime"?

(j) Do you apply rules, warnings, or standards without knowing your own rationale?

You should check these questions to yourself often, especially when you're trying to decide if students feedback is a "con" or not, or a lack of knowledge of the complexities involved in your decision. If you can honestly say "No" to these questions above, you're probably being very fair, and having fewer discipline problems because of it.

F. Especially for Grades K–6

Although following all of the above suggestions will also be helpful to elementary school teachers, because the developmental stages of children aged 5–12 are different, we need to discuss some specific suggestions for grades K–6.

It is especially true in grades K–2 (and somewhat true in grades 3–6) that the teacher's personality is the most influential tool in the classroom. Developmentally (and oversimplifying), children are first motivated by extrinsic rewards (food, toys), then emotional rewards (approval, recognition, attention), then symbolic rewards (gold stars, points, grades), and finally, if they attain this, intrinsic rewards (a feeling of pride, self-satisfaction, enjoying it for its own sake). Of course, at any time, all of these or some of these may be of influence. But it is generally the case that infants are motivated by extrinsic rewards, young children by emotional and symbolic rewards, and adults (if attained) by intrinsic rewards. This oversimplified scheme can be applied to grades K–6, especially K–2. Here, children are most influenced by (emotional rewards) their needs for attention, approval, recognition, and getting symbolic rewards.

Thus, a teacher of this age group needs to be able to emote, show approval, give lots of attention, listen caringly, nurture, and also give symbolic rewards in a systematic (keep track) consistent manner. Often, the ability to say: "Great, John!" or to be dramatic, or give gold stars out fairly and systematically is even more important than the cognitive lesson plan.

Of course, the teacher also needs to be congruent, not make miscalls, follow through, be appropriate and fair, but the interaction between the teacher and the students needs to have a rich, "emotional life."

How can a teacher of K–6 work on this? First of all, re-read Chapter 8, section F where this is reviewed. Just being aware of what you need to do will help. Then, you need to notice your own personality, a powerful tool. Are you too cognitive? Are you not able to express how you feel in positive terms? Is it difficult for you to say: "Wow!" "Great!" "Excellent!" "Good Job!" "Terrific!"? Obviously, if you are withdrawn and not extroverted, you will be more emotionally closed. If you are angry, depressed, not confident, anxious, etc., your emotions will be repressed. To be able to emote, you need to get rid of your anger, get help with your depression, and build confidence. The latter are often helped by getting support to feel less overwhelmed, or you need to find a place to vent your anger and fears. This is tough to work on for people who are introverted. But, unfortunately, it is the case that you will have trouble if you can't also be a "cheerleader" as you teach these grades.

We previously stated that although the teacher's personality is more important in elementary school, it is possible for an elementary school teacher to worry a little less about congruence, since there is more insertion of dramatic excitement or acting allowed (Chapter 8, Section F.). The flip side of this coin is that the elementary school teacher must worry more about consistency. Elementary school children are more immersed than older students in trying to make sense out of their world. With consistent application of fair rules, children can begin to predict the outcomes of their actions, to anticipate them, and finally to enforce consequences themselves. If a child knows in advance what will happen if he/she does "x" then that child will begin to ask him/herself, "Is it worth it for me to do this?" Achieving this goal means a great deal of vigilance early in the year on the part of the teacher and absolute consistency all year, but as the burden of control shifts over time from the teacher to the students, the teacher will be more congruent with him/herself, be freed to teach more, be able to interact in positive ways with his/her students more, and be called on to play the role of "enforcer" less.

Consistency is even more crucial in the elementary school classroom than in the upper grades. I once had a student's mother approach me in my second grade classroom to share something her son had told her about my discipline style when she had (in a moment of anger) accused him of liking me better than he liked her, his own mother. She told me that she had gotten very upset with her son because he always seemed to listen to me, but often ignored her, even when she was clearly angry and meant "it." When she demanded to know why this was true, her son looked at her and said, "I do love you, Mom, but when Mrs. Feller says she is going to do something if we don't stop, I know she will. I never get extra chances from her. You give too many warnings, Mom." Young children need to be able to predict their world to make sense out of it. If what they can predict is that you won't follow through, you are guaranteed to have discipline problems.

Regarding miscalls, remember you need to tolerate a general din of noise and interaction among the students, especially in grades K–2. And, again, you need to keep track of what you promised, to follow through, and be fair. These are especially crucial for this age group since these students not only get angry when these are not done properly but also are learning how to be fair and fulfill promises themselves.

Similarly, the teacher's aide (paraprofessional), especially in grades K–2, needs to be aware of the above and perform them appropriately and effectively.

The aide should review Chapter 1, section D and the last part of Chapter 8, section F. Since you are the <u>assistant</u>, you need to check out with your teacher which kids and specific behaviors your teacher is trying to reward or extinguish. If you are nurturant or sympathetic to a child that is manipulating to get his or her way, you will sabotage the teacher's ability to enforce rules and routines. Children will go for "the weakest link" in the team. Therefore, it is important that you meet with the teacher often. You'll need to share information with your teacher about behaviors s/he may not know about. But then, you both need to be consistent in your decisions about what behaviors do or do not warrant attention, approval, or recognition. Also, regarding symbolic rewards, you <u>both</u> need to keep track of the system, e.g., for getting a gold star, a point, or loss of a privilege.

G. Teachers Share Their Growing Pains[102]

Not Making Miscalls

Displaced anger: I have on many occasions been guilty of this. Something in the hallways (learn to duck, Pam) would upset me and I'd enter the class ready to kill anyone who so much as batted an eye. Now, I let my class know I'm upset and to be patient with me. In return, they are to let me know how they are feeling and I'll take it into consideration.

• • •

Tired of being helpful: How many times have I lost my patience when asked the same thing time and time again. Now I first reevaluate my explanations to make sure I'm being clear.

When I make miscalls, it is usually due to displaced anger. A picture of myself would look like this:

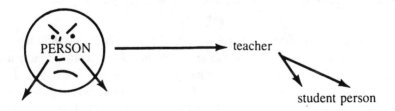

Any little thing got me pissed. It could be a student who just wasn't doing anything but looking out the window, or someone who didn't do their home-

---

[102] These are comments from teachers who have already gone through the training described above.

work. I blew everything out of proportion. At first, I did this very often because I had personal problems and blamed the students for them. Student teaching took up so much of my time (writing lesson plans, making up tests, grading tests, correcting homework, etc.) that I didn't have much time left to spend with my husband. We got into a lot of arguments over this because he felt that I was neglecting him and his wants and needs.

Being Congruent

At the beginning of each school year, I place a great deal of emphasis on my authority in the classroom. In so doing, I block out a great deal of my "person" and exercise authority through my role as a teacher.

I don't quite understand why I've done this, but I have a few ideas. First, it made me feel safer with the students in class. That is to say, I defended myself from reactions by the students, by placing the teacher up in front of the firing line. I thought it deterred students from questioning my reasoning or reactions to classroom situations. When I was a student, I recall my feelings as being "Well he's the teacher and there is nothing I can say about a situation." However, there is more to being a teacher than just teaching. I will have to pull down my defenses and open up. Maybe, this is the "safer" way to go.

However, this poses another problem for me because I don't open myself up like a can of beans for anyone, at least not a casual acquaintance. This is something that unfolds for me naturally over a period of time, as trust and understanding develop. Therefore, my personal interaction with students doesn't begin on the first day. It takes time, I believe you will agree, that personal relationships cannot be achieved in forty-two minutes. However, I am considering opening up more about my feelings and personal reflections to hasten the growth of personal interaction or congruent interaction. Doing this at the start of school I hope will create an understanding more readily between myself and my students than my past experience has shown.

• • •

As far as the curriculum goes, I have not been totally honest with myself or the kids. I know I have to try to approach the subject matter from many different viewpoints to find a way that's congruent to me. Looking back, I can see now that the lessons in which I was congruent were always the best. I know, for example, that I should use the social studies book less and plan more interesting lessons tied to what I feel is important about the subject. I don't have difficulty showing how I feel, but in some areas what I have been projecting is negative feelings. I also must train myself to be more flexible within the lesson.

• • •

My first reaction to the concept of congruence in evaluating myself was that I rated myself as average. I can honestly recall many times when I did not know how I felt and other times when I knew how I felt but could not find the proper words to express it. Also, I have warned the kids about my feelings but have not actually told them what they are.

• • •

I firmly believe that being congruent with a class in the beginning of a semester is a very difficult task, especially when you don't know what their reaction will be. Maybe the problem here could be need for approval on my part. Now, I can clearly see that I have a little more difficulty expressing my feelings about their behavior than expressing my feelings on particular subject matter.

• • •

When examining whether I "say what I feel and feel what I say," I realized that for the most part this is not true.

I find that it is of great importance to think about and evaluate my true feelings on subject matter, rules, warning systems, administrative rules, and personal issues before I begin teaching.

This is something I never did. Consequently, I was faced with many instances of disruptive behavior because the children did not know "where I was at" regarding these areas.

• • •

Having some students older than myself and teaching all boys presented a bit of a problem to me, and I really did hide myself under the cloak of teacher "99.9 percent strength" that first semester. That pressure was really great and it took its toll—I cried often that first term after I came home from trying to banish the "me" from the teacher role.

• • •

The importance of being congruent when dealing with kids cannot be overemphasized. I have come to realize that many times when I stammer and search for the right words, it is exactly those times when I don't really believe or feel what I'm saying. This gets the kids suspicious, and rightly so, and very often leads to discipline problems, either by individual students or the entire class. Since I am not a physically threatening teacher, it is necessary that I consistently convey to the children the kind of "personteacher" I am. As I seek to trust and be trusted by students, I must not talk down to or deceive the students in any way.

• • •

I can speak, I can write, and most times I can understand the way that I feel. At other times, though, when I am removed from being alone with myself,

I have trouble relating my feelings to others. I am afraid that other people will not accept my feelings, and even though I understand how I feel I'm not sure I accept them as being valid myself.

• • •

Congruence is that quality that allows a teacher to express his true feelings about his subject area of teaching or in his personal relationships with his students. When I began teaching, I found that I had many problems expressing my true feelings toward a student if he was being disruptive in my class. Holding my anger inside me usually made matters worse because the student didn't really know where I stood with regard to his behavior. At this time, however, I have very little trouble letting a student know how I feel about him or about something he had done. Also, my attitude toward teaching some topics in mathematics still gives me problems. I do not get very excited about teaching verbal problems in algebra, and I think the students detect this, and sometimes get "turned off." Congruence is a very important quality to have because it can say much about the credibility of the teacher.

• • •

In the beginning of the year, I established some classroom rules that I became uncomfortable with after taking this course. I have changed these rules because it has become impossible for me to congruently enforce these rules. Rules such as "No spiral notebooks," "Math and Spelling must be done in pencil and "No candy for lunch" seem purposeless now. I don't have to prove who is the boss. There is no boss. Regarding school rules, I tell my feeling about them. If I genuinely agree, I say so. If I don't, I say so, adding that they will have to follow these rules in the school, but I am willing to bend them in my classroom.

Following Through

I have trouble being consistent about following through with punishments. This is probably because I am not congruent about them. I still tend to "blurt," and then don't follow through. I am learning not to say, "If you do that again, I'll call your mother, send you to the office, keep you after school every day for a month." Before I call in a third party I have to ask myself if it's necessary.

• • •

I find that at times I forget to give that extra homework assignment or call that parent or talk to a student during the day because I am overwhelmed by the demands and pressures of the job. Sometimes the schedule is changed, something comes up that I must do that day for my supervisor, or I have so many interruptions that the classwork does not get done and everything else is forgotten.

• • •

Sometimes I just didn't want to be bothered with calling a parent. The reason is not that I didn't want to be bothered but that I was afraid. I was afraid of being told that I wasn't doing a good job.

I can remember one parent who couldn't understand why his son was doing so poorly. After I explained the behavior displayed by his child every day, the father blew up at me and told me that it was my job to control his son. I wasn't afraid during this encounter, but I was afraid of having to come in contact with this man again.

• • •

When I threaten to take away a party or some such treat from the children, I usually don't. If I do take it away, I find a reason to give it back to them. This leads the children to believe they can get away with minor infractions. Although I find it difficult to follow through on a threat, I must learn to carry it through. In the long run it will be better for me and the children.

• • •

I tend not to be able to follow through on the warnings I give students when they misbehave. I tend to speak before I think things through, i.e., basically I tend to blurt! For example, a student disrupted the class from learning by talking to her neighbor. I told the student after reprimanding her twice before that if she continued to talk, I would send her to the dean. She continued to talk and I didn't send her to the dean. After I realized what I had said to this student, I knew that I couldn't send her to the dean because in my school we are not supposed to send this type of case to the dean; we are supposed to handle it by ourselves. If I carried through my threat, it would only come back into my lap again. What I should have said to this student is that she should see me after class where we can discuss the matter.

• • •

I am definitely inconsistent and I know it can mess me up. It's just that I'm lazy and so many things need more than one follow-up that I neglect doing it. If I could do it in a one-try-one-follow-up process, I could manage, but as the term progresses, I get bogged down in other stuff and don't follow through the second or third time. The record keeping alone! This is going to be much more difficult for me to do. After all, I'm in control of expressing congruence and there's no paperwork involved. Maybe if I can get those disciplinary steps worked out, I'll be able to see the results that will encourage me to keep it up for the necessary "breaking-in" period.

• • •

This area is definitely the most difficult to be successful in. There are times the thing I tell the students is not quite the same as my follow-through. There are many reasons for this inconsistency, but my problem is mainly that I state more than I really wish to enforce. For example, I have an official class that is very noisy. I warned them that if the noise persists, I will assign seats to the class, even though I'd rather not because it makes extra work for myself. The class ignored my warning, so I repeated my warning about assigned seats and I still didn't do it. There went my consistency. After the third or fourth warning, two days later, I forced myself to assign seats. At this point it was difficult. I am now thinking more clearly about my warnings and not biting too much to chew.

• • •

I find that I am not a consistent person. I do not follow through on my warnings. I have been working on this concept recently. In the past, I felt some of my warnings were too harsh for the type of behavior problem the student exhibited. I also find that I have a tendency toward favoritism. Therefore, I do not always give the same to every child for the same type of behavior.

I would say that I tend to blurt at least two or three times a day, an unfortunate rate. Even though these are spontaneous responses, I sometimes feel I am waiting for an opportunity to respond. To me it is an opportunity to come up with a great line. I have this almost wholly irresistible urge to come up with that great line even though it usually goes over the heads of my students. I believe, this being the case, that it is done just to please and entertain myself, and while I am being momentarily entertained it can lead to chaos.

For example, I'm writing on the board and suddenly I hear a radio blast. If I know where it's coming from, I might wheel and throw a piece of chalk in the direction of the offending student and tell him if he doesn't turn off the radio and put it away I'm going to turn him off and lock him away for good. I don't even know what this means and neither do the kids, but the words sound right and the message is clear. Now, obviously, I'm not going to lock him anywhere but that's not really important at that instant. My kids just stop work and watch the show. With one blurt I have disrupted the class with no chance of following up on that blurt. Fortunately, the student will almost always put the radio away but that does not preclude his bringing it in again another day and forcing me to act again—this time, hopefully, with some sense.

Sometimes the blurt will be truly creative. At one time I would engage in "snapping," the art of putting another person down, but it led to absolute chaos. Now I might be in the middle of a discussion where most people are raising hands while one or two are calling out. They are probably not even calling out answers, just opinions or observations. Perhaps I'll blurt to the few calling out, "Keep yelling out and I'll cut your tongue out." They'll look at me as if I'm crazy. Perhaps I'll say, "Use your hands, you know, the things you use to swing from branch to branch." Or "What's the matter, if you raise your hands your armpits will knock us out." The class falls into instant hysteria. Then I'll say, "If you continue calling out, I'm going to throw you out." They sense immediately that since I helped to create the atmosphere of chaos I won't throw them out. Now most times my blurts do not lead to a situation quite as chaotic as this. But they do lead to my saying things that I know I won't follow up on and my kids know I won't follow up on so another barrier is down, and I am now closer to being at the mercy of my students.

Though blurts might be spontaneous reactions, I feel I can still work on them by working to remain stable and consistent in my teaching without giving into certain whims of my own personality. It is one of my hardest problems.

Being Appropriate

My main focus from now on will be on the growth of the children. There have been many times when I have talked about myself to my class for no purpose but to serve my ego. I have also cheated the class, I am certain, by doing lesson plans that have been more convenient for myself than beneficial to them.

My biggest problem is saying things that are not appropriate for the situation. I enjoy being the center of attention in the class, and many times I make comical statements at the expense of some child. I must try to make appropriate statements to the children.

• • •

Being professional is doing what is good for my classes and not what is convenient for myself. Many times, during the course of a working day, I am tempted to do the easy thing. Sometimes, I am not professional and succumb to my desire to rest and take it easy.

Being Fair

I realize now that I let some students "get by" for subjective reasons.

• • •

I have a bias for students who look like other people in my family.

• • •

For some kids, I have put missing decimal points in on test papers.

• • •

I used to give class punishment assignments and then secretly approach some "goodie-goodies" and tell them they didn't have to do it.

• • •

I think I tend to call on boys more often than girls.

H. Training Exercises and Checklist for Chapter 11

Exercise One: Handling Those Feelings and Needs That Can Lead to Miscalls

(a) Make a list here of areas or responsibilities you feel a lack of pride in or areas you feel irresponsible about because you are procrastinating (in and/or out of school). Then, in the right hand column set a deadline day you will do the item by.

Area	Deadline
1.	
2.	
3.	
4.	
5.	
6.	

(b) To feel less powerless, stop now and make a "to do" list for this week and prioritize the items. Get organized. Decide on a day you will spend after school organizing your desk and classroom. Tell a friend about these plans to feel some support.

(c) To stop storing up angers, make a list here of all the irritations (in and/or out of school) you are feeling.

Angers

1.
2.
3.
4.
5.
6.

Now plan to do one or more of the following with each anger:

A. Meet a friend after school who's a good nonjudgmental listener and just try to vent what's bugging you.
B. Do some strenuous exercise.

C. Get away to a place for a while that is a complete change of environment.

D. Write a nasty letter (you never mail) to a person you're angry with.

E. In a private place, make believe that your pillow is one of the people you're angry with, and yell at it and hit it.

(d) To cope with your loneliness and sense of meaninglessness, you must be with more people and share meanings with them. Write down three persons' names here you will call this week and work on a friendship with them. Also, decide now to try two new meaningful projects this month.

Friend	New Project
1.	1.
2.	2.
3.	

(e) Write down here the names of students to whom you particularly over-react. Then, in the right column try to identify if there is anyone whom each of these students reminds you of (including you).

Students	Remind Me Of
1.	1.
2.	2.
3.	3.
4.	4.

(f) To identify any prejudices you may have, place a ✔ next to those you are most attracted to, an X next to those not attracted to, and an N next to those you find to be neutral or "not sure" for you. Here may be the biases you need to watch in your attitudes and behavior.

_____ Blacks	_____ Fat people	_____ Polish people
_____ Whites	_____ Skinny people	_____ Germans
_____ Orientals	_____ Short people	_____ Physically
_____ Hispanics	_____ Tall people	disabled
_____ WASPS	_____ Heterosexuals	_____ Long-haired males
_____ Jews	_____ Homosexuals	_____ Those with
_____ Protestants	_____ Men	crew cuts
_____ Catholics	_____ Women	_____ Poor dressers
_____ Atheists	_____ Irish people	_____ Cute or pretty
_____ Moslems	_____ Passive students	students

(g) if you feel "curriculum pressure," write out here a short note to the person (you yourself?) who is pushing and rushing you. Then, either really deliver the note, or talk to him or her about the pressures you feel.

_____
_____
_____
_____
_____
_____
_____
_____
_____
_____
_____
_____
_____

Exercise Two: Working on Being Congruent in Your General Interaction with Your Students

Review the congruence diagrams in Chapter 11, section B. Now draw how you are as teacher here (and/or have someone else draw you).

How incongruent are you? Why? (Review the reasons for incongruence on pp. 253–254.) Write yourself some advice here about your own ability to be congruent.

_____
_____
_____
_____

Exercise Three: Working on Being a Real Person with Your Students

Review the ways you can put your "person" into your "teacher" on p. 257. Check off at least four ways you will try this week. Write them down here, and grade yourself on how well you did at the end of the week.

Ways to be more real	Grade
1.	1.
2.	2.
3.	3.
4.	4.

Exercise Four: Working on Being Congruent Regarding Your Rules

Describe five rules you try to enforce in your classroom with each of their warned consequences. Now give them a letter grade: (A) I believe in this very much; (B) somewhat; (C) a little; (D) not at all.

Rule	Warning	Grade
1.	1.	1.
2.	2.	2.
3.	3.	3.
4.	4.	4.
5.	5.	5.

Exercise Five: Working on Congruence Regarding Your Subject Matter

(a) List ten topics you will teach this week. For each give a letter grade: (A) I think this is very important, I care about it; (B) I believe in the importance of this somewhat, care about it somewhat; (C) I don't feel this is valuable, I don't care about it; (D) I think this is useless and boring.

Topic	Grade	Topic	Grade
1.		6.	
2.		7.	
3.		8.	
4.		9.	
5.		10.	

(b) Choose a topic from above you did not give yourself an "A." Now, try to justify it. Why learn this? Give a reason. Then, ask, "why this?" etc. Can you reach some feeling you believe in close to your "heart"?

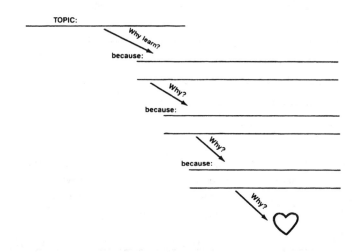

TOPIC:

Why learn?
because:

Why?
because:

Why?
because:

Why?

(c) Close your eyes (after you've read this) and imagine you're in the woods. It's a beautiful day. You hear some children playing off in the distance. Go to them. They are smart, have never been to school, and have never been in the world. You can teach them <u>one</u> thing, only one thing. And they will listen. What would you teach them? Write it here:

This fantasy of what you would teach them may reveal where your "heart" is, what you care about. Try to attach your curriculum to this deep care within you.

(d) Prepare an opening talk to your students about a curriculum topic you gave yourself a "B" on. Try to put your true feelings into this talk. Ask a friend, or a classmate, or colleague to listen to it. Now, ask them to rate you on how congruent, believable, motivating you sound.

Exercise Six: Working on Following Through

Look at your list of rules and warnings you wrote down in Exercise Four above. Give the rule two checkmarks if you always tend to follow through, a single checkmark if <u>sometimes</u>, an "X" if <u>seldom</u>. Why don't you follow through? Are you incongruent, lazy, too busy, worried about anger, hurting someone, forgetful . . . ?

Exercise Seven: Working on Being Appropriate

Look at these rules and warnings again you listed in Exercise Four. For each give them a letter grade: (A) this is for the students' sake; (B) for their sake and my sake; (C) mostly for my sake, somewhat helps them; (D) for my sake, doesn't help them. How appropriate are you?

Exercise Eight: Working on Being Fair

Again, look at your rules and warnings you listed in Exercise Four. Now, look at the questions about fairness listed on pp. 268–269. Can you answer "No" to each question for each of your rules? How fair are you? Which tendencies do you need to watch?

Checklist

1. Are you making any miscalls?
2. Are you handling these situations in a more constructive way?
3. Are you being congruent about your rules and warnings?
4. Are you being congruent about the subject matter in your delivery?
5. Are you acting congruent when you generally interact with your students?
6. Would you feel uncomfortable with your students if they suddenly saw you eating a sloppy pizza at a pizza parlor?
7. Are you following through with your warnings, rewards, and punishments?
8. Are your actions and what you say "appropriate"?
9. Are your rules, warnings, rewards, and punishments "fair"?
10. If you are mostly concerned about grades K–6, did you take the time to revise some of the suggestions in Chapter 11, as advised in section **F** above?

CHAPTER 12: PREVENTING YOUR RULES FROM FALLING APART AND SAVING KIDS

Let us first discuss **warnings and punishments** to enforce our rules. Then, after considering **the debate about: "what's most effective"?** we shall discuss **rewards** to enforce our rules.

A. Twenty-one Guidelines for Effective Rules and Warnings

As I have explained previously, no one can give you your rules; you have to decide them from what you believe in and feel about specific infractions and standards. You must design them congruently with who you are. However, I can give you guidelines that can help you in the formulation of these rules.[103]

1. Decide on a consequence that you will enforce, in the form of a <u>warning, if the rule is</u> broken.[104]

2. Obviously, <u>don't make a rule that enforces a miscall.</u> Check the "typical miscalls" in Chapter 4, section B. You certainly should not make (or have) a rule that helps you go after what is actually not a discipline problem.

3. <u>You should feel congruent with your rules.</u> Don't blurt out something you don't really believe in or that you later realize is too harsh. How do you stop such incongruent blurts? Again, go back to the list of misbehaviors on page 260–261 and formulate a rule now about each that you believe in. If you plan your rule according to your feelings now, you won't be apt to put your foot in your mouth in class.

Of course, your rules must also be in line with the rules of your school, what the administration (and, hopefully, with consent of the staff) has decided.

---

[103] The reader should be reminded here of the point I made at page 140: "One more point . . . ." about "controlling dictators."
[104] As reported in the *American Educator* "The New Research," Summer, 1984, p. 37), recent research indicates that: in the natural course of classroom life, rules will be broken by some students. A good manager plans ahead for these eventualities and builds into the management system a *"hierarchy of consequences."* Just as students should be aware of rules governing their behavior, they should be aware of what will happen when they misbehave (italics mine).

You should be able to feel comfortable with the school's rules, such that they do not cause you to be incongruent with your rules. If you do have problems here, see the discussion on pages 258–262 to help you sort out this problem. Meanwhile, here is a sample of what a typical school's rules might look like:

SCHOOL RULES OF A TYPICAL HIGH SCHOOL
Student Rules and Regulation

1. <u>Every student is to carry his/her program card at all times</u> and <u>must</u> present it <u>immediately</u> upon request by proper school authorities (deans, teachers, school safety officers, etc.). Lost program cards must be replaced in Room B38. There will be a $1 fee. In addition, if the student leaves a program card home, he/she may get a temporary card for one day only. Temporary program cards may be obtained in the deans' office before start of period 3 only.

2. <u>Students must come to school and classes on time.</u> Loitering in the halls will not be tolerated. If a student is repeatedly found in the hall after the late bell, s/he will be asked to bring a parent to school.

3. <u>No student is to be out of class at any time without a pass.</u> Passes will be required to: see a counselor, to go to the library, to go to the G.O. store, or for any other legitimate reason. If students wish to use the telephone, they must either do so during lunch period or have a pass from their subject class teacher.

4. <u>Students entering the building must use Exit 9/10.</u> This will be the only entry into the school. At no time will any other door be used as a student entrance.

5. <u>Every student must remain in the official class for the entire ten-minute period.</u> Having attendance taken and then leaving is unacceptable.

6. <u>Severe penalties will be imposed for cutting.</u>

7. <u>Students are expected to eat lunch in the school cafeteria daily.</u> No food from outside vendors is to be brought into the school.

8. <u>No weapons of any kind are allowed in school.</u> Possession of a weapon will result in a superintendent's suspension and/or arrest (see Chapter 13B, 12).

9. <u>Radios, tape decks, Walkman, bicycles, skateboards, masks, beepers, cellular phones, etc. are not allowed in school.</u> They will be taken by school authorities (deans, security officers) and returned only to parents (see Chapter 13B, 8 and 9).

10. <u>No eating is allowed in class</u> without special permission.

11. <u>Every student is expected to treat all school personnel with respect.</u>

12. Students will be suspended by the principal for the following infractions:
   (a) threatening behavior to school personnel
   (b) stealing of any kind
   (c) use or possession of marijuana, or alcohol, or any other drug (see Chapter 13B, 11)
   (d) gambling
   (e) graffiti, vandalism, fighting, forgery
   (f) verbal abuse, or refusal to identify oneself to school personnel.

13. No children or outsiders may be brought into the school without written permission from the assistant principal.

14. The school policy regarding dress code is listed below. This was formulated and agreed to by student representatives, staff, and administration. Please adhere strictly to these guidelines:

    (a) Shorts will be allowed only if they come no more than 3 inches above the knee. The same holds true for miniskirts.

    (b) No halter tops are allowed. Shirts or blouses must be worn.

    (c) No half shirts (worn by male or female) are allowed.

    (d) No "see-through" garments are allowed unless appropriate undergarments are worn.

    (e) No "gang related" clothing (i.e., bandannas, beads, etc.) may be worn in the building.

(For discussions on the legal parameters regarding many of these kinds of rules, see Appendix C.)

4. You should be able to follow through with the warning you design for each infraction of your rule. Again, don't blurt out "I'll suspend you!" if you can't really do that for, say, calling out. Again, go back to page 285 and decide on a warning you can follow through for each infraction. And keep in mind that not to follow through on one is to weaken your whole system and credibility.

5. Your rule should be one that is for the sake of their education, not just for your convenience. It should be appropriate, professional. If the rule keeps order so you can teach and they can learn, fine. If it only helps you, e.g., get your work done or wash your car, it's inappropriate.

6. The rule should be fair[105]

7. Your first response to an infraction should be as nonverbal as possible, e.g., a disapproving look or no recognition to an answer called out, instead of a verbal reprimand, "John!" Why? Because the latter gives more attention to the misbehavior. You don't want to accidentally award "negative attention" to behaviors you're trying to extinguish. If you have to reprimand, reprimand while giving the misbehavior as little attention as possible. Thus, for example, putting a disruptive student's name on the chalkboard or asking him or her to come to the front of the room, etc., places the student in the limelight. It's a negative limelight, but some students would rather get negative attention than none at all.

8. Along with the above, starve students who seek negative attention, but reward these students immediately as they "turn over a new leaf" and newly try to get attention for being good. Go deaf, dumb, and blind to a call-outer,

[105] According to our criteria listed in questions (a)–(j) on pp. 268–269.

but call on him or her the second s/he does raise his/her hand. (For more on handling "calling out" see pp. 348–349.)

9. Try to deliver your warnings in a place, or in a way, that has the <u>least audience reaction</u>. Don't reprimand a student in front of the class if you can at all help it. Try to remember that a reprimand in front of the class, especially for adolescents, is always much more severe than the same one given in private. Students reprimanded in front of an audience need to revolt against your warning to save face. Always, if you can, deliver your warning after class at the "See me after class!" meeting. Or deliver it at least in the back of the room while others are working. In both these situations, you should have your back to the wall (not the student) so when the student faces you, s/he is not exposed to others as you scold him/her. If you don't do this, the student will be facing you and his/her friends and will resist "facing the music" to save face. Or you might arrange with a teacher next door that if either of you have a disruptive student you'll just send him/her next door with, for instance, a punishment assignment to be done by the end of the period. The student suddenly must sit in the back of the room of a class s/he doesn't know. This strategy is usually better than sending students to the librarian or chairperson who may give the student a task the student enjoys. It's also a better idea than sending the student to the principal, who then wonders if you can handle discipline problems by yourself.

10. <u>Don't deliver your rule in the third person</u>. Be direct and say, "I won't tolerate. . . ." Don't say, "We don't do that. . . ." or "One wouldn't do that in. . . ."

11. Don't design too many rules that involve you in <u>being</u> the "judge <u>and jury" all the time.</u> For instance, don't say, "The rule is you can only go to the bathroom if you have to go badly." What's "badly"? Are you going to try to decide this? Make your rule based on an objective criterion. For example, "You can go to the bathroom only when the pass is not being used, and you can't go more than once a week." You can try to be more lenient, but to do so, and not be conned, will involve you in more and more complex conditions to your rules. For instance, "But you can go more than once a week if you have a note from home." However, the more fair or lenient you are, the more work you will have supervising your rule. Strike a compromised balance on your rules between fairness and objective simplicity. This balance places responsibility on the student (in this case learning useful toilet training), which is educational for coping with how the world often is.

12. Specify concretely and clearly what <u>you mean</u> by each warning. Don't say, "If you call out again, John, you'll see!" Decide now what you specifically will do for each infraction. Decide for each rule: "yes, you can" or "no," or

"maybe." If "maybe," under which conditions? Clear up any cloudy decisions you have now. State the rule clearly, for what, when, and the repercussions. If you have mixed feelings about an infraction, sort your feelings out now, or design a complex rule that fits these mixed feelings. Decide now whether you feel it's O.K. to accept a student's behavior as merely a feeling. Decide now whether you feel certain situations warrant confrontation. Decide now whether certain behaviors should affect the student's grade or not. Also, specify what is bad about the behavior, specify the bad behavior, and clearly indicate the method the student can follow to make amends.

13. Don't make your warnings too long-winded. If you do, the time it takes to reprimand will slow down the train of your lesson. Students will then turn off, and more disruptions will be incited. Say it short and sweet, and then immediately go on with the lesson.

14. As the "new research" indicates design a hierarchy of consequences in the form of warnings if your rule is broken. If a student violates a reprimand the second time, the severity of the consequence should be greater than the first time. The warnings should have graduated consequences. For instance, "If you call out once, I'll let it go. If you call out a second time, you'll see me after class. If you call out after that, you'll have to do a homework assignment"[106] And so on. . . . Work on this fantasy: You say, "Rule #1," and that if you violate it, "#2" will be the consequence. But the student who violates "#1" doesn't do "#2." You warn the student that if he doesn't do "#2, consequence "#3" will follow, and so on. You need to decide what these graduated warning steps will be. For instance, "If you call out again, you'll see me after class. If you don't see me after class, you'll have to do an extra assignment. If you don't do the assignment, I'll call your parents." The understanding here is that if the student does the required reprimand, you'll forget the previous infraction(s). Sometimes you might actually spell out these warning steps. Sometimes, you may just plan them to yourself, so you don't blurt out a warning you may regret.

15. Design the warnings for breaking your rules so that they have as many small step by-step consequences as possible and do not skip warning steps. For instance, an ineffective hierarchy of consequences would be: "If you call out twice, your mother will have to come to school." This consequence is too big and has too few steps. The student has little time to "turn over a new leaf," and the teacher comes near the end of his power too soon. A better

---

[106] If you worry that this warning will give homework a bad name, instead: ask the student to do a "task sheet" (see Ch.15C); or require that s/he must make an entry in a diary recording daily events for the next three days; or that s/he must clean the chalkboard; or graffiti; or you can arrange to rescind a privilege that she has; or have him/her docked from a game in Gym, etc.

system might be: "If you call out more than once, you get a demerit; if you get three demerits you'll see me after class and have to do a punishment assignment; if you don't do the assignment, I'll have to call your mother." Or some similar system that is congruent for you would be effective, as long as it has many small progressive steps.

16. When you warn a student, tell him/her not only the consequence if s/he breaks the rule, but <u>sometimes also explicitly</u> tell him/her the next couple of steps you will follow if s/he continues to misbehave. For instance, "John, if you call out again, you'll have to do this assignment. And, if you don't do that, I'll have to call your parents." This lets the student know you're well thought-out, prepared, and gives him/her a chance to decide, "Maybe I'd better behave."

17. Don't have in your warnings, "If you don't . . . , I'll take it away from you." Don't tell a student who has brought into class a pornographic magazine or who is wearing earphones and listening to a personal stereo: "If you bring that in tomorrow, I'll take it away!" Just as a scolding is very severe in front of an audience (especially for adolescents), taking something away is also very severe. Ownership is an important concern, especially for adolescents. To save themselves from this feeling of being "stripped" in front of others, students may fight back very hard. As a result, you may be involved in a struggle greater than the initial offense. Instead, find another warning that doesn't involve taking the item away and that focuses only on the item's disturbance to your teaching and others' learning. For instance, "John, please put the magazine (or stereo) away; it disturbs my teaching and others' concentration. If you continue the distraction, I'll give you a 'zero'; if you get three 'zeros' we'll have to discuss this with the dean."

18. <u>Don't allow other students to decide who you warn or the nature of your reprimand.</u> You decide whom you will warn and the appropriate warning. Ignore: "Look, Mr. Johnson, Ted has this magazine!" or "Ted just said a curse word!" Here the disruptive student is not Ted, as much as it is the student calling attention to Ted. This student is the discipline problem. Ted's magazine may have been completely undisruptive, and his four-letter word merely a short expression of frustration, had not this student made a big deal of it. Students see these magazines all the time and hear these words often. The student calling attention to Ted is not outraged; s/he is only trying to get you to go after Ted. But, since students can be unjust to each other and aren't the guardians of justice regarding miscalls (you are), the reprimand should be something like: "Mind your own business. You're the one who's disturbing the class, not Ted."

19. Do not argue with or punish a student's emotional reaction to your reprimand or punishment assignment or his/her threat that s/he "won't do it!"
Instead, wait to see what happens, and only reprimand or punish his/her
behavior when s/he actually does not do what you requested. For instance,
let's notice the teacher's responses in the following situation:

> Teacher: "Sue, that's your third demerit, so, as I warned you, tomorrow you'll
> have to bring in the assignment on page 40."
> Sue: "Big deal! I won't do it!" (Sue turns her nose in the air and closes her
> eyes to display a kind of stoic revolt.)
> Teacher: "How dare you refuse! It is a big deal; you've called out three times
> in here. Well, we'll see if you continue that look on your face after I call your
> mother today!"

Here, the teacher has gone on to his or her next consequence because s/he
has punished and reprimanded the emotional reaction to the first reprimand.
As a result, the teacher is involved in a "face-off" in front of the whole class.
The teacher has "upped the ante" by going to a more severe step and now
must follow through for the sake of protecting credibility. We can avoid these
kinds of escalating emotional battles if we simply assume that people under
firing squads do not smile and that to shoot them twice, because they dislike
being under the gun, is ridiculous. A more effective tack in handling Sue's
reaction above would have been to not say anything. "Duck" instead of giving
a rebuttal to her refusal. It would be better to ignore her reaction and only go
to the next step if she actually does not do the assignment by tomorrow. It is
possible that her initial reaction was merely an impulsive emotional response
out of anger. She may tonight cool down, reconsider your hierarchy of consequences, and hand in the assignment. If she doesn't do it by tomorrow, then
you can initiate your next step.

20. Call in a third party to your system as late as possible; if you think you
are nearing the use of a third party, prepare that person ahead of time. For
instance, an ineffective system would be: "If you call out, you'll have to report
to the dean." This tells the student that very quickly you can't handle things
by yourself and leaves the administration with the same impression. You have
too quickly involved a third party who may feel very differently about the
referred misbehavior, even brush it off, or have their own system of consequences. Furthermore, the dean may already be inundated with referrals about
disobedience. A better system might be: "If you call out more than once, you
get a demerit; if you get three, you'll have to do a punishment assignment;
if you don't do the assignment, I'll call your mother; if that does not work,
you'll have to report to the dean." Also, in using the latter system, it is
important to inform the dean of your own system beforehand: what you have
already tried and the hierarchy of misbehaviors that have led to your referral.

If the third party is a parent, also inform him or her ahead of time. You can send a letter home beforehand that outlines your system of warnings and the infractions incurred by their son or daughter. When you call or see the parent, be ready to <u>listen</u> first before you talk. Allow the parent to vent their anger with their child or anger with you or inform you of behavior or reasons that you may not know about. The parent knows the student better than you do. Give the parent respect for their work with this student. Your attitude is to try to form a "team" with this parent so you both may be able to reinforce or extinguish the proper and improper behaviors.

In most cases, the third party to go to <u>first</u> is a person <u>within</u> the school, e.g., the dean and then the parent <u>second</u>. This way, "the parent" is a more intense warning. And, if the parent has no effect, you can go back to the dean (or principal) and try to have the student removed from your class—now with good reason. (If you or the school must even go a step further, e.g., suspension, consult pp. 298–304.)

Most schools set up "school procedures" for referring students to the, e.g., dean. Teachers use a Referral Form which may look like this:

A Typical "Student Referral Form"
John Smith High School   Susanne Warren, Principal
REFERRAL FORM
<u>CHECK ONE</u>: (See "Ladder of Referral" for responsible party)

_____ DEPT CHAIR
_____ DEAN
_____ GUIDANCE COUNSELOR
        PUPIL'S NAME _____   OFFICIAL
CL. _____ OFFICIAL ROOM _____ DATE _____
        DATE OF INCIDENT _____ TIME _____
REFERRER: _____

REASON(S) FOR REFERRAL
_____ ANNOYING TO CLASSMATES   _____ MISCHIEF
_____ UNCOOPERATIVE
_____ RUDE/DISCOURTEOUS
_____ DESTRUCTIVE TO SCHOOL PROPERTY
_____ RESTLESS/INATTENTIVE
_____ UNPREPARED   _____ EXCESSIVE TALKING
_____ OTHER

STEPS TAKEN BY TEACHER
PRIOR TO REFERRAL
_____ CHANGED PUPIL'S SEAT   _____ PARENT CONFERENCE
DATE: _____ PUPIL CONFERENCE, DATE: _____
_____ OTHER: _____

PRESENT ACTION(S) AND/OR
RECOMMENDATION(S) TAKEN

_____ PUPIL INTERVIEWED, DATE: _____

_____ PARENT WRITTEN TO, DATE: _____

_____ GUIDANCE CONFERENCE, DATE: _____

_____ PARENT INTERVIEWED, DATE: _____

_____ REFERRED TO: _____

_____ PARENT TELEPHONED, DATE: _____

_____ PRIN. CONF. (SUSPENSION) DATE _____

_____ PUPIL PLACED ON PROBATION, DATE: _____

_____ OTHER

(Explain) _____

CC. DEAN, GUIDANCE COUNSELOR, DEPT. CHAIR,
PARENT, REFERRER

21. Don't formulate your warnings or feedback to a student by labeling the student. Instead, either try to say how the student's behavior makes you feel, or specify that the behavior is "bad" (disruptive), not the student. Don't say to the student who calls out, "John, are you stupid! Don't you realize. . . ." Instead, you might say (after you have tried some nonverbal method(s)), "John, stop calling out, it really interferes with my teaching." Or, "John, your calling out is very disruptive." Or, if you're giving a student feedback, don't label him with: "You're an inconsiderate person." Instead, say how he makes you feel: "John, I don't feel like you consider what I'm trying to do, and other students feel like you don't consider them."

As you formulate your rules, check with these guidelines. Rules fall apart when they are weak in the areas described above. The more you use these guidelines to design your rules, the longer they will last and the more effective they will be. Of course, the four caveats are very true here: (1) At first, formulating good rules will require more work, e.g., more thoughtfulness, more record keeping, etc. But eventually this work will make your job easier and you'll be more effective. (2) Only do what's congruent for you. (3) But give each a good try before you abandon it. (4) Don't fret if you can't follow or institute every guideline, all the time.[107]

---

[107] A useful resource is the following catalogue of many specific behavior problems. It lists behavior problems and then lists many suggestions of what a teacher might do to handle each problem (along with a reference to the author of the approach). But, make sure, when using this resource, that you heed the twenty-one guidelines above and the four caveats discussed at the opening of Part III. *The Resource Book for Remediating Common Behavior and Learning Problems.* (Allyn and Bacon, Boston) 1989; call: 800-278-3525 or 800-922-0579.

B. The Debates about: "What's Most Effective"?

We shall discuss:

- warnings and punishments
- corporal punishment
- rewards
- inappropriate rewards and punishments
- rules
- suspensions

Warnings and punishments

The literature contains many debates on the value or abuse of punishments, rewards, accepting feelings, etc. I can only touch on these here to heighten your sensitivities to these issues. You should consider these as you develop your own systems. But, ultimately, after you have had an informed debate with yourself about these, you should do what you feel is congruent for you, what you can follow through on and is appropriate and fair according to your judgment (but only after you have also read Chapter 12, B and C.)

Some strategies recommend that a good relationship and empathetic listening is always best. Some recommend rules, rewards, and punishments. Some recommend that confronting the student is best. Probably what is best is eclectic. Some teachers feel best at listening empathetically, others are prone to rewards or confronting. Also, the same teacher may change his/her strategy depending on the situation. Forming a good relationship and listening may affect change too slowly. However, rewards and punishments may affect only immediate behavior and pay too little attention to the causes of the behavior: a student's feelings. Confronting may work but turn the situation into a power struggle. You need to decide your tack for specific situations. It's probably not best to advocate one philosophy for all disruptions.

Some educators argue one should never use "punishment":

> Punishment has critical weaknesses as a tool for teaching. While it can be effective in teaching children what not to do, it is not particularly useful in teaching them to be productive, to take initiative, to be thoughtful. And while children may learn from heavy doses of punishment to avoid a specific behavior, they also learn to avoid the unpleasant situation altogether—in this case, school. And, finally, excessive punishment leads to retaliation and demoralization of student and teacher both.[108]

[108] Paul Chance. "To the Tune of the Hick'ry Stick," *Psychology Today* (Sept. 1985): 80.

Critics of punishments also contend that often the punishment teaches only what <u>not</u> to do; it doesn't teach the <u>correct</u> behavior. Punishment also increases the anxiety level of the student, and/or causes aggression, and/or causes the student to lose interest in the subject matter.[109]

Also, some students perceive a punishment as not as bad as the punisher perceives it. Some students don't mind staying after school or doing extra homework. Some students may even get peer approval for being punished. And again, punishment usually doesn't show the student how s/he should behave or why. However, a teacher can remove a privilege that the student values or reward those who deserve credit (not those who don't) and these "punishments" may be effective. (The critics of using punishment have much fewer objections to rescinding a privilege as a punishment.) Teachers can also deliver punishments before, after, or during instruction on how a student can be more thoughtful and productive, with rationales. Teachers can also accept a student's feelings empathetically, while not accepting the destructive behavior motivated by them: "John, I understand you're bored, but that doesn't mean you can call out jokes all the time. So, the next time you do that. . . ." Finally, asking a student to do a worksheet may not only teach him a lesson, but teach hum a lesson on math or spelling that he then feels pride in, an intrinsic reward. However, you may decide that, wherever possible, misbehavior should be ignored while the good behavior is rewarded. Or you may decide that isolating (not "punishing") the behavior problem is best.

Corporal punishment

"When I get the paddle, I feel I don't want to be in school." (6th grader)

"I got tired of getting hit; it made me feel bad." (school dropout)

"I felt humiliated and violated." (11th grader)

Such reactions to corporal punishment echo in many schools throughout the United States. In the United States (and usually in democracies of a republic of states or provinces), each state, within the U.S. Constitution, can determine its own local education regulations. And, then the cities of each state, and boards of education in these cities, all come under that individual state's regulations. However, federal funding, and how the courts interpret the law vs. students' rights under the Constitution have sometimes taken away, and sometimes given the administrators of schools more or less power.

As of December 1995, twenty-seven states have abolished this form of discipline either by state law or by regulation from State Departments of

---

[109] Chance, Paul, "The Rewards of Learning." *Phi Delta Kappan.* November 1992, pp. 200–207.

Education. In addition, forty-six national associations, including The Council for Exceptional Children, have passed resolutions against corporal punishment.

Despite rising progress, 23 states (as of 12/95) have not enacted statewide legislation against this kind of punishment. According to a survey by the Office of Civil Rights, U.S. Department of Education, the states that reported the largest percentages of school corporal punishment were located in the South and Southwest regions of the United States (Hyman, 1990). The percentages of students paddled in the top 10 states during the 1989–1990 school year were: Mississippi (9.39), Arkansas (7.78).[110]

New York State prohibited the use of corporal punishment against pupils in 1985. Prior to 1985, New York State delegated the use and control of corporal punishment to local school authorities and employees. Under the law then, the only restriction was the requirement that the corporal punishment be "reasonable in manner and moderate in degree." Beginning Sept. 1, 1985, the Board of Regents imposed rules prohibiting any teacher, administrator, employee or officer of a school district or a board of cooperative educational services from using corporal punishment against a pupil.[111]

Also, The Council for Exceptional Children supports the prohibition of the use of corporal punishment in special education. Corporal punishment is here defined as a situation in which all of the following elements are present: an authority accuses a child of violating a rule and seeks from the child an explanation, whereupon a judgment of guilt is made, followed by physical contact and pain inflicted on the child. The Council finds no conditions under which corporal punishment, so defined, would be the treatment of choice in special education.[112]

In short, as educators learn to apply methods of systematic rewards, (emotional and intrinsic, besides extrinsic) the learned tendency to punish is being diminished, especially corporeal punishment, which psychologically (and sometimes physically) scars. The reader should consult this Chapter 12C for further arguments for rewards, instead of punishments.

Rewards

Some teachers feel uncomfortable giving out, e.g., cookies, or gold stars, or credit tokens, or even grades. They feel that learning should not be based on extrinsic motivation but intrinsic motivation. Students should care about learning because they love learning, not to earn a cookie, or even credit.

[110] Evans, E. and Rita Richardson. "Corporeal Punishment: What Teachers Should Know," *Educational Psychology, Annual Editions* (Random House) Article 34, 1996, p. 200.
[111] James Sander and James Brady; General Counsels, New York City, *You and the Law,* p. 122, 1995.
[112] *Teaching Exceptional Children.* Winter 1995, pp. 33–36, 1995. The Council for Exceptional Children.

However, some students who have never tasted their own sense of earned pride have few feelings for intrinsic motivation. These students may only live for immediate gratification, the ease of irresponsibility, and now. They may not have the patience or staying power for long-range goals, honest work, and the ability to earn self-respect through tasks well done. Such students may need to be given extrinsic rewards to motivate them initially. Then, the cookie might be weaned for the "credit," so that if they get three credits, they get a cookie. Here the student is at least motivated by a symbolic reward. (We are motivated by earning credits that get us degrees, that get us money, that get. . .; all are symbolic rewards.) These symbolic rewards may motivate a person to persist in an activity well done. The accomplishment (and the pride of the accomplishment) may be remembered. Then, the pride in the activity may be felt during the activity, i.e., as intrinsic motivation. In other words, some teachers may decide that some extrinsic rewards are means to an end. (For more on using rewards instead of punishments, see this Chapter 12, Sections B and C, below.)

Inappropriate rewards and punishments

Please keep in mind when you are designing your rewards and punishments that there are some "inappropriate" rewards and punishments. (See the definition of "inappropriate" on p. 153.) Accordingly, an inappropriate punishment would be: "You must wash my car," "remove a piece of clothing," "give me some of your money," etc. Also, demanding that the student write 100 times on the chalkboard: e.g., "I will behave," usually only increases the pain in his writing hand, his hate of you, his embarrassment in front of his peers, his desire to get back at you, and s/he probably only learns to <u>spell</u> "behave."

Rules

Regarding rules for your classroom, some educators advocate that the best and most effective rules are ones that are designed by the students. I agree these may be more enforceable, but are they the best and most effective for the teacher and the students? Such total group ownership may be too time consuming, not only at the initial design phase, but during the enforcing of each rule's consequence. Also, students aren't always fair. They may compete with each other, hold personal grudges, have prejudices they don't compensate for, enjoy the power of hurting another, etc. Also, what may be their idea of a good rule you may judge as unprofessional, impossible to enforce, and not congruent with you. Of course, if you can get the students to own what you feel congruent with, is fair, appropriate, etc., all the better.

However, in grades K–6 it is more feasible and educational to let the students learn how to create rules for their whole class. For a discussion on doing this in grades K–6, see Chapter 12, H1.

Suspensions

The first point to make here, as with corporal punishment, in the United States (and usually in democracies of a republic of states or provinces), each state, within the U.S. Constitution, can determine its own local education regulations. And, then the cities of each state, and boards of education in these cities, all come under that individual state's regulations. However, federal funding, and how the courts interpret the law vs. students' rights under the Constitution have sometimes taken away, and sometimes given the administrators of schools more or less power. (See Appendix C, Legal Parameters.)

Regarding suspending students from school, most educators now believe that external (out of school) suspensions are usually ineffective, even counterproductive,[113–115] whereas in-school suspensions allow greater continuity of the educational experience.

The documented advantages of these programs are numerous (Clark, 1578a,b: National School Public Relations, 1576; Meares and Kettle, 1576; McClung, 1575; Mendez, 1577). Protecting the community from vandalism inflicted by suspended students, improving public relations with employed parents who cannot supervise their children during the day, and enhancing school finances through increases in average daily attendance compensation are obvious benefits. In addition, students who would otherwise become further handicapped academically are required to continue their school work; and often the time involved in court procedures is conserved.[116]

These in-school suspensions often involve academic assignments. Unfortunately, those students in these suspension settings are typically deficient in academic skills.[117] All in-school suspension (ISS) models can be classified into punitive, problem-solving, academic, and individual models. The individual model is most reasonable, since it assumes that reasons for misbehavior

---

[113] Edelman, M., "School Suspensions: Are They Helping Children?" *Children's Defense Fund,* Cambridge Mass., 1975.

[114] Mizel, M. H. "Designing and Implementing In-School Alternatives to Suspension." *The Urban Review,* 10, 1978, pp. 213–226.

[115] Williams, Jr. "In-School Alternatives to Suspension: Why Bother?" *In-School Alternatives to Suspension:* Conference Report, edited by A.M. Garibaldi, Washington, D.C.: US. Government Printing Office, 1979.

[116] Linda Nielsen. "Let's Suspend Suspension: Consequences and Alternatives." *Personnel and Guidance Journal,* May 1979, pp. 442–445.

[117] Costenbader, Virginia and Samia Markson. "School Suspension: A Survey of Current Policies and Practices." *NASSP Bulletin,* Oct. 1994, pp. 103–107.

vary from student to student. ISS programs can help modify student misbehavior, protect the overall learning environment by isolating disruptive students, and protect the community by keeping offenders off the streets.[118]

Physical aggression is the most common infraction leading to both internal and external suspensions. In one study, about 40% reported that students were suspended for interfering with other students' learning. The higher the grade level (across the United States) the greater number of suspensions; the average suspension is about two to four days.

Although there is little evidence that out-of-school suspension and expulsion are effective in changing student behavior, their use has increased in schools across the nation. A telephone survey investigated the attitudes and perceptions of 141 regular and special education teachers, principals, and special education coordinators in West Virginia regarding the use of suspension as a disciplinary measure.

(Survey questions addressed typical behaviors leading to suspension, communication, understanding and following regulations, variations among school districts, alternative resources, educators' sense of fairness, effectiveness of discipline codes, and the possible relationship between student suspension and school dropout.)

Findings reveal that the reasons for use of out-of-school suspension often were not related to student violence and that practitioners did not believe that suspension is either effective or equitably administered. School personnel often felt that their attempts to address individual student needs were stymied by policy mandates. Of particular concern is the frequency with which students with disabilities were suspended.[119] The literature on suspension does show that special-education students, non-white male students, and students of single-parent families are disproportionately affected by suspension policies.[120]

In Riverhead Long Island, New York City, disruptive students are sent to an alternative school building, behind the main school. Some advocate that we require districts to create alternative settings (even if it is just a room away from other students or a school within a school). Many feel that we <u>must</u> find the money for these alternatives.[121]

New York City School's Chancellor, Rudy Crew, has recently proposed (Feb. 1997) that students who: carry weapons, drugs, or commit physical acts

---

[118] Sheets, John. "Designing an Effective In-School Suspension Program." *NASSP Bulletin,* v. 80, no. 579, April 1996, pp. 86–90.
[119] Eric Record: EJ522771, Henderson, Joan and Billie Friedland, "Suspension, a Wake-Up Call: Rural Educators" *Attitudes toward Suspension,* 1996.
[120] Eric Record: ED394177, Johns, Beverly-H. et al. "Reduction of School Violence: Alternatives to Suspension," 1995.
[121] "Dealing with a Disruptive Student." Walter Dunn, *Newsday,* March 25, 1996, p. 12.

of violence to students or school staff be placed in alternative SOS schools or be expelled.

Although suspension policies in schools will differ from state to state and school to school, it is helpful to outline an abbreviated version of what might be the wording for a fairly typical suspension policy of, e.g., an urban high school [grades K–6 appear in brackets].

Suspension Policy

Jurisdiction: This policy applies to prohibited actions of students in school, during school hours, before and after school while on school property, while traveling on vehicles funded by the Board of Education, at all school-sponsored events and on other than school property which negatively affect the educational process or endanger the health, morals or welfare of the school community.

Proper response: Guidance considerations and alternative techniques should be used by school personnel in place of disciplinary actions. School officials must consult the Discipline Code in determining what should be the appropriate response.

Discipline Code (sample of items):

1. Classifications of infractions
   1.1 Academic infractions: offenses having to do with learning. Examples: no text, unpreparedness, no homework, absence from class (not cutting).
   1.2 Guidance related infractions: (non-disciplinary) situations which do not interfere with class instruction but require guidance attention. Example: student sleeps in class, suspicion of drug or alcohol use, suspicion of child abuse, knowledge of personal or family problem.
   1.3 Minor behavioral infractions (first instance). Examples: talking with a neighbor, out of seat chewing, wearing a hat and/or Walkman type radio, throwing paper from seat to trash can.
   1.4 Serious infractions: (includes emergency situations) offenses which interfere with instruction or present a danger to the health and safety of staff members, students, or authorized visitors. Examples: abusive language, threats, assaults, littering, vandalism, graffiti, potentially explosive situations, possession of weapons, or possession of controlled substances or alcohol, robbery, improper conduct in the cafeteria, possession of a sounding beeper.
2. Ladder of referral
   Academic infraction
   2.1 Teacher to student

2.2 Teacher parent
2.3 Teacher to department chair
     Guidance-related infractions
3.1 Teacher to guidance counselor
3.2 Guidance to parent and SPARK coordinator
     Minor behavioral infractions
4.1 Teacher to student
4.2 Teacher to parent
4.3 Teacher to departmental chair
     Serious behavioral infractions
5.1 Teacher to dean
5.2 Dean to assistant principal or security staff
5.4 Principal to superintendent

Prevention procedures: School personnel should develop plans for addressing a student's problems and discuss these alternatives with the student and his/her parent. These plans might include the use of alternative instructional materials and/or approaches, alternative classroom management techniques, remedial services, alternative class placement, guidance support and services to address personal and family circumstances. If, after appropriate alternative techniques have been considered, a principal suspects that a student's difficulties may be a manifestation of a handicapping condition that prevents the student from benefiting from general education, the principal shall immediately refer the student to the School-Based Support Team or Committee on Special Education. All preventive efforts should be described in the student's record. The principal should notify the parent and try to remediate the student's behavior with a guidance conference.

Suspension procedures: Suspensions fall into two categories: principal's suspensions and superintendent's suspensions.

A. Principal's suspensions:

1. The principal shall have power to suspend a student when the principal determines that a student's overt behavior presents a clear and present danger of physical injury to the student, other students, or school personnel, or prevents the orderly operation of classes or other school activities. Prior to suspending a student, the principal shall consult the Discipline Code (and obtain the superintendent's approval for grades K–6).

2. Only the principal, or in the principal's absence, the school official designated as "acting principal," may authorize a principal's suspension.

3. A principal must seek the authorization of the superintendent prior to suspending a pupil. Before authorizing the suspension, the superintendent must consider what other disciplinary, guidance and intervention measures the school has considered.

4. A principal may suspend a student from one to five days, but in no case in excess of five school days. Not all behavior warrants a full five-day suspension. A student may not be suspended twice for the same incident. A student cannot be suspended by a principal more than twice in one school year.

5. When a principal believes that a suspension may be warranted, the student shall be removed from classes and informed of the charges against him/her. If the student denies the charges, the principal shall give the student an explanation of the evidence and an opportunity to present his/her side of the event, if it is feasible to do so.

6. If the principal decides that suspension is not warranted, the student shall be returned to class.

7. If the principal decides that suspension is warranted, he/she shall detain the student in school under supervision until either the arrival of the student's parent or until the close of the student's school day. The principal must inform the parent of the location at the school where he/she can pick up the student.

8. The principal shall give immediate written notice of the suspension to the student's parent. Such notice shall be provided by personal delivery, express mail delivery, or any other equivalent means reasonably calculated to ensure receipt of such notice within 24 hours of the suspension.

9. Principal's (superintendent's) suspension conference: The conference presents an opportunity to assess the facts surrounding the incident for which a student was suspended, to determine whether the suspension was justified, to devise collaboratively satisfactory solutions, and to prevent further disruption of the student's education.

   a. The conference is not a formal, contested proceeding and should not become adversarial. A primary purpose of the conference is to design measures to maximize the student's educational development.

   b. The parent and the principal each may bring no more than two persons to assist them in the conference, unless the parent and principal agree to the presence of additional persons. Both parties may also present witnesses and offer statements and other documentary evidence. The additional persons brought by the parties may be attorneys or advocates. Although they may participate only as advisors, they may, like the student and parent, participate freely in the discussion, question all witnesses, and offer objections in a manner consistent with the informal nature of the conference. No participant should become unreasonably contentious or adversarial.

   c. A written summary of the conference must be prepared and maintained by the school.

d. The principal shall notify the parent in writing of his/her decision. This letter shall state whether the suspension was justified and the basis for the decision, and, where necessary, make further recommendations.

e. If the principal determines that the suspension is not justified, the student must be returned to school immediately, and all records relating to the suspension must be expunged.

f. The suspended student is to remain on the register of his/her school and shall not be marked absent during the period of suspension. Appropriate notation of the suspension should be recorded in a manner that will permit expunging, when necessary.

g. A student may not be transferred to another school as a result of a principal's suspension.

h. All students must be reinstated no later than the sixth school day following the suspension regardless of whether a suspension conference has been held.

B. Superintendent's suspension: A superintendent's suspension may result in a period of suspension that <u>exceeds</u> five school to days. Prior to requesting such a suspension, the principal shall consult the Discipline Code. Superintendent's suspensions must be sought when students engage in any of the following behavior:

a. Using any weapon, as defined below in **Categories I and II,** to inflict injury or attempt to inflict injury upon school personnel, students, or others
Category I

- firearm, including pistol and handgun, silencers and electronic dart and stun gun
- shotgun, rifle, machine gun, or any other weapon that simulates or is adaptable for use as a machine gun
- air gun, spring gun, or other instrument or weapon in which the propelling force is a spring or air, and any weapon in which any loaded or blank cartridge may be used (such as a BB gun)
- switchblade knife, gravity knife, plum ballistic knife, and cane sword (a cane that conceals a knife or sword)
- dagger, stiletto, dirk, razor, box cutter, case cutter, utility knife, and other dangerous knives
- explosives, fire crackers, stick, sling shot, metal knuckles, etc.

Category II

- acid or deadly or dangerous chemicals
- imitation gun
- loaded or blank cartridges and other ammunition

- any deadly, dangerous, or sharp pointed instrument that can be used or is intended for use as a weapon (such as scissors, nail file, broken glass, chains, wire)
b. Possessing any weapon, as defined in Category I above
c. Using force against or inflicting serious injury against school personnel
d. Using extreme force or inflicting serious injury upon students or others
e. Selling or distributing illegal drugs or controlled substances
f. Committing arson, causing a riot, possessing or using controlled substances without authorization, or any situation that presents a clear and present danger, or prevents the orderly operation of a school (e.g., theft, vandalism)

Police Involvement: When a student is believed to have committed a crime or is found in possession of a weapon prohibited in Category I, illegal drugs or controlled substances, the police must be summoned. When a student is arrested the principal shall notify the parent immediately.

Some obligations of the principal and superintendent:

1. The suspended student must be provided with classwork and homework assignments during the period of suspension.
2. The student will remain on the register of the school and shall not be marked absent during the suspension, though notation of the suspension will be noted on the record, but in such a way that it can be expunged.
3. The parent/guardian must be informed of the rights to Appeal Procedures.
4. Students may not be academically penalized. (An academic penalty, such as reduction of grade, may only be imposed as a disciplinary measure if the conduct for which a student was suspended is directly related to an academic activity, e.g., plagiarism, cheating on an examination.
5. An academic penalty may not be imposed for absence during the suspension period.
6. Students must be permitted to take any citywide or state examinations that are administered during the period of their suspension for which no makeup examination is permitted by the testing authority, as well as to make up school examinations, such as finals, which may affect their academic records.

Resources

Bailey, R & J. Kackley. *Positive Alternative to Student Suspensions.* St. Petersburg, Fla.: Pupil Personnel Services Project of All Children's Hospital. 1974.

Betteker, D. "Suspensions: Get Rid of Them." *Thrust for Educational Leadership* 5 (1975): 26–27.

Bormanne, S. "In School Suspension Programs" *School and Community* 62 (1976): 36.

Brooks, B. D. "Contingency Contracts with Truants." *Personnel and Guidance Journal.* 52 (1974): 316–320.

Children's Defense Fund. *School Suspensions: Are They Helping Children.* Cambridge, Mass.: Washington Research Project, Inc. 1975.

Clark L [Nielsen]. *Classroom for Development & Change: Teachers Training Handbook.* Winston-Salem, N.C.: Winston-Salem—Forsyth County Schools. June 1978.

Edelman, M., "School Suspensions: Are They Helping Children?" Children's Defense Fund, Cambridge Mass., 1975.

Eric Record: ED394177, Johns, Beverly-H., et al. "Reduction of School Violence: Alternatives to Suspension." 1995.

Eric Record: EJ522771, Henderson, Joan and Billie Friedland. "Suspension, A Wake-Up Call: Rural Educators." *Attitudes toward Suspension.* 1996.

Harvey, D & W. Moosha. "In-School Suspension." *NASSP Bulletin.* 61 (1977): 14–17.

Heaton R. "A Motivational Environment for Behaviorally Deviant Junior High School Students" *Journal of Abnormal Child Psychology.* 4 (1976): 263–275.

Jorgensen, J. "An Alternative to Suspension for Smoking." *Creative Discipline.* 1(4) (1977): 5.

Kelley, W. "Alternative to Suspension: Educational Adjustment Class." *School & Community* 60 (1974): 9.

McClung, M. "Alternatives to Disciplinary Exclusion from School." *Inequality in Education* 20 (1975): 56–73.

Meares, H. & H. Kettle. "In House Suspension." *NASSP Bulletin* 60 (1976): 60–63.

Mendez, R. "School Suspension—Discipline without Failure." *NASSP Bulletin.* 61 (1977): 11–14.

Mizel, M. H. "Designing and Implementing In-School Alternatives to Suspension." *The Urban Review.* 10, 1978,: 213–226.

Mizell, H. *Designing a Positive In-School Suspension Program.* Columbia, S.C. September, 1977.

National School Public Relations. *Suspensions and Expulsions.* Arlington, Va.: Author. 1976.

O'Brien, D. "In School Suspension." *American School Board Journal.* 28 (1976): 36–37.

Costenbader, Virginia and Samia Markson. "School Suspension: A Survey of Current Policies and Practices." *NASSP Bulletin.* Oct. 1994, pp. 103–107.

Sheets, John. "Designing an Effective In-School Suspension Program." *NASSP Bulletin,* v. 80, no. 579, pp. 86–90, April 1996.

Williams, Jr. "In-School Alternatives to Suspension: Why bother?" In-School Alternatives to Suspension: Conference Report. A.M. Garibaldi (ed.). Washington, D.C.: US. Govt. Printing Office, 1979.

Yoakley, R. *Evaluation of In-School Suspensions at Halls High School.* Knoxville, Penn.: Knox County School System 1977.

For a discussion of the Legal Parameters related to suspensions, see Appendix C.

For a discussion on Weapons in Schools, see Chapter 13B. 12.

For School Violence, see Chapter 10A.

For School Rules in General, see Chapter 12A.

C. Systematic Rewards, Instead of Punishments: 43 Suggestions

In 1932, Thorndike revised his famous law of effect to stress that the strengthening effect of reward (positive reinforcement of the appropriate behavior) is much greater than the weakening effect of punishment. In essence, it was advised that rewarding the good behavior is always preferable to punishing the bad behavior. Yet, John Goodlad reports that today, in the elementary grades, an average of only 2% of class time is devoted to positive reinforcement; in the high schools, the figure falls to 1%.[122]

If Thorndike is correct (and most believe that he is), and if it is also true that punishment teaches only what not to do, increases the anxiety and aggression level of the student, and may cause the student to lose interest in the subject matter . . . why is there so much use of punishments, instead of rewards, in our schools ? I think there are several reasons:

1. Infractions to our rules are usually more noticed than respect for our rules. We tend more often to catch our students misbehaving than try to catch them doing the right thing.
2. These infractions make us angry, and our reflexive response is to "get back" at the one that "got us."
3. As discussed above (Section B), many are turned off to rewards, especially extrinsic ones; they equate such rewarding to bribery.
4. Some contend that rewarding the activity takes away the intrinsic interest that the activity would otherwise generate; the child only does the activity for the reward.
5. You can't always reward the good behavior, especially when it is required so frequently. For example, you can't keep giving a child a gold star for

[122] Goodlad. *A Place Called School: Prospects for the Future* (New York: McGraw-Hill, 1984) p. 15.

sitting in her proper seat, whereas you <u>can</u> punish this child for inappropriately getting <u>out</u> of her seat.

6. Rewards, systematically given rewards, take a lot of planning (more than punishing), thus the latter is easier to do.
7. We have mostly been trained at warning and punishing. We tend to imitate the models we had, who mainly used punishments more than rewards.
8. And, finally, you <u>can</u> easily devise rewards for the <u>early</u> grades (although rewards are underused in the elementary grades as well) such as stars, stickers, a party, a free homework pass, etc., whereas it is more difficult to create such age appropriate rewards for, e.g., a 16 year old.

The above have made punishments more prominent in our schools than rewards. But, in an effort to give credence to Thorndike's valuable point, let us at least try to work on these above inhibitions to using rewards (1–8) so that we may be better able to respond by rewarding, instead of reflexively punishing.

Overcoming 1–8 above

<u>Regarding 1 above</u>: We need to catch our students doing the <u>right</u> thing, more than keep our eye out for misbehavior. Begin this attitude early in the semester. Try to ignore the inappropriate behavior at the onset, and compliment and reward the good behavior often and quickly. If this is done early in the class, more students will catch this habit, and you'll have fewer students to notice doing the wrong thing.

<u>Regarding 2 above</u>: Your goal is not to "get back" at the student, but turn his or her behavior around. Try not to take a student's violation of your rule personally. Many of these students are used to getting more attention for doing the wrong thing than the right thing, and/or feel a lack of confidence to be able to do the right thing well, e.g., their homework. Also, many students step over boundaries as a general tendency in their upbringing and are now displacing this normal (for them) behavior onto you.

<u>Regarding 3 and 4 above</u>: I challenge the reader to think of an activity that s/he likes to do that does not involve doing it for some kind of reward. By reward, I think of **extrinsic rewards:** cookies, baseball cards, cars, and material goods in general. There are also **symbolic rewards:** trophies, gold stars, diplomas, stickers, money, etc. that stand for getting extrinsic rewards or **emotional rewards:** compliments, praise, a pat on the back, approval, attention, recognition, acceptance, etc. Then there are **intrinsic rewards** (or as we like to say "intrinsic reasons") for doing the activity: the activity itself is fun, pleasurable, makes us feel good, gives us a sense of pride, or efficacy, or

power, or meaning—even when there are no extrinsic, symbolic, or emotional rewards involved.

Again, I challenge the reader to think of an activity that s/he likes to do that does not involve some kind of reward, now that we understand what we are talking about. This is not just a question of semantics. I believe that students move through all phases of these rewards. And since we all do things for the rewards (as described above), it becomes meaningless to say that rewarding = bribery. What we really don't want to happen is that a student's motivation be mostly **extrinsic;** this is what bothers us. I don't think we mind so much if we motivate by **symbolic** or **emotional rewards,** because that's how we mostly function. What we ultimately want to happen is for the student to do the activity for **intrinsic** reasons.

But, again, I believe that students often move through all phases of these rewards. We may get the student to try a math problem by offering her a little gift, if she can do the problem. Or we may offer her a sticker on her Success Chart, and/or praise, or approval, etc. If the student tries the problem for these rewards, eventually she may do the next math problem just because it makes her feel proud, or more able, or successful at getting the answer. In other words, she may initially engage in the activity for extrinsic, symbolic, or emotional rewards, but these incentives may help her feel an intrinsic liking for the activity.

In other words, we should not shy away from using rewards. Getting rewarded is not bribery, but how we all generally function. And, to the contrary, many rewards actually help grow the intrinsic interest we have now in doing what we like to do and now do well.

Regarding 5 above: Even if the behavior you want to reward is required very frequently (e.g., the student be seated in her proper seat), it is possible (and usually better) to reward this behavior, rather than punish her when she gets out of her seat. Just elongate the reward: e.g., tell her that if she remains in her proper seat for the whole period, you will give her **x** (some **symbolic** reward). If she gets 5 **x's,** she gets **y,** which may add up to, e.g., a privilege, or a note of recognition to the parent, or she can choose her own seat on Monday, etc. Or, if she sits in her proper seat for and entire week, you will give her. . . , etc.

Regarding 6 and 7 above: What would help a great deal here would be actual examples of rewards a teacher can use, but, more importantly, rewards the teacher can use in a systematic way. Systematic rewards are not only the most effective but require the most work and time to implement. I hope the following suggestions below will save teachers valuable time and make this work easier.

Regarding 8 above: Below you will find many specific suggestions for rewards for the upper grades, as well as the lower grades.

Suggestions for systematic rewards

Guidelines

A. As with warnings and punishments above, first make sure you only adopt those rewards that you feel congruent with and can follow through.

B. Reward systems, in general, can involve **(a) competition with others,** or **(b) self-competition.**

(a) Competition with others is a rewards system in which students compete with each other. Implicit in giving grades is students trying to do better than each other. Giving stickers on a chart also involves students competing with each other. Whenever we set up a reward for the student who does the best, or the most . . . , we have a reward system that motivates by competition with others. The motivation gained by this kind of system is often very useful, even exciting to students (whether it is a spelling bee or an essay contest). There are many who do not favor this kind of competition. They feel it encourages students to be against each other, and raises anxiety levels to the point where students demean each other and themselves. However, if used mildly, if team spirit, fairness and good sportsmanship are encouraged, the motivation that comes from this kind of system can be very useful and educational.

(b) Self-competition is a reward system in which the student is encouraged to compete with him/herself. For example, the student has a notebook where she (and the teacher) keep track of her own record: last week she got 4 correct, this week she got 6 correct. The student read 34 pages last week, this week she was able to read 45 pages. The student wrote a one-page essay with 6 errors last week; this week she wrote a two-page essay with only 3 errors. The student sets goals for herself and competes with herself for any of the various kinds of rewards described above.

Most of the suggestions below are of type (a) but can be revised to be more of type (b).

C. With all of these rewards below, you can use a "Behavior Contract." By literally writing out an agreement with the student or students on what behavior will warrant what reward, you will be teaching them how to feel success, and rewarded by the appropriate behavior. In this way, you are also teaching them how to decide what is appropriate behavior and what level of reward is appropriate for what behavior(s). Working with them to make this "contract" will help them (eventually) to be able to go through this process by themselves.

For Grades K–6

1. Try to think of a schedule of **symbolic** rewards that you can use. For example, a sticker, or check for every homework handed in on time. Certainly,

with the symbolic rewards also give **emotional** rewards: approval, compliments, attention (the student can show the rest of the class his work) praise, even applause, etc. Some **extrinsic** rewards that may be more comfortable to teachers than, e.g., candy, maybe a special book for the student, a signed baseball, a special pen, or pencil, a celebrity photo, a special magazine, etc.

2. If necessary, these above rewards can add up to other **symbolic** or **extrinsic** rewards: a higher grade, a certificate, a school jacket, a class trip, a privilege or party, etc. The major point is that you keep track of these, how many equals what other reward, and be systematic and fair. (You will find that some students will start to forget the rewards because they have become so involved in doing the activity itself, **intrinsic** motivation).

3. An example of making use of the above reward system is a homework chart where, each time the student hands in the homework, s/he gets a sticker (it could be a check or a point). Any student that does ten homeworks (it could be five), gets a free homework pass, an actual printed document made on the teacher's computer (it could be a special card or an award xeroxed on special yellow paper). The student, at any time, can hand this special pass in instead of doing the homework and gets full credit for that homework due. (The only caveat is that, even if a student has saved up multiple passes, he/she can only use one per week. This guarantees that a student cannot get too far behind or miss a whole series of homeworks that all build on each other.) Students can save these up for special days (when relatives may be visiting) or hand them in right after they receive them. The teacher of course has the right to announce that a particular assignment may not be fulfilled by a Homework Pass. Alternatively, the teacher might announce, one day, that this project is worth four homeworks passes.

4. The teacher buys, e.g., ten tickets to a concert, small show, a Yankee game, etc. for a Saturday or Sunday afternoon and then sets up a point system of some kind such that the ten students who do **x** get to go with the teacher on this trip. Students who earn the trip get commendation letters sent home to the parents, who sign this letter with their permission for the trip. (The money spent by the teacher (10 × $6?) can motivate students for months worth the price of aspirin.)

5. The same can be done as above, only this time the reward is lunch with the teacher, or an invitation to the teacher's house, or a pizza date, or a basketball game, or ice skating, or a movie with the teacher.

6. If a student, e.g., hands in ten homeworks in a row, s/he gets five extra points on the next test.

7. If the teacher only has to reprimand students, e.g., ten times this week, or less, the whole class gets ten extra points on Friday's test.

8. Same as above, only this time the reward is: "There will be no homework on Friday."

9. Same as above, only this time the reward is: "You will have free time on Friday."

10. Same as above, only this time the reward is: "We will have a party on Friday."

11. Same as all of the above, only this time the rewards may be the same, but to win the reward the goal is <u>not</u> behavior (as in 7–10 above) but the students must finish **x,** or accomplish **y** to get the above rewards.

12. The marble reward system: The teacher puts a small empty glass jar on her desk, out in front of the class. Every time, e.g., a student helps another student, or a group-table does cleanup well, or the class quiets down quickly, or the students accomplish **x,** the teacher places a marble in the jar. When the jar is filled up, on the following day, the class gets a pizza party, instead of going to the cafeteria. The teacher then brings a new jar to be filled for some specified educational goal and offers a new reward (only this time the jar is a little bigger). Notice that with this system the students root for each other, and get not only pizza, but peer approval every time a student earns a marble for the whole class. The students can even vote for the reward they will work for (with teacher approval.)[123]

13. A <u>token system</u>: Every time a student does something well, or, e.g., gets a quiz score over 85, s/he gets a , e.g., gold 3 × 5 card (with the teacher's signature on it). These cards can be saved up to be redeemed for prizes in the "class store" (that the teacher replenishes). Some schools use specially made "school money," and the students can take the earned money to the <u>school</u> store, where items are donated by parents. Or the tokens can be redeemed for lunch with the teacher, or any item in the "catalogue," a book that the students themselves design.

14. The "best" students for this week (whatever goal = best) get their photos posted on the classroom door, or in the hall, under the banner "best this week", with their work also posted for other classmates to see.

15. At the end of every month (or every three days) the teacher gives out special certificates (made on his/her computer) for   , accomplished by   , on   , to be taken home to show the student's parents

---

[123] See Chapter 13H #2, for more details on this system.

and family. (Hopefully, they are posted prominently at home.) Also, try to give a certificate for something that your problem students can do well and give them a certificate for <u>that</u>. Show them (and yourself) that you do notice that they have strengths. You'll find that when you notice their strengths, they will show you more of them.

16. The teacher sets up either a token system or point system whereby, if the student earns **x,** s/he can get free time in the gym to play basketball, help in the library, or nurse's office, or in the computer room (obviously planned out with the personnel involved).

17. Teachers in the lower grades often let students be monitors and have special jobs in the class: feeding the rabbit, giving out the crayons, watering the plants, class leader in line, etc. Some of these jobs are very much enjoyed by the students. The teacher can set up a system such that, to get job **x,** you have to, e.g., earn a certain number of points or accomplish **y.**

18. The teacher designates a bulletin board where students who accomplish **x** get their work displayed there.

19. The three students, who accomplished **x,** get to show their, e.g., answers, ideas, design, etc. in front of the class on the chalkboard tomorrow.

20. The three students, who accomplished **x,** get to be excused from cleanup.

21. Every time a student, e.g., gets higher than 90 on a quiz, solves the class math problem, hands in four homeworks in a row, etc., his/her name is put into this special prize drawing box. The teacher draws, e.g., three names out to the box at the end of every Friday's class, for a reward (any small items that the children value).

(Also, some of the rewards below, that are for the upper grades, may also work for grades K–6, with some revision.)

For the Upper Grades

I agree that it is more difficult to design rewards for the upper grades, but these may be helpful:

22. With very little revision, the above will also work in the upper grades: 4–11, 13, 15, 16, 18–20 (18, and some of the others, may require that you fight for getting all your subject classes to meet in the same room; see Chapter 10C, a.,1.)

23. It was already suggested above that it may be worth it to the teacher to buy a small set of tickets to, e.g., a baseball, or basketball, or hockey game, a rock concert, small show, or coliseum boat or car show, etc., and set up a

point system whereby ten students can earn these rewards over a period of several weeks.

24. A student may earn an exemption from a quiz, or writing a report, or doing a math work sheet, if s/he does **x**.

25. The teacher will drop the lowest test score if a student, e.g., gets over 85 on any three quizzes. (Anyone can have a bad day, especially, if s/he earns it.)

26. The student is exempt from the, e.g., midterm (or final) exam if s/he has above a 90 average on all previous tests. (You may need to check that this can be supported by your department's policy.)

27. At the end of every period, the teacher places a little dot on the Delaney Card of a student who, during that class period, participated well: asked good questions, tried answers, or volunteered in the discussion. At the end of the marking period, if a student has more dots than the average student, s/he gets ten extra points on his/her report card. If a student has the average number of dots, s/he gets five extra points. If a student has below the average number of dots, s/he just gets the average of his/her test scores (plus or minus whatever your system states for handing in homework.)

28. Every time a student hands in the homework on time, s/he gets two extra points on Friday's quiz.

29. If a student scores **x** or accomplishes **y,** the student gets extra help with one subject with the teacher.

30. If a student scores **x** or accomplishes **y,** the student gets one free period in the library.

31. If a student scores **x** or accomplishes **y,** the student gets one free period in class.

32. If a student scores **x** or accomplishes **y,** the student gets to choose the game in Gym.

33. If a student scores **x** or accomplishes **y,** the student gets to sit anywhere in the class for one day, or one week.

34. If a student scores **x** or accomplishes **y,** the student gets to reach into the class grab bag for various rewards (see items below, which often can be gotten cheaply at yard sales).

35. If a student scores **x** or accomplishes **y,** the student gets pens.

36. If a student scores **x** or accomplishes **y,** the student gets pads, stuffed animals, etc.

37. If a student scores **x** or accomplishes **y,** the student gets special book marks.

38. If a student scores **x** or accomplishes **y,** the student gets a T-shirt.

39. If a student scores **x** or accomplishes **y,** the student gets a Granny-Smith apple.

40. If a student scores **x** or accomplishes **y,** the student gets a blank diary book.

41. If a student scores **x** or accomplishes **y,** the student gets a copy of the book or poem that you studied in class.

42. If a student scores **x** or accomplishes **y,** the student gets an address book.

43. If a student scores **x** or accomplishes **y,** the student gets a granola bar.

D. Conflict Resolution (CR) Training

We shall discuss this topic in this order:

1. We need to re-educate the emotional lives of many students.
2. What can schools do to counter these behaviors and re-educate students?
   A. Set Up a School Violence Prevention Code
   B. Train the School Staff in Conflict Resolution (CR)
   C. Train a Cadre of Students for a CR Court
   D. All Students Serve on a CR Court
   E. Teach All Students a CR Curriculum:
      a. Constructive CR Strategies
      b. CR Knowledges and Skills
3. Resources

1. We need to re-educate the emotional lives of many students

Another long-range, but sweeping, strategy to prevent discipline problems is to incorporate conflict resolution procedures and education into the school. The valid rationale here is to introduce and re-educate students to alternative ways they typically, often destructively, learn to deal with conflict and anger.

Unfortunately, a major unhealthy influence on student's learning in this area is TV[124] (and the movies). Half of all U.S. children aged 6–17 have a TV in their room. It is estimated that the average American child watches 4 hours of TV a day and will have watched 100,000 acts of dramatized violence, including 20,000 murders, by the time s/he is 18 years old. These TV programs

---

[124] Recently (Jan. 1997), a rating system for TV programs went into effect so that, along with the V-chip, parents will be able to better control what their children watch; TV programmers will be under pressure to make programs for children more appropriate or lose viewers.

frequently involve the expression of anger and the settlement of conflict by violence, which is often represented as rewarded, inconsequential, painless, and even glamorized. One survey found that 73% of the violent acts on TV were portrayed as unpunished.[125]

Another influence on how students learn to handle conflict and anger is, more importantly, the student's home life, and how their parents/guardians handle these emotions. The conflict strategies that they learn here are often not just ineffective but, in some cases, foster disruptive, even violent behavior in and out of school.

Students inadvertently learn to handle anger and conflict destructively when they watch adults display the following kinds of behavior:

(a) expressing anger physically (e.g., by hitting)
(b) expressing anger by name-calling or "put downs"
(c) not listening to each other's feelings
(d) judging, criticizing, or making fun of each other's feelings
(e) not allowing the constructive verbal expression of frustration or anger
(f) interrupting each other when the other is trying to express important feelings
(g) trying to be strong by not showing feelings in general
(h) trying to win arguments, rather than trying to see the other's point of view
(i) never admitting mistakes, shortcomings, or apologizing
(j) not negotiating when there is a conflict in their wants and preferences.
(k) trying to look good or "cool" to cover feelings of inadequacy
(l) dogmatically insisting that their particular point of view, taste, or value system is better than any other.

2. What can schools do to counter these behaviors and re-educate students?

A. Set Up a School Violence Prevention Code

A school, as a whole, can decide that any student who expresses his or her anger physically (e.g., hits or destroys property) or handles conflict in a "destructive" way, will receive a specific punishment (see Chapter 12A, B [suspensions]). This means that both parties will be punished, regardless of who started, e.g., the fight). The parties involved must use the CR method that is sanctioned by the school (e.g., a school or peer-student "court" [See **3** and **4** below] or they will both be punished.

---

[125] "TV Viewing and Violence: The Impact on Children." Dr. Steven Shelov, Prof. and Vice Chairman of The Dept. of Pediatric Education, Montefiore Hospital; Paper delivered on April 18, 1996, Lehman College, City Univ. of New York.

Versions of this kind of violence prevention are exemplified in the following examples:

(a) Two students are arguing in a 3rd grade class over who gets the good paint brushes. The teacher says, "I will give you both 2 minutes on my watch for both of you to decide how to settle this conflict. If you can't decide by the time the 2 minutes are up, you both lose the brushes (or, you both get time-out)." (Here, the teacher might first explain various constructive conflict strategies [see 5, A below] before she starts her watch.)

(b) Two students on the school newspaper begin to argue and curse over an article they are writing for the paper together. The teacher says, "If you cannot stop arguing over what goes in the article and settle your conflict, then you will both lose: the article will not appear at all in the paper. Teams that cannot work as a team, lose."

(c) Two students begin to call each other names, and then begin to threaten each other physically. The teacher says, "The second one of you touches the other, you will both be sent to the office, and your parents will be called. If you stop now, and refer it to the "court" [see 3 below], no one will be punished." (If this policy is used often, the teacher need only say, "Court!" and the above is understood.)

B. Train School Staff in CR

To back up this violence prevention code, the school staff might be trained in CR strategies, knowledges, and skills. The teachers in the above examples are using such strategies, but many more such tactics can be learned (as we shall discuss in 5, A and B below).

C. Train Students for a CR Court

However, most CR programs are more effective when the students have learned these CR strategies, knowledges, and skills, not just the staff. A few students can be named to serve on a "peer court"; they might be selected by the school staff, or elected by the student body, or a combination of both (where criteria need to be met for election to the court).

This cadre of students is trained in CR skills below [5, A and B] and also learn the following:

(a) mediation skills, wherein they help disputants work out the conflict
(b) to recommend an arbitration decision, if the disputants cannot settle the conflict
(c) to use constructive ground rules: no name calling, sarcasm, nor interrupting of the other's point of view while each has a turn at explaining his or her case

(d) to listen and paraphrase both the fact and feelings of each disputant's point of view
(e) to brain storm solutions
(f) to write out a contract on the agreed upon negotiation, and create consequences to enforce the contract

Peer mediation courts usually take place at lunch time, or at recess, sometimes during class time in a special room. Peer disputes involving, e.g., fist fights, arguments, etc., can be referred to the peer court, whereas more serious problems (weapon possession, violence, illegal activity, etc.) are still negotiated by the school's staff. But the good news is that about 80%–90% of peer-mediated agreements hold, replacing otherwise destructive, even potentially violent student conflicts.[126]

D. All Students Serve on a CR Court

However, the more effective way to resolve more conflicts in a school is to design a procedure whereby all students get a chance to serve on the peer court. Students learn more about constructive CR when they get a chance to be in the mediator's "shoes," especially when they can practice mediating disputes in which they are not personally involved. It is then that they can better practice more objectivity and fairness and see both sides. Later, they may be able to transfer this learning to their own disputes. Students can rotate their membership to such a court, or have to serve on it by some kind of calendar schedule so that as many students as possible are involved in learning to be peer mediators.

E. Teach All Students a CR Curriculum

However, the most ambitious and most effective CR program not only has a non-violence code and mediation court but also teaches CR in the school as part of the school's curriculum.[127] When CR is part of a school's curriculum, class instruction includes learning about constructive CR strategies, knowledges, and skills:

a. Constructive CR strategies: Through lecture,[128] demonstration, role play, class and homework exercises, students learn how to:

(a) use compromise to settle disputes

---

[126] Estimated by The National Assoc. for Mediation in Education, 1996. ED338791 Jun 91 Conflict Resolution Programs in Schools. *ERIC/CUE Digest* Number 74, 1996. Author: Inger, Morton, ERIC Clearinghouse on Urban Education, New York, N.Y.

[127] We may see such a curriculum come to fruition in the next few years if the President of the United States has his way: "Character education must be taught in our schools. We must teach our children to be good citizens." (President Clinton's *State of the Union Address,* Feb. 4, 1997.)

[128] The history of the labor movement, government decisions, etc. are very useful here.

(b) take turns by, e.g., flipping coins, choosing numbers, selecting the neediest or most deserving person, etc.
(c) negotiate and listen to two disputants
(d) conduct the operation of a court
(e) put in place various forms of a non-violence code [See **1** above]
(f) listen empathetically to both content and feelings in disputed points of view
(g) generate options to disputes and create mediated contracts
(h) give constructive feedback
(i) conduct peer counseling

b. CR Knowledges and Skills: Through lecture, demonstration, role play, class and homework exercises,[129] students also learn:

(a) how feelings differ from content statements: That one person can hate the movie and think it's a lousy movie, and another can like the movie and think that it is a good movie. And that they can both be correct, whereas "the cat is on the mat" is either correct or incorrect.
(b) that values and feelings and tastes can differ and can all be respected
(c) that there are patterns of culture (Ruth Benedict's famous book) and that various cultures have different rituals, mores, codes of behavior, arts, customs, holidays, etc.
(d) that many answers to some questions are relative
(e) how to reverse roles with another person's point of view and see it from the other's shoes (empathy training).
(f) how to summarize or paraphrase back to someone what you heard to check if you really understood their point of view.
(g) how to debate well and watch for fallacies in arguments.
(h) how to ask good clarifying questions.
(i) how to describe their own feelings in an honest, appropriate, and sensitive way.
(j) how to handle anger constructively: to say how you felt when s/he did **x,** instead of labeling or "putting down" the other or using threats and/or physical force.
(k) stress management techniques: e.g., Yoga, physical exercise, bioenergetics, meditation, prioritizing, etc.

(Such social education can begin in early childhood. See Chapter 10A.: The First Steps Program, in "Can students be taught nonviolence?")
If you would like to implement some of these ideas in your school, the following resources may be helpful:

---

[129] See "The Social Barometer," Exercise 38 in Chapter 14.

3. Resources: More than 5,000 schools nationwide presently use some kind of CR program that incorporates some or all of the above The programs are in every state, in rural schools as well as inner-city schools, and they involve children from kindergarten through high school. For example:

> Three-fourths of San Francisco's public schools have student conflict managers. In New York City, more than 100 schools with about 80,000 students have some kind of program.
> In Chicago, all students take a dispute resolution course in ninth or tenth grade. In New Mexico, a statewide mediation program involves 30,000 students. In Ann Arbor, a conflict management curriculum reaches all the city's students.[130]

(1) The National Assoc. for Mediation in Education, U.S. Dept. of Education, Washington, D.C.
(2) Deutsch, M. (1973). *The Resolution of Conflict.* New Haven, Conn.: Yale Univ. Press.
(3) Johnson, D.W., *Teaching Students to be Peacemakers* and *Leading the Cooperative School.* Edina, Minn.: Interaction Book Co., 1993.
(4) Tolan, P. *What Works in Reducing Adolescent Violence.* Denver: Center for the Study of Prevention of Violence, Univ. of Colorado.
(5) Wilson-Brewer, R. *Violence Prevention for Young Adolescents.* Eric Clearinghouse, ED356442, 800-443-3742.
(6) Conflict Resolution Consortium, Website: crc@cubldr.colorado.edu

Also see the related Resources at the end of Chapter 13B. 12.

E. Strengthening Students to Be Less Vulnerable to Peer Pressure

We shall discuss this topic in this order:

1. What Kind of Child Is More Vulnerable to Peer Pressure?
2. What Kind of Child Is Less Vulnerable to Peer Pressure?
3. What Parents Can Do
4. What Teachers Can Do

Developmentally, children in the elementary grades generally have a parental transference relationship with their teacher. The teacher becomes a substitute parent for many of the students' psychological needs. In these early school years, the approval or disapproval of the teacher carries more weight with the student than the students' peers. However, during adolescence, what a student's

---

[130] Estimated by The National Assoc. for Mediation in Education, 1996. ED338791 Jun 91 Conflict Resolution Programs in Schools. *ERIC/CUE Digest* Number 74, 1996. Author: Inger, Morton, ERIC Clearinghouse on Urban Education, New York, N.Y.

peers think often becomes more important than any teacher (or parent) reaction. If the teacher says don't do **x,** but the student's peers think it's cool to do **x,** the student is often not strong enough to resist this peer pressure.

To take only one area, research indicates that peer pressure is the major determinant of drug abuse among adolescents.[131] We know that one of the determinate factors in reaching adulthood is when an individual can resist doing what is wrong regardless of peer pressure. So, we ask, what can parents and teachers do to strengthen students to be less vulnerable to peer pressure, as early in the developmental process as possible?

1. What kind of child is more vulnerable to peer pressure?

A. A child who does not feel a sense of belonging and feels alone.

B. This is obviously a child who has few friends. To be accepted by his/her peers, the child may do destructive things to get approval and to become a member.

C. This child does not have enough people in his or her life who support what s/he thinks is right.

D. The child is not used to deciding, by her/himself, what is right or wrong. S/he is not used to weighing values and feelings on an issue. Instead s/he usually depends on others for his/her decision making.

E. The child does not know what s/he is really feeling about an issue. When you ask this child, "How do you feel?" or, "How do you feel about **x**?" s/he usually says, "Fine." or "Dunno." S/he is not aware that s/he is, e.g., irritated, or feels uncomfortable about **x,** or doesn't know how to express it. Thus, s/he has trouble sharing feelings with others or listening to others' feelings supportively. As a result, s/he has trouble making friends, feels more alone, and lacks a sense of belonging.

F. S/he doesn't like her/himself very much. S/he has seldom tried things that s/he felt successful about and, thus, seldom got approval. As a result, s/he needs to be liked by others and needs others' approval more than most people.

G. This child feels a low sense of self-efficacy: s/he doesn't feel that s/he does many (or any) things well. S/he lacks self-confidence.

H. This child has many "blocks" to his/her assertiveness skills (see Chapter 12G).

---

[131] Adler, P.T. and Lotecka, L. (1973). "Drug use among high school students." *Interpersonal Journal of Addictions,* 8, 537–548.

I. The more a child displays these characteristics, the more s/he is vulnerable to peer pressure.

2. What kind of child is less vulnerable to peer pressure?

Let's reverse the process (following the letters above):

H. This child has <u>few</u> "blocks" to his/her assertiveness skills (see Chapter 12G).

G. This child generally feels confident. Early in this child's development, this child felt safe enough to initiate and try things; s/he trusted the world and experimented; s/he got attention and approval (was not overly criticized, corrected, or warned). As a result, this child was able to try many things and was able to find things s/he got approval and encouragement for. Thus, s/he felt confident about many things. This can-do feeling gave the child more ability to try more things to be able to feel successful. Eventually, s/he developed a feeling of self-efficacy, I am able, am good at many things.

F. Thus, this child likes his/herself more. S/he has gotten so many compliments over the years that s/he has these approvals stored, in a way, in his/her "emotional bank." S/he can bank on feeling good about him/herself, even when others (peers) don't like her/him.

E. This child usually <u>does</u> know what s/he is feeling. S/he knows the answer to: "How are you feeling?" And to: "How are you feeling about **x**?" S/he is aware of the fact that s/he is, e.g., irritated, or uncomfortable with **x**, s/he can not only identify his/her feelings but can express these feelings. S/he is not afraid to have feelings. His/her feelings have been listened to and have been supported many times before. As a result, this child has the ability to make friends: s/he is able to express her feelings and knows how to supportively listen to others.

D. This child is used to not only figuring out his /her feelings but sorting out, wrestling, prioritizing, and deciding between mixed and/or conflicting feelings. Someone in this child's history has helped him/her: figure out his/her feelings, asked him/her good questions, not decided everything for him/her, and supported his or her own decision-making process. As a result, s/he needs to depend less on others to make decisions.

C. This child has many friends. These are both adults and peers who know her/him and care and support him/her. This is because the child knows his/her feelings and expresses them openly (see above). Thus, s/he is known by many, who share the same feelings, so that this child does not feel alone. This child can also reciprocate: can listen to other's feelings, and share similar feelings (because s/he has had people in her/his life who have modeled this behavior). Thus, s/he can be a friend and make other friends and, thus, feels a more secure sense of belonging. Peers threatening this child with <u>not belonging</u> can<u>not</u> apply much effective peer pressure to this child.

B. When this child is urged by peers to do something that is potentially destructive and/or threatened with peer disapproval or non-membership, s/he has much past approval in the "bank" and already feels a sense of belonging and enough membership with others.

A. As a result, she does not have so much unsatisfied need to belong and is, therefore, often strong enough to resist peer pressure.

3. What parents can do

a. Early in the child's development, it is important that the parent help the child feel that the world is safe, operates with some kind of regularity, and is generally trustable. The parent/guardian should not let the baby cry too long or get the feeling that his/her needs are in trouble. Consistent routines, that the child can trust, few sudden noises, sides of cribs that do not fall, etc. all give the child the feeling that it can trust the world and that it can depend on the world safely.

b. If the child feels this, the child will venture to try things, new things, and initiate. The parent having provided this sense of safety, can now encourage these new venturesome behaviors and keep the child feeling safe as it experiments.

c. The more the parent provides approval, compliments, and safety at this stage the more the child will attempt to do, make things, and become industrious.

d. It is at these kinds of situations that the parent should "safety-proof" the child's environment. Then, the child can venture out, make things, etc. without parent reprimands (usually done by the anxious parent worried about the child's safety). The latter parent gives the child the message: "be careful, the world is not safe, don't try things, or experiment." As a result, the child makes fewer attempts, produces less, and feels less accomplishments.

e. The parent needs to compliment the child's industry, the things s/he makes, does, produces, tries. Here, the rule of thumb is to notice what the child does <u>well</u>, not to notice and correct everything that the child does wrong.

f. The child's products, tries, and projects should be noticed, hung up, applauded, and listened to. S/he needs to feel that what s/he made, did, said has some importance. If this is done, the child will begin to feel important and good at what s/he did and who s/he is.[132]

g. At these early years, the way to encourage independence is to provide the child with what s/he needs. It is a myth that the child becomes more independent if you don't give in to his/her needs. On the contrary, since children are usually not manipulators at these early years, to neglect these early "cries for help" is to only give the child the message that the world (my caretakers) cannot be trusted. Thus, the child grows more insecure, more dependent.[133]

h. Parents need, from the very start, to notice and listen to the child's feelings. The child needs to feel that his/her feelings are very important. By "listen" I mean more than "hear" these feelings. I mean the parent should try to feel these feelings, if possible, from the child's point of view. Empathize. If you still want to have an influence over your child when s/he becomes a teenager, listen to your child more than chide him or her. A teenager will only listen to the parent that s/he feels understands him or her. S/he won't feel understood if you don't listen. Then, s/he won't listen.

i. The parent should try to separate the content of the child's messages from the affect in the child's messages. For example, what is the feeling in the following message? "Mommy, can I sleep in the bed with you?" One child might say this sadly, another with a tone of anger, another expressing fear. The feeling in the message is often the most important part of the message. The child needs to feel that you hear, understand, and also feel that this part of the message is very important to you.

j. The parent must remember that a child's feeling statement about behavior is not the behavior per se. "I want to hit my sister!" is not the same as the child hitting his sister. The former is a feeling that needs to be understood, not reprimanded. As a matter of fact, if the feeling is reprimanded (rather than understood and listened to), the destructive behavior is sure to follow (as soon as the parent is out of sight).

k. The parent needs to explicitly teach the child about feelings: what they are, how to identify them, the correct vocabulary for their expression; and that it is OK to have them, all kinds: mixed feelings, negative and positive ones.

l. Here, the parent can model his/her own feelings, express his/her joy, sensitivity, disappointment, sadness, jealousy, irritation, etc. The parent can show the child that some feelings last, some pass, get mixed with other feelings, sometimes feel uncomfortable, etc. The parent can say, "Oh, you look like you're

---

[132] The above are extrapolations of Erik Erikson's Theory of Psycho-Social Development.
[133] Spock, Benjamin. *Baby and Child Care.* (Simon and Schuster, New York, 1996) p. 336.

feeling sad, or worried, or that you seem to have two feelings. . . ." The parent can say, "If I were you, I would be feeling jealous or sad that. . . ." In short, the parent needs to help the child locate and express his/her feelings in a supportive, non-judgmental way.

m. The parent needs to teach and model the decision-making process, how one goes about sorting out ones feelings, and deciding about feelings in general. Here, the parent can think out loud about his/her own feelings and decisions. The parent can show the child what one does when one has mixed feelings. The parent can teach the child how to prioritize and sort out conflicting feelings.

n. The parent can ask the child good questions: "How do you feel about that?" "Which is more important to you?" "What do you worry will happen if you do that?" "One part of you feels . . .?" "The other part of you feels . . .?"

o. The parent then can encourage the child to tell their friends what s/he is feeling, e.g., in a dispute or uncomfortable peer situation. If the child has gotten previous support for his/her feelings, the child will be able to stand up for his/her feelings, even be able to tolerate rejection.

p. Generally, the best guideline for these early years is to catch your child being good, not point out what s/he is doing badly.

q. Always give your child tasks and challenges that go from easiest to harder, not the other way around. Your goal is to always leave your child with the feeling of "can-do."

r. Help your child to feel a sense of belonging to his/her family, church, the routines around the house, and the traditions that you create.

s. At each developmental age, from childhood through adolescence, allow the child to try out his/her own independence, as much as possible (within safety). If you have done a good job with the above tasks, this task will be easier and less risky.

t. Finally, teach your child that s/he should always judge the judgers: that people who are jealous of you may call you names and get angry with you; that people who do not like themselves often get inappropriately angry; that needy people may be manipulators; that people may urge you to do something not good for you because they care more about their own needs than yours; that a person may want you to do something with them because they are feeling lonely, etc., etc.

The parent or guardian who can do many of the above for their child will strengthen that child to be less vulnerable to peer pressure.

4. What teachers can do

Teachers can also help a great deal. Teachers can:

1. Work on some of the same abilities that were advised for parents to do above: e, f, h, i, j, k, l, m, n, p, r, s, t
2. Use the specific lesson plan methods suggested in Chapter 14B to make teaching about feelings part of the subject-content lesson.
3. Make the classroom safe for students to try: a question, an answer, a new idea, sharing a feeling, a new project, etc.
4. Protect students' feelings. The teacher should reprimand any student that criticizes (or name-calls) another student. The teacher should support students who attempt answers, especially when the answer turns out to be wrong.
5. Point out to students that there are different opinions, points of view, tastes, values, feelings, etc. The teacher must teach tolerance for these differences.
6. Explicitly teach conflict resolution and ways to negotiate arguments as disputes actually happen in the classroom (see Chapter 12D).
7. Provide students with as many opportunities to feel successful in the classroom.
8. Applaud, notice, post on the bulletin board, etc., student successes and accomplishments.
9. Teach that feelings are more like colors than like facts; that the former are <u>not</u> right or wrong as in: "it is raining or is not raining." Instead, if one person said, "the movie was great" and the other said, "the movie was boring," they can <u>both</u> be correct.
10. Explicitly teach emotional vocabulary; how to spell, use, relate in a story, etc. words such as anxious, ambivalent, envious, frustrated, etc.
11. Model the expression of feelings and share his/her <u>person</u>-teacher with the students. The teacher can often, appropriately, openly show the class his/her feelings that can be educational for the students.
12. Frequently ask students good questions about themselves and their emotions that give them practice sorting out their feelings, values and decisions: e.g., If you could have   , which would you choose first? What is your biggest worry? What frustrates you the most? If one boy wanted to   , and another wanted to   , what could you say to them to help them decide?
13. For what <u>K–6 teachers</u> can especially do, see this Chapter 12**H.**

The more a teacher is able to do these kinds of things, the more s/he will help students be less vulnerable to peer pressure.

These references on this subject may also be useful:

Resisting Peer Pressure Grades 4 to . . . .
URL: http://www.diskovery.com/diskovery/EPG/Products/Videos/1930.html
Interaction and Decision Making: Resisting Peer Pressure
Helps students to see how their feelings of self-worth can influence their behavior.
URL: http://www.diskovery.com/diskovery/EPG/Indices/Videos/ByPublisher/
MindPlay. html
Drug Abuse Resistance Education
URL: http://www.ncia.net/schools/berlin/dare.htm
Summary: The DARE program allows selected Berlin High students to visit with elementary school students.
(The DARE program is now in all fifty states and teaches "peer-refusal skills." There are other similar programs: STAR in Kansas City; SMART in North Carolina; ALERT in California and Oregon; and LST (Life Skills Training) in New York City.)

The reader is referred to the bibliography on affective education at the end of Section H in Chapter 14.

F. Warding off Bullies

There are some things you can do if you have "bullies" in your classroom for grades K–6:

1. Set up warnings and punishments that apply to students who "pick" on other students. In designing these, follow the guidelines above in Chapter 12A. Then, if the "bully" "turns over a new leaf" apply some of the rewards in Chapter 12C.

2. A "bully" is usually a child that feels inadequate in some areas, and/or needs attention, and/or has displaced anger, or "bullies" to feel stronger, or ensure his/her membership in a "strong" group or gang. It is an ambitious task, but you should try to reward and give this student attention for good behavior, and compliment him/her for anything that will boost his/her ego. Try to give him/her a sense of membership through all classroom activities, or "take him/her in" yourself. Provide opportunities for him/her to vent any angers and frustrations that s/he may have that may be coming from outside the classroom. If you are successful at any of these, you will have done more than merely try to stop him/her with warnings, and you'll find that you'll have less "victims" cropping up.

3. Regarding these "victims," (f) It is best to try to strengthen a constantly "picked on" victim than to always try to protect him or her. Trying to always protect the victim will only make that student more dependent, look like the teacher's pet and, thus, be more "picked on" when you're not around. Approach the victim with the attitude, "Sue, why do they always go after you?" "Why you?" "What are you going to do about this?" This tack of working with the victim is more effective than trying to always be around to reprimand the aggressor.

For the upper grades, you can still apply the above: 1, 2, and 3. However, also be diligent with regard to the aggressors to apply the guidelines in Chapter 13B 10: regarding students who "dis" (disrespect) or criticize each other. Do not tolerate a "fight" (see Chapter 13B 2) on school grounds; warn them that, no matter who starts it, if such continues on school grounds (in this classroom), both students involved will be punished (by warnings that you have set up [hopefully, in line with the guidelines in this Chapter 12A]).

G. Working on Asserting Yourself and Taking Stands

Even if you are able to follow all the guidelines and use all the suggestions listed, there will still be a major difficulty if you do not have an important ability: the ability to assert yourself and take stands. However, if you have worked on being more congruent, appropriate, and fair, your ability to assert yourself and take stands will have that much improved. This is because if you are advocating congruent, appropriate, and fair rules and warnings, you will not feel guilty about what you are saying. Guilt weakens your ability to assert yourself. Let's look at other factors that weaken this ability and how we can remedy these problems.

(Parents will also find that working on one's "assertiveness" here will be helpful in working with their children's school problems in general.)

Other Factors That Weaken Assertiveness

1. Guilt from Other Areas: You may not be guilty of incongruence, inappropriateness, or unfairness, but you may be guilty that you said you'd mark and return their tests, but you didn't. Or you owe someone something. Or you lied (in or out of school). Or you haven't done your share of X. Or you should've called your parents. Or you've forgotten to send a card, etc.

2. Conflicting Feelings: You won't be able to say "No" well if you partly feel "Yes." Sort out your feelings in areas you feel ambivalent. Perhaps you need to say "Maybe" and specify your conditions. You can't answer from your

"head" and assert yourself well. Explore your feelings. Standing on your true, clarified feelings will make you stand stronger.

3. Fear of Others' Anger: You won't be able to assert yourself if you are afraid of other people's anger or that they may punish you.

4. Fear of Your Own Anger: You won't be able to assert yourself well if you are afraid that you'll get so angry you won't be able to control yourself.

5. You Have a Low Ego: If you feel a lack of pride in yourself, you'll feel less confidence and strength to assert yourself and take stands.

6. You Need the Class to Like You: Then, you'd rather "give in" than take a stand and lose their approval.

7. You Identify with the Student(s): If you identify with the student to whom you are trying to say "no," you will find it difficult, e.g., to deprive him ("you") of what you want to assent.

How can you work on these "blocks" to your assertiveness?

1. Guilt from Other Areas: You must realize that not doing what you yourself believe in, should do, makes you guilty and, thereby, weakens you. You may get away with, e.g., not paying back, not doing X, etc., but you won't get away from yourself who feels guilty and weakens you in school, in your social life, in your ability to relax, etc. Rectify these guilts if you want to be more assertive.

2. Conflicting Feelings: Discuss these feelings with yourself now. List the pros and cons; prioritize them; tell your ambivalent feelings to a friend and have the friend ask you questions about your emotional conflict. Decide your conditions for your "maybes."

3. Fear of others' anger: What's the worst thing this colleague could do to you if you really say how you feel? Often your fear is based on an unconscious exaggerated fantasy of the consequences. Or you are involved in a "transference" reaction: the other person reminds you of your father or mother, and it feels like s/he will, let us say, send you to bed without dinner. If you feel your friend will punish you by, e.g., leaving you, what kind of friendship is it then anyway?

4. Fear of Your Own Anger: You probably feel that if you let out a little anger, your whole "volcano" will blow. The solution is not to learn to control your angers. Instead, you've got to stop building up a "volcano" of rage. You need to find outlets for your irritations: sports, exercise, aggressive play, friends who will allow you to vent, professional help, etc.

5. You Have a Low Ego: Go out and accomplish something. Work hard on a project or self-assignment that will give you a sense of pride.

6. <u>You Need the Class to Like You</u>: If you had more people who liked you (friends), you'd not need your students' approval so much. Go out and work on improving your friendships. Especially, try to share your "tough" decisions and "stands" with colleagues or friends.

7. You Identify with the Students(s): That's not you. Or tell yourself what you have to do will ultimately help the student (though it hurts you and him/her now). You don't want to teach this student that he/she can "con" the world, do you? Weaning is as important as feeding.

Asserting yourself and taking stands is a complex and difficult skill. It warrants its own book on the subject. Thus, many have been written on this skill. If you feel you need more work and help on this than what I've described above, these books are very helpful:

Alberti, Robert G., and Michael Emmons. *Your Perfect Right: A Guide to Assertive Behavior.* 2nd ed. San Luis Obispo: Impact. 1974.
Adams, Kathleen A. *Assertiveness at Work.* Englewood Cliffs, N.J.: Spectrum, 1982.
Smith, Manuel J. *When I Say No I Feel Guilty.* New York: Dial Press, 1975.

H. Especially for Grades K–6

Most of the above suggestions are also already useful to grades K–6. But this age group requires that we revise some of the above and add a few suggestions that are specific to these grades.

1. Rules and their consequences should be fewer in number and more straightforward than you might use with older students. Children need to be able to remember and understand rules. If these rules get too complicated or numerous, confusion will result, and you may have more discipline problems simply because young children often react to confusion or other negative emotions by acting out. In the elementary grades (contrary to what was said in Section D of this chapter), the children should participate more in creating the rules, and you do have time for this process. The ownership gained will cause them to follow the rules more closely and to enforce them among their peers.

(This is one way to let the center of disciplinary power and control shift from the teacher to the students, encouraging responsibility and self-control. Without this shift, the teacher faces the herculean task of maintaining order alone. This shift is, therefore, necessary if children are to learn to control themselves and develop a sense of right and wrong rather than behaving only as long as the teacher is with them.)

If you find that the students are creating too many rules, as often happens, simply have the students categorize them, e.g., "No Hitting, No Kicking, No Running Indoors, and No Fighting" can all be combined into "No Unsafe Behavior" or, better yet, "Be Safe."

2. In K–6, you will generally do even better with a well-structured system of rewards rather than punishments. One example often used in classrooms that use cooperative learning is to have a "marble jar." I am not saying everyone should use this particular system. Find one that works for you, but the principles of making it work will still hold true. Then start with easily attainable rewards and dole them out plentifully so that your students know you will "deliver" the promised rewards. For example, in a marble jar system,[134] you should start with a small jar and put one marble in it for everything that happens that you want to reinforce. (Every time someone raises their hand instead of calling out, the class lines up properly, a group works well together, someone is helpful to a peer without being asked, etc.) Marbles should flow like water! With a system like this, students can contribute as individuals or as group members, whichever they are capable of. Then, when the jar is full, do something big! The reward has to be worth working for or this will not work. It also has to happen soon enough that the students know you are not lying to them about getting it.

A good rule of thumb is that the first reward should happen by the end of September: Have a pizza party, watch a fun video, take a field trip. Giving a night off of homework is not sufficiently big for a whole jar of good deeds! Once the jar has been filled, start the next jar. This time, make it slightly bigger, but continue to be extremely generous with the marbles. As the year goes on, you can cut back on what you give a marble for.

In September, for example, you might give one marble each for lining up, walking in the hall properly to art, and waiting for the art teacher, i.e., three marbles total.

In January, you might only give one marble for getting to art properly. Explain that as they grow up, you expect more of your students.

To summarize: (1) When in doubt, over-reward rather than under. (2) Each successive jar should be bigger than the last. (3) Make the reward fit all the work that goes into filling a jar; make it big! (4) Never, ever take marbles out of the jar (because this would be a system of punishments). Rather than

---

[134] Also, see **this marble reward system** listed in Chapter 12C.

taking marbles out of the jar, be aware of a situation before it happens and threaten not to put marbles in if they don't fulfill your requirements.

3. Especially in K–6, the teacher can create many situations that <u>encourage independence</u> (and, thus, help students to become less vulnerable to destructive peer pressure; see Chapter 12E):

a. Insist that your students be responsible for preparing themselves for the day, i.e., hanging up their own coat and lunch box, handing in their own homework.
b. After you clearly label all material storage areas in the classroom, insist that the students get their own materials when they need them.
c. Use cooperative learning methods (consult the Index) that encourage students to be responsible for their own learning whenever possible.
d. Assign group and individual projects that respond to open-ended ideas as opposed to short answer or fill-in-the-blank work sheets.
e. Accept and encourage students' questions, even (especially) when they question <u>you.</u> Insist that these questions be phrased with respect, whether directed to you or their peers, and answer these questions openly, thoughtfully, and honestly.

I. Teachers Share Their Growing Pains

Effective Rules and Warnings

I learned a great deal in this course in regard to this topic. I had thought I had a good system of rules and warnings, which I realize was less than adequate. My system was verbal and was not specific enough. At times, depending upon the child, I would bend the rules. I did not have enough warning steps and those that I did have were not really clear cut. I tended to call in an outside party before it was necessary to do so.

• • •

My problem in the warning category is that often when I get in a very pissed-off state, I jump steps and wind up putting myself in a spot. For instance, I'm in a nasty mood and Kim decides to throw a paper across the room into the basket. I snap for Kim to hold the paper until after class. A little while later Kim takes another shot. This time I might make the mistake of blurting out something like, "Kim, if you do that once more I'll have you suspended for a week." What I am trying to say is that quite often I'll get pissed and lose control temporarily and find that my warnings jump steps in a most dramatic fashion.

• • •

Unfortunately, my first response to a misbehavior tends to be a verbal one. I tend to feed negative attention and not reward positive behavior. I do not reprimand with as little attention as possible. I tend to reprimand with a question. I tend to blurt. I tend to have large steps in my warning system. I tend to call in a third person early in my system. I tend not to let students know what is next in my warning system.

• • •

I feel that I need to sit down and set up better rules and a better warning system for each type of infraction. Here is my new warning system for students who "call out":

STUDENT DOES	I DO
1. Calls out	1. I look at the student and call on someone else.
2. Calls out	2. I ignore the student who calls out and call on someone else who raises his/her hand.
3. Calls out	3. I tell the student to see me after class, and if he does not show up he'll lose two points off his grade.
4. Student does not show up after class and calls out the next day in class.	4. I tell the student that he has lost two points off his grade for not coming to see me after class yesterday, and from now on each time he calls out he will lose two more points off his grade.
5. Raises hand	5. I call on the student and I tell him that I'm glad to see that he knows the right way to participate in the class discussion.

This has really been so valuable. One thing I inherited from my mother is my short temper and big mouth. I would start yelling at a kid, throw out ridiculous threats, and not understand why the kid was getting more upset and nastier. He was also winning. I could not imagine why I was not in control. I find when I use these steps I am more relaxed, the kids are more relaxed, the class doesn't get involved, and they work. I have been much calmer, better prepared and enjoy my classes more.

• • •

I find this to be a great weakness of mine. Since I have been teaching I never had a set of warning steps, but I have begun to try them and hope to use them from now on. I have even discussed them with my principal and explained to her how helpful I have found them. In the past, I always found myself threatening or warning a child but very often that was where I stopped. I would sometimes give silly punishments like writing spelling words fifty times each. That might work for a little while, but I find the same thing happening, so 1 know it wasn't very effective. Many times when I'd give punishments, I also found myself not checking them or making sure they got done so many children would not even do them.

The problem I find is to really get enough warning steps. Because of the age of my class (2nd grade) I am limited in their punishment. They are not permitted to stay after school since they cannot get home by themselves. However, as a substitute, I now keep them in during their lunch hour. Taking away a child's playtime proves to be very effective. I also keep in contact more with the parents of the problem kids. This really is helpful. I used to find this more of an inconvenience for me, but it's worthwhile since it seems to be working. My principal is also aware of what I have been doing and agrees to get involved if needed. So far this hasn't happened.

Negative Attention

I can remember many times I put a student in the library because he was a pain in the ass. I know now he loved his punishment. I should have dealt with him in other ways, such as extra homework assignments, detention, zeros, but most importantly not to let anyone see he got attention, never reprimand him publicly. Eventually, he will burn out if I don't feed the negative attention he thrives on.

• • •

I do not have a systematic list of rules and warnings. This is a problem area for me that I have been giving serious thought to. I generally find myself favoring certain children. If a child I like is chewing gum, I will make a light remark about spitting it out. But if a child that "bugged" me chews a piece of gum, I will be much firmer with him/her and make a big problem out of a small issue. This type of inconsistent rule-making is not fair to the class. I am working at laying down the same rules for everyone in all situations.

"See Me after Class!"

The second most interesting and important pan of the course for me was dealing with "see me after class." I have never been good with words and somehow when it got to be after class, I would change what I wanted to say to something nicer. Of course, later, I would be very upset with myself for not telling it like it was. I would:

1. Try to be logical
2. Play a game of "chess"

3. Try to win the person's feelings
4. Have a discussion
5. Put my anger into the form of a question
6. Show inappropriate anger
7. Blurt things out

In the past several weeks I have changed to:

1. Expressing my feelings on the problems
2. Being very brief
3. Stating my follow-up action

Situation 1: In the case of Joe asking me about my belly dancing I told him after class that I did take dancing lessons, that it did not have anything to do with math class, and that I would appreciate it greatly if he not mention it again. He was a little surprised at my reaction and was lost for words. He could not argue with me because I expressed how I felt.

• • •

Although I agree that we should be very direct in telling a student after class what is incorrect about his behavior, I do not think that is enough. I agree that I should not try to change his personality or feelings about me; however, I try to give the child the opportunity to explain the reasons or rationale for his actions, if he so desires. This does not result in a "chessboard" discussion; instead, it represents a cooperative attempt to understand and remove the source of the misbehavior. If a child does not appear to want to discuss the problem, then I think it is correct to simply lay down your feelings, rules, and warnings about continued breaking of those rules.

Calling Out

The most difficult thing that I found was not to give any recognition to those students who called out. Very often I was tempted to look at them or take their answer as they called out and raised their hand. Also, I found it personally difficult not to respond to a question right away. I still feel that students might be turned off if they cannot get their question answered.

• • •

Obviously, I'm not as quick as I should be to observe and reward the person who stops calling out and begins to raise a hand. In the actual classroom, I probably allow questions to be asked sometimes, which interrupt my train of thought.

Indeed, it seems that I need to concentrate and practice the art of being deaf, dumb, and blind to those who do call out and, yet, alert to changes that take place.

• • •

When I tried to follow the guidelines to prevent calling out in my classes, I found it quite challenging. At the beginning of the week, I was very self-conscious because sometimes I would start to frown at students who would call out, when I should have been deaf, dumb, and blind to them. I also forgot to give a lot of attention to students who raised their hands.

By Wednesday I was starting to get the hang of it, though, and the guidelines were becoming effective. The students who almost always call out started to get angry when I ignored them. Most of them just stopped calling out and would not even raise their hand. One student started making comments such as, "I knew that answer," when I would call on someone who was raising their hand.

I also remembered to look straight at the students and thank them.

Fighting

I don't hold students who fight. I once got in trouble because I held the kid with too much force and he claimed he was hurt by me!

• • •

Once I broke up a fight between two seventh grade boys. (I am a female.) I guess I was lucky to come out unharmed.

Cheating

The idea of sitting in the back of the room seems terrific.

I like walking around the room better, but then I can't get much work done during the test.

• • •

I just give essay questions.

• • •

If I see a cheater, I just go up to him/her and look at them and squeeze their arm. They get the idea.

Lateness

I used to stop in the middle of my teaching, walk over to my Delaney book and alter absentees to latenesses for all students who came in late. This drove me crazy!

Now, "a late student must enter through the back door, if there is one, and quietly sit down in his/her seat. The student is marked absent and must see the teacher after class to have the absent mark changed to a lateness; otherwise the absent mark will stay."

I have found this policy to be quite effective in my classes. Students used to come in five to ten minutes late and would interrupt either my instructions or organization of a game. With this new policy the students come in, listen to my instructions, and wait till I have a question period before they ask what they have missed. The repetition is good for the entire class as it reinforces the given instructions. In your policy you do not recommend answering late students' questions. However, I must answer all questions and make sure that everyone fully understands the activity so no one gets hurt.

Homework

Regarding not accepting late homeworks, I wish that I had enforced this rule. The amount of late work I received on the eve of report cards was tremendous, adding stress by doubling my work, correcting papers to get grades to average marks. I penalized late work, but I actually should not have accepted it. I think that I accepted it because I feared that had I not accepted it, some students never would have done any work.

I did use the policy of glancing over homework at the beginning of class and writing the names of those who didn't have it.

I like the idea of commenting on homework without grading it, except occasionally to keep students on their toes. I also like the idea that homework be used as an opening to a class lesson and excluding from discussion those who are on my list as not having done the homework.

• • •

I have not followed the homework policy that was suggested in class; however, I have decided to modify my own homework policy.

This semester I decided to accept late homeworks unconditionally. I still accept late homeworks; however, they must be handed in within three days and they are marked late. I have found that most students now hand homework in on time.

I accept late homework because I feel my homeworks are good for reinforcing what has been learned. No matter when they do the homework, even though we have gone over it in class, they are still reinforcing what has been learned.

I found that when I did not accept late homeworks, many students rarely handed in any homework. This semester, however, most of my students have handed in every homework assigned.

• • •

The homework idea works very well. At the beginning the students were trying to hand m their homeworks at the end of each period, telling me that they forgot to show me at the beginning but soon they realized that I meant what I had said. The only problem is that sometimes I forget the students who had had the assignment and I call on those who hadn't. Then I keep looking in my grade book and time is wasted, but I am working on it.

Some Psychological Considerations

At times, I feel that punishment is necessary to keep obnoxious students in line. I do feel that whatever punishment I give should be educational so that it reinforces my teaching. I would never look down on a student nor belittle a student by giving punishments just to show authority. When I do give punishments, it is always after many warnings and never comes as a surprise. I think that never to punish students would give them every opportunity to misbehave.

• • •

Personally, I don't feel that I would like to give my students an opportunity to formulate their own rules. First of all, I feel that my classes should follow the rules that I feel are appropriate, not the reverse. Second, I've found that there is always a group of clowns in my classes, and I couldn't imagine allowing them to make up rules. I cringe just to think of what they would allow.

• • •

Since I started teaching in the public schools in September, I have been trying to figure out a way to make up class rules that would allow the students to participate in designing them. I feel that a good way may be to ask students to write down the rules they would like to have in different categories (homework, cheating, lateness, etc.). I would then look all of them over and choose the best ones or modify others. I want the rules to be congruent with the way I feel, but I also think that if students help design them, they are placing the responsibility for their behavior on themselves.

Assertiveness

As a student in junior high school as well as high school, I was always anxious to discover what grade I had received on a test. Therefore, when I give a test to my students I feel I should return the corrected papers as soon as possible. If I'm not able to return the papers on the following day, I experience a sense of personal guilt, and I often have trouble telling or reminding my students what they have to do or should have done.

As far as emotional conflicts are concerned, I find that telling a student that he can obtain a bathroom pass only during the third and seventh periods is a bit ridiculous. However, it is one of the rules and yet I have mixed reactions about this rule. In addition to this is another school rule that says that all homework assignments must be signed by a parent. If a child has a parent who works irregular hours and cannot sign the homework, should I penalize the student and give him a zero or an incomplete grade even if his work appears to be correct? These are some of the conflicts I've been confronted with, but it was not until this concept was discussed that I learned why I sometimes have trouble asserting myself.

Fear of my own anger is another variable that sometimes presents a problem for me in asserting myself. I try to control my anger because there have been at least three occasions during my teaching career when I attempted to retaliate to get even for things students did to me.

• • •

Not being able to assert myself most of the time, has something to do with my fear of the kid's anger. Referring to the homework rules, I'll enforce them to the point of being very pushy, knowing beforehand that the kid will never hate me for something he knows is part of school requirements. On the other hand, I would be afraid of the kid's anger if asking to go to the bathroom, I say no because I sense that this is his way of getting out of the classroom. Soon after, I'll be calling him and let him go, only to be in peace with my conscience. I could be more assertive, if sensing his play, I kept my word and let his insistence convince otherwise.

Also, I want the kids to like me. One of the reasons I would handle the bathroom situation the way I did is I would not want the kid to feel that I am insensitive and intransigent. It is like that I am assuring their love, their support.

• • •

I really haven't accepted the idea that it's all right to be angry. I associate anger with immaturity and lack of control. In my mind I've separated "emotional anger" and "intellectual anger." I get "intellectually" angry about a lot of things: racism, sexism, poverty, and I do really feel these things. The way I release the anger is by demonstrating or writing a leaflet or giving a speech. I guess I think anger is okay if it's for the benefit of someone else—or a group of people.

• • •

Asserting myself in certain situations has been a problem that I am trying to overcome. Many times, I have not been as direct and forceful as necessary. The fear of anger and a confrontation is something that has always bothered me, and for these reasons I have developed an attitude that prevents me from asserting myself when the situation calls for it.

• • •

My major block in being assertive is wanting to be liked by my students. I definitely want my students to like me both as a teacher and a person. But will they still like me after I let off some steam at them? I must learn to assert myself more and worry less about their reactions. The problem is that I envy the smooth, easygoing teacher who has a solution for everything and is well-liked by his students. For the most part I am liked, but I don't want to pay a price for that.

My problems with asserting myself in class have gone through stages directly related to my emotional growth. At the beginning of my teaching career, my biggest problem was that of needing the kids to approve of me, like me, etc. I was very unsure of myself both at home (it was the first year of my marriage) and at school. I was then unaware of the extent of my problem. That need continued until recently (though a touch remains), and it caused me to back off many times for the sake of being the "good guy."

As I made progress in therapy and unearthed all the hidden angers of my childhood deprivations, I became terrified of expressing my anger in class because I felt it was a lit fuse to a stick of TNT.

The last two years, I've had problems for other reasons. I felt a lack of accomplishment and an overwhelming sense of loneliness out of school that made me need the children more and affected my ability to assert myself. I also felt guilty over not keeping up with my professional responsibility—that of marking papers, giving tests, etc. I remedied the latter problem of guilt by sitting down with myself and devising a new system that enabled the children to help me out by marking much of their own work. This helped me feel better about me, which naturally reflected itself in the way I related to the kids.

• • •

I have the most trouble asserting myself when I feel guilty. If the lesson that I am teaching is bad, I find it hard to force the students to behave. This is usually a result of lack of proper preparation on my part. However, I question if I should assert myself. My solution to this is to have an appropriate math game or activity handy to substitute for the lesson.

• • •

Another area that I feel has been a weakness is overidentifying with the students. Whenever a student would complain to me about something, my tendency would be to hear the student out thoroughly, even if the complaint did not warrant my giving him as much attention as I did. I came to realize that the student seemed to be like me when I was a kid but not getting the attention that I wanted. I was, in effect, satisfying little Jeff. After speaking to you, I realized that little Jeff is no longer here so I had to get these thoughts and tendencies out of my mind.

J. Training Exercises and Checklist for Chapter 12

Exercise One: Rating Your Present Rules and Warnings

List here six or seven of the rules and warnings you are presently using in your classroom. In the column at the right, place the number of the guideline that is not being followed by you for the rule. (Guidelines 1–21 are listed at the beginning of this chapter, section A.)

Rule	Guideline Not Followed
1.	1.
2.	2.
3.	3.
4.	4.
5.	5.
6.	6.
7.	7.

Which rules are bad ones? Which guidelines do you tend not to heed?

Exercise Two: Not Giving Negative Attention

List your tendencies here where you tend to give negative attention:

1.   4.
2.   5.
3.   6.

Now, write down here three ways you can reprimand a student in a nonaudience setting.

1.
2.
3.

Exercise Three: Deciding Your Limits

With a friend, colleague, or classmate, have them throw demand questions at you, such as: "Can I go to the bathroom during class?" "Can I go twice in one period?" "Can you lend me a dime?' "Do I have to do the homework?" "Can I call you by your first name?" Ask them to make all their questions answerable by either: "yes," "no," "maybe," or "none of your business." You must answer each question as fast as you can, on the spot. However, if you take the easy road of "maybe," you must answer, "If what?" You must state your conditions. Since teachers often can't give rationales, you can't justify your judgments. Just answer "yes," "no," "maybe" (if what?) or "none of your business." Do this exercise with your partner. Then reverse roles: the other person be "the teacher," the other person be "the demanding, questioning student."

Where are you cloudy on your limits? Do you say "yes" more often than you mean because of fear of anger or of being disliked? Could you follow through with your "no's"? (Have your partner see if s/he can change your answer by acting angry, sad, seductive, etc.)

Exercise Four: Deciding Your Warning Steps and Consequences

Try to fill in the chart below by trying this "nightmare." Assume that (in the left column) you are "teaching and all is going well," and the students (in the right column 1) are all "paying attention." However, suddenly, in 2 "a student calls out." What would you do at this time? Write your response in 2, the left column. Now assume that the student violates whatever warning (or whatever you did) in 2. Imagine what it is s/he does to violate you (write it out as 3 in the right column). Now, what do you do about this 3? Write your next graduated response in 3 (left column). Again, assume in 4 that s/he violates your 3. Imagine the student's 4, write it out, and respond with your 4. And so on. Continue until you run out of power. When you finish the "nightmare," see if your warning steps followed the guidelines (1–21) discussed in this chapter, section A.

I do:	Student does:
1. teaching, and all is going well	1. paying attention
	2. student calls out
2. _____	
	3. _____
3. _____	
	4. _____
4. _____	
	5. _____
5. _____	
	6. _____
6. _____	

Exercise Five: Preparing Your Warnings and Rules

Write down a rule in the left column. Word it as you would actually say it to the class. In the right column, list at least four steps of consequences you would use to enforce the rule. Do this for six or seven rules. (Certainly decide a rule for calling out, lateness, talking and disturbing the class, and gum chewing). Do your warned consequences follow the guidelines 1–21 discussed in this chapter?

Rule	Consequences
I.	1.
	2.
	3.
	4.
II.	1.
	2.
	3.
	4.
III.	1.
	2.
	3.
	4.
IV.	1.
	2.
	3.
	4.
V.	1.
	2.
	3.
	4.
VI.	1.
	2.
	3.
	4.
VII.	1.
	2.
	3.
	4.

Exercise Six: Evaluating Your Rules

Look at your rules objectively. Try to write down every single rule that you would like to see followed in your classroom. If you have a list that is so long that you can't remember them all right away, then you will probably have trouble enforcing all of them. In addition, if there are too many for you to handle effectively, then there are certainly too many for your students to remember and follow to the letter.

Try going through your list to see which of those rules are truly important to you personally. Which you consider important because that's how you were taught? Or because it's always been done that way? Which ones really enhance your teaching? Versus giving you a false sense of power or control? Which rules could be combined into a more general rule that would be easier to remember and follow?

Exercise Seven: Clarifying Your Policies in Light of Some Psychological Considerations

These issues discussed in Chapter 12, section D are difficult and complex. Write out a short speech you believe in for each of the following issues:

1. The Use of Empathetic Listening
2. The Use of Rewards and Punishments
3. When Confronting Is Best
4. Using Punishments
5. Using Extrinsic Rewards
6. Should the Students Decide the Rules?
7. Out-of-School Suspensions
8. In-School Suspensions

Exercise Eight: Working on Asserting Yourself and Taking Stands

Below are the "blocks" to assertiveness that weaken this ability. Place an A next to the ones that are usually your problem, B if sometimes, C if seldom, D if never. Which is your problem(s)?

Blocks to Assertiveness	Rating
1. Incongruence, thus Guilty	
2. Inappropriateness, thus Guilty	
3. Unfairness, thus Guilty	
4. Guilt for Other Areas	
5. Conflicting Feelings	
6. Fear of Other's Anger	
7. Fear of Your Own Anger	
8. Low Ego	
9. I Need the Class to Like Me	
10. Identification with the Student(s)	

Notice which ones received A's and B's. You should read the suggestions for working on these on pp. 327–329 and try to follow them.

Checklist

1. Are you following as many of the twenty-one guidelines as you can that are suggested in this chapter?
2. Which guideline do you have trouble following?
3. Are you trying to reinforce the appropriate behavior with some kind of rewards as much as possible, rather than always punish the inappropriate behavior?
4. Are your rewards and punishments systematic, and do you keep track of them?
5. Have you tried to apply some conflict resolution strategies to conflicts in your classroom?
6. Are you applying any of the strategies suggested in this chapter to strengthen students to be less vulnerable to peer pressure?
7. Are you keeping an eye to trying to strengthen any victims that you may have in your class?
8. Are you trying to "unblock" any areas that are weak for you personally that you may become more assertive?
9. If you are mainly concerned about grades K–6, have you taken time to revise some of the suggestions in this chapter that have been advised in section **H** above?

CHAPTER 13: SPECIFICS

Besides the above guidelines for preventing discipline problems, let us look at some specific problems encountered in most schools, and suggest some ways of handling these.[135]

A. How to Handle the "See Me after Class!"

It is appropriate at this point to spend more time on a specific reprimand that is typical for most classes. One effective and often-used reprimand is, "See me after class!" If you feel congruent with this reprimand, it can be effective, appropriate, and deliver your warning in a helpful non-audience setting. However, some teachers don't know exactly what to say or do at the "See me after class!" or what not to do when they are actually alone with the student. Here are some specific suggestions for handling the student when s/he sees you after class:

(a) Specify what it is you are annoyed with that the student did that has caused you to see him/her after class.

(b) Don't get into an argument, "arm wrestle," about: "But I didn't do any-thing!" or "But John did the same thing. How come you're not blaming him?" Don't justify yourself. Ignore the invitation to this debate, trust your judgment, and just deliver your reprimand and warning.

(c) Don't answer a "Why?!" challenge. But you may explain a "Why?" if you think the student sincerely doesn't understand.

---

[135] A useful resource is the following catalogue of many specific behavior problems. It lists behavior problems and then lists many suggestions of what a teacher might do to handle each problem (along with a reference to the author of the approach). But make sure, when using this resource, that you heed the twenty-one guidelines above and the four caveats discussed at the opening of Part III. *The Resource Book for Remediating Common Behavior and Learning Problems* (Allyn and Bacon, Boston) 1989. Call: 800-278-3525 or 800-922-0579.

(d) Of course, say only what you really feel (i.e., feel congruent with). And don't do this in the form of a question, such as: "Don't you realize. . .?"

(e) Warn what you feel is appropriate.

(f) Warn what you can actually follow through with.

(g) Warn what you feel is fair.

(h) Have your back to the wall so the student looks at you and the wall instead of facing you and his/her peers' observations of the scolding.

(i) You might explain that you can understand the student's feelings, e.g., "That you're bored with math," or "That John was bugging you." But then, explain you can accept this feeling, but not the disruptive behavior, e.g., "But you can't call out," or "You can't hit John."

(j) Make your reprimand direct. Don't deliver it in the third person, e.g., "We don't do that. . . ." Or don't deliver it in the form of a question, e.g., "Do you know what you were doing?" "Would you tolerate this if you were the teacher?" "How would you like it if . . .?" Such questions may give a red carpet to a wise-guy answer you don't want to do battle with.

(k) Don't label the student, e.g., "John, you're a pain in the ass." Instead, say how his specific behavior makes you feel, e.g., "John, your calling out gets me very angry. I can't concentrate. . . ." A student will find it more difficult to argue with your feeling than your label.

(1) This is not the time to give a lecture on morals. Specify the bad behavior, your reprimand and warning, and that's it. This is not a time for argument or to teach a lesson on proper values or feelings.

(m) Don't try to convince with logic, e.g., "Don't you see if you do X, then he does Y, then I do Z?" This situation is not the best place where logic can change behavior. Logic seldom changes feelings or behavior, especially in a place of reprimand.

(n) Don't ask, "Why did you do this?" Reasoning or trying to create guilt doesn't go very far here.

(o) Don't try to win the student's feeling, e.g., "And don't smirk like that when I talk to you!" Just go after the behavior.

(p) Don't reprimand the student's reaction to your reprimand, e.g., "And for smirking at my warning, here's another warning."

(q) Specify the punishment for the infraction, and, perhaps, mention the next step in your system if s/he doesn't "shape up."

(r) If, after you're done, the student starts, "But . . . , but . . . ," say, "That's it!" Don't accept this challenge to explain yourself and discuss the whole thing again. The "See me after class!" is not a discussion.

These guidelines may be difficult to remember and to put into practice. Ideally, you need to practice these. It's not easy to do the "See me after class!" well all the time. But a good one might sound like this:
"John, your calling out has gotten me very annoyed. I can't concentrate."
John: "But I wasn't. . . ."
"I don't care, no buts! If you call out again tomorrow, you'll have to do all the exercises on page 21. And, if you don't do that, I'll have to write to your parents."
John: "Big deal!"
"Fine. Let's see what you do tomorrow."
John: "Why me?"
"I won't answer this question. You know why, and that's it. I understand you want to be called on, or you forget to raise your hand, but you can't continue this behavior."
(John smirks.)
"You can smirk all you want, but now at least you understand me."
John. "But. . . ."
"That's it. I'll see you tomorrow."
John: "But I. . . ."
(Teacher walks away.)
But, you may ask, what if, after I say, "See me after class," the student just continues to curse at me or continues to call out? If there are only ten minutes left to the class period, follow the guidelines in section A above: 7, 8, and 19. Just ignore the student and speak to the class. Instruct them to ignore the disruptive student. Try to wait out the student until after the class is over. Do not go on to your next warning. Only go to your next warning if he doesn't see you after class (which you may have to shout as he runs out of your class). If there are 20 or 30 minutes left to the period, you may first try to ignore him with the hope his anger will cool down. If it doesn't, let him know: "Tom, if you cool it now, you'll only have to talk to me after class and it'll be over. But, if you continue, I'll have to . . . (your next step)." The next step might be, "call your father" or "give you this homework assignment." What if this has no effect and you still have a long way to go before the period ends? Then, I suggest you put a "do-now" on the chalkboard (which you tell the class you will collect) and open your classroom door. Place one foot outside

the door and one inside the classroom,[136] and signal some staff member, e.g., a hall-duty person, to come and escort your disruptive student out of your class. If the rest of the class starts to cause you problems as you try to get help, remind them: "John! Are you doing the do-now? Do you also want to be escorted out of this class?" Or another less drastic method is as follows: Again, put a "do-now" on the chalkboard, take the same foot-stance as above, but now tell Tom to come to you and have him stand outside the classroom, along the wall, but facing you as you stand in the doorway. You can now reprimand Tom out of view of his peers, and yet you never leave the room. Again, you can warn a "John" as happened above to do the do-now. In a way, this tactic allows you to do the "see me after class" during the class (because you've decided nothing is working and you can't wait the student out).

B. How to Handle Students Who . . .

Although it's best for you to figure out how you feel for each infraction so that you don't adopt one that you don't feel congruent with, I have some concrete suggestions about some specific problems. Read these, and if they are a problem for you, try them. However, though these suggestions may save you time and be easier than formulating your own, don t e them if you can't own them. These suggestions are only as effective as they are congruent with you.

1. Students who call out

(a) Don't call on the first person who raises his/her hand. This only encourages a "horse race" of who can give the answer first. Then, the slower ("losers") just feel like withdrawing. Instead, wait, nod your head in recognition as one hand comes up, two, three, etc. Wait till five or six think they know the answer. Then, call on someone. This will give them all time to think.

(b) Only respond to students who raise their hand. And that means don't respond to a student who calls out as s/he raises her/his hand.

(c) Go deaf, dumb, and blind to any questions, answers, comments that come without a hand raised, that you have not called on. Just don't hear his/her answer or see the student, even if s/he is the only person calling out the right answer.

---

[136] You can be sued for negligence if you leave a classroom and a student is, e.g., hurt or has an accident. This stance keeps you responsible to the rest of the class while you work on handling the disruptive student.

(d) Don't say to the call-outer, "John, stop it. I won't call on you." That is already giving John "negative attention." In a way, you have then called on him. Just ignore him, as if he doesn't exist, and call on a hand raiser (even if the hand raiser says the same thing John said).

(e) Don't feel like you need to respond to every response. You can't feed all students all the time. After you get some responses, go on with your lesson. If you try to respond to every response, the train of your lesson will slow down to the point where students will "turn off" (get off) and withdraw.

(f) While you go deaf, dumb, and blind to call-outers, give a lot of attention to the hand raisers: look at the person you call on; call him/her by name; write his or her answer on the chalkboard; perhaps, put his/her initial(s) next to the answer; thank him/her for the answer.

(g) Meanwhile, keep aware of any students who were calling out who may try raising their hand to get the recognition you are giving out to the hand raisers. The second a former call-outer decides to "turn over a new leaf" call on him/her immediately to reward this new behavior.

(h) If you feel you must say, "I won't call on anyone unless they raise their hand," don't say it to anyone or to the class. Say it as you're writing on the chalkboard, or say it looking at the floor. If you say it to the class, you'll again be giving "negative attention" to the call-outers.

These guidelines require practice. You are trying to train yourself to train the students. Work at it. Catch yourself making the mistakes I've described above and persist. The class will "come around" if you're consistent about these guidelines. However, don't get starved for lack of class participation. Don't recognize someone who calls out just because no one else is participating.[137]

2. Students who fight

(a) Of course, the best method is prevention. If you spot two students who seem to be building up hostility for each other, separate them, before they start to fight.

(b) As mentioned above, don't have a policy that depends on your finding out who started the fight. You usually will be unable to be the "judge and jury," and often the provocation for the fight may go back to what happened days ago.

---

[137] If you suffer from this, you need more participation techniques so you don't give in out of "starvation" for responses. We'll discuss many participation techniques in Chapter 14, section E.

(c) Either tell them that you will reprimand the person you saw who throws the first punch or that you will punish <u>both</u> fighters no matter who started it. This policy will at least inhibit them from continuing the fight in school. You might even say, "I can't stop all fights. But the person I see start it (even if s/he really didn't) is in trouble." Or "I want you to know, no matter who starts it, if you both fight, you're <u>both</u> in trouble. So get away from the one who started it, and then I'll get the one who wants to keep fighting."

(d) Plan out steps of punishment you believe in. For instance, "If you are caught fighting, you go to the dean." Or "If you are caught fighting, you get a <u>special demerit</u>; two of these and you, e.g., go to the dean, or I call your parents, or I start suspension procedures, or you lose ten points from your report card." Decide which warning step you'll use.

(e) Certainly try to talk with students who fight, after they cool down. Listen— don't give advice right away. Let their rage subside.

(f) Don't try to stop a fight that is already in progress by yourself. You can only hold one student, which only enrages him or her more and makes him or her more of a target. However, if you can grab and stop the aggressive one (not the passive one), you might be able to stop the fight with one of the reprimands in (c) above. But you've got to decide who's who accurately.

(g) Get help. If there are two teachers, you can both pull the students apart and then warn, "The next person to throw a punch gets punished."

(Regarding "bullies," see Chapter 12 F.)

3. Students who cheat[138]

(a) When you give a test, have the desks in neat rows and sit in the back of the room. When they can't see you so well, they are usually more nervous about trying to cheat. Those that are tempted to cheat will usually try to turn around to see where you are. This will make it easy for you to spot potential cheaters.

(b) If you are giving a short-answer test (true/false, fill-in-the-blank, or multiple choice), cheating is easier. So try to give short essay (paragraph) tests. The former kind is more work to design and less work to mark. If you still prefer the former, make one set of tests so that the questions run, e.g., 1–10 for one and 10–1 for the other. This way the test is given out in two forms: Question 1 on one test is question 10 on the other; question 2 is 9; question 3 is 8; and

---

[138] This is a discipline problem. Since it interferes with your giving just credit where credit belongs, it interferes with your ability to motivate their learning.

so on. You might mimeograph one set on white paper, the other on yellow paper. Then, give row one the white version, row two the yellow version, row three the white version, etc. Tell them you have done this so that if they copy an answer, it'll be from the wrong question!

(c) If you have no time to make up two forms of the test, you might still print some on yellow paper, some on white. Then, tell them that, "Some of the test questions are in different order on some papers; so don't cheat." (However, you may not find that this lie is worth your loss of congruence.)

(d) Don't take away the paper of a suspected cheat. Such action will usually cause more disturbance during the test. and give more students the opportunity to cheat. Instead, inform them that, "If I suspect anyone of cheating, I'll note it down while I sit here in the back of the room. If you get your paper back with ten points off, you'll know why."

(e) Say to the class at the start of the test, "Cover up your answers. Sue, Tom, Jack, etc., cover up your answers. Those who help anyone cheat will, e.g., see me after class." By encouraging students to cover up their own papers, they will probably do what they want to do. But, now, they'll be able to do this with less peer disapproval since the action was directed by you. Also, the ones who are likely to follow your "cover up" direction are usually the ones with the correct answers who do want their own credit. Thus, you've cut off from view the major sources of correct "cheatable" answers.

(f) Don't tell your students how you'll handle cheating the day of the test, right before the test. By then, for the students who did not study, it's too late. Instead, lay down these warnings about cheating the day or two before the test. In this way, you may motivate a potential cheater to study.

(g) Give back the test papers at the end (not the beginning) of the period. This will be helpful in two ways: (1) the students will be anxious to listen while you review the test answers before you return their papers; (2) if you return papers at the beginning of the period, the cheaters (who got zeros) may vent anger with you the whole period, thus disrupting your class. If cheaters get back papers at the end of the period, they can talk to you after class. Or they may go home, vent at home, cool off, realize the consequences, and be more handleable by the time you see them the next day.

4. Students who come in late

(a) As was mentioned above, leave one or two empty chairs by the front or back door for latecomers. Students who are late are not to walk in front of the room or to go to their regular seats. They must take one of the "late seats" by the door. This will limit latecomers from disturbing the class already in progress.

(b) Do not talk to latecomers who come in late. Don't accept a late pass or a comment during the class. Ignore them and motion to them to take the "late seat."

(c) At the bell, mark anyone not in his or her seat "absent" with an "a" in your Delaney book. Then, let the students know this policy: "If you come in late after I've taken attendance, you've been marked 'absent.' If you want me to change your 'absence' to a 'late,' you must see me after class. Then, I'll change your 'a' to an 'L.' If you forget to see me after class, your 'a' remains." This shifts the responsibility of being on time to the student, who now has the burden of remembering to remain after class to change the "a" to an "l."

(d) Decide on some system like: 3 'l's = an 'a,' and if you are absent 3 times, 3 'a's = 5 points off your grade. This will motivate them to be on time, and bother to remain after class to change an "a" to an "l."

(e) In some schools the system is already in place. If a student receives an "absence" in a class period, but was present in homeroom, s/he gets a "cut." Then, "cutting" receives its own school penalties.

(f) And/or you might have a "do-now!" at the beginning of every period that is always collected five minutes after you take attendance. If a student comes in late and can't complete the "do-now!" s/he doesn't get credit for it.

(g) And/or give tests back at the beginning of the period. If you're late, you get your test back at the end of the period or tomorrow. (However, sometimes it's best to give tests back at the end of the period. In this way they can look them over that night, get over their anger, and understand the review of the test the next day when they've cooled down.)

(h) Penalize any latecomer who comes in and then proceeds to talk to his/her neighbor. Now use the system you've decided on for "talking in class." If a latecomer has a question about what s/he missed, s/he can ask another student or you after class.

(i) Sometimes the coordination of an entire school policy on lateness to class is the most effective strategy. For instance, one school worked collaboratively to institute a strict policy of locking the classroom doors as soon as the late bell rang, coupled with "hall sweeps" of any stragglers by deans and security guards. Latecomers were channeled to a detention room, where careful records of each lateness was kept, with consequences for each infraction. After the first lateness, the student got a warning, but after the second lateness in a day or the third at any time, the student's ID card was held until a parent came to school. Parents got first-class letters informing them about the plan and enlisting their cooperation.

The first day, about 500 kids got "swept." But within a few days, students realized the school meant business. So many students were on time the next week that the Transit Authority called to ask the school if it had changed its morning schedule!

5. Students who don't do the homework

1. The Traditional Way

(a) What many teachers do is that they collect the homework immediately, when they start the class. The thinking is that they want to catch students who did not do the homework quickly, before they can copy it from another student.

(b) Then, they go over the homework, with usually only a few students participating; this may be due, in part, because the students can't refer to their homework any more.

(c) Then, the teacher desperately calls on everyone possible (not knowing whether the student called on has done the homework or not). This method motivates the students who did not do the homework to fake answers and may even discourage students who actually did the homework.

(d) Then, the teacher takes home the homework (if there's 36 in a class, and all did it, that's 36 times five classes = 180 papers, a day!) The teacher may be "glad" that not everyone (or few!) actually did the homework.

(e) S/he then not only tries to enter into her mark book those who did/didn't do the homework, for five subject classes, but also tries to correct and comment on each paper!

(f) Eventually, overwhelmed by the paper work, s/he falls behind handing the homework back, which irritates the students.

(g) who become more motivated not to do the homework. ("If s/he's not doing her homework, why should we?!").

(h) Then, the teacher begins to give up on correcting all the homework and is even motivated not to give homework or give much less.

(i) Of course, she accepts late homework; s/he's glad to get anything!

(j) The students then know that they can always hand it in late, so they are less motivated to do it on time.

(k) Since, now, most are handing it in late (just before the marking period ends) or not doing it at all, the class discussions about the homework have less and less student participants.

(l) At the end of the marking period, the teacher is swamped with late homework, with all different makeup dates on the papers, from all different assignments, from all different classes!

(m) Since it's impossible to sort these all out, nor read all of them, or comment on all of them, s/he accepts them all, even if s/he hasn't read them!

(n) This procedure only encourages the students again, at the next marking period, to hand in late homework (even copied homework from another student) or hand in any scribble at all!

It's obvious that this system is educationally ineffective for the students and overwhelming for the teacher. Is there a better way? Yes.

2. A Better Homework Policy

Below are suggestions for a better way to handle homework. The explanation indicates why the suggestion is better than the traditional way just described above.

(a) Don't accept or give any credit for late homework. If you presently have a policy that you can make up homework, you are probably swamped with late homework coming in as the marking period comes to an end. You are also, accidentally, encouraging students not to do homework on time, since they can still get credit for homework even if it's late. Also, you are then giving little credit for those who are doing it on time. Also, you probably have poor participation in class when you start to discuss today's homework. Your "forgiveness" about late homework doesn't do much good. If you find that you are not congruent with giving no credit for late homework, at least give less credit for late homework.

(b) While they are doing the "do-now!" go around and check who has not done the homework. (Instruct them to put it out on their desks facing you.) Only give an "X" in your Delaney book for not having it, not a ✔ to each who has it. The former system will be faster. When you collect the homework (after you discuss it), you do not have to go down your marking book for each class to enter who did or didn't do the homework; you did that already in class, while they were doing the "do-now." You need only skim through them, perhaps make a few comments, and see what the class is or is not understanding.

(c) Then, discuss the homework allowing only those who didn't get an "X" to participate. This policy will give you better class participation because they can look at their homework to participate in the discussion. And students who didn't do the homework now can't get credit for the discussion on the homework. Also, those who try to make up the homework during class time are already too late. You already have given credit to those who did it on time, and you don't accept late homework.

(d) Have a system like: "three missing homeworks = five points off your grade (with no late homeworks): That is if you and the administration believe in mixing grades and conduct. You may decide that such students are not "discipline problems" since they only disturb their own grades. But you may feel that this negligence may spread; thus, it is not a miscall.

(e) Collect all homework after the discussion on the homework, not before the discussion. This will again let them use the homework for the discussion. And you don't need to worry about collecting it right away since no one can "cheat" your system by doing it during class, since you've already given credit where credit is due.

(f) Collect it by rows and instruct them to pass from back seat to front keeping papers in the order they are seated. Then, the front person of each row places the whole row (in order) in the folder for that row. You then collect, e.g., five folders, one for row one, one for row two, etc. When you mark them, keep them in this collected order. Then, return them by returning each row's folder to the student in the front seat, who passes them back in order.

With this system, you will not be overwhelmed with late homework, students will be more motivated to hand the homework in on time, the discussions about the homework will have more participants, and you'll be able to hand the homework back quickly, which will give the students more immediate feedback and encouragement to do the homework.

Regarding all these suggestions, remember the four caveats: (1) Integrating these suggestions into your style will first be more work, but will be worth it in the long run. (2) Only use those suggestions that are congruent for you. (3) However, give each a good try before you abandon it. (4) Don't fret if you can't employ all of the suggestions.

6. Students who have "crushes" on you

Although this is strictly not a discipline problem, if it is handled improperly, it can result in behavior that is disruptive to the learning of the rest of the class and/or your teaching. More importantly, if handled improperly, it can be upsetting, even damaging, to a young student. Of course, it is irrelevant what the sexual orientation of the student is or the gender of the student. But, for example, if a female student has a "crush" on you (a male teacher), you need to be sensitive to the situation and handle it appropriately. "Appropriately" means (see pp. 153 and 267) you do what is best for the welfare of the student, obviously not use it for your own satisfaction. Explicitly, this imperatively means that it is always unprofessional, unethical, even criminal, to date or engage in sexual activity with a student. Why? Because it is usually the case that "crushes" involve "psychological transference." This means that there is not only a sexual-affectionate attraction for the teacher, but also a powerful, substitute parental reaction involved. Often, a student who has childhood parental needs unmet will transfer these needs onto a present authority figure. These needs are not only primal and powerful but are usually "blinding," out of control, and potentially harmful to the student's future development. If the "crush" is handled improperly, a student may feel abandoned, inadequate, depressed, and very angry—not only presently and in the future, but "historically" (affect his/her childhood and adolescent developmental stages).

   I don't want to be too alarming. The crush is often handled by the student fairly well over time. But this adjustment is not easily done if the teacher handles it improperly. I suggest a number of guidelines here you can follow to help the student:

1. You need to display an attitude of distance and lack of interest in her affections, yet not be so cold as to be angry with her.
2. Anything you can say or do to let her know you are her teacher (not her boyfriend or just another man) will help.
3. Do not do anything that is a "fathering" role. You are her teacher. "Fathers" ask about her social life, drive her home from school, have meals with her. "Teachers" ask her about her school work, do not drive her anywhere, and do not "hang out" with her in social situations. You may protest: "But sometimes doing these latter kinds of things is often good to do with a student!" Yes, sometimes. But not with a student who has a crush on you.
4. Avoid physical contact. With some students, giving them "five," patting them on the head or shoulder, even a wink and a hug (at graduation) may be appropriate. But such behavior with a student who has a crush on you will cloud the relationship that you need to keep clearly defined.
5. Avoid being alone with the student.
6. Anything you can do to demystify yourself to the student will help. She probably has an ideal image of you. You need to let her know, in subtle ways, you're not: that great, able to do anything, able to care for her

(beyond her academics), or that you would be a great boyfriend, lover, or husband. She probably has these fantasies. You need to derail them.
7. Finally, you need to do all these things and yet not abandon her, at least, as her teacher. In many ways, you are her substitute parent (as her teacher) who tries to cultivate her intellectual, even emotional-social growth. But, with this student, it may be best to support her academic growth and allow other teachers or counselors (that she does not have a crush on) to help her with these other needs.

7. Students who wear hats

This situation is complicated. In one way, you may consider it to be a miscall if Tom in row 5, the last seat, is wearing a Yankee hat. After all, he is not disturbing your teaching or the learning of the rest of the class. But, usually, this permission can become potentially disruptive (see the definition on pp. 53–54), thus, a "discipline problem." Tom wears his hat, John then brings in his Dodger hat, Sue a tennis hat, etc. And, since most kids feel some identity-attachment to their hats, any criticism of a kid's hat or attempt by one student to take another's will be disruptive (besides the fact that if the hat is big, the person sitting behind it may not be able to see the chalkboard). So, it's probably best not to treat a student wearing a hat as a miscall. Usually, the school has a policy: "no hats worn in school." Usually, they must be put in students' lockers when they arrive at school or in homeroom (section class). If the hat is carried with the student from period to period, it must be put away. If any student is seen wearing a hat (s/he may have forgotten it's on), the teacher just points to his or her head, gives a "reminder look," and signals the student to remove it. You may wish to carry out a similar policy: "If you wear (or even bring) a hat to my class, I will confiscate it, and it will be returned to you after class." You can back this policy up with the guidelines we discussed in this chapter, section A. But the fear of the possible loss of the property is usually enough to deter the problem. (For help with students who wear sunglasses in class, see Chapter 4, section C, #2.)

8. Students who bring personal stereos to class

It is generally the case that what I advised above about hats in 7 is also advisable if a student brings or wears a "Walkman" to class. What we said in 7 about hats regarding whether it's a miscall, its potential disruption, the school policy, and doing your "signal," with the same backup warnings, also goes for personal stereos. Sometimes you can just walk around the room (while the class is copying notes from the board) and give a nonverbal signal to the student with the "Walkman." Often, just the fear engendered by your approach is enough to make the student put it away. Since the personal property is more monetarily valuable than a hat, most schools not only forbid students to wear them or have them (which means: "don't let us see them in school") but also have a security guard confiscate them. Then, it can only be reclaimed by the student's parents. The strictness of this latter policy is often enough to keep students on guard from bringing them (or showing them) in school.

9. Students who have beepers

Unfortunately, it is becoming increasingly the case that students come to school with beepers. The worry is that these students are often drug dealers. But we can't arrest a student for just having a beeper. What we can do is warn such students with the same policy we outlined above in 8 for personal stereos. Only here, confiscation would take place if the equipment is either seen or heard (goes off in the classroom or hallway or in school in general).

10. Students who criticize, "dis," each other

In many city schools you'll hear, "He 'dissed' me!" Or, if you criticize a student, you may hear the class shout: "Dis, dis, dis!" The latter is easy to handle: don't label or criticize students in such a way that they look bad in front of their peers, especially in grades 9–12. If a student "disses" another student, treat such disturbances as "fighting" in class, a nonverbal form of fighting. Many of the guidelines in 2 above are relevant; review these. There in 2 above, (a) is applicable. So is (b). With (c), tell them you will reprimand the first person you hear who starts the "dissing." The rest of (c) is applicable for this nonverbal fight. You also might encourage them to "hold it" until after school, "or you both will get in trouble."

11. Students who are "high" or dealing drugs

This problem has become a serious one in many schools. It is serious enough that often local law, the school board, or, at least, the school itself dictates a rigorous policy to be followed by all school staff. A new teacher needs to learn that policy first. He or she is then obligated to follow it. However, I believe the best guidelines for such a policy are the following:

1. Distinguish between a student who is "high," a user (perhaps even a victim), and a student who is a dealer, who is selling drugs in the school (or school zone).
2. The user should be treated differently than the dealer.

3. Often, the user is withdrawn, falling asleep in class, red-eyed, and "out-of-it." The student needs help, not anger, nor for you to call the police. In this case, follow the guidelines for "withdrawn students" in Chapter 4, section C, where you can help him her to get professional help. (If the student is on "uppers," s/he may be hyper and a discipline problem. Then, handle him/her with the guidelines in Chapter 12, section A, but also try to get him/her professional help. (See "referring" in the Index.)

4. The dealer is different. He or she is a menace to other students. Often, the student may also be carrying a weapon. Unless you are sure you have the skills to warn and stop this person by yourself, you should not take him or her on yourself. It is best to confidentially report him or her to school security personnel and let these authorities approach this student according to their planned procedures.

12. Students who carry weapons

We will discuss handling this very serious issue in this order:

a. Extent of the Problem
b. Kinds of "Weapons"
c. What a School Can Do
d. A Sample Policy Statement
e. What a Teacher Should Do
f. Resources

a. Extent of the Problem

Let us first place the problem in the context of our society as a whole. Violent crime among 14–17 year olds is up 46.3%.[139] The number of gun homicides by juveniles nationally has tripled since 1983.[140] One survey (in New York State) found that 35% of male high school students in high crime urban neighborhoods said they carry a gun![141]

Thus, the problem of weapons in our schools is a very serious upshot of what is going on in our entire culture, especially among our youth. The figures that pertain to our schools are frightening: Research indicates that in the United States one teacher in five has been assaulted or threatened with violence.[142]

---

[139] James Alan Fox, "Trends in Juvenile Violence," *A Report to the U.S. Attorney General,* June, 1996.
[140] *The New York Post.* Suzanne Fields' Column; Oct. 17, 1996.
[141] *The New York Teacher.* Feb. 21, 1994, p. 9.
[142] Wild, Jerry. *Anger Management in Schools* (Technomic Publ. Co., 1996).

In 1996, in one city (New York City) a staggering 3,905 weapons were confiscated in the school system:146 handguns, 4 rifles, 1,643 knives, and 1,402 dangerous implements (box cutters, etc.).[143]

However, it would be <u>more</u> frightening if it were the case that students bring weapons to school with the actual intention of hurting another student or a school staff member. Research indicates that this is <u>not</u> the case. Instead, students usually bring a weapon into a school for <u>protection</u>, not to commit crimes. The research demonstrates that the problem is the perception of crime. Perhaps, 16,000–17,000 students said that they "bring a weapon to school everyday, <u>for protection</u>."[144] Ironically then, their safety is put in jeopardy because of their <u>own fear,</u> (not necessarily because of their aggression) and the feeling among students of powerlessness.[145]

b. Kinds of "Weapons"

As we consider ways to curtail weapons in our schools, we need to be clear about the wording of our policies. The following is a list of items considered "weapons" that can be grounds for a Superintendent's Suspension (see Chapter 12B).

- firearm, including pistol and handgun
- silencers
- electronic dart and stun gun
- shotgun
- rifle
- machine gun
- air gun
- spring gun (or other instrument or weapon in which the propelling force is a spring or air, and any weapon in which any loaded or blank cartridge may be used, e.g., BB gun)
- switchblade knife, or gravity knife, plum ballistic knife, cane sword
- dagger, or stiletto, dirk
- razor, case cutter, utility knife, <u>box cutter</u> (recently the weapon of choice among high school students, although it is now against the law, in many states, to sell one to a minor)
- imitation gun

---

[143] "A Violent Season in Schools," *New York Newsday,* Aug. 18, 1994, p. B7.
[144] Danny L. Coe. "We Must Act Now To Make Our Schools Safe." *National Association of Secondary School Principals Bulletin,* Oct., 1994, pp. 108–110.
[145] Wood, Craig, and Mark Chestnut. "Violence in U.S. School: The Problem and Some Responses." *West's Education Law Quarterly,* v. 4, no.3, pp. 414, 416, Jul., 1995.

- loaded or blank cartridges and other ammunition
- any deadly, dangerous, or sharp pointed instrument that can be used or is intended for use as a weapon, e.g., scissors, nail file, broken glass, chains, wire, etc.

c. What a School Can Do

When we think of how to handle this serious issue, our responses should match the perceptual problem: students bring weapons because it is their perception that they are not safe. Students' fears are often the major motivation for their carrying weapons into schools. Then, this presence of weapons increases their fear, which, in turn, causes more weapons to be brought into schools.[146]

Therefore, it is this self-fulfilling prophecy that needs to be broken by somehow making interventions into this cycle. One is reminded of the rationale that the N.R.A uses to justify the ownership of guns by "peace loving citizens who need guns to feel safe, and protect themselves." Similarly, we are familiar with the portrayal of, e.g., all the cowboys of the Old West who carried guns as the norm, again, for self-defense. But, then, either a tough sheriff or U.S. Marshall came along and forbid people in the town to carry a gun. He had to also guarantee that he would protect the people and bring law and order to the town. In the Old West movies, if the peace officer was able to enforce the "no-gun" rule, and people believed that he could keep them safe, the movie ended with peace in the town. The lack of guns made people safer, which helped them feel safe enough to give up their guns, which made them feel even safer, especially if the peace officer did show them that he could protect them. Then, the self-fulfilling prophecy went the right way.

It seems that we need to make students feel safer in our schools, which would decrease the number of weapons in schools, which would further reduce their fear and their motivation to carry weapons. We must have as one of our goals: to give students the reassurance that we can protect them and provide them with the "law and order" they need to feel safe to be able to focus on their education.

However, this will not be enough. There are other motivations that contribute to (especially teenage) students bringing weapons into school: (a) to show other students that they have a weapon to enhance their image among some students; (b) to show that they "belong" (to a gang, or to the "non-weak group"); (c) to show that they are "cool"; (d) to display that they have power and are not powerless.

---

[146] Wood, Craig, and Mark Chestnut. "Violence in U.S. School: The Problem and Some Responses." *West's Education Law Quarterly,* v. 4, no.3, p. 414, 416, Jul., 1995.

Although it is an oversimplification, most of the above motivations stem from students feeling inadequate, powerless, and a sense of non-belonging. These feelings (which Erik Erikson describes as key developmental tasks during adolescence [see Chapter 6A]), coupled with students feeling that they need protection, create a synergistic set of motives for students to carry weapons in school. In short, we must also have as our goal, though an ambitious one, to help students master some key psychological, developmental tasks, especially before and during adolescence.

What strategies will help meet these goals?

Although the above clarifies some of the causes of the problem, several strategies (not all in agreement) have been suggested and are currently being tried in our schools: (1) Needs Assessment; (2) A Sense of "Order" in the School, and Security Measures; (3) Character Education; (4) Procedures for When Prevention Fails; (5) Designing and Enforcing Policy Statements.

(1) Needs Assessment: First of all, it would be helpful if administrators could have more timely and accurate security data. A school should, at least, have a uniform method of recording the information on an, e.g., "Incident Profile Form." Such a form could ask for the recording of the exact nature, time, and place of the offense, descriptions of the offender and victim, and actions taken by the school. Robert J. Rubel, director of the National Alliance for Safe Schools (NASS), has developed a "Process Guide" that adapts crime analysis techniques to the school environment. With this guide, disciplinary infractions and incidents of crime are documented and coded according to specific parameters. The data can then be analyzed to identify patterns or trends to develop intervention and prevention strategies.

For example, The Duval County Public Schools in Florida used these recording methods and identified the noon hour as the time of most thefts. Shortening the lunch period and posting off-limit areas dramatically decreased petty thefts (Smith, 1984). Also, The American Association of School Administrators (AASA) has examples of "Model Report Systems" developed by five school districts, which give suggestions for assessment and reporting systems (AASA, 1981).[147]

(2) A Sense of "Order" in the School, and Security Measures: There needs to be established a clear and consistent discipline policy in the school, not just set up by the administration, but also owned by the school's staff. (For

---

[147] Gaustad, Joan. ERIC No.:ED321343. "School Security." *ERIC Digest* Series Number EA 46, from the Eric Clearing House on Educational Management, Eugene, OR, 1990.

help with this, see Chapter 12A, B, C, and 5 just below.) There needs to be clear expectations, respect shown to students and staff, and there needs to be a feeling of trust in the school, where positive reinforcement is more frequent than criticism. If, on the other hand, the atmosphere in the school is one of hostility and insensitivity, in which students are continually subjected to criticism and failure, the research indicates that serious disciplinary problems and criminal behaviors are more likely. Also, the principal should set the tone of the school, including encouraging cooperation among staff members, being personally visible, promoting student involvement. S/he also needs to see that students and staff with personal problems get help. Emergency drills in the school are also useful to reinforce a sense of order and safety.

Cooperation between school and community is also important. It would be helpful if a multifaceted, comprehensive approach was used, one that involves students, teachers, administrators, parents, community leaders, the police, and courts.[148]

And, of course, also implementing security measures will both secure a school's clear and consistent discipline policy and make students feel safer. Alarm systems can effectively reduce vandalism and burglaries. Metal detectors are sometimes effective but are expensive and controversial. In a 1988 New York City pilot program, security guards checked for weapons with handheld metal detectors. No guns were confiscated in the schools, but approximately 200 weapons were found nearby, apparently dropped by students when they saw the detectors (Suzanne Harper, 1989). A Detroit program using metal detectors was challenged legally) and ultimately abandoned, "partly because of the difficulties in herding students through the gates in time for class" (Del Stover, 1988).

Other security measures that may be helpful are: heavy-duty locks, special key-handling procedures, fences, identification cards, hall passes, visitor policies, inventory procedures, and teachers collecting school related money during the first period. Schools should assign staff to patrol halls and cafeterias and have parents and community volunteers monitor reception areas, or the school should (also) hire security guards.[149]

(3) Character Education: Of course, though an ambitious goal, remediating the "sources" of violent behavior in our society would go much further (than just security measures) at stemming the unsafe environmental factors in

[148] Gaustad, Joan. ERIC No.:ED321343. "School Security." *ERIC Digest* Series Number EA 46, from the Eric Clearing House on Educational Management, Eugene, OR, 1990.
[149] Gaustad, Joan. ERIC No.:ED321343. "School Security." *ERIC Digest* Series Number EA 46, from the Eric Clearing House on Educational Management, Eugene, OR, 1990.

schools. As discussed above, besides making students feel more safe, we need to help students with their feelings of inadequacy, powerlessness, and their sense of non-belonging. In short, we need to do some "character education" in our schools. What might this involve?

It would at least involve some of these elements:

(a) Counteracting how some students inadvertently learn to handle anger and conflict from watching adults (e.g., their parents) communicate destructively
(b) Perhaps, training the school staff in conflict resolution techniques
(c) Teaching students a conflict resolution curriculum, e.g., how to use compromise to settle disputes, to listen empathetically, to give constructive feedback, etc.
(d) Using more techniques in our classrooms that teach "emotional education," that enhance ego development and help students feel a sense of belonging. (See the bibliography in Chapter 14, at the end of section H.)

(The reader should consult Chapter 10A on Violence in Our Schools, and especially Chapter 12D on Conflict Resolution Training where the above elements are discussed in greater detail.)

Re-educating the emotional life of students with violent tendencies and teaching them basic social skills and conflict resolution often produce very concrete results. For example, an anti-bullying campaign initiated in 1983 in Norway reduced bullying and victim problems by 50 percent in two years (Stuart Greenbaum, 1989).[150]

(4) Procedures for When Prevention Fails: Despite careful efforts, acts of violence will occur. Each school should have a written crisis plan in place that assigns staff members to specific roles in case of emergency. Schools should have intercom systems and access to cellular phones. (Recently federal funds have been made available for such crime prevention equipment [Fall, 1996].) The school should also have procedures in place for contacting, e.g., parents, staff, law enforcement personnel, emergency medical services, the media, and hospitals. Administrators and staff should have training regarding the care and needs of victims, before assaults occur. An entire community

---

[150] Gaustad, Joan. ERIC No.:ED321343. "School Security." *ERIC Digest* Series Number EA 46, from the Eric Clearing House on Educational Management, Eugene, OR, 1990.

may need therapeutic care after a crisis such as the shooting at Cleveland Elementary School in Stockton, California.[151]

(5) Designing and Enforcing Policy Statements: Besides (1)–(4) above, one of the most effective and immediate safety measure a school can enact is to design and enforce a clear and strong Policy Statement regarding weapons and school safety.

The first point to make here is that in the United States (and usually in democracies of a republic of states or provinces), each state within the U.S. Constitution, can determine its own local education policies. The cities of each state and boards of education in these cities, all come under that individual state's regulations. However, federal funding, and how the courts interpret the law vs. students' rights under the Constitution have sometimes taken away, and sometimes given the administrators of schools more or less power (see S.F. 3, Legal Parameters).

Although the specifics of Policy Statements may vary somewhat, in almost all schools the following parameters are usually the case:

1. Possession of a weapon is grounds for suspension.
2. Immediate referral to the local police (although the student's rights must be protected regarding suspension procedures (see Chapter 12B and Appendix C).
3. When the student returns from the suspension, s/he is usually placed under the supervision of the, e.g., dean of that school.
4. If the student is transferred, the receiving school is usually notified of the incident.
5. It is the obligation of the principal to update yearly the school's Safety Plan, usually by October, and establish a School Safety Committee for the school.
6. The administration must follow the usual Suspension Policy process (see Chapter 12B).

There are many other similarities in these policies. Probably the best way to see the details of the proper wording of a policy (that both tries to handle the problem and respects student rights) is to look at a Sample Policy Statement that may be helpful to administrators (who must design these) and helpful to the safety of school staff and students.

---

[151] Gaustad, Joan. ERIC No.:ED321343. "School Security." *ERIC Digest* Series Number EA 46, from the Eric Clearing House on Educational Management, Eugene, OR, 1990.

d. A Sample Policy Statement[152]

(This Policy will be disseminated to all students and parents, and employees, and in all the languages that are prevalent for this school district.)

A. Policy

It is the policy of the school district to maintain a positive, safe, secure learning and working environment. In striving to attain such an environment, the district takes the position of no tolerance for weapons in our schools, except as specifically stated below. All weapons or instruments that have the appearance of a weapon are prohibited within all school environments and the school zone. School environments include, but are not limited to, district-owned buildings; leased or rented facilities; school-sponsored activities; field trips; school vehicles and school buses, rented or owned; and school bus stops. Anyone found to be in possession of a weapon in any area defined in this policy, before, during, or after school hours is subject to the following administrative and/or legal action.

B. Possession

Students and non-students, including employees and other adults, are forbidden to knowingly or voluntarily possess, store in any area subject to one's control, handle, transmit, or use any instrument that is considered a weapon or a look-alike weapon in any of the school environments listed above. (See the sample list above in b. above)

C. Violations of the above policy

(Students who see or become aware of a weapon at school must not touch it nor remain in the presence of a person or group who possesses a weapon. Students must notify an adult immediately for the safety of all concerned.)

1. Violation by Students

The procedure for all offenses is:

- confiscation of the weapon (if it can be done safely) or call 911 and request assistance if needed.
- notification of the superintendent or designees.
- proceed with the usual suspension-evaluation process.[153] (see Chapter 12B.)

2. Violation by Other Youths and Adults, Including Employees

- immediate police involvement with recommendation to charge
- employees also subject to the same

---

[152] This is an eclectic, edited, amalgam version from policies gathered from various schools, e.g., DeWitt Clinton High School, Scarsdale High School, and other New York City schools; and from 390 public schools in 1994 in Minnesota (Clifford P. Hooker, *NASSP Bulletin.* Jan. 1995, 100–103). The Policy complies with federal law, but state statutes may require modifications. It is an educational statement, not a legal document. (The reader should also consult Chapter 12B on Suspension Policies, and Appendix C on Legal Parameters.)

[153] In accordance with the Gun-Free Schools Act of 1994, any student who, after a hearing held pursuant to Education Law §3214, is found guilty of bringing a weapon onto the premises of any school owned or controlled by this District, will be subject to a penalty of at least a one-year suspension from school.

3. Weapons-Possession of Objects That May or May Not Be Considered Weapons

While this policy represents a "no-tolerance" position on weapons and/or look-alike weapons, there are several objects that are questionable. The administrator may use his or her discretion when interpreting use and intent with such objects:

- small pocket knives
- fireworks, fire crackers, and smoke bombs
- throwing darts
- nuisance items and toys
- unauthorized tools
- mace[154]

D. Administrative Discretion Regarding Possession

1. A student who finds a weapon on the way to school, on school property, or in the school building and takes the weapon immediately to the principal's office shall not be considered in possession of a weapon.

2. When it is determined that a "weapon" was inadvertently brought onto school property, this situation shall not be considered: "in possession of a weapon."

3. This policy is not meant to interfere with the use of appropriate equipment and tools by employees, teachers, and students. Such equipment, when properly used and stored, shall not be considered a weapon for purposes of this policy. However, when authorized instructional and work equipment and tools are used in a potentially dangerous or threatening manner, the guidelines and consequences of this policy will take effect.

E. Exceptions

- licensed peace officers, military personnel
- school district-approved starter guns for athletic contests

---

The reader should take note of the fact that no school policy is self-implementing. The strongest policies in the hands of weak administrators are not effective. Moreover, policies that are overly prescriptive make insufficient allowance for administrator discretion, an ingredient that is essential in school discipline situations.[155]

(It should be noted that recently, New York City's School's Chancellor, Rudy Crew, has proposed that students who carry weapons, drugs, or commit

---

[154] Although Mace is considered a potential weapon under this policy, parents of a student may make special arrangements with the principal if a student feels he or she needs to carry Mace for defensive purposes outside the school setting. Such arrangements shall be made in advance for the student to check the Mace into the school office.

[155] Clifford P. Hooker, *NASSP Bulletin*, Jan. 1995, 100–103.

physical acts of violence to students or school staff be placed in alternative SOS schools, or be expelled [Feb. 1997].)

e. What a Teacher Should Do

The following are some <u>general</u> guidelines for teachers:

1. If you suspect or notice that a student is carrying a weapon, <u>do not</u> confront the student, whether the student is alone or with peers.
2. Try <u>not</u> to let the student know that you suspect or know that s/he may be carrying a weapon.
3. Instead (unless there is an immediate danger or use of this weapon[156]), <u>wait</u>, make note of the suspicion inconspicuously, and do not take action until the class period is over, or the student has left your immediate presence.
4. Then, immediately, alert a security officer in your school with a description of the student and the weapon.
5. Follow your school's Policy Statement.

The reasons why the above guidelines are best, are the following:

(a) If you confront the student alone or with peers present (especially in the case of the latter), you risk a confrontation that may incite the student (depending on his/her anger level) to use the weapon.

(b) If the student suspects that you know that s/he has a weapon, s/he may be inclined to dispose of it before you are able to call a security officer and may target you as the person that ratted on him/her.

(c) If you wait till the student is out of your presence, when a security officer <u>does</u> search the student, the student will have little idea of who called the officer. (Students who carry weapons are generally always worried about being fingered. Thus, without specific suspicion of <u>you</u>, the student may wonder if the rat is one of a dozen possible teachers or students.) Thereby, your confidentiality and safety will not be compromised.

(d) The security officer is, hopefully, trained in the law regarding search and seizure,[157] safe-search procedures, self-defense, etc. <u>You are probably not.</u> A

---

[156] If there is an immediate danger that the student may use the weapon, urge the victims of the student wielding the weapon to: give in, back off, and be non-confrontive to the student with the weapon. <u>Do not</u> verbally or physically fight with the student. (A student who has a weapon, who is confronted, especially in front of his/her peers, may need to <u>show</u> his/her power to save face. And, generally, students who carry weapons already feel <u>powerless</u>, such that, to use the weapon, compensates for their feeling of weakness.) Of course, try to alert someone for help (e.g., a security officer) but try to do this without inciting the student with the weapon. If the weapon is already, actually being used, of course, get help at all costs.

[157] See Appendix C, Legal Parameters.

mistake, and you not only risk violation of the law (therefore the inability to properly prosecute the incident), but your own and other students' safety.

However, teachers can do little alone. Nor can school administrators without the support of families, who, themselves, need much more support. In short, "It takes a village!" our First Lady, Hillary Rodham Clinton, has urged. We must not give up on educating, cognitively and emotionally, our whole society. Fortunately, we do have some powerful cheerleaders.

"Character education must be taught in our schools. We must teach our children to be good citizens. And we must continue to promote order and discipline, supporting communities . . . remove disruptive students from the classroom, and have zero tolerance for guns and drugs." (President Clinton's *State of the Union Address,* Feb. 4, 1997.)

f. Resources

If students feel unsafe, there are now national hotline numbers that students can call: 1-800-552-4867 or 1-800-467-7719 where they can talk to either a counselor or police officer with complete confidentiality.

1. *Reporting Violence, Vandalism and Other Incidents in Schools,* American Association of School Administrators, Arlington, Virginia 39 pages, 1981 [ERIC No. ED 208 603].

2. Blauvelt, Peter D. "School Security Management." *The Practitioner.* 13,4 (June 1987) p.1–11. Reston, Virginia: National Association of Secondary School Principals [ERIC ED 284 344].

3. Feder, June. "Crime's Aftermath." *School Safety.* (Spring 1989):26–29. [Eric EJ 398 977].

4. Gamble, Lanny R., Curtis P. Sellers, and Charles E. Bone. "School Building Intrusions: Prevention Strategies." *School Business Affairs* 53,6 (June 1987):18–21 [EJ 357 978].

5. Greenbaum, Stuart, et al. *Set Straight on Bullies.* Malibu, California: National School Safety Center, September 1989. 89 pages [ED 312 744].

6. Harper, Suzanne. *School Crisis Prevention and Response.* Resource Paper. Malibu, California: National School Safety Center, September 1989. 24 pages [ED 311 600].

7. Moles, Oliver C. (Ed.) *Strategies to Reduce Student Misbehavior.* Washington, D.C.: Office of Educational Research and Improvement, U.S. Department of Education, September 1989.

8. Moriarty, Anthony R., and Patrick J. Fitzgerald. "We Made Police Power a Positive Force in Our Schools." *Executive Educator* 11, 2 (February 1989): 13–14, 25. [EJ 385 245].

9. Smith, Valerie. "Tracking School Crime." *American School and University* 57,1 (September 1984): 54, 58–59 [EJ 306 700].

10. Stover, Del. "School Violence Is Rising, and Your Staff Is the Target." *Executive Educator* 10,10 (October 1988) pp. 15–16, 19–21, 33. [EJ378 719].

11. Gun-Free Schools Act of 1994 found in ERIC no. ED 391227.

12. Kadel, Stephanie, et al. "Reducing School Violence: Building a Framework for School Safety." *Florida State Dept. of Education.* Tallahassee: SERVE: SouthEastern Regional Vision for Education, 1995.

13. The National School Safety Center (NSSC)
    4165 Thousand Oaks Blvd., Suite 290
    Westlake Village, CA 91362

14. Website: blackbird.iss.indiana.edu
    Offers both text and multimedia files providing information on school violence: films, videos, etc.

15. Hayes, Diane Williams, "Reading, Writing, and Arithmetic—An Educaton in Violence." *Crisis,* vol. 100, no. 4, pp. 8–10 April–May, 1993.

16. John Eddowes, "Violence: A Crisis in Homes and Schools." *Childhood Education.* vol. 67, pp. 4–7, Fall 1990.

17. The American Association of School Administrators (AASA) has suggestions for "reporting systems" and "incident report forms."

(Also consult the Resources at the end of Chapter 10A: School Violence. The reader may also find it helpful to consult these related chapters: Chapter 10A. on School Violence; Chapter 12B on Suspensions; and S.F. 3 on Legal Parameters.)

C. Especially for Grades K–6

Most of the above suggestions are also already useful to grades K–6. But this age group requires that we revise some of the above and add a few suggestions that are specific to these grades.

1. Regarding rules, warnings, rewards, and punishments, things are sometimes different. Instead of: "See me after class!" since you are with the class for the whole day, it might be helpful to locate a private space (behind a room divider) for these kinds of reprimands or "time out." For rewards, again, your attention, recognition, and approval are usually very influential. Or you may wish to create a system of how one gets, e.g., gold stars, smiling-face stickers, points, grates, baseball cards, etc.[158] Punishments can be in the form of not getting these symbolic rewards or can be loss of a privilege, e.g., not being a monitor. Or "If you are disruptive, you won't be called on!" Or "You must

[158] You may want to create a "token economy" where make-believe money or special tokens that are earned can "buy" prizes.

leave the reading circle." Or "I won't put your work up on the bulletin board." Or "You will have to sit on the bench at recess."

2. Calling out may or may not be a problem in K–6, especially K–1; here, you must decide if this is really disruptive or part of their "steam" (see pp. 69–70) or their need to interact and learn socialization.

3. Fighting and cheating should be handled as suggested above; however, since the kids are much smaller, it is probably advisable to step in and stop the fight. If one student is particularly out of control, you may grab him, hold him, and hug the child nurturingly (to calm him down). This is true especially if you have a good relationship with the student. (Be careful that the other student he fought doesn't get jealous and feel treated unfairly.)

4. Lateness requires a less angry reprimand than it does in grades 7–12 because in grades K–6, the latecomer doesn't enter a short 40-minute period where you are usually working on an academic lesson. Although latecomers in grades 2–6 can be treated as suggested on pp. 351–352, in K–1 things are often different. Here, the lateness may not be the student's fault. Younger children depend on parents, grandparents, and babysitters to get them to school on time. Thus, you might find it more useful to speak with the caregiver than to the student.

5. Regarding homework in grades 2–6, the suggestions above are still applicable. With grades K–1 you'll need to demonstrate how to do the homework; perhaps, let them start the homework in class with a buddy, as you walk around and give individual help. It is helpful to always write the "homework assignment" in the same special place on the chalkboard. Tell the class the rewards for doing the homework and what will happen if they don't do it. Connect this assignment to your rewards, e.g., a certain kind of recognition. Return the homework promptly with a sticker or your personal, "OK good job!" Hold personal conferences about undone assignments while others are working. Be more lenient with "make-up" work than in grades 7–12. (Also, some of what I've suggested above for K–1 is somewhat applicable to grades 2–6, depending on the seriousness of the academic work.)

D. Training Exercises and Checklist for Chapter 13

Exercise One: Working on Your "See Me after Class!"
You should role play the exercise with a friend, colleague, or classmate. You play "the teacher," and your partner should play a student who: (1) has called out too much; (2) started to fight; (3) threw something across the room; (4) cursed at you, consecutively. You must say "See me after class!" and then assume it's the end of the period, after class. What do you say now? Your

partner should try to be as unmanageable as students are sometimes. After situation (1), see if you have followed the guidelines (a)–(r) on pages 345–347. Then, try situation (2). Check the guidelines again. Try all four situations. Which guidelines reveal your pitfalls? (Reverse roles and let your partner try being "the teacher.")

Exercise Two: Handling Calling Out

If you are in an education class or workshop, get up in front of the class. In this role play, some students should call out, some raise their hands. Now teach a simple lesson on, e.g., names of cars or names of flowers. Ask, "Who knows the name of a car, a flower?" Respond to the class and try to stop the calling out. Which guidelines do you not follow (your pitfall) from those described in Chapter 13, section B, 1.

Exercise Three: Handling Fighting, Cheating, Latecomers, Late Homework

Review Chapter 12, section C. Place a "c" next to each suggestion made about these problems if you feel congruent with the suggestion. Then, try the suggestion for a week. Check the suggestion periodically. If after a week, you feel this is not tryout revise it or drop it (ask others for other suggestions).

Checklist

1. Have you reviewed your warnings so that you know what you need to say if you have to see a student after class?
2. Have you practiced ignoring the "caller-outer" and only responding to those who raise their hands?
3. Do you know how and where to get quick help from a staff member if you need help to break up a fight?
4. Before you plan to give a test, have you reviewed the guidelines for preventing cheating?
5. Have you thought through your "late policy"?
6. Have you thought through your "homework policy"?
7. Have you decided on your policies (and reviewed the schools policies) regarding hats, personal stereos, beepers, drugs, and weapons?
8. Have you decided on what you will do if you suspect a student is "high" in your class?
9. Have you planned how you will handle students who "dis" each other in your class?

CHAPTER 14: REPAIRING THE DELIVERY OF YOUR LESSON PLAN (89 METHODS)

In Chapter 9 we discussed the sources of disruptive behavior that can come from the delivery of the lesson plan. They were: (A) from incongruent content; (B) from the lesson not being affective enough; (C) from not being actional or experiential enough; (D) not being inductive enough; (E) not being interactive enough; (F) from a lack of a felt sense of order, reward, and momentum; (G) from a mismanaged distribution of attention; or (H) from not being explained well enough.

Your lesson delivery may at times suffer some of these problems or all of these. Some teachers might do best to work on the delivery problem they need most help with first. In any event, we shall work on each one of these problems by offering a series of methods that repair each area in its turn. Where a method might repair two or more of the above delivery problems, such will be indicated.

A. Delivering the Subject Matter Congruently

When you deliver the subject matter and you are teaching congruently, you have more of a chance of calling it to the attention of your class. Congruent delivery of content enlivens and has more impact. In a way, the congruence heard by the students announces, trumpets, that here comes something significant that enlivens you, that has care. Care is the surging essence of human nature.[159] Students need and want also to care and be enlivened (as they see you expressing) too. Congruence attracts. How might you deliver the subject matter congruently?

Method

1. Give a Preface Statement: Before you launch into the content of the curriculum, level with the students and tell them how you honestly feel about

---

[159] Martin Heiddeger. *Being and Time.* New York: Harper and Row 1962: Section VI.

teaching them what you are about to teach. Or tell them how you honestly feel about the importance or value of the content you are about to teach. If you find that this is one of the areas among the, e.g., eighty percent you believe in, you should have no trouble. If it's in the twenty percent area of topics you don't care about, level with them without precoloring those students' interest who might just love this topic more than you.

2. Share a Personal Experience: Before you teach the topic (if you do care about it), research inside yourself, "Why is this important (to me)?" Dig in and keep asking for each academic answer you give, "But why important to me?" You can often discover that it matters to you personally because of some deep value or care you hold (Exercise 5[b] in Chapter 11 may also help). This care or value may be due to a personal experience you had. Try to share as much of this experience as you can with your class as a lead-in to why you value or care about what you are about to teach.

3. Use "I": Talk in the first person. Use "I" a lot. Even if the topic is applicable to many people or all or "we" use "I." If it is applicable to many or all, use yourself as an example as often as you can. This tack will present you more as *teacherperson*.

4. Comment on the Progress of the Lesson: As the lesson proceeds, every once in a while comment on how you are feeling as you are teaching it. For instance: "This is taking longer than I thought; I also feel a little tired of this part, but. . . ." Or "I find this interesting, how we got here from there" Or "I also find this part interesting."

5. Talk to Their Personstudent: Every once in a while say things like: "Folks, are you following me?" "I need you to hang in there a little longer." "Hello out there, you guys tired of this?" "I know you folks are getting a little impatient, right?" This will connect you more as teacherperson to their studentperson.

B. Making the Lesson Affective

Knowing is not just possessing factual or cognitive knowledge that is retrievable abstract data. Knowing is also (maybe even more primordially) feeling, acting, owning, and using experience. Experience is owning, actional, affective, living perception that is more than sight. And although the label, or cognitive handle, we put on our experience by conceptualizing it makes it more knowledge, this knowledge is not these labels or concepts per se. For instance, knowing "imperialism" is not to take notes on this label, but to know experientially, affectively, emotionally (even in action) the feel for this verbal label. We must therefore give our students more than notes; notes aren't learnings.

There has been much resistance to teaching the affective-experiential side of knowledge. Cognitive knowledge can be fixed and static in concepts and even mathematized and measured. Affective-experiential knowledge is a dipping into the flux of the stream of consciousness. The referring concept can be fixed, but the referent (what the concept refers to in experience) is always changing. Feelings don't last, though their labels may, thus, the preference for the latter, not the tenuous former. And for most teachers, cognitive knowledge is easier to teach than affective-experiential learning. The latter can't be noted and lectured on as well. To teach affective-experiential learning might even mean that the teacher has to follow the class's feelings, not the teacher's lesson; then, the teacher, besides the students, might have to take notes too! Such teaching might involve action, role playing, and simulation, which may be too "noisy" for some teachers.

However, it may be more important "to learn from one bird how to sing" than mathematically calculate the heavens "to teach 10,000 stars how not to dance" (e. e. cummings). To influence behavior, knowledge needs to be related to some affect in the learner.[160] That's why it's not so much the case that children tend to learn to read easily what's in their speaking vocabulary, but that they tend to learn words that have personal meaning for them in their world. Therefore, "significant contact with pupils is most effectively established and maintained when the content and the method of instruction have an affective basis."[161]

How might you make your lessons more affective?

Method

6. Follow Student Digressions: Though you may have to watch out for digressions that take you too far from the subject or ones that are sheer manipulations away from work, often these "digressions" are the motivational feelings to support the lesson. Let students share the feelings, personal experiences, etc., that are kicked off by the lesson. However, be diligent in channeling these feelings and experiences into transferable knowledge. There's no harm in noting on the chalkboard their feelings (and ideas) besides yours and the curriculum's.

7. Using Journals: If you see a topic that you will teach coming up that can relate to their everyday experiences, give them an assignment to keep a journal

---

[160] Gerald Weinstein and Mario Fontini. *Toward Humanistic Education: A Curriculum of Affect.* New York: Praeger. 1970: 28.
[161] Ibid., 10.

on their experience from a specific point of view. For instance, if you will be discussing the causes of World War II, ask them to keep a journal on conflicts they notice in their everyday dealings. Then, to start this lesson, let them share some of their feelings and experiences about the conflicts they noted.

8. How does this feel? Simply stop from time to time in your lesson and ask: "How do you feel about this topic, this part of the lesson?" "Which seems more meaningful to you, valuable?" "Why?"

9. Write a Poem: Perhaps at the end of a unit, ask them to write a poem about the topic. Instruct them not to try to make it rhyme, or be abstract, but to put feelings into it. Have them read these poems aloud. Don't judge these poems for transferable knowledge, but, instead, accept them as personally shared experiences of having all gone down the same "road" (topic) together. (Or, if poetry seems alien to them, have them write "a letter" to the topic. For instance, "Dear World War II, I didn't like. . . .")

10. Prioritize Values: Ask them to list the valuable information learned in the lesson. Now, ask them to prioritize these from most valuable to least by giving each one a number, e.g., 1–8. Then they might share their prioritized list and explain their feelings for their priorities. Again, acceptance and sharing of these feelings is the goal here, not right or wrong answers.

11. Relationship Analysis: Ask the students to choose items in the topic that have influence on each other. Then, ask them to place these on a blank sheet of paper and to draw arrows between items that represent the relationship each exerts on the other. For instance:

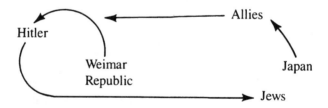

Then ask them to explain their arrows.

12. Draw a Picture: Ask the students to draw a picture of how this topic feels. Let them use colors and be impressionistic. Then, do a "show and tell" and ask each to share the reasons for their impressions.

13. Make a Statue: Ask the students to picture a statue that might be constructed "in memoriam" to this topic (besides history topics, this can be done for literary, science, or even math or grammar topics). Then, ask one or two students to explain how their statue might look. If a student is comfortable enough, ask him/her to show you and the class the statue or be the statue.

14. <u>Stop Distancing</u>: Students tend to talk in the third person, e.g., "You kind of feel sad when you think about this topic." This is called "distancing." Stop such distancing. Don't let them say "we," "one tends to. . . ," etc. Encourage, "You mean, I feel sad when . . . ?" Turn their "you's" and "one's" into "I feel. . . ." Such will bring their feelings into the lesson more and stop inappropriate generalizations about "you," "one," and, thereby, help avoid tiresome, wasteful arguments.

15. <u>Philosophizing</u>: Every once in a while, ask them to write a short composition on how the topic relates to a basic human philosophical area such as death, values, love, impermanence, truth, guilt, goodness, human needs, evil, man's search for meaning, irrationality, freedom, faith and belief, courage, understanding the nature of the universe, time, self-knowledge, growth, reason, intuition, the future, communication, ethics, etc. Allow them to stretch the topic to relate to one of these. Such an exercise will force them to relate the topic more to life.

16. <u>Allow Irritations</u>: Every once in a while just ask them, "Which item in this topic irritates you, bugs you the most?" Then, just allow them to complain. Understand and accept these feelings; maybe even share with them.

Method **2** above will also make your lesson more affective.

Some guidelines for introducing affective-experiential education are to be heeded: (a) Don't allow students to judge each other's feelings. Protect students' feelings and insist that feelings are personal. (b) Don't process a student's shared feeling so that it becomes a scene for an inappropriate therapeutic intervention. (c) Don't call on students to share feelings. Instead, keep the class a safe place for feelings and volunteers will appear. (d) The energy and excitement that is generated by such lessons is not "smoke" before the "fire" of discipline problems. It's "steam" engine motivation. Channel, instead of cut off, this energy.

C. Making the Lesson Actional and Experiential

Again, here we want to bolster mere cognitive learning. The resistance to actionalizing the content of the curriculum, e.g., role playing to experientialize it, is the same resistance we described earlier. Against this resistance we must remember that knowledge acted out, experienced, and made more concrete is knowledge that lasts and is internalized. Kant pointed out that experiences without concepts are blind, but mere concepts without experiences are empty.[162] We too often see the world from an observer's stance. For instance, students would learn more about conflicts by not just reading about them, but by experiencing them, e.g., in a simulation. We need to teach the experience that fills the learning "bucket," not just the notes and labels that are the cognitive handles that make this experience transferable.

How might you make your lessons more actional and experiential?

Method

17. Role Play: Have students role play famous people in history, characters in literature, famous people in science, etc. Also, have them personify concepts, even parts of speech, e.g., be a verb, a gerund. What would it say, dress like, do? Personify any abstraction: infinity, chemical elements, the earth, the sun, the "woods" in Frosts "Stopping by the Woods," democracy, a law, Congress, France, the Alps, the Pythagorean theorem, an axiom in geometry, etc. Students might role play a person or topic while the class guesses who they are.

Role playing is a skill. You just can't tell students to be, e.g., George Washington. This skill takes training and practice. Some tips here will be helpful. Follow these steps: (a) Do a warm up; discuss the topic and relax the class; let them discuss it intellectually, even unfeelingly. (b) Look for a student who seems most open, "most ready" somewhat extroverted. (c) Ask this person to picture, e.g., George Washington. (d) Ask this student some questions that define the role, e.g., "What would he be wearing?" "How would he sit?" (e) Ask the student to show you what he means, e.g., "You mean he'd sit

---

[162] Immanuel Kant. *Critique of Pure Reason.* translated by N.K. Smith. London (1933).

like this'?" "No?" "Then, how?" "Show me." (f) Now, talk to the student (supportively) as if he is George Washington.

18. Sense Saturate: Ask the class to imagine that an abstraction could be smelled, tasted, touched, have a color, weigh something, etc. For instance, what would "infinity" weigh? What color would it be? How would "democracy" smell or taste? What shape or color would it be?

19. Simulation: Try to devise a simulation of a problem, event, or decision-making process. For instance, set up a Congress, or Supreme Court, or a jury that judges characters in history or literature. You might even set up a chemical process where students go through the process as if they were elements in it. Good simulations also require skill and practice. Follow the guidelines I offered regarding role playing in #17. (You can also refer to the bibliography listed on p. 399 for some helpful books on these kinds of exercises.)

20. Sociodrama: Similarly, you might set up a sociodrama. Here you only tell students their societal role, e.g., father, mother, teacher, and the problem, e.g., the teacher is calling the parent. Then, the players "wing it" and play out what they imagine. Here you set the roles and the problem, and have the class take notes on what happens for class discussion when the exercise is over.

21. The Empty Chair: Place an empty chair in front of the room. Ask students to imagine, e.g., a historical figure in the chair, or a character from a work of literature, or a famous scientist sitting in the chair. Ask volunteers to talk to him or her. Thank this person, tell him or her what you think of them, ask them a question, etc. You might even ask the class to imagine how the person in the chair would respond. Let someone then sit in the chair and respond. You can take notes on this imaginative discussion, and use your notes for a full class discussion after the exercise is over. (Here, again, the guidelines I gave above for Role Play might be helpful.)

22. Force Field Analysis: Using the diagrammed columns below, have the students do a "force field analysis" of specific variables. For instance, the illustration shown is a "force field analysis" of environmental issues:

Pros	Cons	Ideal
		Better Environment
solar power	coal mining	clean air
wind power	acid rain	clean water
Ralph Nader	car manufacturers	low radioactivity

Any topic that has forces that push or pull in different directions and move away or toward a goal can be placed into the columns: Pros, <u>Cons</u>, <u>Ideal</u>. Then, students can show and tell their analyses, and explain their reasons for their placements into the columns.

Methods **12** and **13** above will also make your lessons more actional and experiential.

The same guidelines that I described for affective-experiential education (p. 377) should also be heeded for Methods **17–22**. Additionally, the teacher should be guided by the following general outline of the process of experiential learning for all of these methods: (a) Always begin with a "warm-up"; relax the class by first discussing the topic academically and casually. (b) Then, do the <u>action</u> part of the exercise that is experiential. (c) During the action, have the class (and you) take notes on what is observed during the action (perhaps guided by a question you put to the class). (d) After the action, discuss all notes (placing them on the chalkboard) to venerate <u>knowledge</u> from the exercise. The process looks like this:

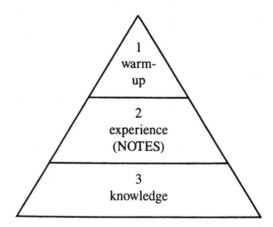

Of course, the longer the warm-up, the wider the role-played experience, the wider the knowledge. Also, notice that each class may derive its own "knowledge-findings" from the experience. Therefore, you need to be <u>not only</u> a facilitator but also a record keeper of what each class "discovered." In other words, you'll need to follow your lesson plan and their learning.

D. Making the Lesson More Inductive

The traditional lesson teaches the curriculum content, e.g., the causes of the Civil War and then at the end of the unit spends some time asking the students, "How does this relate to you and the present?" Such a lesson is deductive. During such a lesson, students' associations to events in their lives are usually barely tolerated or considered "digressions" off the topic. Another version of the traditional lesson starts out by giving the students a motivation or an enticement to be interested in the topic. Such a tack tries to get the students "concerned" about the subject, or at least attracted away from their mundane concerns.

On the other hand, an inductive lesson starts with the students' real present concerns, experiences, perceptions, and analyzes or correlates these via various methods that inductively pull together a curricula generalization that is useful knowledge. For instance, the class might explore conflicts they now experience, real economic and ethnic pressures, and be guided to relate these to understand the causes of the Civil War. In an inductive lesson, the students relate their lives first, and the curriculum content later becomes examples of truths and/or a medium for insights into the present. There is no need to get them concerned about the lesson; their concerns are the premises and foundation for the content to be studied.

An inductive lesson taught well takes skill and practice. The teacher cannot plan the whole lesson for the students to simply take notes on. Instead, the teacher can only plan ways to facilitate the relating of students' experiences to the curriculum. Here, some students have different experiences and different paths to knowledge from these experiences; the teacher (as well as the students) must take notes on what each class period "discovers." This inductive process will become clearer if we take a look at some ways you might make your lessons more inductive.

Method

23. A Confluent Lesson: A "confluent lesson" is an inductive lesson that teaches affective and cognitive learning simultaneously. The teacher should proceed as follows: (a) Choose a real concern that your students have or a set of experiences that have a common denominator. Some concerns might be: dealing with conflicts, future worries, being understood, being bored, etc. Some useful experiences might be their present conflicts, angers, money problems, arguments with their parents, or not having a good weekend. (b) Invite your students to share these concerns and experiences in some structured way. For instance, ask them to list their conflicts and angers, future worries, areas they feel misunderstood, what they find boring. (c) Ask them to either prioritize these, correlate them, or notice similarities among them. For instance, "Which conflicts have to do with power, money, rules, lifestyles?" Or "What kinds of future worries do you notice, any categories?" Or "How do these misunderstandings happen?" Or "What makes some things meaningful, others meaningless?" (d) The class might analyze all of these by listing them

382   Preventing and Handling the Sources of Disruptive Behavior

on the chalkboard. Here, the whole class might inductively find similarities, differences, correlations, and causes between the items. The teacher simply, for example, draws arrows relating items 1 and 6, or 7 and 2, or circles 3 and 7. (e) Finally, the class is asked to make generalizations from noticing the relations they do find among their own shared experiences. Regarding their conflicts, they may be led by you to discover that many conflicts they presently experience can also be found in historic wars. You might then assign them to, e.g., "Write down three things about the causes of the Civil War that are similar to conflicts we listed on the chalkboard today." Regarding future worries or angers, they may be led to notice categories of fears and angers. You might then assign them to "Choose three characters in *Tale of Two Cities* who have worries and angers similar to those we named on the chalkboard today." Regarding money problems, they may be led by you to discover supply and demand factors. You might then assign them, "Which nations in Europe in Chapter 12 of your history book have the same problems we identified on the chalkboard?" Regarding being misunderstood, you might ask them to identify these into "areas," and write a composition or poem on an "area" that better explains it. Regarding meaning and boredom, you might ask them to read three poems in their literature text and to discover, "What did the poet find meaningful, and why?"

Of course, each class will discuss different learnings. And although you must now follow them and take notes (besides them), they are now concerned about the lesson because the lesson was built on and out of their own concerns.

24. Learning to Read Using Life-Experience Material: Most traditional lessons that are designed to build reading skills involve literature that has no apparent relation to the students' immediate concerns. Although such classical literature builds vocabulary, it suffers from inability to motivate the student to read it. At times, it is better to give students reading materials that are not the best in literature but are self-motivating because they involve the students' immediate concerns. Below are some suggested reading materials that may be useful in building reading skills inductively:

1. Schedules
2. Sports Magazines
3. Comics
4. Postal Service Forms
5. Tax Forms
6. Advertisements
7. Maps
8. Job Application Forms
9. Bills

10. Travel Folders
11. Table Games Instructions
12. Food Advertisements
13. Menus
14. Cook Book Recipes
15. Weather Reports
16. Sports Pages of a Newspaper
17. Telephone Directory
18. Coupons
19. Order Forms
20. Signs
21. Labels
22. Cereal Boxes
23. Credit Card Information
24. Banking Information
25. Apartment Advertisements
26. Apartment Leases
27. Auto Advertisements
28. Driver's Manuals and Handbooks
29. Newspaper Classified Ads
30. Washing Instructions
31. Tables of Contents of Books
32. Record Jackets and Labels
33. Rock Magazines
34. Driver's License
35. Car Manual for New Cars

25. <u>Life Problem</u>: Either by using student journals or by just orally brainstorming, have students suggest "life problems," and write them on the chalkboard. They might suggest: careers, making money, becoming famous, problems regarding dating, boredom, resolving conflicts, etc. Have them choose one of these to focus on. Then, as a first assignment, you might ask them to write a short composition on the problem. Allow them to write in the third person, e.g., "Teenagers tend to. . . ." In actuality, they will probably be relating their own concerns. Then, assign them to locate a bibliography for this "life problem." You might request that the bibliography contain at least three poems that relate to this problem, one short story, three historic events, one nonfiction essay, etc. You can also, of course, compile your own list of suggested readings. Finally, you and the class design the reading assignments that you will all read and discuss that work on the problem. Of course, this method works best for an English class or Social Studies class, but the life problem can have scientific aspects and be used in a science class or even as a small unit in a math class. The life problem is the aim here, not to learn the subject matter of the curriculum. Instead, the latter is the means to the former.

26. Future Projection: Ask the students to write a letter imagining it is five years or ten years later. Ask them to write out where they are living, what they are doing with their time: Are they married? Have children? They write the letter dated, e.g., May 6, 2003, and write it in the present tense. If you're teaching an English class, the class shares these compositions in a non-judgmental atmosphere, and only later do you evaluate them for grammar. If it's a literature class, you might assign a poem or short story or play that also struggles with future projection: e.g., Frost's "Stopping by the Woods," Wilder's *Our Town,* Orwell's *1984.* Then, you'll need to assign "theme questions" that relate their own future projections to the work of literature. If you're teaching Social Studies, you might ask that the future projection composition guess about political matters: Who's president? Are countries at war? Why? What are the economic conditions? You might then assign them readings that explore these predictions. Or they might have to find facts that make these predictions plausible.

27. Follow "Digressions": Either follow the class's sporadic associations to the topic as they arise or periodically ask the class, "What does this remind you of?" as you teach the curriculum subject matter. In order not to lose track, just write these "digressions" and associations on the chalkboard with lines drawn from the curriculum to their association. When you feel you are at a good stopping point in your lesson, allow free venting of these associations. However, as they discuss these associations, require that they justify the relation of their association to the curriculum topic. You might even devise an assignment that requires them to write on this relation. This method allows the students to relate their present lives during the lesson rather than too late; after it is taught.

Methods **6, 7, 14, 15, 17, 19, 20,** and **22** above will also help make your lesson delivery more inductive.

Keep in mind that, although during such inductive lessons the teacher has the added jobs of record keeping, taking notes on what the students discover, following the class, etc., the task of motivating students and keeping them attentive and non-disruptive is lessened. (You might simply "✔" or "X" your own lesson plan to keep track of what you covered for each period while you follow each period's discoveries.) Such extra work is often worth it: (a) the students get a chance to relate their own knowledge; (b) they are "with you" more; (c) inductive lessons allow them also to "be the teacher"; (d) it is thereby ego-supportive; (e) it allows learning that is at once affective-experiential and cognitive.[163]

E. Involving the Students: Participation Methods

The more the class is involved in the lesson, the more they have to "act into" rather than "act out" and be disruptive. The more you do all the talking, the more you teach passivity, withdrawal, and either suppress their energy into hostility or invite truancy. Here are some ways to make the lesson delivery more participatory.

Method

28. Working in a Horseshoe or Circle: We spoke of using a horseshoe or circle seating arrangement in Chapter 10, section C. Besides using these seating arrangements as improvements to the environment of the classroom, they also increase student participation. Students can see each other and hear each other's comments and questions better. They also have the benefit of being able to see nonverbal reactions that often support their courage to speak up. However, working in a highly participatory circle or horseshoe requires much skill on the part of the teacher. Here is some help for working in these seating arrangements: (a) Get into the habit of standing up and giving very short lectures on the curriculum topic (no longer than five minutes). (b) Then, direct the class to react to what you just said, and sit down and don't talk; let the class talk, share, and react. Stay out of this discussion. (c) However, you might call on people, disentangle mislistenings, and just be a "gatekeeper" of the flow of the discussion. (d) When you think the discussion has served its purpose of reacting to your little lecture, stand up again, and summarize the class reactions. (e) Then, deliver another short lecture, and sit down and repeat the above procedures. No one interrupts you when you're standing, and you don't interrupt them when you sit down. Enforce this routine with rules and warnings. In this way you can channel the participatory energy of the circle or horseshoe arrangement. Tell the students that you will not call on the first people to raise their hands because you are giving the whole class time to think. Validate the slower thinkers by reminding the class (and yourself) that the fastest answer is rarely well thought out and is certainly not always right. Real thought takes effort. If you expect thoughtful answers from your students, you have to give them the time to formulate them.

---

[163] Since some of these methods become very affective-experiential, the teacher might also follow those guidelines given at the end of section B, p. 377.

29. Be Aware of Poor Questioning Techniques: Asking the class questions does get them to participate. However, often teachers ask poor questions or fall into certain pitfalls that curtail the participation questioning can encourage. Be aware of these mistakes: (a) Don't ask a "complex question," e.g., "Who knows a cause of the Civil War and how the South reacted to it?" Instead, ask one question as simply as you can at a time. (b) Don't ask "railroading" questions that push the answer you want, e.g., "Who knows a cause of the Civil War, that was an economic one, that had to do with Southern agriculture?" (c) Avoid questions that require simply memory answers, e.g., "Who was president during the Civil War?" "What was the final battle of the Civil War?" or "What do you call the 'ing' form of a verb?" Such questions do not encourage class participation. The class's involvement is over as soon as someone has the remembered answer. (d) Avoid questions that can be answered by simply "Yes" or "No," e.g., "Did the South win the Civil War?" (e) Don't call on the first person who raises his/her hand. Instead, wait until a few hands are up before you call on someone. This will discourage the competitive race to the correct answer and give students a chance to think and get courage to raise their hands. (f) Don't always respond "correct" to the first student's answer. Allow a few answers to be tried before you let them know who is correct. This will encourage them to listen to each other more. If you use the kinds of questions suggested in **(a)** above, there will usually be many comments that students can offer that fall into the category of "right" answers. It is hard to acknowledge an answer without giving feedback on it. You might want to say something like "OK, anyone else have a comment?" or simply "Mmm-hmm, and what else?" Use a positive tone of voice so the students know you are not dismissing their thinking, but use your body language to show that you are looking for more than one "right" answer. (g) Ask them to raise their hands high and look around the room when they raise their hands. Then, they will see that they are not alone with their answer or question, which will encourage more students to risk their answer or question. (h) Don't repeat every comment, answer, or question each student gives or asks so the other students can hear them. Don't become a P.A. system for the class. If you repeat their responses for the rest of the class, you encourage them not to listen to each other and only listen to you. Instead, say, "good" to John's answer, and leave it at that. If students didn't hear John's answer, ask them to ask John, and John talks to the class, not you.

30. Ask Questions That Require Listing: Ask students to, e.g., "Name three causes of. . . ." Or "List three factors that. . . ." Or "Describe two situations that. . . ." These kinds of questions tend to avoid the above pitfalls.

31. Ask Questions That Require Verbalizations: Ask students to imagine, e.g., "What would you say to Lincoln when . . . ?" Or "What would you say to

the South regarding . . . ?" Or "What would you say to the main character in
. . . ?" Or "What would you say to someone who wanted to know the meaning
of the Pythagorean theorem?"

32. Stop "Distancing": Try to wean your students away from talking in the
third person, e.g., "you tend to . . . ," "one generally feels. . . ." Instead, encourage them to use "I" and to express their feelings openly. "I" statements will
be more interesting to the other students and may kick off similar feelings
that they can share with each other. Also, by avoiding "you" and "one" you'll
avoid tiresome, mock arguments. If one student says, "You tend to find this
boring" and another says, "One could say this is very important," these students
may argue. But if each in turn says, "I found it boring," "I was interested in
it," the argument is avoided because now they are both right, from his or her
own point of view. Also, when a student says, "I feel . . ." you can encourage
participation by asking the class, "Who feels similarly?"

33. Ask the Feeling behind the Question: Teach the class that when we ask
a question, often the question is motivated by a feeling behind the question.
For instance, a student might ask: "Do you think the North was fair in the
Civil War?" Such a question might be motivated by a feeling or opinion about
the subject of the question. In such situations, say: "John, that's a good
question. You seem to have a feeling or opinion here. What is it? And then,
John, we'll see how the others feel about your question or point."

34. Note Student Responses on the Chalkboard: Don't just use the chalkboard
for your notes. Also, record their ideas on the chalkboard, perhaps in response
to a question you put to them. And don't revise their responses into the "correct
way" to say it. That'll turn them off. Keep it in their language. Write their
responses by listing them by letter: A, B. C, not 1, 2, 3. Then, after all
responses are on the chalkboard, ask the class to prioritize them. Should "A"
be 3 or 1 or 2? Should "C" be 1? Ask them to number the lettered items in
order of most important or most valuable or most difficult. Then discuss their
opinions of their ordering of these lettered items. Or ask them to "✔" the
item they most understand or agree with, "X" items they don't understand or
disagree with, and "?" items they have questions about. Then, discuss their
markings per item.

35. Have Them Teach Each Other: From the above method, you might ask
those who made a checkmark on an item, e.g., B, to talk to those who made
an "X." Or ask all of those who marked a "?" to raise their hands. Now have
a student who marked a check for this item teach the one who has the
"?" question.

36. <u>Use 3 × 5 Cards</u>: To encourage free responses, you might ask the class a question and have them all respond on 3 × 5 cards that you hand out. The students write their question or answer on the 3 × 5 card anonymously. You then collect them face down and shuffle them. You can then read them all, or some, or pass them back out to the class who reads them to the class. The class might try to guess who wrote each comment or answer.

37. <u>Walk around the Room</u>: If you work with a class in rows, get into the habit of asking a question and then letting the class discuss it while you walk around the room. If you can get away from standing up in front of the class all the time, they won't tend to look at you while they respond. This will be the case especially as you stand in the back of the room during the discussion. Such will force them to turn around more and see each other and talk to each other more. Also, this will stop them from talking to you, especially if a student is responding to something Susan said. Say, "John, tell Susan, or ask her, not me."

38. <u>The Social Barometer</u>: Place across the chalkboard this scale:

| −4 | −3 | −2 | −1 | 0 | +1 | +2 | +3 | +4 |

Now, ask the class to get out of their seats and to make a single line all lining up facing the "0." Ask them, at first, some non-threatening questions, e.g., "How do you like summer?" If a student feels very positive, he moves over to the right end of the room and stands at "+4." If he feels somewhat good about the summer, he stands at "+3" or "+2." If he hates the summer, he stands at "−4." If he has no opinion, or feels neutral, he stands at "0." Each time you ask a question, students stand where they feel. Each response will produce a social barometer or map of the opinions of the students in the class. After they have gotten the idea with some non-threatening questions, you can also ask, e.g., "How do you feel about capital punishment? Abortion? The president? Frost's poem? The use of nuclear power?" Sometimes the question will divide the room in about half. At those times, you can initiate a debate with one side talking to the other. If one side convinces some of the others, they can change their stand, and move from, e.g., "+3" to "−2." Also, you might give each student a 3 × 5 card so that they can write down a question anonymously they can give you to ask the class. The social barometer also is affected by peer pressure. It's difficult for a minority of students to stand at "−4" when the majority is standing at "+4." However, you can discuss this social or peer pressure as "food for thought" in a very educational way.

39. <u>Paired-Off Interviews</u>: Ask the class a question. Then, ask them to turn to their neighbor and interview each other about their answer to this question. Instruct them that when they finish the interview of their neighbor, they will have to summarize what their neighbor said. This will not only encourage more participation but force them to listen to each other.

40. Forced Paraphrasing: Tell the students that during the next discussion of a topic they cannot comment, answer, or ask a question unless they can paraphrase satisfactorily what the last student said. If the next student can't give such a summary of what was just said, s/he cannot go. You then call on someone else who tries to paraphrase correctly. Students cannot give their opinion until each understands the other person's opinion correctly. This method also forces them to listen to each other.

41. Correct Each Other's Papers: Give the class a short task or quiz. Now ask them to trade papers with their neighbor. Go over the answer to each item and stop. Allow them to correct each other's papers and discuss the correction with each other. Then, discuss the next item, stop, and they correct and discuss. At the end of the entire quiz, you can ask what they noticed while marking each other's papers.

42. Use Cooperative Learning: Structure lessons so that students work together to achieve shared goals. Use questions and research projects that require students to work in teams to learn the material you want to cover, and, also, make sure that all the members of their group learn the material as well. If you teach this way, you can have each team working on a separate project and use the final products to teach the material to the other teams.

Some examples of projects might be: (a) Each team will represent a state delegation to the Continental Congress. At the end of the week we will try to work together to write a constitution. Make sure that your state's particular concerns and needs are addressed. You will need to work together to research your state's concerns just after the revolution. (b) How many different figures can your group make that have an area of 36 cm sq. with one side of the figure having a length of 4 cm? (c) (for a language class) Write a play in Spanish that uses all of this week's vocabulary and at least three verb tenses. The play must make sense.

In **cooperative learning,** all the students are responsible for making sure that each member of the group contributes something to the project; however, it's OK that not everyone will contribute in the same way.

The following are some general guidelines:

1. The number of students in each group (never more than six) will depend on the age of the students and the nature of the task to be completed. In early elementary grades, start with groups of two or three.
2. In general, each group should have a leader, a reporter/recorder, a materials monitor (materials must be shared for cooperative learning to work), and

participants. Each role must be both assigned and clearly defined in advance. For example, the leader is not "the boss" but rather a member of the group whose responsibility is to make sure that the project gets done and that all the members participate. The reporter/recorder cannot tell the class what s/he wants to say but rather must report faithfully the conclusions the group agreed on. In addition, the students may also have roles that change from project to project, i.e., researchers, writers, illustrators, choreographers, dancers, and musicians.

3. Rotate the group jobs/roles so all students get to experience them.
4. Role play a cooperative group in action with the class before you ask them to work in one to complete a real project.

Working together is a goal that has been increasingly in the media as a requirement for success in today's workforce. You can help your students succeed with a better understanding of the content of your subject by teaching them to be personally responsible for their own learning, and that of their peers. By using **cooperative learning** students will gain a better understanding of the material, as well as learn group skills necessary to succeed as part of a team. (For more information on **cooperative learning,** see the book *Circles of Learning* listed at the end of Section H in this chapter.)

Methods **7, 9, 10, 11, 12, 13, 16, 17, 18, 19, 20, 21, 22, 23, 25, 26,** and **27** above will also help you deliver a lesson that will encourage more class participation.

Teachers who attempt these participation methods should try to keep the train of their lesson moving. If you stop for every response, the lesson will lose momentum. Students will peer out the "window" of your slowed down "train" to see "where it is we are going. If you then respond to these "turned-off" students, you stop the train of your lesson, and students will "get off." So, keep your lesson moving. Also, you will have to actively distinguish "smoke" from "steam." The latter is the energy encouraged by these participation methods. The former may be signs of real discipline problems that need to be extinguished before the real trouble starts. Your challenge will be to channel this participation energy (or go back to a repressed, non-participatory lesson delivery that can be the source of discipline problems).

F. Creating Lessons That Feel Orderly and Have Rewards and Momentum

Although your written lesson plan may seem orderly to you, the important thing is that the delivery of the lesson plan feel orderly to the class. They need to feel where you are going, and while they are going there, the class needs to feel some sense of rewards during the "ride." Often they cannot wait until you finally "get there," at the end of the lesson. Also, this ride needs to have momentum. They need to feel they and you are moving; "we're getting somewhere." What are some ways you can make your lesson plan delivery orderly, have rewards and momentum?

43. Write on the Chalkboard a "Felt Goal." Not an "Aim" for the Lesson: Don't write on the chalkboard, e.g., "Aim: To learn about imperialism." Since the class doesn't understand "imperialism," they have no real feeling for where you are going. Instead of presenting an abstraction as your "Aim," give them a "felt goal," some goal they can understand or feel. For instance: "We will learn how and why people sometimes push their ideas, feelings, and power on others." They can understand and feel this goal. Here, you can start the lesson with examples of this "push of ideas, feelings, and power on others," and then lead to an understanding of "imperialism" as an international phenomenon. Similarly, in an English class, an "Aim" such as "to study Orwell's *1984*" would not be as helpful as the felt goal: "to discover how losing freedom feels." Similarly, in a math class, an "Aim" such as "to study the Pythagorean theorem" would not be as helpful as the felt goal: "to figure out the length of side A of the triangle, when we only know sides B and C." A felt goal rather than an abstract "Aim" gives the lesson a sense of felt order.

44. Give an Overview When You Begin: Besides presenting a "felt goal," also give a brief overview of where you intend to go. You might even give your overview in an outline form. For instance, "Class, today we will . . . (felt goal), then (A) we will . . . , then (B) we'll try to . . . , (C) finally we'll see. . . ." The overview will give students a felt sense of order.

45. Stop Every Once in Awhile and Review "What We've Covered, Where We Are. and Where We're Going": After you've covered some material, refer back to your "felt goal," point to where you are now (perhaps at a certain point on the chalkboard notes), and point to (or say) where you are going. Do this two or three times during your lesson. Also ask, "How many see where we are? Raise your hands." This procedure will keep the students on track with the train of your lesson.

46. Deliver Your Lesson in Short Verbal Steps: Don't talk or explain for longer than five minutes. Long verbal statements are hard to digest. Instead, explain an aspect or piece of the subject matter, get responses from the students, and then go on to the next verbal explanation of the subject matter. If you do this talk, stop, wait for responses, talk, stop, wait for responses . . . etc., in progressive short steps, the class will be able to follow you better.

47. Let Students Know How They Can Be "Good" During Your Lesson: You not only need to let students know when they are being "good" or "bad" regarding classroom rules, but when they are being "good" according to the train of the lesson. Students need to have a sense of the answer to such questions as: "Does the teacher want me to listen, take notes, then comment or ask questions?" "Am I supposed to try to offer a strategy or suggestion?" "Should I respond to the comments my fellow students are making?" "Should I now comment on my emotional reaction to this fact just presented?" "Is this the proper time for me to disagree?" "Is it appropriate to say what this presented fact reminds me of?" Students, to be "good," need to feel a clear sense of what is "being good" during your lesson. You need to make clear what you approve of, want, are after, what is success, and the subtle rules of the game for doing well during your lesson. Sometimes students are "bad" because they don't know what being "good" is in period three vs. period seven in their many class periods during the day. Verbalize how you'd like to proceed and your standards for your procedures. For instance: "Class, I'd like to explain the causes of the Civil War. Please write these points down, and stop me if you have a question. But hold your comments for now. We'll discuss these after we get some of these points down in our notes."

48. Recognize Students on the Chalkboard: As we mentioned above, use the chalkboard for their comments and questions, as well as your own. Write their ideas and questions on the chalkboard as a way of rewarding them with ongoing recognition during the lesson. Students need this ongoing recognition; the recognition of a good grade on an exam often comes too late to motivate them to behave during the lesson. You might even put their names (or at least their initials) on the chalkboard beside their volunteered answer or question.

49. Ownership: Students can also have a sense of ongoing reward during the lesson if they can "own" something during the lesson. If your lesson is about Asia, allow them to, e.g., own a small map of Asia as they learn it. If your lesson is about comma errors in writing sentences, go over the grammar errors involving the comma in sentences, e.g., on 3 × 5 cards. Then, give these cards to each student who sees the error or who can correct it. If you are teaching something using a science experiment, give a piece of the apparatus, or some material to the students who participate well in the lesson. By designing your lessons into 3 × 5 or 5 × 8 cards, or onto newsprint, you can have pieces of your lesson you can give away to your students so that they can feel that they "own" the learning. This can be an ongoing reward during the lesson.

50. Task Sheets: Midst your lesson, hand out short "task sheets," a one-page puzzle, diagram, or set of short questions that relate to your teaching. If you are teaching grammar, hand out a sheet that has sentences, e.g., where the commas are missing. If you are teaching the causes of the Civil War, hand out a sheet that has events, dates, and famous people on it, and ask students to draw lines connecting these. If you are teaching math, hand out a sheet that has equations on it and ask them to circle those equations that relate to what you just taught. These "task sheets" should be short and sweet. They might be multiple choice, matching, fill-in-the-blank, puzzles, diagrams to be designed, etc. They are not tests or quizzes. They should provide immediate rewarding opportunity for students to apply the knowledge you just taught. (Also see Chapter 14, section C for more on task sheets.)

51. Being a Detective: Any lesson you can devise that involves them in being a detective, with clues, and discovering the missing parts will give students ongoing reward during the lesson. For instance, "Class, which cause of the Civil War is missing here on the chalkboard? Let me give you a clue." Or "These words on the chalkboard all refer to a point we made yesterday. Can you guess what it is? Let me give you a clue."

52. Let Them Be the Teacher Sometimes: After you have taught a segment of your lesson, ask: "Who knows it well enough to teach it?" Get a volunteer and ask him/her to now "be the teacher." Ask the class to make believe they don't understand the segment just taught and to ask this "teacher" some questions. By having the opportunity to briefly be the teacher, students can be continually rewarded for their learning.

53. Use Self-Competition: Students too often compete with each other. Set up ways so students can measure their present self against their old self. For instance, ask them to notice how many comma errors they made on this composition compared to their last composition. Or ask them to notice the errors in multiplication they made on this test compared to their last test. Any way you can help students to keep track of their own work so they can compare their work of yesterday with today will encourage a self-competition. This will give them a sense of reward during the learning.

54. Demarcate Points in Your Lesson: Try to keep numbering or giving letters to segments or points in your lesson. Call this idea, or fact, or concept #1, the next #2, then #3, etc. Or use letters: A, B. C, etc. Then, refer to the points you've made by number or letter as you show them where you were and are going. This procedure will give the train of your lesson a sense of movement and momentum.

55. Summarize Often: After you have taught a few segments of the subject matter, summarize what you have taught within a brief statement, then move on. Do this often. This will give your lesson momentum.

56. Don't Respond to Every Response or Question: You probably often feel that you are being inconsiderate (or you get worried that they won't like you) if you don't respond to every comment or question. However, if you do respond to every comment or question, the lesson slows down. Students' attention wanders "out the window" as the train of your lesson slows down. Now, you tend to talk to the students whose heads are "out the window." Thereby your lesson slows to a stop. Now the train of your lesson has stopped and people "get off." You become more involved in not losing "passengers" than your lesson. Instead, keep your lesson moving. People hurry to get on, or don't likely jump off of, a moving train. Instruct students to hold their questions or comments ("write them down if you tend to forget them") until you find a good stopping place. If you worry too much about each passenger's pleasure, you may lose the whole train load.

Methods **17, 19, 20, 24, 27, 34,** and **41** can also be used to give your lesson delivery a sense of order, reward, and momentum. Also, to make your lesson delivery replete with rewards of all kinds, see Chapter 12C for many suggestions.

G. Managing the Distribution of Attention

When the lesson is teacher-centered, the teacher needs to be the major feeder of attention and approval. In such cases, it is very difficult to feed all students satisfactorily, especially when it is the case for adolescents that attention from <u>each other</u> is more important. As a result, students who don't get enough attention or approval <u>in</u> the lesson find it by <u>acting</u> out. Rather than work against this current (students' need of attention from each other) and rather than try the impossible job of feeding all satisfactorily, teachers need methods that better manage the distribution of attention so that students can feed each other.

Method

57. <u>Sit Down after Your Lecture and Allow the Circle or Horseshoe to Discuss It</u>: We discussed in Method 28 above how you can use a circle or horseshoe seating arrangement to involve the students. The only reminder here is that you should often sit down (after your brief explanations and, perhaps, a question) and shut up. Let the students talk to each other; even direct them to look at each other, not you, e.g., to "speak to John whom you are responding to, not me."

58. <u>Encourage Them to Summarize Each Other</u>: Ask: "Who can summarize what Sue said?" Or "Do you all agree with what Sue said?" Don't you repeat what Sue said. Again, if you become a "P.A. system" for students' comments and questions, they won't listen to each other.

59. Create a Stage: "Show and tell" is probably one of the oldest and best ways for students to give each other attention. Ask students to come up in front of the room and "show us what you mean," or have them put their homework on the chalkboard, etc.

60. Work in Small Groups: Every so often allow the class for a brief time to break off into small groups to discuss something you've initiated. When they return to the large groups, have a representative of each small group present his/her group's findings. This procedure will encourage each group to listen to the other groups' comments.

61. Panel Discussions: Set up a panel of students to discuss an issue. Also give the class a sheet of questions they should keep in' mind as the panel discussion proceeds. Then, the whole class responds to the panel. If it's a debate, the class can argue from side to side, and vote.

62. Have the Class Create Questions for the Class: After you have taught a short unit, ask the class to create some good questions one might ask on this unit. Then, students ask each other questions. (You should hold yourself back as long as you can if you hear wrong answers being given; the attention to each other may be more useful than your always taking over with the right answer. You can always make some corrections at the end of the period. Take notes if you must.)

63. Team Games: Spelling bees, team competition over math problems, games where two teams ask each other questions for points, etc., all distribute attention from student to student.

64. Detective Role Play: After teaching, e.g., the parts of speech, ask students to assume the personality of a "part of speech": be a gerund, verb, article, etc. Students introduce themselves, e.g., "I stand still yet am very active. What am I?" "A gerund!" You can do this for characters in history, literature, famous scientists, and even abstractions personified.

65. Have Students Bring in Articles: Like "show and tell," after a lesson is taught, you might assign students to bring in current events clippings from newspapers that they must explain to the class. They might also bring in photos or clippings from magazines that show a scientific or mathematical principle, a literary or grammatical point, etc.

66. A Class Project: Design a project that requires the cooperation of the whole class to put together. It could simply be a collage on a large piece of paper or a large chalkboard drawing. It could also be a science project or a drama that the class writes about a history event, etc.

67. Students Test the Class: As in Method 61, you can also have students write incorrect sentences or incorrect statements of fact on the chalkboard, and each challenges the class to discover the mistake(s).

68. Have Students Give Speeches: These speeches can either be debatable opinions on the curriculum topic or simply a situation in which students read their compositions or short essays that you assigned.

69. Simulations: Conduct a mock trial. Have the class be the Congress. Have them make believe they are in a "life boat," at an auction of important items, etc.

70. Students Create Detective Stories or Puzzles: You might ask students to create short stories to be solved with clues about the subject matter, or word puzzles or diagrams or charts to be figured out—that they present to the class.

71. Who Am I? Interview: A student comes up to the front of the class unidentified regarding who or what she will role play. The class can ask, e.g., twenty questions that the role player can only answer with a "yes" or "no." The class must figure out who s/he is. S/he might be a character in history, a part of speech, a poet, a scientific concept, an axiom in geometry, etc.

72. Students Go Step by Step: A student writes down the first step, e.g., in a geometry proof. The next student must be able to write down the next logical step. This can also be done in a set of grammar rules sentences or for chronological events in history, etc.

73. Have Students Call on Each Other: Sometimes ask students, "Whom would you like to hear from?" Or, when two students raise their hands at the same time, ask them to look at each other, and they decide who goes first.

74. Students Exchange Papers: They can mark each other's papers, write comments on each other's papers, etc. They can either do this with their neighbor, or you shuffle all papers and redistribute them randomly to the class. Then, the student-evaluators discuss what they found and report to the class.

Methods **7, 9, 11, 12, 13, 17, 18, 19, 20, 21, 22, 23, 25, 26, 27, 28, 32, 34, 35, 36, 37, 38, 39, 40, 41, 51,** and **52** will also help manage the distribution of attention from students to students.

With many of the above methods, as the lesson proceeds, the teacher along with the students, needs to take notes during the discussion to keep track of what each class period covered in the curriculum.

H. Making the Lesson Supportive and Explained Well

When is a lesson delivery supportive? Let's review (from Chapter 9H) when it's not. A lesson is not supportive when it unfortunately, perhaps, inadvertently does one or all of the following:

1. Pushes students to do tasks that they are not ready to do
2. Pushes students to do tasks that make them feel inadequate
3. Doesn't provide the students with adequate protection from feeling uncomfortable in front of their peers
4. Doesn't explain the content to be learned, or the tasks required, well enough
5. Doesn't provide students with ways to give the teacher feedback as to when any of the above may be happening

Such a lesson raises student anxiety levels, wears down their frustration tolerance, and can become the source of disruptive behavior.

It figures then that a <u>supportive</u> lesson delivery:

1. Makes sure that it is only demanding learning and tasks that have been preceded by the teacher checking that the students have mastered the <u>prerequisite</u> knowledges and skills
2. Bolsters their ego, that starts with giving the students a feeling of "can-do" (efficacy), that goes from easy to harder, is paced in small "digestible" pieces, and is replete with positive, encouraging feedback
3. Protects students from feeling uncomfortable in front of their peers
4. Explains the content to be mastered and tasks to be performed, well
5. Provides students with ample ways and opportunities to let the teacher know when they may: not be ready, feel inadequate, uncomfortable, or, simply, not understand.

The following methods will help make the lesson delivery more supportive:

75. <u>Before you move on to the next task or content to be taught, review what you just taught</u>, or have the students give a summary of what was just explained, or ask a brief question that will give you feedback as to whether they are ready or not.

76. <u>Compliment the students a lot.</u> Don't overcorrect. Notice and tell them what they are doing <u>well</u>, not what they are doing wrong. Deliver the lesson in small units, with as much visual, tactile, drama, or role play as possible.

77. <u>Always ask for volunteers, rather than pick on students</u> who feel uncomfortable. Then, treat the volunteers very supportively. The shy ones will be watching as to whether it's safe to venture volunteering. If you treat the students who even give wrong answers well, you will get more volunteers. Provide safe ways for students to respond:

78. <u>Before you require them to, e.g., say their answer in front of the class let them: write it privately</u> (you will not collect it) at their own desk; tell their neighbor their answer; work out the answer in a small group; write it anonymously on a 3 × 5 card which you collect, shuffle, and read to the class, protecting the author of the card.

79. Instead of asking students all the time to raise their hands "if you don't understand," ask those who do understand to raise their hands. The former asks the most inadequate and least confident to do a very uncomfortable task. The latter asks the more confident students to do a task that inherently is easier for them. You can even say, "If you understand it very well, raise your hand very high, not so well, not as high, etc." It will be much easier for the students who lack confidence to simply not raise their hands. And, more importantly, you'll get much better feedback as to how much the class really understands what you've taught.

80. Total Responses: Instead of asking, e.g., "Does anyone have any questions?" say, "Raise your hand very high if you follow me, or not so high if you follow me only somewhat. Don't raise your hand if you feel a little lost. Ready? Go. Now, look around the room. See? You're not alone." This procedure will show you more than the procedure of asking the ones with low confidence to do the most, viz., "raise your hand." Eventually, you only need to say: "How many follow me well, not so well?" Or "Got me?" Students will readily learn to raise their hands high or not at all to show you where they are. This will give you easy ongoing feedback about their learning.

81. Where Lost? After you've finished a small unit that consisted of notes on the chalkboard, point to parts of the notes and say: "How many feel they understand this well?" Then point to another set of the notes: "And how many get this well?" "And this well?" This procedure will show you where in the notes you may have lost some students. Place a check next to notes that seem to be understood well. Mark a "?" beside notes where there may be problems. Append an "X" to notes where the students seem lost.

82. Let Them Teach Each Other: Again, as we suggested above, let some students explain the material to those who indicated they have questions, or to those who just don't raise their hands when you ask for a show of confidence (in 73). You'll learn a lot as teacher when you hear students teach back what you think you taught.

Methods **15–22, 27, 29, 30, 31, 33, 35, 36, 37, 39–45, 49, 51, 53, 54, 57, 61, 63, 66, 69, 70, 71,** and **73** will also help explain the lesson better and provide ongoing feedback to you about their learning during the lesson.

Again, you must be reminded here that with these methods, like many of the above, you'll need to take notes (not just the students) on what each class period has learned.

For those teachers who would like more methods that make your lesson delivery affective, actional, experiential, inductive, more participatory, and evocative of a sense of order, reward, momentum, a distribution of attention—I offer below a list of some further resource books that contain many more methods that accomplish these purposes:

Borton, Terry. *Reach, Touch and Teach.* New York: McGraw Hill. 1970.

Brown, George. *Human Teaching for Human Learning: An Introduction to Confluent Education.* Boston: Viking Press. 1974.

Canfield, Jack. *100 Ways to Enhance Self Concept in the Classroom.* New Jersey: Prentice Hall. 1976.

Cullum, Albert. *Push Back the Desks.* New York: Citation Press. 1968.

Demise, Richard. *Put Your Mother on the Ceiling: Children's Imagination Games.* Walker Publishing Co., 1975.

F.P.A. School Services Publication. *Simulation Games for the Social Studies Classroom.* Vol. 1, No 1. 1974.

Johnson, David W., Roger T. Johnson, Edythe Johnson Holubee, and Patricia Roy. *Circles of Learning, Cooperation in the Classroom.* Association for Supervision and Curriculum Development. 1984.

Kirschenbaum, Howard and Sidney Simon. *Clarifying Values Through Subject Matter.* New York: Winston Press. 1973.

Koch, Kenneth. *Wishes, Lies, and Dreams.* New York: Chelsea House Publication. 1970.

Schild, E. O., and Sarane Boocock. *Simulation Games in Learning.* Beverly Hills, CA: Sage Publication. 1971.

Simon, S. L. Howe, and H. Kirschenbaum. *Values Clarification Handbook.* New York: Hart Publishing Co. 1975.

Stanford, Gene and Barbara Stanford. *Learning Discussion Skills Through Games.* New York: Citation Press 1969.

Zackerman, Everett L. *Guide to Simulation Games.* Washington, DC: Information Resources, Inc. 1978.

Good luck with all of these new methods. If done well, they will incite fewer discipline problems by repairing the delivery of your lesson plan. However, remember the four caveats as you try these: (1) At first, these methods will require more work before they make your job easier. (2) Only use those methods that are congruent for your style. (3) However, give the method a good try before you abandon it. (4) Don't fret if you cannot successfully use many of the methods suggested above.

I. Especially for Grades K–6

Although many of the methods above will also enhance the delivery of the lesson plan in K–6 (especially grades 2–6) in the lower grades, there are some special things you should do:

83. Try to Emote as You Teach: Dramatize and give lots of attention and recognition.

400 Preventing and Handling the Sources of Disruptive Behavior

84. <u>Turn Lessons into Games</u>: Use short, clear, step by step instructions with small rewards after one or two steps.

85. <u>Use Computer-Assisted Instruction</u>: Use software designed to give students immediate feedback.

86. <u>Concretize the Learning So Students Can Touch and Manipulate It</u>: Use colors, photos, drawn pictures, arrows indicating direction, stencils, tracing paper, index cards they can organize, and cardboard they can cut into fractions, puzzles, etc.

87. <u>Use Worksheets</u> (task sheets, see pp. 410–414) <u>and Workbooks</u>: Many publishers (Scholastic) specialize in these for every subject matter. However, premade sheets from a book are limited in how well they relate to the lesson you actually taught that day, unless you are following the textbook lessons exactly. If you teach to student needs, then one of those needs is to have their worksheets tailored to the lesson they received. This is not to say that you cannot sometimes find premade worksheets that will fit your lesson. If you can, then there is, of course, no need to "reinvent the wheel." However, do not slip into the habit of making <u>your lessons</u> conform to the worksheet you found, so that you won't have to make one.

It is always better to make your own worksheet. And, while making your worksheets to really match your lessons is an initial output of work, it will have both an immediate relevance for your students, and will have a long-term payoff for you.

Or better yet, have hands-on projects or games planned for the middle of the lesson that give your students a chance to practice, experientially, what you have covered. Elementary school children need to participate more than they need to sit and listen. Make sure that these concrete projects actually correlate to what you taught, not just to today's page in the book. Often projects can look similar to "Do-Now" assignments in the older grades. They can be done individually, or better yet, in cooperative groups.

Some examples are:

- "Create a silly phrase (mnemonic) that will help you remember the names of the planets in order, for example My Very Excellent Mother Just Simply Uses No Perfume (Mercury, Venus, Earth, Mars, Jupiter, Saturn, Uranus, Neptune, Pluto)."
- "Sally works in a tricycle factory. In one week she makes 12 tricycles. How many wheels does she use?"
- "List five ways you personally can help not pollute the environment."
- "Find the five mistakes in this sentence: I usually do my homework after dinner but by, then I am so tyrd that I make mistakes alot."

• Games could be a Spelling Bee, Multiplication Catch (You call out a multiplication problem, throw a ball, and the student you threw it to has to give the answer before catching the ball), MadLibs (for parts of speech), etc.

88. Teach in "Themes": Do a whole unit on government, where students make pictures of Congress, write about laws, do math about government economics, read about politics, sing about George Washington, etc.

89. Give Individual Attention: Of course, in grades K–2, even 3–6, you can go around the room and give individual instruction and approval while others are working on their, e.g., workbooks.

Methods **1–84** (especially **42**) can all be used in the lower grades, with some revisions.

J. Teachers Share Their Growing Pains

Discussing your analogy of keeping during a lesson, I remember that I did not do that very well when I was in charge of the third grade class I worked with. I used to try to pay close attention to each student's actions, and while I was doing that, twenty other students would start doing their own thing and suddenly the whole class was out of control.

• • •

Not actional enough—I talk too much! I have, since taking this course, asked for students to summarize, respond, react to other students' answers or to the lesson. I have not gotten into debates and role playing, but this is an excellent way to get kids motivated and to have some mobility and freedom to speak.

• • •

I realized during our discussion on attention flow that rarely have I asked students to come to the chalkboard this semester. My feeling had been that it takes too much time and results in too much movement. This is wrong. During the past month, I have asked students to solve problems at the board, explaining their work if possible, and have other students ask questions and comment on it. Students enjoy the recognition and usually strive to meet the challenge. It also keeps the rest of the class interested as it represents a change—seeing someone else talk math after seeing me 150 times. I have also used the suggestion of writing students' answers and ideas on the board more often, even if they are wrong.

I have used games involving teams and the like, but they take a lot out of me. The kids get very excited and I have to keep control in addition to playing referee in the game.

• • •

One of the ways I can motivate the students is by creating learning situations that involve students relating to each other.

For example, I would introduce the information about the properties of air. Then, I would ask each student to quiz each other on the properties of air. Then, I would ask someone to write the properties of air on the chalkboard. And finally, I would ask the class to determine whether these properties this student wrote on the board are correct or not. I feel that this approach takes me (teacher) off the stage and puts the students into the limelight. I feel that this approach will result in the student being "turned on" to my lesson.

• • •

As an introduction to teaching coordinates last month, I distributed maps of the United States and asked the kids to locate the place of their birth or the home of some out-of-state relative where they spent a vacation. Many of the kids took a very personal interest in this activity. In general, I am glad that we discussed the need to relate lessons to children's lives.

• • •

This past week I taught mitosis and meiosis to my Regents Biology classes. I tried very hard to think of ways to use the participation techniques mentioned in class. Although I find it extremely difficult to role play, I decided to use this technique because I have a few "hams" in my classes.

After going through the stages of mitosis, I said, "I can't imagine what it would be like to be a chromosome going through mitosis. Let's think about it." We thought about it for a minute and I said, "Who can imagine being a chromosome?" A few students raised their hands and I chose Nadine. I asked Nadine what stage of mitosis she was in, and then I asked her to describe herself. The students thought this was great. Other students wanted to get in on the act. We were laughing so hard at one point that I thought the floor dean would come to the door. They really enjoyed role playing, but most of all it seemed to help them understand the topic. I have asked students to imagine themselves in certain situations, but this was the first time I asked them to role play. I would certainly recommend this technique.

K. Training Exercises and Checklist for Chapter 14

Exercise One: Delivering the Subject Matter Congruently

Prepare a preface to a particular unit of the curriculum by either expressing how you really feel about the subject matter or by sharing a relevant personal experience. Make your preface talk from your "I" personally to the student's person. Now present this preface to either a friend or colleague or another participant in your education class or workshop. Allow them to rate your congruence. Practice these kinds of prefaces for better congruence.

Exercise Two: Making Your Lesson Affective, Actional, Experiential
If you are in an education class or workshop, each participant can present a lesson plan to the rest of the group. The group gives each lesson a −1 point every time a full minute goes by that the lesson is only cognitive, verbal, and only the teacher is doing something. (A situation in which the students are only taking notes, also gets a −1 rating.) Each presenter tries to receive the least minus points in score in a given ten-minute lesson.

Exercise Three: Making the Lesson Inductive
If you are in an education course or workshop, participants should volunteer curriculum topics that are written on the chalkboard. For every three placed on the chalkboard, the class must brainstorm a way to teach one of them by starting inductively with the students' experiences. Each time a successful inductive strategy is described, all three topics are erased, and the participants offer another three. Again, the class tries to offer a successful inductive strategy that teaches one of these by starting with the students' experiences. Continue this exercise until most of the participants can construct at least some inductive strategies for some of the curricula.

Exercise Four: Practicing Involving the Students
If you are in an education course or workshop, each participant presents a lesson to the other participants who role play being "students." The presenting teacher conducts the lesson for ten minutes and then closes by explaining where he or she would've gone with this lesson had s/he had time to continue. The "students" make a checkmark in their notes each time the lesson delivery made them want to participate. And the "students" also grade the lesson A, B, C, etc. as to whether it would encourage them to participate upon hearing the explanation of the direction of the rest of the lesson. Each presenter tries to get as many vats as possible and to get as high a grade as possible.

Exercise Five: Practicing Creating Lessons That Feel Orderly and Have Rewards and Momentum
If you are in an education course or workshop, each participant presents the opening three minutes of a lesson to the others who listen as "students." The listeners then report to the presenter: (a) where they think s/he was going with this introduction; (b) how they think one goes about being good in this lesson; and (c) tells whether they would have been interested in staying on the "ride" of the movement of this lesson. The presenter hopefully gets guesses that are correct for (a) and (b) for what s/he intended in the presentation and gets a high rating in terms of who would've liked to take the "ride" offered in the presenter's lesson.

Exercise Six: Managing the Distribution of Attention

You can either role play this to each other if you are in an education course or workshop, or you and a friend or colleague can observe each other's lessons. Every time you as teacher are the one who is giving the attention or approval in the lesson, you receive a −1 from the observer. Every time the students are able to give each other attention or approval in the lesson, you receive a +1 from the observer(s). The object is to deliver a lesson in which the teacher's score is a total that is positive, on the + side.

Exercise Seven: Explaining the Lesson Well

If you are in an education course or workshop, each participant can teach a lesson to the others as "students." Here, the "students" give a checkmark to the teacher every time they feel the comfortable opportunity to let the teacher know where they are in the learning, or let the teacher know how well they are following him or her. The teacher teaches for ten minutes and tries to score as many ✔s as possible indicating that the lesson provides feedback opportunities for the "students."

Checklist for Chapter 14: Improving Your Lesson Plan Delivery

Below you can fill in the lesson topic each day that you teach. Then, for each lesson each day you can check off whether your lesson contained the elements discussed in Chapter 14. You may notice that consistently your lesson lacks elements (E) and (I), as in the example below. Try to place these elements into your next day's lesson.

TOPIC	Causes of World War II (Mon)	Tue	Wed	Thu	Fri	Mon	Tue	Wed	Thu	Fri
A. Congruent Delivery	✔									
B. Affective	✔									
C. Actional, Experiential	✔									
D. Inductive	✔									
E. Participatory										
F. Felt Order	✔									
G. Sensed Reward	✔									
H. Momentum	✔									
I. Distributed Attention										
J. Student-Opportunity for Feedback	✔									
K. Explained Well	✔									

CHAPTER 15: THE SUBSTITUTE TEACHER

Being a regular teacher is hard enough. However, being a <u>substitute teacher</u> deserves a "purple heart"! Like the tradition of complaining about the school lunch, the substitute teacher has been the "pin cushion" of students for ages. I loved to test them and give them trouble, and so did you. The persistence of this tendency over generations has good reason. Students experience their regular teacher's absence as a "leaving," even an abandonment of them. If their regular teacher was any good, students have made an attachment to their teacher's congruent openness, his/her caretaking of the environment, fairness, the class's order, and rewards. Now s/he just doesn't show up. Anger and revolt (even repressed hurt) is an understandable response on the part of the students. However, understandable or not, if we are called upon to be a substitute teacher (or do a "coverage" or are a "cluster teacher"), we must, as best we can, protect the education of students.

What can a substitute teacher do to do this job as best as possible? Generally, substitute teachers are at a great disadvantage: (1) they get the displaced anger and revolt of the students caused by the regular teacher's leaving; (2) they have almost no control over the classroom environment; (3) they have no time to establish their own procedures or learn the regular teacher's; (4) they usually can't gain easy access to equipment; (5) they have little time to establish the influence of a congruent, fair relationship with the students; (6) they learn last minute about the subject matter they must teach; (7) they, therefore, have almost no time to work on a good lesson delivery; (8) and, if they are not a regular faculty member (not doing a "coverage" or not a "cluster teacher"), if they are only a per diem substitute, they have almost no support to enable them to follow through on any of their warnings and rules. No wonder the job is well done if the substitute survives, let alone teaches anything. However, there are ways to deal with this difficult job.

A. Securing Your Place

1. If you tend to call schools or send them post cards to alert them that you are available, try to sub, as much as possible, at the <u>same school</u>. This will

enable you to get the routine down more easily. You'll also be familiar with where the clock is, the faculty bathroom, cafeteria, etc., and learn names of some key personnel. Also, if you are in the same school often, the students will begin to feel your credibility and your ability to follow through.

2. Be nice to the school secretary. Often s/he is in charge of calling substitutes 7 A.M. to fill in every day. S/he usually can decide who to call. If you can help her in any way when you're there, do so. She may decide whether you return to the school again or whether you keep getting a different class each day, or the same class for a week. The latter situation is, of course, the more manageable job. You can also ask her/him to try to place you in the subject areas you feel most comfortable.

3. Get a see-through pencil case and get all the items (44–60) of equipment I recommended as little tools of survival on pages 215–216 in Chapter 10.

4. Get there early, at least twenty minutes before the first period. You'll need to locate the main entrance, perhaps sign in, find the school secretary, get your assignment, learn where the rooms are, learn your schedule, etc. By the time the bell rings to meet your first class, you'll need to feel organized and ready.

5. Try to get the regular teacher's roll book and/or marking book and/or Delaney book. Besides the fact that these are useful, when the students see that you actually have their teacher's books, there is often some legitimate transfer of respect to you as their teacher.

6. Get to the classroom before the students get there. Stand outside the door and, as each one enters, look him or her straight in the face and give them some kind of handout "do-now" that they must do immediately.[164] Don't talk to them, don't answer their: "Who are you?" "Are you a sub?" "Where's our teacher?" "Do you know Mr. Smith?"

7. Try to select out two or three students who don't seem to be angry or aggressive and say "hello" to them and ask, "What's your name?" and thank them. Try to memorize two or three students' names.

B. Some Helpful Techniques

1. At the very opening of the class session, level with the students as congruently as you can. Tell them how you feel about this job. Let them know that you understand how they feel about "subs," and then explain what you'll do

---

[164] In section C of this chapter, we will discuss handouts that can be useful here, viz., "task sheets."

this period with them. Tell them how you feel about what you'll go over or teach. Try to talk TEACHER_person, stern but as a real person, as yourself.

2. Briefly, in a sentence or two, tell them what you will and won't tolerate. Again, make sure you express these sentences as congruently as possible. But don't preach rules; be very brief and then start some kind of lesson.

3. Get the train of your lesson moving as fast as you can. Do not get bogged down by questions or comments. Start teaching, write notes on the chalkboard, ask questions, call on students. Move.

4. Call on the two or three students whose names you memorized, and thank each one for his response, whether the answers are correct or not. That you know students' names and treat them well will immediately give you credibility with the class and some influence on the class's need for attention and approval.

5. Get and give out "commendation cards," if this school uses this system. Or give students "credit" by noting their names on a piece of paper or in the Delaney or marking book. Tell them that this "credit" record will be given to their regular teacher. Any questions the students ask, e.g., "Will this count?" answer "Yes."

6. Make sure you try to carry over, follow through, any credit or demerits to the regular teacher. You can leave the regular teacher a short letter in his or her mailbox or in the Delaney book.

Even better would be to do this and call the regular teacher at home (if possible) that evening to fill him or her in on disruptive kids, warnings, or credits you gave. Since you may teach this class again or at least teach in the same school, it is imperative that you try to communicate with the regular teacher so that you develop a reputation that you do follow through, what you say counts.

7. For severe disruptions, learn the name of the dean and learn how one sends a student there. Or, if you can become friendly with a teacher next door (perhaps you can do something for him or her?), ask if you ever have a very disruptive student, could you place the student in her/his room with some work?

8. Regarding what you should teach, often it is best to teach what you have prepared and know best. This is true especially if you will only be their teacher, this one day, one period for forty minutes. To try to teach the regular teacher's lesson often is too difficult to do well, especially in his/her own style, incongruently for you. Prepare a short lesson (or go over a "task sheet" we shall discuss immediately below) that you really care about and teach it your own congruent way. This will ensure fewer disruptions and is more apt to successfully teach something. It is better than trying to teach someone else's

lesson and subject matter. If you go over grammar, math fundamentals, or teach one scientific or social concept, you will have served the students well, no matter what the regular teacher was working on.

C. Some Useful "Task Sheets"

A task sheet is a one-page handout that asks the student to complete a few fairly simple educational tasks. They are best used when given out at the very beginning of the class period, completed in about ten minutes or less, and then gone over by the teacher. They can be used as "do-nows!" as a warm-up to the day's lesson, for immediate reward or feedback to students on a specific learning unit, or can be a complete lesson for a substitute teacher. Here's an example of a good task sheet:

....

_____   _____   _____
Regular Teacher   Print Your Name: First, Last   Today's Date

_____   _____
This Class Period   Your Homeroom Section #

Fill in the correct answers in the blanks below by writing the <u>letter</u> of the correct word in the blank.

A. there   B. their   C. they're   D. its
E. it's   F. whose   G. who's

For example: A.   they are.

1. _____ he goes.
2. This is _____ book.
3. I want to be _____.
4. _____ going to school.
5. I wonder if _____ going to _____ house.
6. _____ a great day.
7. The dog wagged _____ tail.
8. _____ book is this?
9. _____ at the door?
10. Where is your book? over _____

Place an X next to those sentences that are wrong, a ✔ if correct.

_____ 1. There going with me.
_____ 2. It's his book.

_____ 3. Whose at the door?
_____ 4. Their he goes again!
_____ 5. It's nicer over there.

....

Notice that a good task sheet does not ask the student to do too much. A good task sheet might be a fill-in-the-blank, or matching exercise, a true-false set of questions, multiple choice questions, etc. It should not ask for an essay or paragraph answer. It should engage the student immediately and feel easy to do. The first questions should be the easiest, the more difficult ones at the end. It's always helpful to give an example of the correct way to do the sheet at the beginning. Also, there should be a place at the top of the sheet where students have to fill in easy information as soon as they receive the sheet. This will immediately get them busy and help settle them down. When students see others working and hear a silence among the other students, the silence and the work become contagious. You might place the date, the class period, and the regular teacher's name on the chalkboard that they can copy to fill in the top of the sheet. While they fill out and work on the task sheet, don't answer questions or start discussions. Just tell the class that this work will count, it'll be given to their regular teacher, and that you will go over all answers after they are done. You might also let them know that they'd better fill out one because you will only count them "present" if you get a task sheet from them completed with their name on it. Some students may shout out: "Is this a test?" Answer something like: "No. If you behave, I'll just give you the answers and the credit for the work. No one will be graded. Just try your best." However, if some students become unruly, you may threaten that you'll use it as a test if they don't stop being disruptive. Go over the answers and teach the subject matter of the task sheet while they score (or their neighbors score) their paper. Then, you can ask them how they did and discuss the subject matter further. Usually the doing of the task sheet, its review, its teaching and discussion will last the whole period. You then should collect them at the end of the period for your feedback to the regular teacher.

I suggest that often it is best that you don't try to teach the lesson the regular teacher leaves for the substitute. Instead, I suggest you prepare a battery of possible task sheets that you can use for any substitute assignment (like the one above). As long as the subject matter is useful to students, and the sheet is "short and sweet," it'll provide an educational experience for the students and help you survive this difficult job. A teacher that may have to sub every day and for many subjects might prepare another English task sheet like the one above and also have in his/her briefcase, one on social studies, science, and even music. The former ones might simply ask students to put historical dates in order or state a list of facts that are either true or false. A music task sheet might have the following tasks:

....

I. Arrange the following tempo markings in ascending order from slowest to fastest: Allegretto, Lento, Largo, Allegro, Adagio, Presto, Moderato, Andante.

1. _____, 2. _____, 3. _____, 4. _____,
5. _____, 6. _____, 7. _____, 8. _____.

2. Match each composer with his nationality and his stylistic period.
        Example: Robert Schumann ___a___ ___3___

		Nationalities	Stylistic Periods
Debussy	____ ____	a. German/Austrian	1. Baroque
Brahms	____ ____	b. French	2. Classical
Beethoven	____ ____	c. Italian	3. Romantic
Mussorgsky	____ ____	d. American	4. Impressionistic
Copeland	____ ____	e. Russian	5. 20th Century

....

Or, you may choose a task sheet that feels more like a puzzle:

....

DIRECTIONS
1. Write the alphabet in a horizontal line in the blank spaces below.

A B C D E F   Z
1 2 3

2. Place a number under each letter, beginning with number 1 under the letter A and ending with number 26 under the letter Z.

3. Solve this message:
   25, 15, 21,   _____
    1, 18, 5,   _____
   22, 5, 18, 25,   _____
   19, 13, 1, 18, 20   _____

....

In 3 above, you might write a fact, a question, or a description of a famous historical figure that then leads into your lesson.

If you have to teach a math class, you might want to construct something like this:[165]

. . . .

Find the route that
when you multiply each
number in the path, the
answer is: 30,240 .

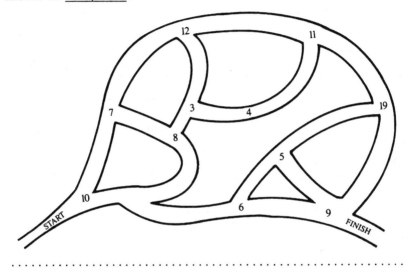

. . . .

Of course, the path-puzzle might only be the practice of addition, or it may contain fractions, decimals, or even equations.

Substitute teaching is very difficult. Some principals are satisfied if you are just able to keep order and do not have to use them to manage the students you are assigned to. However, if you follow some of the suggestions above, you will be more able to manage them as well as protect each student's education.

D. Especially for Grades K–6

Many of the above suggestions will also help people who are substituting for grades K–6. But these grades are special, luckily, usually easier than the upper grades. First of all, since congruence is easier or matters less than the emotion and approval you can give, you can more effectively follow the planned lessons the regular teacher has left for you. Also, since lessons in

---

[165] It's easiest to make this puzzle if you just fill in the correct path first, figure out its answer, and fill in the rest of the irrelevant paths.

grades K–6 usually are general knowledge for most teachers, you probably will already know the subject matter well. So, you don't have to prepare your own task sheets (though you may have one that fits what the regular teacher wants you to go over). If you come in to the class with a warm, emotively nurturant attitude, the students will receive you and accept you as their substitute (substitute parent). You need not worry about the classroom environment as much as in the upper grades (where it changes every period). Instead, the students will keep the assurance that they get from being in their own classroom (their "world"), though they have a different teacher today. Many elementary school teachers leave a list of helpful students for the substitute. Use this list. Ask these students how they usually do things. Enlist their help as "assistants" to keep the routines as normal as possible. (You will generally be able to tell in the lower grades if they are guiding you honestly or "pulling your leg.") They are used to having different teachers, e.g., for music, for art, who come to their classroom. If the regular teacher has been prepared for his or her absence, usually you will find all of the lessons and equipment you need right there. Or, if you are substituting for grades K–2, the teacher's aide (paraprofessional) will usually help you, or even do most of the job while you become the "aide." Also, any follow-through will be much easier, since there is only one teacher, not one for each period. You will be able to use most of the suggestions in all the chapters in the text, sections "Especially for Grades K–6" because the students will transfer to you if you are nurturant. So, review these.

E. Training Exercises and Checklist for Chapter 15

Exercise One: Securing Your Place

Below, write out what you plan to say to the, e.g., secretary of the school where you wish to substitute. Then, orally rehearse it a little.

_____

_____

_____

_____

Exercise Two: Your Opening Remarks to the Class

Below, write out what you will generally say to the class when you first meet them. Then, orally rehearse it a little.

_____

_____

_____

_____

_____

Exercise Three: Preparing Some Task Sheets

Write out two or three "task sheets" (according to the guidelines in this chapter) that you can use when you sub, and make enough copies to teach classes for one or two days.

Checklist

1. Have you reread the second paragraph of this chapter to be prepared for students' anger that will be displaced at you?
2. Have you followed the suggestions in Section A, above for "securing you place?"
3. Have you prepared what you will congruently say to the class when you first see them?
4. Do you have some good "task sheets" ready that you can use?
5. Are you ready to use techniques 4–7 of Section B, above?
6. If you are going to sub in grades K–6, have you reviewed Section D, above?

CHAPTER 16: EPILOGUE: "YOU MATTER!"

I understand. You are tired, frustrated, and angry at the injustices of low salaries, low status, and lack of support. You deserve much better. Unfortunately, our society doesn't realize how much you matter. And sometimes you feel what you try doesn't matter: "How can I be expected to follow some of the suggestions in this book when all I do might not matter or be appreciated? Even if I do a good job on Monday, the students' peers or home life may wreck it by Friday. What I do doesn't really matter. So why should I work so hard at this?"

You do matter. When you made Johnny feel good or proud for only a few minutes at 1:10 P.M. last Thursday, it mattered. His friends may push him to irresponsibility, and he may be neglected at home, but that short feeling you gave him that day, he'll remember. That feeling of possibly a new way to feel and be becomes a student's hope: "I want to feel that way again in my life." Such moments, when you got to him or her, become remembered feelings that evolve into goals of: "How I would like to be." What you did in those few minutes does matter.

You are the custodians of our society. You are the caretakers of the children who are our future. The divorce rate in this country is now exceeding one in every three marriages.[166] The rising rate of teenage pregnancy and children born out of wedlock is leaving us with both troubled parents and youth. In 1984, one out of five children was born out of marriage.[167] And, within the past two decades, the suicide rate among children and adolescents has increased threefold,[168] and a teenager commits suicide every 90 minutes![169] In these troubled societal waters, you are our lifeguards. Our schools are the incubators of our culture, the transmitters of all our history and knowledge of human striving for well-being and meaningfulness for our species. You are its guard-

---

[166] B. Beth Hess, Elizabeth W. Markson, and Peter J Stein. *Sociology*. New York: Macmillan Publishing Co. 1985: 273.

[167] Ibid., p. 282.

[168] Youth Suicide National Center, as reported in *New York Magazine* (June 2, 1986): 39.

[169] Hess, Markson and Stein, *Sociology,* 5th edition (Allyn and Bacon, 1996) p. 155.

ians. In concrete terms, the students who turn off today become truant and end up in trouble in juvenile or criminal court tomorrow. You matter!

This is not just cheerleading conjecture. For instance, the importance of interacting with professional role models (such as teachers) for increasing student interest and achievement in, e.g., mathematics and science (especially for women and racial minorities) has been well documented.[170] In two studies, more than twenty-five years later, there was a significant relationship between a person's adult success level or status and the positive effect of that person's first-grade teacher.[171]

Sometimes teachers have the chance to realize their impact:

> One parent wrote me a personal letter in which she said, "Your classes are affecting my son's life." I could hardly wait to get to school the next day to see which boy it was. I looked at the seating charts. He wasn't in the first class. In the second, there he was! That boy? Short, overweight—the one in the corner in the last seat. The one who rocked his chair back and forth the entire period. I had no idea he'd even been listening.[172]
>
> One boy who had been bused in sat over next to the window. There I was, giving my all, and he was just looking out the window. Once in a while, he'd look at me, almost with hostility, and then out the window again.
>
> I wondered what it would take to get through to that boy. At the end of the class, when I asked the students to write "What These Ideas Meant to Me," he didn't even have paper and pencil.
>
> I gave him a piece of paper and a red pen, which was all I had. I didn't mean to set him up, but I do know what he wrote that day. Only one answer was in red ink. He wrote: "I was thinking about cutting out and going to California, but since you rapped with us today I might just stay and get my education. I just don't know." He wasn't merely looking out the window. He wasn't looking at me with hostility. He was listening to every word.[173]

Teachers are the inspiration of great careers and strength:

> BETTY FORD, First Lady of the United States: Martha Graham, my former dance teacher, is my very, very favorite person, one of the outstanding women

---

[170] H. A Young and B. H. Young. *Scientists in the Black Perspective.* Louisville, KY: The Lincoln Foundation. 1974; L. W. Sells, "The Mathematics Filter and the Education of Women and Minorities." Paper presented at the annual meeting of the American Association for the Advancement of Science, Boston, MA, 1976; Jane Stallings and Ann Robertson. *Factors Affecting Women's Decisions to Enroll in Advanced Mathematics Courses.* Menlo Park, CA: SRI International, 1979; Westina Matthews. *Influences on the Learning and Participation of Minorities in Mathematics.* Wisconsin: Wisconsin Center for Educational Research, 1983.

[171] Eigel Penderson. "The Lifelong Impact of a First-Grade Teacher." *Instructor.* Vol. LXXXIX, No. 5 (December 1979): 62–66; and Eigel Pendersen, Therese Faucher, and William Eaton. "A New Perspective on the Effects of First Grade Teachers on Children's Subsequent Adult Status." *Harvard Educational Review.* Vol. 48, No 1 (February 1978): 1–30.

[172] Marilyn van Derbur. "Never Underestimate Your Influence," *Today's Education.* Vol. 65, No. 3. (September-October 1976): 52.

[173] Ibid.

of the world. As my teacher, she helped shape my life. She gave me the ability to stand up to all the things I have had to go through with much more courage than I would ever have had without her.[174]

WARREN E. BURGER, Chief Justice of the United States: A number of teachers made great impressions on me. Elizabeth K. Gill, my eighth grade teacher, was one. She was new to the school and a few students tried to test her. She let them disrupt the class for several days and then firmly stopped the disorderly conduct, demonstrating that she could do so. Then she told us since we would soon be voting citizens, we had better learn to govern ourselves. She outlined a form of class government and told us the majority would make the rules and she would carry out the enforcement. We did and she did. This was my first—and lasting—lesson in ordered liberty.[175]

EDWARD ASNER, actor and activist: I remember the effect Miss Timmer . . . had on me. I was a class clown in high school. She meted out punishment by having me memorize and recite long poems . . . but I found myself looking forward to the punishment. Years later, I realized that she had given me the chance to find my facility with lines in front of groups, and that her character helped me with my strength and new found (and sorely needed) pride.[176]

JIMMY CARTER, President of the United States: My life was heavily influenced by our school superintendent, Miss Julia Coleman, who encouraged me to learn about music, art, and especially, literature. As a schoolboy who lived in an isolated farm community, my exposure to classical literature, art, and music was ensured by this superlative teacher. She prescribed my reading list (War and Peace when I was 12 years old!) and gave me a silver star for every five books read and a gold star for ten book reports. I went on to read War and Peace (at first thinking it would be a short cowboys and Indians story) three times.[176]

ERMA BOMBECK, humorist: Rosamund Moak . . . taught English in a vocational school where auto mechanics, nursing, and retailing had precedence over the written word. She was rigid; she was tough; her teeth didn't fit. But when we got out of her class, we could communicate on every level. To say that she had an impact on my life would be the understatement of the century. [You emerged] from her classes with a feeling of pride.[176]

HERMAN WOUK, novelist: My eighth grade English teacher, Miss Sarah Dickson, a superb teacher, at P.S. 75, The Bronx, told me when I was eleven that I would be a writer. . . . I remember well her reading aloud of "Evangeline," and her perceptive appreciation of my early composition efforts.[176]

HAIM GINOTT, teacher and child: I have come to a frightening conclusion: I am the decisive element in the classroom. It is my daily mood that makes the weather. As a teacher, I possess tremendous power to make a child's life miserable or joyous. I can be a tool of torture or an instrument of inspiration. I can humiliate or humor, hurt or heal. In all situations, it is my response that decides

---

[174] "My Favorite Teacher," *Instructor.* Vol. LXXXVI, No. 1. (August-September 1976): 24.
[175] "My Favorite Teacher," *Instructor.* Vol. LXXXVI, No. 1. (August-September 1976): 24.
[176] A Celebration of Teachers for the Diamond Jubilee of the National Council of Teachers of English, 1986, pp. 3, 5, 6, 54.

whether a crisis will be escalated or de-escalated and a child humanized or dehumanized.

A Second Grade Teacher[177]: I once had a student who was the victim of an abusive home and had a lot of behavior problems and poor academic performance as a result. His kindergarten and first grade teachers "warned" me about him and basically told me not to worry if he failed again this year. In the course of a private conversation in the beginning of the year, I asked him if he thought of himself as a good kid or a bad kid or as a good kid who sometimes did bad things? It brought tears to my eyes when this seven year old replied, "Oh, I know I'm a bad kid." There was no question in my mind that he honestly believed that, with all his heart. At the end of the year (and after a lot of hard work from both of us), I asked him the same question. He smiled, and said, "I know that I make bad choices about my behavior sometimes, but I'm a good kid inside now."

His academic performance had come up to above grade level as well! Every year after that I made a point of checking on his progress both with him and with his current teacher. He is now in fifth grade and still maintaining his work at grade level. His behavior is still not what you might call exemplary, but he is no longer violent nor in trouble. I will always remember that boy, and I know that I do make a difference.

A Tutor: I used to go on the train to Brooklyn every Thursday at 3 P.M. to tutor this little eight-year-old foster child (who had now been transferred to his second family). One day, I found out that little Edward had suddenly been cutting school and was beginning to hang around with other truant students (many who already had police records). After about an hour of listening to him and consoling him, he told me that: about two weeks ago, he had a multiplication test, and he was scared he didn't know his times tables. So, he wrote the nine times table on his wrist. The teacher bawled him out in front of the class, and he began to cry. The next day, he faked a stomach ache, and the next. When that didn't work, he made believe he went to school. We worked on the times tables that day with flash cards for an hour, to the point where he not only knew the tables, but began laughing, and we tickled each other. The next day, he went to class and had another Math test. He did very well. He never cut classes after that, never got in any trouble with any kids, and did very well, . . . and since that was over thirty years ago, he may not even remember my name. (He gave me a lot.)

A Teacher in a Private School for the Emotionally Disturbed: After many years of teaching, I felt discouraged because I seldom saw any observable gains. I found my energy and enthusiasm dwindling. But one morning a

---

[177] Mary-Ann L. Feller (Bio. at the back of this book).

message from a former student came to our school's website on the Internet. The student wrote that he was now a father and cub scout leader and taught his children what I had taught him: that to be of value to the community, one must first feel valued. I only teach eight students at a time. But, now I realize that each of them grows up and influences others, which affects their children, families, and communities, . . . and that **what I do, does matter!**

Arnold Willens: On March 7, 1997 a 51-year-old teacher died. He had been merely a 5th grade teacher and theater arts teacher for about 17 years in a small public school in New York City. (Oh, he also, apparently, made it a point to be at school early each day to greet students and staff in the morning.) The school handed out a brief letter, unfortunately, with only two days notice, that a small service would be held in the auditorium of the school for Mr. Willens. To the shock of some (but not all) over 600 people showed up at the auditorium (which could hold only about 400). So, the rest just stood in the back of the auditorium, in the halls outside, for over an hour and a half. Most of the people who came were in tears, many had flown in from as far as California. After the hour and a half, they had to end the service because present and past students, parents, and fellow teachers kept going on, speaking about him (e.g., how he came to school to take the kids on a bird watch dressed as a cardinal), and there was no end in sight of the stories of how his work with students had changed and enriched their lives.

I know of many others as well: Albert Cullum (see the dedication of this book); Carmen Mason, who is "god-mother" to hundreds of students in the Bronx; Elizabeth Kasowitz; Mary-Ann Feller; Robert Weintraub; my 8th grade teacher, Mrs. Morris, ...

There should also be statues and monuments of teachers (not just soldiers) in all our parks, libraries, museums, ...

So, try to watch your miscalls; to duck; to work on the environment of your classroom; to repair your interactions with your students, your rules, and the delivery of your lesson plans—as best as you can. What you do does matter. And, since you must be congruent with these attempts, who you are matters. You matter to all of us.

PART IV

Special Features:
Training Tools That Can Be
Used with This Book

APPENDIX A: A QUESTIONNAIRE FOR YOUR STAFF—"ASSESSING THE PROBLEMS AND NEEDS OF YOUR TEACHERS REGARDING DISCIPLINE PROBLEMS"

You may wish to make copies of the questionnaire below to assess the problems and needs of teachers in your school. This should be done anonymously, tallied, and the results posted for teachers to learn they are not alone. Then, you might follow up with a workshop and make this book, H. Seeman's *Preventing Classroom Discipline Problems,* available to your staff. You can call Technomic Publishing Company at 1-900-233-9936 for the book. A training **video** for your staff, cued to this book, is also available: See Appendix B.

Problems and Needs Regarding Discipline Problems

Please indicate the extent to which the following are problems for you.

Always—3	Often—2	Sometimes—1	Never—0

_____ 1. Disruptive behavior
_____ 2. Deciding whether I should call certain behaviors discipline problems versus letting a behavior "slide"
_____ 3. Withdrawn students
_____ 4. Winning over students' feelings
_____ 5. Sarcastic nonverbal reactions from students
_____ 6. Getting the lessons done on a time schedule
_____ 7. Getting students to participate in the lesson
_____ 8. Cursing by the students
_____ 9. Deciding the best seating arrangements
_____ 10. Bathroom going and a proper bathroom policy
_____ 11. Homework not being done
_____ 12. Marking all the homeworks handed in
_____ 13. Late homework
_____ 14. My homework policy in general
_____ 15. Latecomers
_____ 16. Calling out

_____ 17. Class clowns

_____ 18. Handing out papers and materials

_____ 19. Students talking to each other during the lesson

_____ 20. Cheating

_____ 21. Fighting among students

_____ 22. Verbal "put-downs" among students

_____ 23. Verbal wisecracks at me

_____ 24. Students throwing things

_____ 25. Students who wear hats

_____ 26. Students with "Walkmans" (personal stereos)

_____ 27. Students with beepers

_____ 28. Students with weapons

_____ 29. Students who are high

_____ 30. Students who carry drugs

_____ 31. Students who are dealing drugs

_____ 32. Keeping students motivated

_____ 33. Parents coming into my class

_____ 34. Confrontational students

_____ 35. Students getting out of their seats

_____ 36. Feeling better related to the students

_____ 37. Losing my patience

_____ 38. Some of my procedures (like: _____ ,
            _____ , _____)

_____ 39. Lack of equipment and materials (like: _____ ,
            _____ , _____)

_____ 40. Deciding whether to confront a student during class or let it slide
            until after class, or just to overlook the behavior

_____ 41. Being completely honest with myself and the class about the
            subject matter

_____ 42. Being honest about all rules

_____ 43. Being honest in general interactions with the students

_____ 44. Following through on any warnings

_____ 45. Getting support from the administration on my rewards and pun-
            ishments

_____ 46. Being accused of being unfair

_____ 47. Not believing in the whole curriculum I'm teaching

_____ 48. Putting emotions into some of my lessons

_____ 49. Making my lessons relate to students' experiences

_____ 50. Getting the students to interact with each other, besides me

_____ 51. Helping the students feel a sense of direction and the goal of
            the lesson

_____ 52. Explaining everything very well

_____ 53. Handling students' anger

_____ 54. Disturbances right outside my classroom

_____ 55. My rules falling apart

_____ 56. Handling the "See me after class!"

_____ 57. Deciding the proper rewards and punishments

_____ 58. Asserting myself

_____ 59. Students when I'm substituting or doing a "coverage"

_____ 60. Designing good "do-nows" or short worksheets

_____ 61. I feel as though I'm alone with these problems.

_____ 62. I feel frustrated in my efforts about handling "discipline problems."

_____ 63. I feel the problem is always the students.

_____ 64. I feel the problem is the administration.

_____ 65. I feel the problem is the parents and home life.

_____ 66. I feel the problem is the students' peers.

_____ 67. I feel the problem is none of these.

_____ 68. I feel the problem is sometimes my own personal style.

_____ 69. I feel the problem is the environment of my classroom.

_____ 70. I feel the problem is sometimes in procedures.

_____ 71. I feel the problem is in the delivery of my lessons.

_____ 72. Other: _____

_____

_____

Please indicate the numbers of the three items that are most important to you from the above list 1–72.

1. _____ Very important to me.

2. _____ Important to me.

3. _____ Somewhat important to me.

For help with these issues consult the **video** in Appendix B, then Appendix E and the Index of *Preventing Classroom Discipline Problems, Third Edition,* H. Seeman, published by Technomic Publishing Company. Call: 1-800-233-9936, or e-mail: HOKAJA@aol.com

APPENDIX B: A COMPANION TRAINING VIDEO, CUED TO THIS BOOK

A companion training video is available, cued to this book, which:

1. Actually demonstrates the effective vs. the ineffective teacher.
2. Is perfect for training school staff or future educators.
3. Teaches practical skills for specific, frequent problems.
4. Trains educators for the diagnosis and prevention of actual discipline problems.
5. Is not "ivory tower" theory, but actually shows what to do and what not to do.
6. Cuts down the referral of disruptive students to the dean or principal's office.
7. Teaches practical suggestions, by example, for handling disruptive behavior without the need for revamping the entire school's procedures.

The Video has Successfully Been Used in Over 300 public and private schools across the United States; teacher education courses in many United States universities; Canadian public schools and universities in five provinces; and international schools in Japan, Ghana, Mexico, Malaysia, Greece, Singapore, Switzerland, Iceland, and Kuwait, and many other countries.

Reviews:

"This video is a powerful change agent! . . . enables teachers to feel less alone and more empowered to prevent and constructively respond to discipline problems! Rich . . . far reaching and practical."

—Susan G. Roth, Ed.D., Chief School Psychologist; Governor's Committee on Children's Planning for New Jersey; Senior Coordinating Supervisor, Rutgers University Graduate School of Applied Professional Psychology

". . . essential truths, invaluable for new or experienced teachers; priceless keys to rewarding teaching, beautifully demonstrated! . . . a guide to successful discipline-free teaching, no matter what your style."

—Carmen H. Mason, Teacher Trainer for the New York City Board of Education. Teacher of the Year, 1993 and New York City High School Teacher of English for 21 years.

"Excellent examples of troublesome situations, skillfully demonstrated . . . provides very practical discussion and learning for very real classroom problems."

—Ronald Manyin, Director of Student Teachers, City University of New York.

"Every parent should see this video and have this book to evaluate their child's teacher and help their child's emotional development."

—Steve and Linda Wilhelm, parents of four children, N.Y.C.

"A comprehensive treatment of classroom discipline. . . . not about controlling children, but rather about humanistic education with ample regard for practical solutions to disruptive behavior."

—*Journal of Staff Development*

"Seeman has created a text that can be used as a self-help guide or training manual for preventing and solving discipline problems."

—*Educational Leadership*

"All the suggestions . . . are skillfully presented and can easily be executed. . . . I thoroughly recommend this book to every teacher. In reading and practicing what Seeman is telling us (and showing us) to do, we will reduce the number of discipline problems in schools."

—*The Journal of Educational Thought*

"Well received! . . . Both the book and the video are recommended to all schools in Saskatchewan, Canada, that need help with emotional and behavior disorders. Also, recommended to the College of Education, University of Regina, Canada."

—Gail Saunders, Coordinator of Materials Evaluation and Acquisition, Saskatchewan Department of Education, Canada

Guidelines for Training:

1. Post the announcement (see the next pages) of the showing of the **video** for your staff to see.
2. About one week prior to the showing of the **video,** distribute the questionnaire for your staff (S.F.1) so that they may anonymously fill it out and hand it in (e.g., to a box with a slot).
3. Tally the results of the questionnaire and post it to be read just before the showing of the **video.**
4. Show the **video** (46 min.) without stopping it.

5. At the end of the showing, take comments and questions, but do not attempt to answer these concerns here. Just allow your staff to vent their concerns so that they can here that each of them is not alone.
6. Before the viewing audience leaves, distribute "Am I Going to Have a Lot of Discipline Problems? A Pretest (S.F.4).
7. Now, make available (in the faculty lounge, or library) several copies of this book so that your staff can look through the book for their particular concerns that were prompted by the **video,** the questionnaire, and the pretest.[178]
8. About one week after the distribution of the pretest, post the answers, which are all: No!
9. This will prompt a very useful discussion among your staff and refer them to the particular chapters that they got "wrong."
10. Each teacher can read their own concern and chapter and work on these problems by using the exercises and checklists at the end of every chapter.
11. Show the **video** once more; this time stop it after each section for staff discussion.
12. For further workshops, and in-service training for your staff with the **video** and this book, I recommend that each person below read their specific chapter, before the **video** is shown:
    - Education Majors and Student Teachers read Chapter 1A.
    - New Teachers and Veteran Teachers read Chapter 1B.
    - Instructors and Consultants read Chapter 1F.
    - School Psychologists and Guidance Counselors read Chapter 1G.
    - Administrators read Chapter 1H.
    - Supervisors of Student Teachers read Chapter 1I.
    - Instructors of Education Courses read Chapter 1J.
    - Parents (for a PTA meeting) read Chapter 1K.

To Order the Video:

Enclosed is my check* (or purchase order) of $_____ for _____ copies of the VIDEO [at $119 per copy], plus $3/copy for shipping & handling.
(*shipping is faster if paid by check than by purchase order)

MAIL (make check payable) TO: "Pro-Education Media" c/o Prof. Karen Beatty, 19 West 8th Street, No. 4, New York, NY 10011.
SHIP TO:
Your Name _____
School _____

[178] For a school discount set of books, cued to this video, call: 800-233-9936. For more information about the *video,* call (718) 960-8007, or e-mail: HOKAJA@aol.com

Address _____ Phone( ) _____
_____ ZIP _____
Sorry, preview copies of the video are no longer available.
Availability of the video is limited.

For more information about the **video,** call (718) 960-8007 or e-mail us at:
HOKAJA@aol.com

Post this notice, after you have filled in the information, whited out these
instructions, and enlarged, all before you show the **video** (see previous page).

ANNOUNCEMENT

A VIDEO ON:

PREVENTING CLASSROOM
DISCIPLINE PROBLEMS

WILL BE SHOWN ON:_____

IN:_____

Your attendance is very much appreciated.

I think that you will all find it valuable, for yourself and our school.
We will also distribute, at the showing, some useful handouts.
 Thank you.

APPENDIX C: LEGAL PARAMETERS

In this chapter, we shall discuss these topics regarding only the legal parameters (For the initial, fuller discussions of these topics, see Chapters 10A, 12B, and 13B, 12.):

1. **Search and Seizure**
2. **Locker Searches**
3. **Metal Detectors**
4. **Weapons in Schools**
5. **Corporal Punishment**
6. **Suspensions**
7. **Disabled Students**
8. **Student Records**
9. **Gangs**
10. **Dress Codes**
11. **Freedom of Speech**
12. **Graffiti, Vandalism, and Arson**
13. **Conclusions**
14. **Resources**

The first point to make here is that in the United States (and usually in democracies of a republic of states or provinces), each state, within the U.S. Constitution, can determine its own local education policies. The cities of each state, and boards of education in these cities, all come under that individual state's regulations. However, federal funding, and how the courts interpret the law vs. students' rights under the Constitution have sometimes taken away, and sometimes given the administrators of schools more or less power.

1. Search and Seizure

The issues involved here are unfortunately in opposition: students' rights to privacy vs. school administrators' needs to find ways to ensure the safety of a school. How much should the Fourth Amendment[179] be invoked regarding the rights of students?

The courts have been flexible in accommodating the fourth amendment to the special situation presented by the public schools, where school officials have both a right and a duty to provide a safe environment conducive to education.[180] For example, in a case that has set the standard on this issue (New Jersey v. T.L.O., 469 U.S. 325, 83 L. Ed.2d 720, 105 S. Ct. 733, 740 (1985) The court noted that:

> against the child's interest of privacy must be set the substantial interest of teachers and administrators in maintaining discipline in the classroom and on school grounds. . . . Accordingly, we have recognized that maintaining security and order in the schools requires a certain degree of flexibility in school disciplinary procedures. . .

These kinds of decisions have created a key criterion for search and seizures in schools: students are entitled to protection from <u>unreasonable</u> searches and seizures. The legality of a search of a student should depend simply on the <u>reasonableness</u>, under all the circumstances of the search. (T.L.O., 469 U.S. at 341;105 S. Ct. at 742.)

Considering this criterion, the following policies are probably best[181] regarding this issue:

1. The administrators of a school and the school board should write up a search and seizure policy that spells out the criterion of the T.L.O. case regarding reasonableness. It should clearly state that the following kinds of decisions should be made in determining whether a search should be conducted:
   a. Whether a student's conduct creates a reasonable suspicion that a regulation or law has been violated.
   b. Whether the measures contemplated for the search are reasonably related to the search objectives and not excessively intrusive or harsh in light of the suspected infraction and the age and sex of the student.
2. Administrators and faculty should receive in-service training regarding the school's search and seizure policy.
3. When contemplating a search of a student's person, belongings, or locker, a teacher or school administrator should consult with an objective third

---

[179] The right of the people to be secure in their persons, houses, papers, and effects against unreasonable searches and seizures, shall not be violated, and no warrant shall issue, but upon probable cause, supported by oath or affirmation, and particularly describing the place to be searched, and the persons or things to be seized.

[180] Horton v. Goose Creek Indep. Sch. Dist., 690 F.2d 470 (5th Cir. 1982); ruling denied, 693 F.2d 524 (5th Cir. 1982).

[181] Day, Reed, B. *Legal Issues Surrounding Safe Schools,* National Organization on Legal Problems of Education, pp. 30–31.

party (preferably another administrator or teacher). These professionals should discuss whether a search is reasonable,[182] given the immediate situation and the methods by which the search will be conducted. All searches should be conducted by at least two faculty members of the same sex as the student being searched.

4. Notes detailing the method and nature of the search should be made during or immediately after the search.

5. The school board should publish a notice to all students that student lockers are school property and that school authorities may search student lockers with or without cause.

Some factors that might be considered in determining whether reasonable suspicion to search exists include the child's age, history and record in school; the prevalence and seriousness of the problem in the school to which the search was directed; the exigencies in making a search without delay, and further investigation; also, the probative value and reliability of the information used as a justification for the search; and the particular teacher or school official's experience with the student.[183] Also, the more that law enforcement officers are involved the more likely "probable cause" must be evident.[184]

2. Locker Searches

School lockers are generally the property of the school and therefore many courts have found that schools have a right to control and search them. In fact, the courts in these cases often do not even consider an inspection of a student's locker to be a "search" within the Fourth Amendment, especially if it is written in a public statement that: "school lockers are school property".[185] In these kinds of searches, school officials do not even need "reasonable" suspicion. (There are states, however, such as Massachusetts, that recognize that students do have some reasonable expectation of privacy in their school lockers and therefore provide some protection against unreasonable searches.)[186]

---

[182] Regarding "reasonable" in 3 above: a search must be justified at its inception; that is, the school official must have reasonable grounds to suspect that the search will turn up evidence that the student has violated, or is violating, either the law, or the rules of the school. And, such a search must be limited and related in scope to the circumstance which gave rise to the inference that a school rule or the law was being violated in the first place. (T.L.O., 469 U.S. AT 342, 105 s. Ct. at 473.)

[183] Wood, Craig, and Mark Chestnut. "Violence in U.S. Schools: The Problems and Some Responses." *West's Education-Law Quarterly*. V. 4, No. 3, pp. 417–418, July, 1995.

[184] Wood and Chestnut, p. 420.

[185] Bjorklun, Eugene. "School Locker Searches and the Fourth Amendment." *West's Education-Law Quarterly*. V.4, No. 1, Jan. 1995, p. 8.

[186] Wood and Chestnut, pp. 419–420.

As a result of such policies regarding lockers, students may be more likely to keep weapons on their persons than in their lockers, especially when they are aware of the possibility of "suspicionless" locker searches. Or, the end result may be that, with this policy regarding lockers and the use of metal detectors, more weapons may be kept out of school, since there are fewer places to hide them.[187]

3. Metal Detectors

There are few problems in using metal detectors in schools as attempts to keep a school safer. But, they are an expensive technology, and at times, ineffective (see Chapter 13B, 12, c., 2) p. 363. However, regarding their legality, funds for their use and installation in schools are provided by federal law (Public Law 103-227,108 Stat 204) which, thus, lends an approval to their use. And school administrators usually need only to show that there is a need for such a measure to justify their installation.[188]

4. Weapons in Schools

In an effort to prevent guns from being brought onto school grounds, Congress enacted the "Gun-Free School Zones Act of 1990." It requires every local educational agency to have some kind of policy and procedure for the expulsion of any student (for a minimum of one year) who is determined to have brought a weapon to school. (An exception may be made on a case-by-case basis by the chief administering officer of the school. This would normally be the district superintendent.) This Act has been upheld by most courts, but some cases that have invoked this act are still (1997) in appeal, mostly regarding whether the item in question should be considered a "weapon."[189] (For examples of what may count as a "weapon," see Chapter 13B, 12)

5. Corporal Punishment

As of December 1995, 27 states have abolished "corporal punishment," either by state law or by regulation from State Departments of Education. In addition, 46 national associations, including The Council for Exceptional Children, have passed resolutions against corporal punishment.[190] Paddling is

---

[187] Ibid, p. 420.
[188] Ibid, p. 420–421.
[189] Day, Reed, B., p. 49.
[190] Evans, E. and Rita Richardson. "Corporeal Punishment: What Teachers Should Know." *Educational Psychology, Annual Editions* (Random House) Article 34, 1996, p. 200.

the most common form of corporal punishment, although "corporal" may mean anything physical (see Chapter 12B, p. 295) This was the breakdown as of December 1995 (with more states joining the list every month):

By State:[191]

BY STATUTE:

1. California	8. Massachusetts	15. North Dakota
2. Connecticut	9. Michigan	16. Oregon
3. Hawaii	10. Minnesota	17. Vermont
4. Illinois	11. Montana	18. Virginia
5. Iowa	12. Nebraska	19. Washington
6. Maine	13. Nevada	20. West Virginia
7. Maryland	14. New Jersey	21. Wisconsin

BY STATE REGULATION:

1. Alaska
2. New Hampshire
3. New York
4. Utah

BY SCHOOL BOARD:

1. Rhode Island
2. South Dakota

By City:[192]

Prohibited by regulation in these cities:

Atlanta; Baltimore; Chicago; Cincinnati; Cleveland; Miami; New Orleans; Oklahoma City; Philadelphia; Pittsburgh; St. Louis; Seattle, WA; Austin, TX; Boulder, CO; Charleston, SC; Charlotte-Mechienberg, NC; Columbia, MO; Little Rock, AK; Ogden, UT; Raleigh, NC; Reno, NV; Spokane, WA; Tampa, FL; Topeka, KS; Walla Walla, WA; and Wichita, KS.

6. Suspensions

The courts have decided that, under the Fourteenth Amendment, no student may be denied entitlement to an education without some fair procedure of due process.[193] However, the courts have never required, e.g., hearings in connection with short (less than ten days) suspensions. Also, the courts gener-

---

[191] The National Center for the Study of Corporal Punishment and Alternatives, Temple University, School Psychology Program, Philadelphia.

[192] National School Safety Center. "Corporeal Punishment in Schools" (1993). Like the other issues above, the legal decisions on suspensions is always in process.

[193] The federal Civil Rights Act, 42, U.S.C. section 1983.

ally have decided that suspensions need not be "strictly" by rules of evidence, as it is with cases in outside schools.[194] However, the courts have not upheld suspensions for, e.g., truancy, poor academic behavior, smoking cigarettes, etc. (For more details on a generally court sanctioned, "proper" suspension policy, see Chapter 12B: Suspension Policy).

In New York State, the governor has recently introduced legislation authorizing teachers and principals to remove disruptive students from the classroom for up to ten days without formal hearings.[195]

The West Virginia State Legislature recently enacted the Safe Schools Act, which specifically mandates suspension for no less than twelve consecutive months for possession of a deadly weapon, assaulting a school employee, or attempting to sell illegal drugs.[196]

7. Disabled Students

School districts should proceed carefully when contemplating discipline of a student who is deemed to have a disability. A disabled student has distinct and special rights with respect to discipline and what kinds of proceedings can be imposed. (Individuals with Disabilities Education Act, 200 U.S.C., 400, et. seq.).

The Supreme Court has provided a threshold standard for the administration of discipline to a student with a disability. Any exclusion from school of a student with a disability for more than ten days is considered "a change in the placement of that student." This means that students with disabilities may neither be suspended nor otherwise excluded from school for over ten days without complying with special requirements in the above act., e.g., placement procedures, parental agreement, and the disallowance of punishment for conduct that is a manifestation of the child's disability.[197]

However, the courts have found legal basis for stipulating that students with disabilities can be treated in the same manner as students without disabilities for short-term suspensions and other typical disciplinary measures. For example, one can petition the court to temporarily change the student's placement when: the individual presents a continuing threat of disruption; uses drugs or alcohol; or is carrying a weapon in school.[198]

[194] Day, Reed, B., p. 41.
[195] *The New York State Teacher,* March 1995, p. 6.
[196] Henderson, Joan, Friedland, Billie. "Attitudes toward Suspension, a Wake-Up Call: Rural Educators." (ERIC NO. ED 394749), 1996.
[197] Day, Reed, B., p. 44.
[198] ERIC NO. ED384192. Sorensen, Gail. "Discipline of Students with Disabilities: An Update." (A Legal-Memorandum) National Association of Secondary School Principals, Reston, VA. June 1995.

8. Student Records

School records can be released only on specified conditions of access. The school cannot permit anyone except the parent/guardian or eligible student to have access to protected information without written consent, except:

- other school officials with legitimate educational interest
- officials of other schools in which the student intends to enroll
- state and local officials to whom the information is required by statute
- authorized federal officials
- persons in connection with the student's application for financial aid
- testing services
- accrediting agencies
- persons in compliance with a judicial order
- persons in connection with an emergency to protect "health and safety."

In all the above cases , the confidentiality of records given to the authorized person(s) must be protected.[199]

9. Gangs

School districts are recently adopting a variety of methods designed to eliminate or restrict gang activity, and these methods are being upheld by the courts. For example, the prohibition of wearing certain jewelry, as an attempt to ban gang activities, was sustained in an Illinois court. The court asserted that the school had convincingly enunciated a rationale with regard to such jewelry which directly related to the safety and well-being of its students.[200] And, in California, the prohibition of wearing gang-related apparel was authorized by the legislature (Jan. 1, 1995),[201] and its Supreme Court also ruled (Jan. 31, 1996) that cities can prohibit suspected gang members from standing together on streets, wearing beepers, etc.[202] (See also 12 below.)

10. Dress Codes

There is an increasing body of opinion, as recognized by recent California legislation, that: "Many educators believe that school dress significantly influences pupil behavior." Apparel that relates to gang membership (as discussed above) is only one instance. The courts are beginning to support educators

---

[199] Furtwingler, Willis and William Konnert. *Improving School Discipline: An Administrators Guide.* Chapter: 9 "Legal Parameters." (Allyn and Bacon, Boston, 1982) pp. 206–207.
[200] Day, Reed, B., p. 71.
[201] Ibid., p. 53.
[202] *The New York Times,* Feb. 1, 1997, p.6.

regarding dress codes in general. For example, the courts have recently sustained rules by schools to prohibit the wearing of immodest clothing that impacts upon relationships between student and student, and student and teacher. Similarly, the prohibition of the wearing of certain buttons was sustained by a court that found that some buttons did relate to boisterous conduct and the undermining of school authority. To eliminate clothing-related school problems, the California legislature has also authorized schools to adopt the wearing of school uniforms.[203]

However, in many cases the courts have not sustained the schools' prohibitions: with regard to, e.g., wearing certain pants, pantsuits, dungarees, etc. where it was judged that such were not disruptive to school discipline or detrimental to morals.[204]

The President of the United States agrees with educators, "that school dress significantly influences pupil behavior." For example: ". . . we must continue to promote order and discipline, supporting communities that introduce school uniforms. . . ." (President Clinton's *State of the Union Address,* Feb. 4, 1997.) And, recently (Feb. 24, 1996) President Clinton instructed the Secretary of Education to issue a Manual on School Uniforms to the nation's 16,000 school districts on how they can legally enforce the use of such uniforms.

11. Freedom of Speech

The courts have upheld the rights of students to express their opinions, even on controversial subjects (Tinker v. DesMoines Indep. Comm. Sch. Dist., 393 U.S. 503,21 L. Ed.2d 731,89 S. Ct. 733 [1969]). The only way to bar students of these rights is to show that the students' activities would materially and substantially disrupt the work and discipline of the school (Id., 393 U.S. at 513; 21 l. Ed.2d at 742). Thus, for example, it has been ruled that freedom of speech (and the freedom to distribute literature on school grounds) does not extend to the privilege of cursing one's teachers and school administrators, nor can a student, e.g., post a cartoon that is deemed to be offensive to other students,[205] or obscene, or libelous.[206]

12. Graffiti, Vandalism, and Arson

Gangs use graffiti to claim territory. To restrict gang activity, schools who budget funds to immediately eradicate graffiti, have been supported by the

---

[203] Day, Reed, B., p. 71.
[204] Day, Reed, B., pp. 53, 55–56.
[205] Ibid., p. 59.
[206] Furtwingler, Willis and William Konnert. *Improving School Discipline: An Administrators Guide.* Chapter: 9 "Legal Parameters." (Allyn and Bacon, Boston, 1982) p. 202.

courts. And, the courts have also deemed vandalism and arson as acts that justify schools' policies of mandatory suspension.[207]

13. Conclusions

Presently, it seems as though our society is generally opting on the side of safety and violence prevention in our schools as opposed to an overconcern for students' rights (although the A.C.L.U continues to fight for the latter).

For example, regarding school safety and weapons in schools, with relaxed rules on student searches, combined with low-intrusive detector searches and zero-tolerance policies, schools have more legal support to, e.g., curtail weapons in schools and, therefore, eliminate some of the more dangerous crimes. (However, easy access to guns, usually from the home, is still a huge problem that is difficult for schools to control.)[208] However, several state legislatures (e.g., California, Connecticut, Florida, Iowa, North Carolina, Ohio, Pennsylvania) have enacted laws making parents responsible for the actions of their children.[209]

Also, in the Anti-Crime Bill signed by the President (Aug. 26, 1994) there are substantial grants to be used for alternative punishment for young offenders, e.g., requiring young offenders to reimburse the victims of their crimes, weekend incarceration, community service, and programs to deal with serious substance abuse and gang-related crime. Also provided are funds to state and local governments which have a law or policy that (1) punishes any student caught with a firearm with the loss of driver's license privileges and suspension from school; and (2) bans guns and other weapons within one hundred yards of a school. The bill also provided funds for new "drug courts" to be established by state and local governments, and public and private organizations. There are also provisions here for substantial funding for after-school programs for youth, offering education, tutoring, job preparation, athletics, culture, and arts and crafts.

14. Resources

1. The Education Law Association (formerly National Organization on Legal Problems of Education) 300 College Park; Dayton, OH, 45469-2280 phone: (937) 229-3589
2. The National Council on Crime Prevention at: http://www.weprevent.org

---

[207] Day, Reed, B., p. 62.
[208] Wood and Chestnut, p. 427.
[209] Day, Reed, B., p. 77.

3. The National School Safety Center (NSSC)
   4165 Thousand Oaks Blvd., Suite 290
   Westlake Village, CA 91362
4. The National Report on School Violence (800) 274-6737 at: http://www.bpinews.com or e-mail at: bpinews@bpinews.com (includes information on innovative programs, contact persons, phone numbers, etc.)

For other relevant resources, also see Chapters 10A and 13B, 12: Resources.

APPENDIX D: "AM I GOING TO HAVE A LOT OF DISCIPLINE PROBLEMS?" A PRETEST FOR DIAGNOSIS AND PREVENTION

This is an assessment questionnaire for new and beginning teachers. It is also a good test to take for experienced teachers who want to make sure they are not falling into some bad pitfalls as they start the new semester.

It is a fact that often the average new teacher goes through almost five years of trial and error trying to learn how to manage a class to best eliminate many discipline problems. Some teachers, during this time, just give up and quit teaching. Among these teachers are often potentially good teachers, people who really care about students, but, because of the stress in this area of the job, just give up. It shouldn't take five years to better manage disruptive behavior, and we shouldn't lose these caring, ill-prepared teachers. By answering the questions below, you will be helped to find our where your weaknesses, and pitfalls may be beforehand. This can save you from a lot of unnessary years of upset, save many responsible students' learning from many disruptions, and help all of us keep you, a caring potentially effective educator.

Directions

(a) Below, answer Yes or No as honestly as you can. (b) After you answer the questions, consult the upside-down answers at the end of the questionnaire. (c) Then, read the chapter and section that refers to your pitfall or potential weakness (the answers you got wrong).

	Pitfalls		
	Yes	No	Chapter and Section
1. I think that if I am myself, and often very honest with the class, that this openness with my class can often cause discipline problems.			8B, 11B
2. I should try to do and say what other good teachers have said and done.			8B, 11B

	Yes	No	Chapter and Section
3. Almost always, if I feel disrupted by a student, I should <u>not</u> let that behavior slide.			4
4. I should "go after" students who withdraw, e.g., fall asleep in my class.			4
5. It's important for me to be a good teacher, to try to always "win" students' feelings, not just get their correct behavior, so that they have the correct feelings about school.			4B
6. If a student from outside my class is disrupting my class by waving at one of my students through the classroom door window, I should first "go after" the student outside my door.			6C, 10B
7. It's best to have my class sit in rows, rather than in circle.			7C, 10C
8. It's fine if I usually don't express emotions in my class; it's better if I'm mostly cognitive and get across the ideas presented in the lesson.			9B, 14B
9. It's always important that I have everyone's attention.			4B
10. It's very important that I stop students' digressions and "off-the-lesson questions" to get my lesson plan done.			4B, 9D, 14D
11. Exercising control in almost all situations is very important.			4B
12. I shouldn't really be "myself" with a class. Instead, I should try to be the "teacher."			8B, 11B
13. Keeping track of things is not so important as being able to explain abstract ideas.			8C, 11C
14. It's okay if I don't believe in all of the curriculum that I'm teaching, as long as I can convince my students to study the material.			9A, 14A
15. It's best if I can often go from the curriculum, then to examples of how the curriculm relates to students' lives.			9D, 14D
16. It's better if the students (in the lesson) interact with <u>me</u> (the teacher) than each other.			9E, G, 14E, G
17. I know some good rules that I can implement used by a good teacher I once had.			8B, 11B, 12A
18. I remember some effective lectures to give students who violate my rules (that my past teachers used to give me).			8B, 11B, 12A
19. I have no problem calling a parent the second a child violates one of my rules.			12A

	Yes	No	Chapter and Section
20. If I am reprimanding a student, and the student says: "I won't do it, big deal!" I should know how to give the next punishment (for such an attitude).			12A
21. I know how to reprimand students who call out.			13B-1
22. I know how to go after students during a test who are cheating.			13B-3
23. It's important for me to not smile or laugh when a student in my class is being funny as a "class clown."			8B, 11B
24. I know how to break up a fight between two students by myself.			13B-2
25. I know how to speak warmly to a student who might have a crush on me.			13B-6
26. If I'm a substitute teacher, I can usually follow the lesson left for me by the regular teacher.			15B, C, D
27. It's OK for me to let elementary school students rely on their parents somewhat to help them enter the class in the morning (hang up their coats, turn in their homework, read the problem of the day, etc.) since it will help them and me to have them ready for work in the morning.			10E, b

ANSWERS:
The better answers are all **No!** If you answered **Yes** to any of these, read chapter and section indicated for the question you answered **Yes**, so that you might rethink your teaching methods and attitudes in that area.

APPENDIX E: AN INDEXED INVENTORY OF THE SOURCES OF DISRUPTIVE BEHAVIOR AND THEIR REMEDIES

Source by Chapter & Section	Sources of Disruptive Behavior	Description (page)	Prevention and/or Dealing with (page)
4A	You make a miscall.	51, 146	73, 241
4B-1	You reprimand a withdrawn student.	62	73, 241
4B-2	You overreact to a rule.	62–63	73, 241
4B-3	You try to win students' feelings.	64–65	73, 241
4B-4	You need their attention inappropriately.	65	73, 241
4B-5	You reprimand a student because your ego is hurt.	65–66	73, 241
4B-6	You reprimand students because they're interfering with your getting your lesson done.	66–67	73, 241
4B-7	You displace your anger.	67	73, 241
4B-8	You are tired of trying to be understanding all the time.	67–68	73, 241
4B-9	You reprimand because of the "mirror effect."	68	73, 241
4B-10	You need to control, inappropriately.	68–69	73, 241
4B-11	You mistake "steam" for "smoke."	69–70	73, 241
4B-12	You mistake "venting" for "cursing."	70–71	73, 241
4B-13	You make a prejudicial mistake.	71	73, 241
4B-14	You hold a grudge.	71	73, 241
4B-15	You punish an education problem.	72	73, 241
6A-1	Students cope with physical and sexual maturation.	118–119	125
6A-2	Students cope with the development of self-identity.	119–120	125
6A-3	Students cope with realizations of mortality and finitude.	121–122	125

447

Source by Chapter & Section	Sources of Disruptive Behavior	Description (page)	Prevention and/or Dealing with (page)
6A-4	Students cope with anxiety about the future.	122	125
6A-4	Students attempt to develop a *system* of ideas.	122	125
6B-1	Problems are from home.	123–124	125
6B-2	Students need peer-group support.	124	125
6C-1	Problems are from right outside your classroom.	126	125
7A	Disorder breeds disorder in the physical environment.	135	204–215
7B-1	Each class period is not in the same room.	135–137	204–215
7B-2	You get to your classroom after the students get there.	135–137	204–215
7B-3	The classroom is located too near a noisy area.	135–137	204–215
7B-4	The windows face a distraction.	135–137	204–215
7B-5	The lighting in your classroom is bad.	135–137	204–215
7B-6	The floor is noisy.	135–137	204–215
7B-7	There are papers all over the floor.	135–137	204–215
7B-8	The room is too warm.	135–137	204–215
7B-9	The sun is glaring into the windows.	135–137	204–215
7B-10	The room has only one entrance-way door.	135–137	204–215
7B-11	The front entrance-way door has a window.	135–137	204–215
7B-12	There is no place in your classroom for privacy.	135–137	204–215
7B-13	There's either no chalkboard or eraser or chalk.	135–137	204–215
7B-14	There are no bulletin boards.	135–137	204–215
7B-15	The bulletin boards and walls are a mess.	135–137	204–215
7B-16	The bulletin boards are distracting.	135–137	204–215
7B-17	There's no garbage can, or it's in "basketball" range.	135–137	204–215
7B-18	The pencil sharpener is usable in class.	135–137	204–215
7B-19	There aren't enough chairs and desks.	135–137	204–215

Source by Chapter & Section	Sources of Disruptive Behavior	Description (page)	Prevention and/or Dealing with (page)
7B-20	The desks and chairs squeak or are broken.	135–137	204–215
7B-21	The room is cluttered with nonessential furniture.	135–137	204–215
7C-1	The seats are in sloppy rows.	137–138	204–215
7C-2	The seats are in rows that inhibit student interaction.	137–138	204–215
7C-3	The seating arrangement promotes an adversary relationship.	137–138	204–215
7C-4	The seating arrangement makes you the major feeder of attention.	137–138	204–215
7C-5	You and the students are too far from each other.	137–138	204–215
7C-6	The students are sitting too close to each other.	137–138	204–215
7C-7	The seating arrangement has a poor traffic pattern.	137–138	204–215
7C-8	The seats face too much toward the door or windows.	137–138	204–215
7C-9	The seating arrangement promotes too much interaction.	137–138	204–215
7C-11	The students keep taking different seats.	137–138	204–215
7C-12	There are no empty seats near the door for latecomers.	137–138	204–215
7D-1	You don't put a "do-now!" assignment on the chalkboard.	138	204–215
7D-2	You don't use task sheets.	138	204–215
7D-3	You don't post rules or routines.	138	204–215
7D-4	There aren't predictable routines in your style.	138	204–215
7D-5	You don't demarcate time, use a calendar, or list topics covered or to be covered.	138	204–215
7D-6	You haven't written a lesson plan with a felt sense of order.	138	204–215
7D-7	You ask for their attention while you give out papers.	138	204–215
7D-8	Your handouts are unclear or too difficult.	138	204–215

Source by Chapter & Section	Sources of Disruptive Behavior	Description (page)	Prevention and/or Dealing with (page)
7D-9	You have a poor policy for latecomers.	138	204–215
7D-10	You have a poor homework policy.	138	204–215
7D-11	You have an unclear grading system.	138	204–215
7D-12	You have a poor policy for going to the bathroom.	138	204–215
7E-1	You don't carry a piece of chalk and/or an eraser with you.	138–141	215–218
7E-2	You don't have a piece of colored chalk.	138–141	215–218
7E-3	You don't use newsprint, or 5 × 8 cards.	138–141	215–218
7E-4	You don't use or have a large calendar for class.	138–141	215–218
7E-5	You don't carry the "little tools of survival" in a pencil case.	138–141	215–218
7E-6	You don't use an appointment book.	138–141	215–218
7E-7	You don't carry change for making phone calls.	138–141	215–218
7E-8	You don't use a Delaney book.	138–141	215–218
8A	You have some needs and feelings that lead to miscalls.	146–149	241–248
8B	You tend to be incongruent in some areas.	149–152	248–265
8C	You tend not to follow through.	152–153	265–267
8D	You tend to be inappropriate.	153–154	267
8E	You tend to be unfair.	154–155	267
9 and 14A	You have a lesson delivery that has incongruent content.	165–166	373
9 and 14B	You have a lesson delivery that is not affective enough.	167–168	374
9 and 14C	You have a lesson delivery that is not actional or experiential enough.	170	377
9 and 14D	You have a lesson delivery that is not inductive enough.	170	380
9 and 14E	You have a lesson delivery where students don't participate enough.	171	385
9 and 14F	You have a lesson delivery that lacks a felt sense of order, rewards, or momentum.	172	390

Source by Chapter & Section	Sources of Disruptive Behavior	Description (page)	Prevention and/or Dealing with (page)
9 and 14G	You have a lesson delivery that mismanages the distribution of attention.	174	394
9 and 14H	You have a lesson delivery that is not explained well enough.	175	396
12A	Your rules fall apart.	285	285
12B	You handle the "See me after class!" wrong.	345	345
13B-1	You mishandle students who call out.	348	348
13B-2	You mishandle fighting.	349	349
13B-3	You mishandle cheating.	350	350
13B-4	You mishandle latecomers.	351	351
13B-5	You mishandle homework.	353	353
12B, C	You are confused about rewards, punishments, and suspensions.	294–312	294–312
12G	You have trouble asserting yourself and taking stands.	327–328	327–328

APPENDIX F: A CHECKLIST FOR STUDENT TEACHERS, "YOUR FIRST DAY!"

Checklist

A few days (or a week) before you start your student-teaching experience (or your first teaching job), it'll be helpful to prepare many areas. First, you should observe the class as much as possible with your supervisor's help. Then, you might consider these:

1. Have you reviewed the definitions of a "discipline problem" and "miscall" (Chapter 4, section A)?
2. Which typical miscalls might you fall into making?
3. Have you re-sensitized yourself to remembering the developmental problems of your students (Chapter 6)?
4. Have you looked into how you might prevent disruptions from coming into your classroom from the outside (Chapters 6, section C and 10, section B)?
5. Have you decided on your seating plan(s) (Chapters 7, section C and 10, section C)?
6. Have you decided what procedures you will institute for the many tasks you will have to carry out (Chapters 7, section D and 10, section C)?
7. Have you obtained all of the survival tools and equipment that you will need (Chapters 7, section E and 10, section D)?
8. Have you decided how you feel and what you will say about your rules and subject matter (and how you will generally interact with your students) so you will deliver these congruently (Chapters 8, section B, 11, section B, 12, section A, and 13, section A)?
9. Have you reviewed how important it is to:
   - follow through (Chapters 8, section C and 11, section C)
   - be appropriate (Chapters 8, section D and 11, section D)
   - be fair (Chapters 8, section E amd 11, section E)
10. Have you reviewed Chapter 9 and selected, planned, and practiced some of the methods you might use to enhance the delivery of your lesson plan?
11. Have you reviewed the technical terms in Appendix G?

12. Have you set up a weekly time to meet with your cooperating teacher to plan and discuss your progress, the progress of students, and any difficulties you are having?

Your First Day!

Re-read Chapter 3, 1. on pp. 36–37, the list of uncertainties and fears of student teachers. Locate which listed question is your personal worry. Below are some general guidelines for each concern listed. (Hopefully, you knew the answer from having read it already in this book.)

For items 1, 10, 11, 16, 17, 24, 27

These generally have to do with being congruent. Figure out how you feel about things, and plan to talk to the students about these honestly as both a teacher and real person. Being congruent will not conflict with your enforcing rules and teaching; it will actually add credibility to them.

For items 2, 3, 4, 13, 25, and all of 30

These generally have to do with clearly formulating fair rules and routines for your classes, that are congruent for you, and making sure that you can and do follow through with your warnings, rewards and punishments for each of these rules (see Chapter 12A, B, C).

For items 19, 28, 29

These will require that you be for the other person while you are yourself at the same time. You will need to do and say what the cooperating teacher, principal, and parent need, while you also say and do what you believe in. You should be able to find a middle ground that is also honest for you. If you feel that to be for the other will involve you in being untrue to yourself, try to express your feelings to these people as tactfully as you can, before you push "your way." (For more help with this concern, review Chapter 11, B. 2, pp. 258–262.)

For items 5, 6, 7, 8, 14, 15, 18, 21

All of these are just normal feelings and anxieties. Most beginning teachers worry about these. If you can follow many of the guidelines in this book, you'll be fine.

For items 9, 12, 20

These generally involve using methods for an effective lesson plan delivery. See Chapter 14.

For item 22

Read Chapter 11E, page 268.

For items 23 and 26

It is worth your time to, at least, learn to use a computer, perhaps a projector, and certainly a VCR, to be able to show educational videos. But, these are not necessary. Regarding a piano, usually you need not know how to play one, though, if you have limited time, it's worth learning to read and play, at least, the melody line of songs.

APPENDIX G: A GLOSSARY OF TECHNICAL TERMS USED IN SCHOOLS

achievement test   Standardized test designed to measure how much has been learned about a particular subject.

ADHD   Attention deficit and hyperactivity disorder. A behavioral disorder that many researchers believe stems from a brain chemistry imbalance that often shows up as impulsive behavior, inattentiveness, hyperactivity, and occasionally violence. It is often treated with the drug Ritalin. ADHD has recently become exceedingly overdiagnosed. True ADHD children are not merely hyperactive; they have many symptoms that must be evaluated by a trained professional.

administrative period (prep. period)   A non-teaching period during which the school administration may assign particular duties.

androgynous   Having both masculine and feminine psychological characteristics.

anecdotal record   A written report of specific incidents occurring in the classroom or elsewhere.

aptitude test   Standardized test designed to supply an estimate of a student's potential ability in a particular area of study.

assembly schedule   The assembly schedule may consist of two parts: the dates, times, and topics or programs, and the rows in which each class is to sit. Stairways and entrances may also be included. In some schools, assemblies are attended by official classes, in others by designated subject classes. In either case, the schedule will indicate the period or time of the assembly.

at risk   A term used for any student who is likely to have difficulty succeeding in a mainstream classroom, or is "at risk of dropping out," or "in danger of, e.g., failing" for one or more reasons, (a diagnosed learning disability, developmental lag(s), non-English speaking, behavioral disorder, emotional disturbance, etc.) or who is suspected of having these potential difficulties due to poor classroom performance.

autistic   Lacking responsiveness to normal visual and auditory stimuli, despite absence of sensory defect.

behavior modification   Correction or change of conduct by means of rewards and reinforcements of desired behaviors, or approximations thereof and ignoring of undesirable actions. Based on the phenomenon of operant conditioning, behavior modification focuses on change of action rather than on change of attitude or motivation.

cooperative learning   A teaching method emphasizing students exploring concepts and materials by teaching each other in heterogeneous groups. All aspects of learning

457

are shared, students take on group functional role, e.g., leader, secretary, etc., and share materials, work responsibilities, projects, rewards, etc. The teacher in this method guides exploration and discovery rather than imparting knowledge directly. Students learn to get along, explain their ideas to each other, influence, follow, and help each other to reach a "team" solution to the learning assignment.

decoding   The process of reading a word using phonetic cues, context, illustrations, etc.

decoding   Decoding is the initial stage of reading, in which the reader obtains the meaning of individual words or sounds of letters.

deficiency needs   In Maslow's hierarchy, deficiency needs are needs that humans are motivated to fulfill as a result of their lacking them (physiological needs, safety needs, needs for love, needs for esteem).

Delaney card   This small oblong card contains lines and boxes for student's name, relevant information and data, and records of the student's marks and work. The cards for each subject or recitation class are kept in the Delaney book.

developmental lag   When a student does not show normal progress in a specific area with no diagnosed reason, e.g., a student who is not reading at age seven but does not show any reading-related learning disability under testing has a developmental lag in reading.

developmental readiness   A psychological term referring to when a student has matured sufficiently to be able to accomplish a specific task, e.g., reading.

distar   A direct instructional model used primarily to teach elementary level reading and math to low-achieving students.

Down's syndrome (mongolism)   One known organic cause for retardation in which the individual has an extra chromosome.

educable mentally retarded   Category of mental retardation applied to those with mild handicaps, whose learning problems are often identified only after school entry.

emotionally disturbed   A student who cannot maintain satisfactory interpersonal relationships with peers and teachers; s/he has inappropriate behavior or feelings under normal circumstances, has pervasive mood of unhappiness or depression, and has physical symptoms or fears associated with personal or school problems, and these are not due to sensory or circumstantial health reasons.

encoding   The process of putting parts of words together (syllables) to read a word.

ESL   English as a Second Language, usually used to indicate that the person learning English is learning it as his/her second language; the student is fluent in their first, native language.

extrinsic motivation   Doing something to earn some sort of concrete reward.

G.O. card   The student government or student organization in a secondary school is called the General Organization or the G.O. for short. All students who join by paying their dues are given a G.O. card.

gifted student   A gifted student is one who possesses superior intellectual or other abilities. The specific definitions vary from state to state but usually consist of criteria based on intelligence test results, achievement test results, or creativity test results.

gross motor activity   A physical action, such as running or throwing, which involves the limbs and large muscles.

halo effect   Tendency for an initial impression or one characteristic of an individual to influence another person's perceptions of the behavior of that person.

Hawthorne effect   A major research error that is due to response differences resulting not from the action of the independent variable but from the bakery or attention paid to the subjects by the experimenter.

hearing impaired   Hearing impaired people have partial hearing.

humanistic education   Approach to instruction that stresses affect, emotional learning, attitudes, values, personal fulfillment, and relationship with others.

hyperactivity   Hyperactivity (hyperkinesis) is a learning disorder characterized by excessive activity, inattentiveness, and impulsiveness.

individualized education program (IEP)   A program written for the student by the teacher, parents, a qualified school official, and the student (whenever possible). This program should set forth goals, services, and teaching strategies for that student.

integrated learning/teaching or theme study   A method of teaching that uses theme units, usually in social studies or science, to provide material for all areas of the curriculum, e.g., in a unit on the solar system, reading would be taught in books on the planets; math would be a unit on scale and distances, writing might look at the genre of science fiction, etc.

intelligence quotient (IQ)   A score determined by dividing the individual's mental age by chronological age and multiplying by 100. The formula is $IQ = MA/CA \times 100$.

intrinsic motivation   Doing something for its own sake, a feeling of pride.

invented spelling   In early writing attempts in elementary school, the teacher may accept "invented spelling" or phonetic attempts at writing words. The purpose is to encourage the flow of writing rather than emphasizing dictionary spellings on a first draft. Dictionary spellings and editing are taught as separate skills applied in second or third drafts.

Keller plan   Teaching technique in which students proceed at their own pace in mastering a series of units in some subject (also called the Personalized System of Instruction or PSI).

kinesthetic method   Technique for teaching learning disabled pupils that makes use of several sense modalities.

learning disability   Disorder that impedes academic progress of people who are not mentally retarded or emotionally disturbed.

learning disabled   A student who has problems with understanding or using language, spoken or written, to listen with inabilities, speak, write, spell, or do mathematical calculations or read. It includes perceptual problems, brain or neurological impairment, brain dysfunction, dyslexia, and developmental aphasia. It does not include students who have visual, hearing, or motor handicaps or mental retardation. Nor does it mean emotional disturbance or economic disadvantage.

learning environment   The physical classroom, including unchangeable structures such as windows and closets, re-arrangeable objects such as furniture, and items under the teacher's control such as materials and their storage. Discussion of the "learning environment" also examines how these physical items impact on student learning.

mainstreaming   Public Law 94-142 dictates that students in special education be given the least restrictive environment. It is a term describing the social and instructional integration of students with disabilities into a general education class for at least a portion of the school day.

manipulatives   Manipulatives refer to materials that students physically manipulate to better understand a concept, e.g., pattern blocks, cuisenaire rods, unifix cubes, bean counters, etc.

mean   Arithmetical average of a distribution computed by adding together all scores and dividing by the number of scores.

median   Middle score of a distribution. If the median number of items correct for children in the norm group who were exactly ten years old was fifty items, then children later taking the test who get fifty items right would receive a mental age score of 10.0.

mental age   Mental age refers to the average raw score of children in the norm group of a specific age on measures of intelligence.

mentally retarded   A student who has deficits in adaptive behavior and intellectual ability 1.5 standard deviations (or more) below the mean determined by an individual psychological evaluation.

miscues   A reading term referring to when a student makes an attempt at decoding a word using his/her prior knowledge of language structure or letter sounds but reads it incorrectly, e.g., reads "home" or "horse" instead of "house."

multiple intelligences   A theory devised by Howard Gardner in which he identifies seven types of intelligence a person can have: verbal-linguistic, logical-mathematical, interpersonal, intrapersonal, bodily-kinesthetic, musical, and spatial. Knowing these areas of strength and how they influence a student's learning helps teachers to tap into the different ways students access knowledge.

negative reinforcement   Any stimulus, the removal of which increases the rate of responding. If a rat is in a cage with an electrified floor grid and the electricity is turned off only after the rat presses a lever, the rate of the lever-pressing responses will tend to increase dramatically. Unlike punishment, which reduces response rates, negative reinforcement often increases response rates even more quickly than would positive reinforcement.

normal curve   In a normal curve (or normal distribution), the mean, the median, and the mode are identical, and they all fall at the same place on the curve, the center. The curve is symmetrical around this point with the number of scores decreasing away from the midpoint.

norms   In referring to groups, the standards for acceptable or "normal" behavior in the group.

objective tests   Tests using multiple choice, fill-in, true-false, or any similar format. Knowledge comprehension, application, and analysis objectives are best measured through the use of objective tests.

open classroom   A general concept rather than a precisely defined idea of how classes might be organized and conducted. Among the notions denoted by this concept are freedom for pupils to follow their own interests, self-evaluation, the teacher as a facilitator of learning, work outside the walls of the school, and encouragement of pupil choice in the conduct of learning.

open education   Form of instruction stressing student activity, learning areas, multiage grouping, self-selection, and individualized teaching.

orthopedic devices   Devices such as braces, crutches, wheelchairs, etc., used by physically handicapped students.

P.I.P.   A personal improvement plan asked for from a teacher, usually, by the principal in the lower grades. The teacher proposes what he or she plans to work on or do by June to improve himself or herself educationally for the school and students. For example, a teacher may plan to: learn to play the piano, take a workshop on drug abuse prevention, or learn to use new software for computer instruction. The P.I.P. then is considered in the teacher's end-of-the-year evaluation.

para   Paraprofessional, teacher, assistant.

percentile rank   A comparison of an individual's raw score with raw scores of the norming sample. This comparison tells the test taker the percent of students in the norming sample whose scores fall at or below his or her own score.

PL 94-142   United States Congress: The Education of All Handicapped Students Act mandated full free public education and due process rights for exceptional students.

portfolio assessment   A method of assessing students that involves compiling a wide variety of work samples as well as anecdotal records, tests, and other materials that give a complete picture of the student's performance. Usually, both students and teacher are involved in selecting the work to go into the portfolio. Students are then evaluated based on all their work and demonstrated strengths, rather than on the mathematical average of test scores.

pretest   A formative test given before instruction to determine what the students already know and what they are ready to learn.

programmed instruction   Structured lessons that students can work on individually at their own pace.

projective tests   An indirect method for obtaining a diagnosis of personality organization by interpreting an individual's responses to relatively ambiguous stimuli. These tests are based on the assumption that subjects will project their own needs, attitudes, or fears into their responses.

PSI   (See Keller Plan.)

pull-out programs   Any of a number of programs designed to help students who are at risk or failing for one or more reasons, e.g., ESL, reading recovery, resource room, etc.

pygmalion effect   Tendency for individuals who are treated as capable (or incapable) to act that way (essentially the same as self-fulfilling prophecy). What you expect a child to do influences what he'll do.

reading recovery   A pull-out program that targets early childhood students who are at risk in reading.

reliability   How consistent scores are if the same test is given to the same students a second time.

replication   Duplication of an original experiment to determine if the same results will be obtained by a different experimenter working with different subjects.

repression   Explanation of forgetting stressing tendency; the inability to remember disagreeable experiences because they are "pushed" into the unconscious.

resource room   A separate classroom in which a student can receive extra help in a problem area. A resource room is generally equipped with special materials and a specially trained teacher.

running record   A method of recording a child's performance while reading aloud. The teacher has a second copy of the text and marks any miscues or self-corrections using a specific system of notations.

seat work   That portion of students' school work that is done independently. Seat work often includes reading, drills, answering questions, completing worksheets, etc.

self-fulfilling prophecy   (See pygmalion effect.)

sociometry   The study of interpersonal likes and preferences of members of a group by means of columnar or schematic plotting of attractions or isolations. The graphs or columns are called sociograms.

standard deviation (σ)   A measure of the variability of a distribution of scores. The more the scores cluster about the mean, the smaller the standard deviation. For a normal distribution, about two thirds of the scores are within 1 standard deviation below the mean to 1 standard deviation above the mean.

standard error of measurement   An estimation of how much an individual's score would vary if the test were given repeatedly. A reliable test would have a small standard error of measurement.

standardized tests   Tests that have been tried out with many students and revised based upon these trials. Standardized tests have standard administration and scoring procedures.

task analysis   A system for breaking down a task into fundamental subskills. The first step is to define the final performance goal and then list the skills necessary to attain that goal. These skills are then broken down into subskills until a full picture is attained of all abilities (in proper sequence) necessary to achieve the ultimate goal.

time out   Placing a student in a room where as many opportunities for positive reinforcement as possible are eliminated.

token system   A system of reinforcement used by proponents of behavior modification, in which tokens of varying point values are awarded to students for fulfilling specific behavior objectives. The tokens (conditioned reinforces) may be different colored pieces of cardboard or poker chips that the student may earn to achieve some desired prize or privilege. The system is said to have two main advantages: (1) it maintains a high daily rate of desirable responses, and (2) it teaches delayed gratification.

trainable mentally retarded   Category of mental retardation applied to those with moderate handicaps, whose education usually focuses on self-help skills.

values clarification   Techniques of humanistic education designed to help students choose, prize, and act on their beliefs.

WAIS (Wechsler Adult Intelligence Scale) Individual IQ test developed by David Wechsler (along with the WISC—Wechsler intelligent Scale for Children and the WPPSI—Wechsler Preschool and Primary Scale of intelligence). All the Wechsler tests are administered by a trained examiner to one person at a time. All the tests yield three scores: a verbal IQ, a performance IQ, and a full-scale IQ. Wechsler believed that many of the intelligence tests of the day were too heavily laden with verbal items, and, to correct for that, the Wechsler tests all include a Performance section that tests an individual's visual motor abilities.

whole language A method of teaching reading that presents reading skills such as phonics, picture cues, predicting, etc. when they show up in appropriate texts rather than on a predetermined schedule from a textbook or workbook. The philosophy emphasizes learning written language the way children learn spoken language: by doing it in context rather than as isolated skills, e.g., learning phonics and apply this sound decoding to isolated words.

writing process A method of teaching writing designed by Lucy Calkins at Teachers College, Columbia University, that treats beginning writers (even in kindergarten) as authors who use writers' notebooks, get their thoughts on paper using invented spelling, participate in collaborative editing, and engage in multiple drafts of their work.

BIBLIOGRAPHY

See Chapter 2B for summaries and critiques of some major books on classroom discipline problems. At the end of many chapters, see Resources for other useful books, articles, and organizations for that chapter's particular topic.

Allen, C. and R. Mendler. *Taking Charge in the Classroom.* VA:Reston (1983).

Anderson, L., C. Evertson and E. Emmer. "Dimensions in Classroom Management Derived from Recent Research." *Journal of Curriculum Studies,* 12:343–356 (1980).

Aspy, D. N. and F. N. Roebuck. *Kids Don't Learn from People They Don't Like.* Amherst MA:Human Resource Development Press (1977).

Axelrod, S. *Behavioral Modification for the Classroom Teacher.* New York:McGraw-Hill (1977).

Blackwood, R. O. *Operant Control of Behavior: Elimination of Misbehavior and Motivation of Children.* Akron, OH:Exordium Press (1971).

Bloom, R. B. "Teachers and Students in Conflict: The CREED Approach." *Phi Delta Kappan,* 61:624–626 (1980).

Bossert, S. T. "Tasks, Group Management, and Teacher Control Behavior: A Study of Classroom Organization and Teacher Style." *School Review,* 85:552–565 (1977).

Brodinsky, B. *Student Discipline: Problems and Solutions.* Arlington, VA:American Association of School Administrators (1980).

Brophy, J and J. Putnam. *Classroom Management in the Elementary Grades.* Research Series Number 32. East Lansing, MI:Institute for Research on Teaching, Michigan State University (1978).

Brophy, J. and M. Rohrkemper. *Teachers' Specific Strategies for Dealing with Hostile and Aggressive Students.* Research Series Number 86. East Lansing, MI:Institute for Research on Teaching, Michigan State University (1980).

Brophy, J. "On Praising Effectively." *The Elementary School Journal,* 81:269–278 (1981).

Brown, A. R. and C. Avery, eds. *Modifying Children's Behavior: A Book of Readings.* Springfield, IL:Charles C Thomas Publisher (1974).

Brown, D. Changing Student Behavior: A New Approach to Discipline. Dubuque, lO:William C. Brown Company (1971).

Buckley, N. K. and H. M. Walker. *Modifying Classroom Behavior: A Manual of Procedures for Classroom Teachers.* Champaign, IL:Research Press Company (1978).

Buckley, P. K. and J M. Cooper. "Classroom Management: A Rule Establishment and Enforcement Model." *The Elementary School Journal,* 78:255–263 (1978).

Burke, J. C. *Decreasing Classroom Behavior Problems.* San Diego:Senglar Publishing Co. (1992).

465

Canter, L. and M. Canter. *Assertive Discipline: A Take-Charge Approach for Today's Educator.* Seal Beach, CA:Canter and Associates (1976).

Carducci, D. J. *The Caring Classroom.* Palo Alto, CA:Beill Publ. Co. (1984)

Carter, R. *Help! These Kids Are Driving Me Crazy.* Champaign, IL:Research Press (1972).

Charles, C. M. *Building Classroom Discipline.* New York:Longman Inc. (1981).

Charles, C. M. *Elementary Classroom Management.* New York:Longman Inc. (1983)

Chernow, Fred and Carol Chernow. *Classroom Discipline and Control: 101 Practical Techniques.* West Nyack, NY:Parker Publ. Co. (1981).

Clarizio, H. F. *Toward Positive Classroom Discipline.* New York:John Wiley and Sons (1980).

Collins, M. *Survival Kit for Teachers.* CA: Goodyear Publ. Co. (1975).

Crawford, J. and C. Robinson. *The Empirically Defined Domain of Effective Classroom Management: Final Report.* Princeton, NJ:Educational Testing Service (1981).

Curvin, R. L. and A. N. Mendler. *The Discipline Book: A Complete Guide to School and Classroom Management.* Reston, VA:Reston Publishing Company (1980).

Curvin, R. L. *Classroom Discipline.* Bloomington, IN:Agency for Instructional Technology (1991).

Davis, J. E. *Coping with Disruptive Behavior.* Washington, DC:National Education Association (1974).

Deitz, S. and J. Hummel. *Discipline in the Schools: A Guide to Reducing Misbehavior.* Englewood Cliffs, NJ:Educational Technology Publishers, Inc. (1978).

Dobson, J. *Dare to Discipline.* Wheaton, IL:Tyndale House Publishers (1970).

Dollar, B. *Humanizing Classroom Discipline: A Behavioral Approach.* New York:Harper and Row (1972)

Doyle, W. *Classroom Management.* West Lafayette, IN:Kappa Delta Pi (1980).

Dreikurs, R. *Psychology in the Classroom.* New York:Harper and Row (1968).

Dreikurs, R. and L. Grey. *A New Approach to Discipline: Logical Consequences.* New York:Hawthorn Books (1969).

Dreikurs, R. and P. Cassel. *Discipline without Tears.* New York:Hawthorn Books (1972)

Dreikurs, R., B. Grunwald and F. Pepper. *Maintaining Sanity in the Classroom.* New York:Harper and Row (1981).

Duke, D. L. and V. F. Iones. "What Can Schools Do to Foster Student Responsibility?" *Theory into Practice,* 24(4):277–285 (1985).

Duke, D. L. *Managing Student Behavior Problems.* New York:Teachers College Press (1981).

Duke, D. L., ed. *Classroom Management. The Seventy-Eighth Yearbook of the National Society for the Study of Education.* Chicago:University of Chicago Press (1979).

Duke, D. L., ed. *Helping Teachers Manage Classrooms.* Alexandria, VA:Association for Supervision and Curriculum Development (1982).

Emmer, E. and C. Evertson. *Effective Management at the Beginning of the School Year in Junior High Classes.* Report Number 6107. Austin, TX:Research and Development Center for Teacher Education, The University of Texas at Austin (1980).

Emmer, E. and C. Evertson. "Synthesis of Research on Classroom Management." *Educational Leadership,* 342–347 (1981).

Emmer, E., C. Evenson and L. Anderson. "Effective Management at the Beginning of the School Year." *The Elementary School Journal,* 80:219–231 (1980).

Emmer, E.T. *Classroom Management for Secondary Teachers.* Boston:Allyn and Bacon (1994).

Epstein, C. *Classroom Management and Teaching: Persistent Problems and Rational Solutions.* Reston,VA:Reston Publishing Company (1979).

Ernst, K. *Games Students Play and What to Do About Them.* CA:Celestial Arts (1973).

Faust, N F. *Discipline and the Classroom Teacher.* Port Washington, NY:Kennikat Press (1977).

Galloway, D. *Case Studies in Classroom Management.* London:Longman Group Limited (1976).

Givener, A. and P. S. Graubard. *A Handbook of Behavior Modification for the Classroom.* New York:Holt, Rinehart & Winston (1974).

Glasser, W. *Schools without Failure.* New York:Harper and Row (1969).

Gnagey, W. J. *The Psychology of Discipline in the Classroom.* New York:Macmillan Company (1968).

Gnagey, W. J. *Motivating Classroom Discipline.* New York:Macmillan Company (1981).

Good, J. E., and Brophy, T. L., *Looking in Classrooms.* New York:Harper Collins (1994).

Gordon, T. with N. Burch. *T.E.T: Teacher Effectiveness Training.* New York:McKay Publishing Co. (1974).

Grey, L. *Discipline without Fear.* New York:Hawthorn Books (1974).

Hair, H. and others. "Development of Internal Structure in Elementary Students: A System of Classroom Management and Class Control." ERIC Document ED 1829 067 (1980).

Harring, N. G. and E. L. Phillips. *Analysis and Modifications of Classroom Behavior.* Englewood Cliffs. NJ:Prentice-Hall (1972).

Harris, M. B., ed. *Classroom Uses of Behavior Modification.* Columbus, OH:Charles E. Merrill Publishing Company (1972).

Hill, P. L. *Solving Behavior Problems.* Danville, NY:The Instructor Publications (1973).

Homme, L. with A. P. Csanyi, M. A. Gonzales and J. R. Rechs. *How to Use Contingency Contracting in the Classroom.* Champaign, IL:Research Press (1970).

Hoover, K H. "Motivation-Discipline Techniques." Chapter 4 in *Secondary/Middle School Teaching: A Handbook for Beginning Teachers and Teacher Self-Renewal.* Boston:Allyn and Bacon, 71–100 (1977).

Hoover, K. H. and P. M. Hollingsworth. "Classroom Discipline and Behavior." Chapter 6 in *A Handbook for Elementary School Teachers.* Boston:Allyn and Bacon, 57–64 (1973).

Howard, E. R. *School Discipline Desk Book.* West Nyack, NY:Parker Publishing Company (1978).

Howell, R. G. and P. L. Howell. *Discipline in the Classroom: Solving the Teacher Puzzle.* Reston, VA:Reston Publishing Company (1979).

James, V. *Comprehensive Classroom Management.* Boston:Allyn and Bacon (1990).

Johns, A. F. *School Discipline Guidebook.* Boston:Allyn and Bacon (1988).

Johnson, David and Roger Johnson and Edythe Holubec and Particia Roy. *Circles of Learning, Cooperation in the Classroom.* The Association for Supervision and Curriculum Development, 1984.

Johnson, L. V. and M. A. Bany. *Classroom Management: Theory and Skill Training.* New York:Macmillan Company (1970).

Jones, V. F. *Adolescents with Behavior Problems: Strategies for Teaching, Counseling, and Parent Involvement.* Boston:Allyn and Bacon (1980).

Karlin, M. S. and R. Berger. *Discipline and the Disruptive Child.* West Nyack, NY:Parker Publishing Company, Inc. (1972).

Kelley, E. C. "The Place of Affective Learning." *Educational Leadership,* Vol. XXI:455 (1965).

Kline, J. A. *Classroom Management.* Dansville, NY:The Instructor Publications. (1974).

Kohut, S., Jr. and D. G. Range. *Classroom Discipline: Case Studies and Viewpoints.* Washington, D.C.:National Education Association (1979).

Kounin, J. S. *Discipline and Group Management in Classrooms.* New York:Holt, Rinehart & Winston (1970).

Krajuoski, R. 1. and R. B. Shuman. *The Beginning Teacher: A Practical Guide to Problem Solving.* Washington, D.C.:National Educational Association (1979).

Krumboltz, J. D. and H. B. Krumboltz. *Changing Children's Behavior.* Englewood Cliffs, NJ: Prentice-Hall (1972).

Kyriacov, C and J. Sutcliffe. "Teacher Stress: Prevalence, Sources and Symptoms." *British Journal of Educational Psychology,* 48:159–167 (1978).

Lasley, T. J. and W. W. Warpon. "Characteristics of Schools with Good Discipline." *Educational Leadership* (December):28–31(1992).

Lemlech, J. K. *Classroom Management.* New York:Harper and Row (1979).

Long, J. D. and V. H. Frye. *Making it Till Friday: A Guide to Successful Classroom Management.* Princeton, NJ:Princeton Book Company (1977).

Long, N. J., W. C. Morse and R. G. Newman. *Conflict in the Classroom.* Belmont, CA:Wadsworth Publishing Company (1980).

Loughlin, Catherine and Joseph Suina. *The Learning Environment.* New York:Teachers College Press, 1982.

Macht, J. *Managing Classroom Behavior.* New York:Longman (1990).

Madsen, C. C. *Teaching Discipline: Behavioral Principles Towards a Positive Approach, 2nd Ed.* Boston:Allyn and Bacon (1974).

Madsen, C. H., Jr. and C. K. Madsen. *Teaching-Discipline: A Positive Approach for Educational Development.* Boston:Allyn and Bacon (1981)

McDaniel, T. R. "Exploring Alternatives to Punishment: The Keys to Effective Discipline: *Phi Delta Kappan,* 61:455–458 (1980).

McIntyre, T. *A Resource Book for Remediating Common Behavior and Learning Problems.* Boston:Allyn and Bacon (1992).

McIntyre, T. *The Behavior Management Handbook.* Boston:Allyn and Bacon (1991).

McLemore, W. P. "The ABC's of Classroom Discipline." *The Clearing House,* 54:205–206 (1981).

Mirthes, C. *Can't You Hear Me Talking to You?* New York:Bantam (1971).

Morales, C. A. "Discipline: Applicable Techniques for Student Teachers" *Education,* 101:115–117 (1980).

Morris, R. C. "Creating Effective Classroom Discipline." *The Clearing House,* 52:122–124 (1978).

Muir, Edward. *Security in the Schools.* NY:UFT (1979).

National Education Association. *Discipline and Learning: An Inquiry into Student-Teacher Relationships.* Washington, D.C.:National Education Association (1975).

National Educational Association. *Discipline in the Classroom.* Washington, D.C.:National Educational Association (1974).

New York City Board of Education. *Getting Started in the New York City Public Schools.* (1992).

Nielsen, L. "Let's Suspend Suspension: Consequences and Alternatives." *Personnel and Guidance Journal* (May 1979).

O'Banion, D. R. and D. L. Whaley. *Behavior Contracting: Arranging Contingencies of Reinforcement.* New York:Springer Publishing Company (1981).

O'Leary, K. D. and S. G. O'Leary, eds. *Classroom Management: The Successful Use of Behavior Modification.* Elmsland, NY:Pergamon Press (1977).

Popham, W. J. and E. L. Baker. "Classroom Management." Chapter 8, in *Systematic Instruction.* Englewood Cliffs, NJ:Prentice-Hall, 117–128 (1970).

Presbie, R. J. and P. L. Brown. *Behavior Modification.* Washington, D.C.:National Education Association (1976).

Raths, L. *Values and Teaching.* Columbus, OH:Charles E. Merrill Publishing Co. (1966).

Rice, D. L. *Classroom Behavior from A to Z.* Belmont, CA:Fearon-Pitman Publishers, Inc. (1974).

Rogen, C. *On Encounter Groups.* New York:Harper and Row (1970).

Rogers, C. and B. Stevens. *Person to Person: The Problem of Being Human.* IUT:Real People Press (1969).

Rohrkemper, M. and J. Brophy. *Teachers' General Strategies for Dealing with Problem Students.* Research Series Number 87. East Lansing, MI:Institute for Research on Teaching, Michigan State University (1980).

Safer, D. J. *School Programs for Disruptive Adolescents.* MD:University Park Press (1982).

Saunders, M. *Class Control and Behavior Problems.* Maidenhead, Berkshire, England:McGrawill Book Company (UK) Limited (1979).

Shipman, H. and E. Foley. *Any Teacher Can . . . A Systematic Approach to Behavior Management and Positive Teaching.* Chicago:Loyola University Press (1973).

Sloane, H. N., D. R. Buckholdt, W. R. Jenson and J. A. Crandall. *Structured Teaching: A Design for Classroom Management and Instruction.* Champaign, IL:Research Press (1979).

Stainback, S. B. and W. C. Stainback, eds. *Classroom Discipline: A Positive Approach.* Springfield, IL:Charles C Thomas Publisher (1974).

Stoops, E. and J. King-Stoops. *Discipline or Disaster?* Bloomington, IN:Phi Delta Kappa Educational Foundation (1972).

Sulzer, B. and G. R. Mayer. *Behavior Modification Procedures for School Personnel.* Hinsdale, IL:Dryden Press (1972).

Tanaka, J. *Classroom Management: A Guide for the School Consultant.* Springfield, IL: Charles C Thomas Publisher (1979).

Tanner, L. N. *Classroom Discipline for Effective Teaching and Learning.* New York:Holt, Rinehart & Winston (1978).

The Harvard Education Letter (Jan./Feb., 1995) "The debate over incentives heats up." 11(1),6.

Trouer, R. "This is Going to Hurt You More Than it Hurts Me." *Science News,* 102:332–333 (Nov. 18, 1972).

Turner, R. L. "Teacher Characteristics and Classroom Behavior." *ERIC Clearing House Report,* ED 015-886 (February 1966).

Walch, J. W. *Alternatives to Suspension.* Portland, ME:J. Weston Walch, Publisher (1979).

Walker, J. E. and T. M. Shea. *Behavior Modification: A Practical Approach for Educators.* St. Louis:The C. V. Mosby Company (1980).

Walker, H. M. *The Acting-Out Child: Coping with Classroom Disruption.* Boston:Allyn and Bacon (1979).

Wallen, C. J. and L. L. Wallen. *Effective Classroom Management.* Boston:Allyn and Bacon (1978).

Weber, W. A: "Classroom Management." Chapter 8, in *Classroom Teaching Skills: A Handbook.* J. M. Cooper, ed. Lexington, MA:D. C. Heath and Company, 284–348 (1977).

Weber, W. A. "Classroom Management." Chapter 8 in *Classroom Teaching Skills.* J. M. Cooper, ed. Lexington, MA:D. C. Heath and Company, 281–363 (1982).

Weber, W. A. "Teacher Perceptions of Effective Classroom Management Strategies." Paper presented at the annual meeting of the American Educational Research Association, Los Angeles (April 1981).

Weber, W. A. and others. *Classroom Management: Reviews of the Teacher Education and Research Literature.* Princeton, NJ:Educational Testing Service (1983).

Weber, W. A. with L. A. Roff. *The Classroom Management Project: A Brief Summary.* Princeton, NJ:Educational Testing Service (1981).

Weber, W. A. with L. A. Roff. *The Classroom Management Project: A Technical Report.* Princeton, NJ:Educational Testing Service (1982).

Weiner, D. N. *Classroom Management and Discipline.* Iuasca, IL:F. E. Peacock Publishers (1972).

Weinstein, G., and M. Fontini. *Toward Humanistic Education: A Curriculum of Affect.* New York:Praeger (1970)

Weiss, M. and P. Weiss. "Taking Another Look at Teaching: How Lower-Class Children Influence Middle-Class Teachers." Paper presented at the annual meeting of the American Anthropological Association (1975).

Welch, J. David. *Discipline: A Shared Experience.* CO:Shields Publ. Co, Inc. (1973).

Welch, F. C. and J. D. Halfacre. "Ten Better Ways to Classroom Management," *Teacher,* 96:86–87 (1978).

Wolfgang, C H. and C. D. Glickman. *Solving Discipline Problems: Strategies for Classroom Teachers.* Boston:Allyn and Bacon (1980).

Yinger, R. J. "A Study of Teacher Planning." *Elementary School Journal,* 80:107–127 (1980).

INDEX

ABOUT THE AUTHOR

Howard Seeman, Ph.D., is a Professor of Education (at Lehman College, City University of New York, Bronx, N.Y. 10468; 718-960-8007) who has taught and supervised teachers and student teachers since 1970. He has published more than twenty articles in professional journals on education, counseling, philosophy and psychology. He has been the invited keynote speaker at many national education conferences and radio shows, and has given more than fifty workshops and lectures throughout the United States on classroom management and emotional education. He was a visiting professor in Japan from 1990 to 1992. Dr. Seeman was also a licensed English, Social Studies, and Substitute teacher in the New York City public schools from 1965 to 1970.

Consultant to 3rd Edition's K–6 Sections

Mary-Ann L. Feller, M.A., an elementary teacher in New York City since 1991, is one of the first teachers in the country to be certified by the National Board for Professional Teaching Standards. She has presented at many staff development conferences, including the National New Standards Project. She served as a consultant to the National Center for Reforming Education, Schools, and Teaching; the Professional Development School Project, Dist. 3, N.Y.C.; Scholastic's *Magic School Bus* television show; and *Super Science Red* magazine.